The Elevator Effect

The Elevator Effect

Contact and Collegiality in the American Judiciary

MORGAN L.W. HAZELTON
Associate Professor
Department of Political Science
Saint Louis University
morgan.hazelton@slu.edu

RACHAEL K. HINKLE
Associate Professor
Department of Political Science
University at Buffalo, SUNY
rkhinkle@buffalo.edu

MICHAEL J. NELSON
Professor
Department of Political Science
Pennsylvania State University
mjn15@psu.edu

Oxford University Press is a department of the University of Oxford. It furthers the University's objective of excellence in research, scholarship, and education by publishing worldwide. Oxford is a registered trade mark of Oxford University Press in the UK and certain other countries.

Published in the United States of America by Oxford University Press
198 Madison Avenue, New York, NY 10016, United States of America.

© Oxford University Press 2023

All rights reserved. No part of this publication may be reproduced, stored in a retrieval system, or transmitted, in any form or by any means, without the prior permission in writing of Oxford University Press, or as expressly permitted by law, by license, or under terms agreed with the appropriate reproduction rights organization. Inquiries concerning reproduction outside the scope of the above should be sent to the Rights Department, Oxford University Press, at the address above.

You must not circulate this work in any other form
and you must impose this same condition on any acquirer.

CIP data is on file at the Library of Congress

ISBN 978-0-19-762540-8

DOI: 10.1093/oso/9780197625408.001.0001

Printed by Integrated Books International, United States of America

Note to Readers

This publication is designed to provide accurate and authoritative information in regard to the subject matter covered. It is based upon sources believed to be accurate and reliable and is intended to be current as of the time it was written. It is sold with the understanding that the publisher is not engaged in rendering legal, accounting, or other professional services. If legal advice or other expert assistance is required, the services of a competent professional person should be sought. Also, to confirm that the information has not been affected or changed by recent developments, traditional legal research techniques should be used, including checking primary sources where appropriate.

(Based on the Declaration of Principles jointly adopted by a Committee of the American Bar Association and a Committee of Publishers and Associations.)

You may order this or any other Oxford University Press publication by visiting the Oxford University Press website at www.oup.com.

MLWH: For Henry Paoli and in memory of Lisa Vinson, my first collegials-in-crime.
RKH: In memory of Judge Robert C. Broomfield, a great judge and an even better person.
MJN: For Matthew Schill, my longest-tenured friend.

Summary Contents

List of Figures	xiii
List of Tables	xv
Acknowledgments	xvii

1. The Missing Link: The Importance of Collegiality for Judicial Behavior	1
2. Understanding Collegiality	15
3. Interpersonal Contact and Publicizing Disagreement	49
4. Why Does Collegiality Matter?	75
5. The Supreme Court: From the Boarding House to the Marble Temple	107
6. The Lunchroom Politics of Intercourt Relations	137
7. Collegiality and the Language of Dissent	159
8. The Impact of Relationships on the Use of Precedent	199
9. Taking Collegiality Seriously in Designing and Studying Courts	227

Bibliography	251
Index	273

Detailed Contents

List of Figures	xiii
List of Tables	xv
Acknowledgments	xvii

1. **The Missing Link: The Importance of Collegiality for Judicial Behavior** — 1
   - Introduction — 1
   - What Influences Judicial Behavior? — 5
     - Law — 6
     - Attitudes — 7
     - Strategy: Internal and External Constraints — 8
     - Background Characteristics — 10
   - Judicial Behavior Is Collaborative — 11
   - Roadmap of the Book — 12

2. **Understanding Collegiality** — 15
   - Introduction — 15
   - What Is Collegiality? — 17
   - Collegiality Is Important — 18
     - Collegiality in Our Everyday Lives — 18
     - The Importance of Collegiality in Courts — 19
   - Existing Evidence on the Effects of Collegiality — 27
     - Studies of Collegiality in Policymaking and Contact — 27
     - The Potential Mechanisms Tying Contact and Collegiality to Outcomes — 28
     - Is Collegiality Always Good? — 33
   - Our Theory — 34
     - Relationship of Collegiality to Contact — 34
     - The Role of Ideology — 38
     - Institutional Differences in Balancing Ideology and Collegiality — 40
     - Collegiality and Different Types of Colleagues — 42
   - Conclusion — 42
   - Appendix 2.A: Interview Methods — 43
   - Appendix 2.B: Interview Questions — 44
     - Court of Appeals Judges — 44
     - Supreme Court Clerks — 45
     - Court of Appeals Clerks — 46
   - Appendix 2.C: Clerks' Perspectives on Collegiality — 47

3. **Interpersonal Contact and Publicizing Disagreement** — 49
   - Introduction — 49
   - Collegiality and the Costs of Publicizing Disagreement — 50
   - Collegiality and Ideological Disagreement — 53

X DETAILED CONTENTS

The Differences Between Concurring and Dissenting	55
Proximity and Collegiality	55
A Measure of Collegiality: Same Courthouse	58
Data and Research Design	60
Descriptive Results	63
Multivariate Analysis	64
Conclusions	69
Appendix 3.A: Regression Results	71
Appendix 3.B: Detailed Data Collection Description	72
Appendix 3.C: Interview Evidence on Panel Assignment	72

4. Why Does Collegiality Matter? 75

Introduction	75
Personal and Professional Relationships	76
Persuasion and Suppression	77
Measuring the Mechanisms	79
Personal Relationships	79
Professional Relationships	80
Empirical Strategy	85
Results	86
The Direct Effects of Collegiality	87
The Conditional Effect of Collegiality	88
The Conditional Effect of Ideology	91
The Cumulative Effect of Collegiality	94
Control Variables	99
Conclusions	99
Appendix 4.A: Summary Statistics	103
Appendix 4.B: Regression Results	104

5. The Supreme Court: From the Boarding House to the Marble Temple 107

Introduction	107
Collegiality and Institutional Context	108
Historical Accounts Regarding the Operation and Importance of Collegiality	110
Interview Evidence Regarding the Operation and Importance of Collegiality	113
Institutional Differences	113
Clerk Professionalization and Socialization and the Importance of Collegiality	114
Contact and Relationships among Clerks and Justices	116
Observations about Justices, Their Interactions, and Collegiality	117
Contact and Collegiality	118
The Consequences of Collegiality	121
Data and Research Design	122
Results	125
Descriptive Statistics	125
Multivariate Research	125

Conclusions	128
Appendix 5.A: Interview Results	129
Collegiality among Clerks	129
Clerks as Conduits	131
Appendix 5.B: Summary Statistics	132
Appendix 5.C: Regression Results	133

6. The Lunchroom Politics of Intercourt Relations	137
Introduction	137
Reversal and Reputation	139
Building Assessments	141
Assessments, Collegiality, and Ideology	144
Measuring Hierarchical Collegiality	145
Data and Research Design	148
Results	150
Direct Effects of Reputation	150
Conditional Effect of Ideology by Assessments	150
Control Variables	154
Conclusions	154
Appendix 6.A: Summary Statistics	156
Appendix 6.B: Regression Results	157

7. Collegiality and the Language of Dissent	159
Introduction	159
The Context and Complexity of Dissent	160
The Impact of Language on Relationships	163
Collegiality and the Language of Dissent	167
Measuring Politeness and Rudeness	169
Data and Methods	172
Results: U.S. Courts of Appeals	175
Results: Supreme Court	181
Conclusions	188
Appendix 7.A: Summary Statistics	190
Appendix 7.B: Regression Results	192

8. The Impact of Relationships on the Use of Precedent	199
Introduction	199
The Importance of Studying Citations	201
Reasons to Cite a Precedent	202
The Impact of Collegial Relationships on Citation	204
Relationships with Former Colleagues	205
Relationships with Current Colleagues	207
Research Design	209
Collegiality and Citation in the Circuit Courts	211
Data	211
Results	212

xii DETAILED CONTENTS

Collegiality and Citation in the U.S. Supreme Court	217
Data	217
Results	218
Conclusions	221
Appendix 8.A: Summary Statistics	223
Appendix 8.B: Regression Results	225

9. Taking Collegiality Seriously in Designing and Studying Courts — 227
   Introduction — 227
   Summary of Findings — 227
   Increased Collegiality May Foster Consensus — 228
   The Effect of Collegiality Increases with Ideological Distance — 229
   Collegiality Dampens the Effect of Ideological Disagreement — 230
   Mechanisms — 231
   Differences in Institutional Context — 232
   Highlights of Our Findings — 233
   Implications — 235
   Implications for Theories of Judicial Behavior — 235
   Implications for Institutional Reforms — 236
   Potential Reforms to Judicial Norms — 238
   Opportunities for Future Research — 241
   Generalizability — 241
   Collegiality and Judge Characteristics — 242
   Building and Maintaining Collegiality — 243
   Collegiality in Other Contexts — 246
   Final Thoughts — 248

Bibliography — 251
Index — 273

List of Figures

3.1. Location of Courts of Appeals Chambers in 2010	58
3.2. Number of Cases, by Year and Circuit, in the Courts of Appeals Search and Seizure Dataset	61
3.3. Summary of Same Courthouse Pairs	63
3.4. Distribution of Dissenting or Concurring Votes, by Ideological Distance Quartile	64
3.5. Effect of Same Courthouse on Concurring and Dissenting, Courts of Appeals	67
3.6. Conditional Effect of Ideological Distance on Concurring and Dissenting, Courts of Appeals	69
4.1. Relationship between Circuit Size and Probability of Future Panel Service	83
4.2. Trends in Collegiality Indicators over Time	86
4.3. Direct Effects of Cotenure and Pr(Future Panel) on Concurring and Dissenting, Courts of Appeals	88
4.4. Effect of Same Courthouse on Concurring and Dissenting, Courts of Appeals	89
4.5. Effect of Cotenure on Concurring and Dissenting, Courts of Appeals	90
4.6. Effect of Pr(Future Panel) on Concurring and Dissenting, Courts of Appeals	91
4.7. Effect of Ideological Distance, by Same Courthouse, on Concurring and Dissenting, Courts of Appeals	92
4.8. Effect of Ideological Distance, by Cotenure, on Concurring and Dissenting, Courts of Appeals	92
4.9. Effect of Ideological Distance, by Pr(Future Panel), on Concurring and Dissenting, Courts of Appeals	93
4.10. Cumulative Effects of Collegiality on Concurring and Dissenting, Courts of Appeals	95
4.11. Conditional Effect of Ideological Distance on Concurring and Dissenting, Courts of Appeals	97
4.12. Changes in Predicted Probability of Concurring and Dissenting, Court of Appeals	100
5.1. Dissent in the Early Years of the Supreme Court	111
5.2. Trends in Cotenure over Time, Supreme Court	123
5.3. Changes in Predicted Probability of Concurring and Dissenting, Supreme Court	126
5.4. Effect of Cotenure on Concurring and Dissenting, Supreme Court	126
6.1. Predicted Probability of Vote to Reverse for Each Determinant of Assessment	151

xiv LIST OF FIGURES

6.2.	Predicted Probability of Vote to Reverse over Range of Aligned	152
6.3.	Conditional Effect of Each Determinant of Assessment on the Probability of a Vote to Reverse	153
6.4.	Changes in Predicted Probability of a Vote to Reverse	155
7.1.	Tone of Dissents over Time	172
7.2.	Changes in Predicted Number of Positive and Negative Emotion Words, Courts of Appeals	176
7.3.	Effect of Same Courthouse on Negative Emotional Language, Courts of Appeals	177
7.4.	Effect of Ideology on Positive Emotional Language, Courts of Appeals	178
7.5.	Changes in Predicted Probability of a Polite or Rude Sign-Off, Courts of Appeals	180
7.6.	Direct Effect of Pr(Future Panel) on Rude Sign-Offs, Courts of Appeals	181
7.7.	Effect of Ideology on Polite Sign-Offs, Courts of Appeals	182
7.8.	Changes in Predicted Number of Direct References to Majority, Courts of Appeals	183
7.9.	Changes in Predicted Number of Positive and Negative Emotion Words, Supreme Court	184
7.10.	Changes in Predicted Probability of a Polite or Rude Sign-Off, Supreme Court	185
7.11.	Conditional Effect of Cotenure on Polite and Rude Sign-Offs, Supreme Court	185
7.12.	Conditional Effect of Ideological Distance on Polite Sign-Offs, Supreme Court	186
7.13.	Changes in Predicted Number of Direct References to Majority, Supreme Court	187
8.1.	Changes in Predicted Probability of Citation, Courts of Appeals, Main Explanatory Variables	213
8.2.	Direct Effects of Precedent Author Participating and Pr(Future Panel) on Citation, Courts of Appeals	214
8.3.	Changes in Predicted Probability of Citation, Courts of Appeals, Control Variables	216
8.4.	Changes in Predicted Probability of Citation, Supreme Court	219
8.5.	Effect of Current Colleague on Citation, Supreme Court	220

List of Tables

2.1. Description of Interviewees and Identification Codes	22
3.A.1. Model Results	71
4.1. Indicators of Collegiality	85
4.2. The Combined Effects of Collegiality on Concurring and Dissenting, Courts of Appeals	98
4.3. Summary of Results	101
4.A.1. Summary Statistics for Courts of Appeals Search and Seizure Vote Dataset	103
4.B.1. Model Results	104
5.B.1. Summary Statistics for Supreme Court Vote Dataset	132
5.C.1. Model Results	133
5.C.2. Model Results	135
6.1. Distribution of District Judges	147
6.2. Distribution of Votes and Same Courthouse Pairs, by Circuit	149
6.A.1. Summary Statistics for Courts of Appeals Search and Seizure Reversal Vote Dataset	156
6.B.1. Model Results	157
7.1. Summary of Results, Dissenting Language	188
7.A.1. Summary Statistics for Courts of Appeals Search and Seizure Dissenting Opinion Dataset	190
7.A.2. Summary Statistics for Supreme Court Dissenting Opinion Dataset	191
7.B.1. Emotional Language Model, Courts of Appeals	192
7.B.2. Sign-Off Model, Courts of Appeals	193
7.B.3. Direct Address Model, Courts of Appeals	194
7.B.4. Emotional Language Model, Supreme Court	195
7.B.5. Sign-Off Model, Supreme Court	196
7.B.6. Direct Address Model, Supreme Court	197
8.1. Summary of Collegiality Mechanisms for Citation	208
8.2. Summary of Results, Citing Precedent	222
8.A.1. Summary Statistics for Courts of Appeals Search and Seizure Citation Dataset	223
8.A.2. Summary Statistics for Supreme Court Citation Dataset	224
8.B.1. Precedent Citation Model, Circuit Courts	225
8.B.2. Precedent Citation Model, Supreme Court	226

Acknowledgments

This is a book about the importance of collegiality and contact written by former officemates.

The three of us met as Ph.D. students in the Department of Political Science at Washington University in St. Louis where we spent three years working on coursework, meeting with students, and writing our dissertations as Graduate Student Associates of Andrew Martin's Center for Empirical Research in the Law (CERL). This experience taught us the importance of collegial relationships as we edited each other's papers, debugged each other's R code, troubleshot student issues, and coauthored with each other.

We didn't begin work on this project until after we had completed our Ph.D.s and moved on to our new academic homes, Hazelton at Saint Louis University, Hinkle at the University at Buffalo, and Nelson at Penn State. We first planned this project in the lobby of the Palmer House—a place where interpersonal contact among political scientists is all too common—and what started as a single paper (now Chapter 3) became several conference papers as helpful discussants and audience members pushed us to explore collegiality in different ways. Before we knew it, we realized that we were well on the way to writing a book.

We also had individual interests in judicial collegiality. Hazelton collaborated with Emerson Tiller (Northwestern Law) and Kristin Hickman (Minnesota Law) on work regarding panel effects in the federal courts of appeals. Hinkle's work on the circuit courts, both alone and with various coauthors, often touched on panel effects and other aspects of interactions among panel mates. Nelson wrote his undergraduate thesis on the potential for a "consensus-building justice," and his first conference presentation (in an empty Palmer House conference room) was a paper on that topic coauthored with Rachel Paine Caufield.

This book has been enriched by the contributions of so many people. We've had a small army of fantastic research assistants—including Trevor Bachus, Rachael Behling, Andrew Brown, Emma Cohen, Nathaniel Flemming, Michael Hunter, Patience Kapfer, Sangyeon Kim, David Miller, Steven Morgan, Kaleb Rasmussen, Charles Ryan, Steven Saroka, Caleb Petry, Taran Samarth, and Jamie VandenOever—who coded courthouse locations and judges' biographical information, compiled news articles about judges' spats and COVID-19 courthouse procedures, coded text in dissents, and helped us proofread and polish our prose.

We have also benefited from feedback from many colleagues and friends (with apologies in advance for those we have forgotten to list here): Christina Boyd, Paul Collins, Erin Delaney, Amanda Driscoll, Lee Epstein, Jim Gibson, Susan Haire, Tim Johnson, Alyx Mark, Lynn Mather, Jud Matthews, Laura Moyer, Eric Plutzer, Steve Puro, Keith Schnakenberg, Maya Sen, John Szmer, Steve Wasby, Albert Yoon, Mike Zilis, and Chris Zorn. We are also indebted to panel participants and discussants at the 2017, 2018, and 2022 Midwest Political Science Association meetings, the 2017 and

2022 Conferences on Empirical Legal Studies, and departmental seminar participants at Penn State's Department of Political Science and Penn State Law, the University at Buffalo, SUNY and its Baldy Center for Law and Social Policy, University of Chicago School of Law, and Saint Louis University School of Law.

Some of the data used in this research was originally collected using support provided by National Science Foundation Dissertation Improvement Grant SES-1155066. Any opinions, findings, and conclusions or recommendations expressed in this material are those of the authors and do not necessarily reflect the views of the National Science Foundation.

Hazelton would like to thank the many collaborators, both academic and professional, who helped teach her about collegiality. In law school, she had the good fortune to study, collude, and work with Beverly Bond, Kristen Huff, Kristina Rollins, and many others. Her days as a lawyer were made fuller by associate colleagues, including Katari Buck, Sheri Crosby, Tom Erickson, Henry Paoli, and Lisa Vinson. In addition to Rachael Hinkle and Michael Nelson, she is grateful to Amanda Driscoll, Xun Pang, Keith Schnackenberg, Alicia Uribe-McGuire, Greg Whitfield, and her other fellow graduate students. Finally, she is lucky to be surrounded by a faculty— including both past and current members of her department, the law school, and the legal history reading group—who enrich her personal and professional lives.

Hinkle would like to express her gratitude to a parade of amazing colleagues throughout the years. Amy Smith Reeves studied with her for countless history exams, Marshall Shelton was a daily fixture in law school, and her co-clerks (Will, Carmen, Paul, Martha, and Brock) provided much-needed camaraderie and support in the midst of hectic and demanding work. She is further grateful for all the laughs, struggles, and triumphs shared with her coauthors as well as Alicia Uribe-McGuire, Jee Seon Jeon, Cristian Pérez Muñoz, and her other fellow graduate students. Lastly, she appreciates her fellow professors both within her own university and scattered around the world. An astonishingly large number of people have brought joy and light to her professional world.

Nelson has also benefited from the help of many colleagues, coauthors, and friends over the years. Amanda Driscoll, Keith Schnakenberg, Jay Krehbiel, Jim Gibson, Dan Tavana, Rachel Paine Caufield, Amy Sentementes, and Erin Heidt-Forsythe have been the model of supportive friends and colleagues over the years, and his friends outside of the academy, including Matt Schill, Ellen Schill, Johnny Gallagher, Tyler Buller, Erik Baxter, and Brandon Harper, have provided support and laughs along the way. Nelson has also has benefited from the opportunity to work with fantastic colleagues at Penn State. Particularly, Nelson would like to thank Lee Ann Banaszak for her support of this research as department head and Michael Berkman for his support as director of the Center for American Political Responsiveness and McCourtney Institute for Democracy.

1

The Missing Link: The Importance of Collegiality for Judicial Behavior

Introduction

John W. Byrd, Jr. was convicted of killing a store clerk in 1983 and sentenced to death.[1] In 2001, he was still on death row, and the U.S. Court of Appeals for the Sixth Circuit considered his appeal.[2] A panel of three circuit judges heard Byrd's request for a stay of execution, and two of the judges rejected his claim. But, in an unusual procedural move, the majority granted a temporary stay of execution to accommodate the judge on the panel who disagreed.[3]

Writing that it was "simply lawless to stay an execution as a matter of comity to one member of the panel," Judge Danny J. Boggs, a Sixth Circuit judge who was not on the panel who heard Byrd's case, demanded on September 10 that the full Sixth Circuit decide whether the execution should be stayed. The next day, terrorists attacked the World Trade Center in New York City and the nation's capital in Washington, D.C. The chief judge of the Sixth Circuit was in Washington, D.C., on official business during the attack (Lane 2001). He lost his cell phone in the aftermath, rendering him unable to communicate with his colleagues in the Midwest. Byrd's execution was scheduled for 10 a.m. on September 12, making time of the essence. Late in the afternoon of September 11, Judge Nathaniel R. Jones, the judge who originally requested the stay, allegedly told the clerk of the court that a majority of judges had voted to grant the stay, resulting in the clerk issuing an order granting a longer stay (c.f. Lane 2001; *In re Byrd*).[4]

This series of events set off a firestorm (Lane 2001). Accusations flew among the Sixth Circuit's judges. There were allegations that normal voting procedures were not followed, and some judges who opposed the stay claimed that they had not been contacted to register their dissent. In a solo dissent, Judge Boggs accused Judge Jones of lying and wrote that "for *this* prisoner, a majority of the active members of *this* court would grant a stay based on a hot dog menu. This, however, is not a correct statement of the law (nor is it any sort of law at all)."[5] In a second dissent, joined by other judges,

---

[1] *In re Byrd*, 269 F.3d 544 (6th Cir. 2001).
[2] The Sixth Circuit is a court in the middle rung of the U.S. federal judiciary and hears appeals from federal district courts in Michigan, Ohio, Kentucky, and Tennessee.
[3] *In re Byrd*, 269 F.3d 561 (6th Cir. 2001).
[4] 269 F.3d 578 (6th Cir. 2001). The Ohio Attorney General's office asked the U.S. Supreme Court, in a faxed document, to overrule the Sixth Circuit's decision; there was no one at the Court on the morning of September 11, 2001, to receive the request due to the attacks (Lane 2001), though the Court did eventually vote to allow the stay to remain in place.
[5] *In re Byrd*, 269 F.3d 578, 582 (6th Cir. 2001) (italicized text appears in bold face in original text).

The Elevator Effect. Morgan L.W. Hazelton, Rachael K. Hinkle, and Michael J. Nelson, Oxford University Press.
© Oxford University Press 2023. DOI: 10.1093/oso/9780197625408.003.0001

2 THE ELEVATOR EFFECT

Boggs went on to write: "This type of secret undocumented decision-making by exclusive in-groups is the way decisions are made in totalitarian countries, not usually in the United States."[6] In fact, Judge Alice Batchelder, one of the original panel members, claimed that she had not been asked to vote on the stay and decried the lack of documentation for the vote, calling the Court's process a "cabal."[7]

Countering Judges Boggs and Batchelder, Judge Jones responded in an opinion that "[t]his case has stirred a disturbing degree of acrimony within the court which reflects the politicization of the issues by some political officials with motives open to serious question."[8] In a later opinion in the case, Jones went on to criticize the dissenters, writing that "they constitute a fanciful exegesis that bears little relationship to the facts of this case or the requirements of the law. Each dissenter accuses the en banc majority of 'lawless' actions or of acting without a lawful basis."[9] Privately, Jones wrote to Boggs that Boggs's behavior was "totally unwarranted, unprofessional, and wrong"; three other members of the court circulated a letter calling Boggs "patronizing and condescending" (Lane 2001).

Just a few months after deciding *In re Byrd*, the Sixth Circuit heard oral argument in *Grutter v. Bolinger*, a case about affirmative action at the University of Michigan.[10] In a story about the *Byrd* dispute among the Sixth Circuit's judges, a *Washington Post* reporter quoted an attorney making a prediction: "If the temperature is this high on this court, the affirmative action case could be really incendiary" (Lane 2001). He was right.

In *Grutter*, Judge Boggs dissented from the Court's majority opinion, finding that the University of Michigan's affirmative action plan was constitutional.[11] He included a "procedural appendix" accusing the Court's chief judge of manipulating the assignment of judges to hear the case and also slow-walking the case until two other judges on the circuit had retired from full-time service on the court, thereby stacking the deck in favor of the chief judge's preferred outcome.

In response, Judge Karen Nelson Moore wrote a concurring opinion in *Grutter*.[12] Moore decried Boggs's "unfounded assertion that the majority's decision today is the result of political maneuvering and manipulation."[13] Moore wrote:

> Judge Boggs's opinion marks a new low point in the history of the Sixth Circuit. It will irreparably damage the already strained working relationships among the judges of this court, and . . . serve to undermine public confidence in our ability to perform our important role in American democracy.[14]

Moore went on to note that her opinion "is truly a recourse of last resort, as several members of this court have endeavored to persuade Judge Boggs to withdraw [his

---

[6] *Id.* at 583.

[7] *Id.* at 584.

[8] *Id.* at 580.

[9] *In re Byrd*, 269 F.3d 585, 586 (6th Cir. 2001).

[10] 288 F.3d 732 (6th Cir. 2002).

[11] 288 F.3d at 780.

[12] *Id.* at 752.

[13] *Id.* at 753.

[14] *Id.* at 758.

opinion]. He has steadfastly refused to do so."[15] Moore's colleague, Judge Eric Clay, also concurred, writing that Boggs's opinion "constitutes an embarrassing attack on the integrity of the Chief Judge and this Court as a whole."[16]

This peek into the Sixth Circuit shows us a moment when collegiality on a court was remarkably low. Judges were accusing each other of dishonesty and manipulative tactics, and they were airing their disagreements in public. The behavior was so remarkable that both the *New York Times* (Liptak 2003) and *Washington Post* (Lane 2001) chronicled the drama on this regional court for their national readership. One can imagine the chilly silence when these judges found themselves riding in the same elevator.

Compare the Sixth Circuit's behavior with the image that U.S. Supreme Court justices are at pains to present to the public. Chief Justice Roberts, for example, noted in a 2018 talk at the University of Minnesota that the justices shake hands before each argument and are committed to mutual respect, saying:

> Those of us on the court know that the best way to do our job is to work together in a collegial way ... I am not talking about mere civility, although that helps. I am instead talking about a shared commitment to a genuine exchange of ideas and views through each step of the decision process. We need to know at each step that we are in this together (Biskupic 2018).

Roberts went on to discuss the important role that collegiality plays in the Court's operations. During a question-and-answer session, Roberts stated:

> I think the collegiality on the Court is very, very good ... In many ways, it's unlike any other job. There aren't many jobs where everybody is doing exactly the same thing. I mean if you are at a company, and you are all in sales but you are selling to different people and all that kind of thing.
>
> We do exactly the same thing. We read the same briefs and go to the same arguments and read the same cases, and that does cause a real bond to develop between you and also, because of obvious reasons, we are often the only people we can talk to about certain subjects because you don't want to talk about a lot of different things with members of the public. Certainly not politics or other things like that.
>
> But we can talk to each other about it and again that forms a bond. And I think we appreciate the pressures that each other are under and that creates a certain amount of empathy that you may not have in other enterprises. There have been times on the court where there have been unpleasant people there and that has made life unpleasant because you do work in such close quarters. But now is not one of those times (C-SPAN 2018).

His statements emphasize how the confidential nature of the Court's work makes it important to be able to speak freely with one's colleagues and suggesting that the members of the Court liked each other on a personal level.

---

[15] *Id.* at 754, fn. 2.
[16] *Id.* at 772.

4 THE ELEVATOR EFFECT

Roberts is not alone. Justices across the ideological spectrum laud the Court's commitment to positive interpersonal relationships. Consider testimony by Justice Alito to a House of Representatives subcommittee during a hearing about the Court's budget:

> We have developed a very open style of debating issues back and forth among the Justices when there is a majority opinion and a dissent. We argue the issues robustly, let me put it that way, and increasingly we don't pull any punches.
>
> And we don't take it personally. When one of my colleagues attacks my reasoning and says it doesn't make any sense, I don't take it personally, and I hope that the same is true when I reciprocate.
>
> But I think sometimes people who read what we write may get the wrong impression that we are at each other's throats in a personal sense, and that is certainly not true. And this is not just something that we say for public consumption. This is the complete truth (Financial Services 2020).

Likewise, Justice Kagan often emphasizes the Court's collegiality when she speaks to public groups. Consider her remarks in a speech at the University of Colorado:

> There are really good friends upon the court among people who disagree with each other about many things ... Justice Scalia, he used to have a line where he said, if you take this personally, you are in the wrong business. I think that is basically true. We are dealing with important matters. Of course, we are going to criticize each other. Of course we are going to tell each other, you got the law really wrong today. That doesn't mean that we can't think that the other person is operating in good faith and is a good person. And is—it seems to me that you can have very good friendships with people you disagree with (C-SPAN 2019).

These statements by Justices Roberts, Alito, and Kagan all speak to the central role that collegiality plays in the craft of judging. That's also the central argument of this book: how judges interact with each other has important effects at every stage of the judicial process. Appellate judges wield enormous influence in the United States. Their decisions define the scope of legislative and executive power, adjudicate relationships between the federal government and the states, and determine the breadth of individuals' rights and liberties. But, compared to their colleagues on trial courts, they face a significant constraint on their power: their colleagues. After all, judges on appellate courts make decisions in small groups, and their opinions only carry the force of precedent when a majority of judges can agree on both the outcome of a case and its rationale (Martinek 2010). Thus, the collegial environment on appellate courts may shape the decisions these courts produce and, by extension, legal development.

Surprisingly, leading theories of judicial behavior relegate collegiality to the background. Attitudinal explanations for judicial behavior prioritize the preferences of individual judges, treating each judge's decisions as basically independent from those of her colleagues. Strategic explanations acknowledge that judges may sometimes need to act against their short-term preferences but theorize that those deviations are in service of longer-term policy gains (e.g., Maltzman, Spriggs, and Wahlbeck 2000).

THE MISSING LINK 5

Neither approach emphasizes the possibility that the small-group decision-making environment may produce genuine changes in belief with respect to a case or a willingness to temper one's disagreement to prevent souring working relationships. In fact, because judges on appellate courts often serve for long terms, the long-run collegiality calculation is especially important: two judges might serve together for decades and might adapt their behavior to maintain positive relationships with their colleagues. After all, who wants a lifetime of frosty, awkward elevator rides?

And consider a simple fact: appellate court judges say collegiality affects their decisions. As U.S. Court of Appeals Judge Harry Edwards (2003, 1645) has written, "collegiality plays an important part in mitigating the role of partisan politics and personal ideology by allowing judges of differing perspectives and philosophies to communicate with, listen to, and ultimately influence one another." Former Third Circuit Judge Walter K. Stapleton (1995, 36–37) noted how interpersonal relationships, built over time, affect judicial behavior. He wrote:

> It is difficult to listen, much less give up something important to you in compromise,
> if you are dealing with strangers. It is only when you come to know a colleague in
> some depth as a human being that you accept without question his or her good faith.
> Only when the good faith of your colleagues is taken as a given is it possible to find
> wisdom in a thought of another in conflict with your own.

While there are strong theoretical reasons to expect collegiality to affect consensual judicial decision-making, quantitative tests of its effects have been scant. The lack of empirical evidence on this point is so acute that Epstein, Landes, and Posner (2013, 48) implored scholars to account for collegiality in studies of judicial behavior: "[J]udges frequently refer to the importance of collegiality (e.g., Edwards 2003; Wald 1987), and just as frequently, scholars reject it. We should not."

Taking collegiality seriously is the goal of this book. We present a comprehensive, first of its kind, examination of the importance of interpersonal relationships among judges for judicial decision-making and legal development. Our overriding argument is that collegiality affects nearly every aspect of judicial behavior. With respect to how judges resolve cases, we demonstrate that more frequent interpersonal contact among judges diminishes the role of ideology to the point where it is both substantively and statistically imperceptible. This finding stands in stark contrast to scholarly accounts that privilege ideology as the predominant determinant of judicial choice. With regard to legal development, we show that collegiality affects both the language that judges use to express their disagreement with one another and the precedents they choose to support their arguments.

What Influences Judicial Behavior?

Explaining why judges behave the way they do has long been the central concern of political scientists who study the judicial branch of government. The voluminous literature on judicial behavior has identified four major factors—law, attitudes, strategic concerns, and personal characteristics—that explain judicial behavior. The central

6 THE ELEVATOR EFFECT

argument of this book is that interpersonal relationships among judges—what we term "collegiality concerns"—are another, equally important factor in the judicial calculus. We begin by summarizing some of the major conclusions of the existing judicial behavior literature.[17]

Law

Judges are asked to decide cases by interpreting or applying the law to the facts before them. Thus, it stands to reason that judges' actions in particular cases are shaped by legal considerations. The evidence suggests that it does. In an early study, Segal (1984) identified features of search and seizure decisions that should make Supreme Court justices more (or less) likely to uphold a search as constitutional. After coding each case for the presence or absence of these features, his statistical analysis demonstrated that, true to form, the Court's decisions in these cases followed directly from the facts of the case. George and Epstein (1992) showed that legal considerations also affect the Court's jurisprudence in death penalty cases. As another example, in a series of projects Richards and Kritzer looked for the effects of "jurisprudential regimes" on Supreme Court decision-making and found that once the Court identifies a particular fact as important, its presence or absence becomes a strong predictor of judicial behavior (Kritzer and Richards 2005, 2003; Richards and Kritzer 2002; Pang et al. 2012).

Legal considerations have an even greater effect in the lower courts. Studies have shown that circuit courts demonstrate a fairly high degree of compliance with Supreme Court doctrine (e.g., Benesh and Reddick 2002; Songer and Haire 1992). Johnson (1987) provides evidence that legal considerations explain most of the variation in how both district and circuit courts implement Supreme Court precedent. Hinkle (2015) demonstrates that circuit judges are less likely to explicitly narrow or reject precedents that are binding under legal doctrine compared to those that are merely persuasive. This indicates judges are constrained by that legal doctrine.

While legal concerns provide a strong intuitive basis for the large proportion of decisions, there is variation in judicial behavior that is not explained by legal considerations. Efforts to explain or predict outcomes based on legal factors still contain considerable error. The Supreme Court Forecasting Project tested the ability of legal experts to predict the outcome of cases in the 2002 term and found that 59 percent of their predictions were accurate (Martin et al. 2004). Efforts in the legal industry to write algorithms that automate decision-making processes have faced substantial difficulties and are often viewed as impractical or undesirable (Morison and Harkens 2019). At least part of the reason for these shortcomings is likely that determining the "right" legal outcome in any given case is not always easy. As a result, even jurists fully dedicated to applying the law will sometimes face situations in which they have

---

[17] We do not mean to imply that these four factors are the *only* factors that influence judicial behavior. Certainly, a variety of case-level factors, such as attorney experience (Hazelton and Hinkle 2022; Nelson and Epstein 2022; Songer and Sheehan 1992) and litigant resources (Galanter 1974; Songer, Sheehan, and Haire 1999; Brace and Hall 2001; Gibson and Nelson 2021), might also affect judicial behavior. Additionally, other important theoretical lenses exist, such as the historical-interpretative approach (Gillman 1999). We focus on these four factors because they represent the four leading classes of explanations for judicial behavior.

to make a close call. This suggests that other factors beyond the law also influence decision-making.

Attitudes

Judges' ideological considerations provide a second class of explanations for judicial behavior. The classic statement of this factor is Segal and Spaeth's (2002, 65) attitudinal model. As they explain:

> This model holds that the Supreme Court decides disputes in light of the facts of the case vis-à-vis the ideological attitudes and values of the justices. Simply put, Rehnquist votes the way he does because he is extremely conservative; Marshall voted the way he did because he is extremely liberal.

Segal and Spaeth argue that the institutional structure of the U.S. Supreme Court makes that court a particularly likely case to find that ideological considerations affect judicial voting decisions. For example, the justices can pick their own cases, and they prioritize cases in which lower courts have come to opposite conclusions on the same legal questions. This means that there are strong legal arguments on both sides of most Supreme Court cases, providing considerable leeway for judges' preferences to influence their decisions. Further, because Supreme Court justices are appointed for life, they have no need to worry about re-election or reappointment. Nor are they angling for promotion. And the fact that intercircuit conflict is a predominant predictor of whether the Court will agree to hear a case suggests that there are plausible liberal and conservative legal arguments on both sides of many cases. Still, Segal and Spaeth assert that law has some effect; they argue that judicial opinions are based upon the personal preferences of the justices and the constraints of the case facts.

There is a large body of evidence demonstrating the importance of attitudinal considerations in U.S. Supreme Court decision-making.[18] Many studies have found evidence that justices' votes in cases heard on the merits correlate with their ideological predispositions (e.g., Segal and Cover 1989; Segal and Spaeth 2002; Martin et al. 2004; Baum 2017). The influence of attitudes is also apparent in many other types of judicial behavior on the Court. For example, Black and Owens (2009a) found evidence that ideology influences which cases the Court agrees to hear. Attitudes have also been shown to influence which precedents justices choose to cite (Hansford and Spriggs 2006) and which they overrule (Spriggs and Hansford 2001). Additionally, Maltzman, Spriggs, and Wahlbeck (2000) provide evidence that ideological considerations are involved in a vast array of decisions, including authorship assignments and responses to draft opinions. Overall, the influence of attitudes is well established.

---

[18] It should be noted that the attitudinal model and the strategic model we describe in the next section have theoretical overlap regarding the importance of ideological factors in driving justices' decisions, though the theories vary in the extent to which they anticipate justices behaving sincerely or without regard to internal and external constraints (Epstein and Knight 1998). Thus, we discuss studies that find an effect for ideology as part of a strategic investigation alongside those that fall more directly under the auspices of attitudinalism.

8 THE ELEVATOR EFFECT

But evidence supporting the primacy of attitudinal considerations declines as one moves down the judicial hierarchy (Zorn and Bowie 2010). For example, Johnson (1987) finds that ideological factors are a stronger predictor of how circuit judges apply Supreme Court precedent than it is for district judges. Epstein, Landes, and Posner (2013) directly compare the impact of ideology on both the district and circuit judges who resolved the same set of cases; they find that ideology is a larger motivation for circuit judges than it is for district judges. Epstein, Landes, and Posner (2013) also examine the role of ideology in district judges' sentencing decisions, and while they do find that it matters, they also conclude that the size of that effect is quite modest. Thus, overall, it appears that the influence of ideology on judicial decision-making weakens as one moves down the judicial hierarchy. This is consistent with Segal and Spaeth's (2002) theory that the factors that make justices the most independent of federal judges also make them the most attitudinal.

Attitudinal explanations do a compelling job explaining the outcomes of many cases in which the Supreme Court's decisions are divided. But in the many cases which the Court decides unanimously, attitudinal explanations can come up short: attitudinal explanations suggest that a unanimous decision only happens when a judicial decision aligns with the ideological proclivities of the entire court, perhaps because the lower court decision is ideologically extreme; yet many of the cases the Court decides are ones on which lower courts have come to opposite conclusions, suggesting that it is unlikely that the plurality of cases the Court hears are ideological outliers. Further, in many cases, especially in lower courts, judges seem to vote against their sincere policy preferences (Maltzman, Spriggs, and Wahlbeck 2000); attitudinal explanations fail to explain these cases as well.

Strategy: Internal and External Constraints

A third class of explanations seeks to understand why judges may sometimes vote against their sincere policy goals. As Epstein and Knight (1998, 10) explain:

> Justices may be primarily seekers of legal policy, but they are not unconstrained actors who make decisions based only on their own ideological attitudes. Rather, justices are strategic actors who realize that their ability to achieve their goals depends on a consideration of the preferences of other actors, and the choices they expect others to make, and the institutional context in which they act.

Thus, strategic explanations highlight both *external* and *internal* constraints on judicial behavior (Murphy 1964). Surprisingly, empirical evidence regarding the effect of external constraints (at least with respect to the Supreme Court) is scant, with many studies demonstrating that justices do not adjust their voting behavior in the face of changing congressional preferences as many formal theoretic, spatial models of politics would suggest (Owens 2010; Sala and Spriggs 2004; Segal 1997). Still, some evidence does indicate that the justices adapt their behavior, becoming less likely to exercise the power of judicial review when Congress is considering a larger number of court-curbing bills (Clark 2011). Justices also exercise their agenda control power in strategic ways, avoiding issues in which their preferences are opposed to those of the current Congress (Harvey and Friedman 2009).

Public opinion is another potential avenue of external constraint on judges (Epstein and Knight 1998). Because courts do not have independent sources of financial support to sustain themselves or direct control over martial forces to enforce their edicts, they are generally at the mercy of the other branches of government (e.g., Hazelton and Hinkle 2022). Under the theory, courts must rely on public support and perceptions of legitimacy to help ensure compliance with their decisions when the other branches would otherwise be disinclined to follow them (e.g., Friedman 2009; Gibson and Nelson 2014; Gibson, Caldeira, and Spence 2005).[19] Many researchers have studied whether the Supreme Court appears to follow public opinion (e.g., Casillas, Enns, and Wohlfarth 2011; Giles, Blackstone, and Vining 2008; McGuire and Stimson 2004; Johnson and Strother 2021). Overall, there is controversy regarding evidence of a link between public opinion and Supreme Court decision-making and the mechanism by which opinion and decisions might be related.[20]

On the lower federal courts, the possibility of review by judges higher in the judicial hierarchy drives external strategic concerns. While there is some evidence of such strategic behavior in the lower courts, the empirical results are mixed. For example, some scholars have found that circuit court judges who are more closely aligned with the potential reviewing courts are more likely to dissent, blowing the whistle on their colleagues to gain the attention of the higher court (Blackstone and Collins 2014; Cross and Tiller 1998; Kim 2009). However, several other studies fail to find any such evidence of strategic dissent (Bowie and Songer 2009; Bowie, Songer, and Szmer 2014; Hettinger, Lindquist, and Martinek 2004, 2006; Klein 2002; Klein and Hume 2003).

There are also indications that external constraints affect opinion writing. Smith and Tiller (2002) show that circuit judges strategically select legal grounds that are more difficult to overturn when facing potential review from an ideological opponent. Under such conditions, district judges use more hedging language, which is phrasing that makes it more difficult to disprove their conclusions (Hinkle et al. 2012). There is also evidence that circuit judges' treatment of precedent is shaped by the preferences of potential reviewing courts (Boston 2020; Hinkle and Nelson 2016; Westerland et al. 2010). And in state supreme courts—where most judges must face the electorate to

---

[19] In order for judicial legitimacy to help judges secure acceptance for their decisions, the institution's public support must persist even in the face of unpopular decisions. The extent to which judicial legitimacy is tied to performance satisfaction is a subject of some debate (c.f. Bartels and Johnston 2013, 2020; Gibson and Nelson 2015, 2017, 2018; Nelson and Gibson 2020). Historically, the U.S. Supreme Court's legitimacy has been stable (e.g., Nelson and Tucker 2021) and high in comparison to other national high courts (Driscoll and Nelson 2018; Gibson, Caldeira, and Baird 1998), in part because the Court has been seen as nonpartisan and apolitical (Nelson and Gibson 2019; Gibson and Nelson 2017).

[20] Scholars have also studied the relationship between public opinion and judicial behavior in lower courts, demonstrating that public opinion affects the behavior of U.S. courts of appeals judges (e.g., Owens and Wohlfarth 2019). Where judges are directly connected to public sentiment through judicial elections (in the U.S. states), public opinion is also a powerful predictor of judicial behavior; this influence is particularly potent when judges must run in nonpartisan elections (Canes-Wrone and Clark 2009; Canes-Wrone, Clark, and Park 2012; Canes-Wrone, Clark, and Kelly 2014; Gibson and Nelson 2021).

10   THE ELEVATOR EFFECT

keep their jobs—there is a rich body of evidence that judges change their behavior to appease voters (Hall 1987; Canes-Wrone, Clark, and Kelly 2014).

Strategic explanations also relate to *internal* deliberations among judges. Maltzman, Spriggs, and Wahlbeck (2000), for example, demonstrate that the internal bargaining process through which final versions of Supreme Court opinions are created generates a complex strategic situation. As one example, judges may choose to vote against their personal preferences in the short term to narrow the implications of an opinion rather than to dissent against a broader, "worse" version of the same opinion. As another example, chief justices, who can assign the opinion author if they are in the majority, may also act strategically in how they go about utilizing their opinion assignment power (Benesh, Sheehan, and Spaeth 1998; Lax and Cameron 2007; Maltzman and Wahlbeck 2004; Wahlbeck 2006). In fact, their calculations can extend beyond internal factors to include external considerations as well (Li 2020).

Internal strategic calculations are also important in the federal circuit courts. Many scholars have observed that there is a strong norm of dissent avoidance in the circuit courts (Epstein, Landes, and Posner 2011; Posner 2008; Fischman 2015). As a result, when considering one's vote, it is strategic for a circuit judge to consider that a dissent could rock the boat. Dissents not only have the potential to undermine the legitimacy of the court, they also often cause more work for the majority (Bowie, Songer, and Szmer 2014). Cross (2007) finds that majority opinions are longer in cases that include a dissent. Internal strategy is not just for judges who find themselves alone in their perspective. Their colleagues may be motivated by norms of consensus to reach a compromise position that is satisfactory to all (Cross 2007; Hettinger, Lindquist, and Martinek 2006; Hinkle 2021).

Background Characteristics

A final class of explanations centers around the identity of the judge, suggesting that a judge's gender, race, and prior professional experiences affect their on-the-bench behavior. Regarding demographic characteristics, evidence in the lower courts has demonstrated that background characteristics matter, at least in certain types of cases.[21] For example, Boyd, Epstein, and Martin (2010) investigate the effect of a court of appeals judge's sex on their decisions, demonstrating that female judges are more sympathetic to plaintiffs in sexual harassment cases than male judges, though there are no differences between men and women on most issues. Kastellec (2011) reaches a similar conclusion about black judges (compared to white) deciding affirmative action disputes, and Glynn and Sen (2015) find that male judges with daughters vote differently on cases related to women's issues than those without daughters.

The evidence with respect to judges' prior professional experiences is mixed.[22] Some studies have found that service as a prosecutor or as a public defender affects judges' behavior (Nagel 1974; Tate 1981), while other studies find no evidence of

---

[21] For a review of this literature, see Harris and Sen (2019).
[22] For a review of this research, see George (2008).

this sort of effect (Gibson and Nelson 2021). Previous service as a judge can explain voting behavior, although some studies find it leads to more conservative behavior (Johnston and Peabody 1976), while others report that it generates more liberal votes (Tate 1981). In the circuit courts, Hinkle, Nelson, and Hazelton (2020) fail to find that judges with a background as a prosecutor or public defender have any additional sway over their colleagues in search and seizure cases.

Judicial Behavior Is Collaborative

What unifies all these explanations is an emphasis on the individual judge: it is the individual judge that has a set of background characteristics and professional experiences, policy preferences, and strategic calculations. These, the judicial behavior literature tells us, aggregate across judges to create case outcomes. What is largely missing from these explanations is the fact that appellate court decisions are a group effort. Even internal strategic explanations focus on the ability of individual judges to achieve their individual policy goals, not how group dynamics affect judicial behavior.

The most sustained efforts to understand how group dynamics shape judicial behavior have examined panel effects in the U.S. Courts of Appeals. In these courts, most cases are initially resolved by a panel of three judges (Hinkle 2015). This institutional feature generates variation in group dynamics since different three-judge combinations hear different cases. Studies in this vein demonstrate that the diversity of a set of judges—along racial, gender, and partisan lines—affects the decisions panels reach in particular types of cases (Boyd, Epstein, and Martin 2010; Hinkle, Nelson, and Hazelton 2020; Kastellec 2013; Sunstein et al. 2006). While these studies demonstrate that the diversity of a panel can affect case outcomes, they largely sidestep the interpersonal dynamics among panel members (but see Hinkle, Nelson, and Hazelton 2020).

We go one step further to incorporate the complexity of human relationships. Federal appellate judges are co-workers with life tenure, and the relationships they build over time (and that they would like to preserve for future interactions) might affect judicial behavior. Indeed, there are important reasons to suspect that changes in the amount of contact that policymakers have with each other influence how they make decisions. Early members of Congress and Supreme Court justices lived together in boardinghouses in the country's nascent years (e.g., Morgan 1953), a practice that some modern-day commentators have suggested as a potential cure for the polarization, gridlock, and dysfunction that seemingly grips Washington today (Cooper 2018). Even without living under the same roof, personal relationships forged despite ideological differences can ease policymaking. Hakeem Jeffries, a Democrat in the House, and Doug Collins, a Republican member, enjoy a close friendship and have cosponsored bills, including prison reform legislation (the First Step Act) which passed in 2018 (Grisales 2019; Prison Fellowship 2019). Or consider the close collegial relationship between Justices Scalia and Ginsburg, ideological rivals, that so captured the popular imagination (e.g., Wolf 2020). In an era of heightened polarization, such incidents stand out. Furthermore, they indicate that understanding how variation in interpersonal interactions can affect the way policymakers work with each other is a critical element of comprehending how policy is made.

Roadmap of the Book

We begin in Chapter 2 by developing a theory to explain how collegiality can affect judicial policy and introducing original interviews with court of appeals judges and former court of appeals and Supreme Court clerks that we conducted. We start by defining collegiality in terms of cooperative relationships among co-workers. In doing so, we place collegiality in a general context that virtually everyone can relate to their own personal experiences. Next, we survey and integrate existing theories regarding collegiality in policymaking, broadly speaking. Building on work in political psychology, small-group decision-making, and beyond, we assert that collegial interactions can lead to either genuine persuasion through the deliberative process or the suppression of disagreement, that is, "going along" in order to prevent ruffling feathers. Both processes are more likely to play a role when the relevant decision makers come into contact more frequently and spend more time with one another. Critically, the relative ideologies of the policymakers should play a key role in the influence of collegiality on policy outcomes. Collegiality is unlikely to exert much influence in decision-making among policymakers who share similar ideological views (as they tend to agree from the beginning). Rather, the effects of collegiality should operate most noticeably among colleagues who tend to disagree. In other words, collegiality dampens the effect of ideology. Finally, we outline features specific to the judiciary that make collegial relationships important and more likely to form.

In Chapters 3 and 4, we begin to examine this theory empirically. We begin by examining collegiality's effects in the courts of appeals with a specific focus on when judges publicize disharmony with a colleague by publishing a separate opinion. We examine three major empirical implications of our theory. First, we expect judges with greater collegiality concerns to be less likely to dissent or concur from a majority opinion. Second, we expect collegiality concerns to be most important when contention with the opinion author is highest. Finally, increased collegiality concerns can dampen the role of ideological disagreement on a judge's decision to write separately. Further, in Chapter 4, we distinguish between two mechanisms that may explain *why* collegiality affects judicial behavior. We focus our attention on two major possible mechanisms: *persuasion* and *suppression*. First, collegial relations with colleagues may enable judges to make effective private arguments that change the content of the majority opinion during the opinion-drafting process, thereby negating the need to dissent or concur. In this way, *persuasion* may lead to sincere consensus. Second, the existence of collegial relationships increases the costs of publicizing disagreements with fellow judges (see Epstein, Segal, and Spaeth 2001; Goelzhauser 2015). Some judges see each other often, may socialize together, and could therefore have a desire to maintain a positive personal relationship. This desire may affect how they decide a particular case. Even when there is only a cursory personal relationship, a judge may have a desire to maintain a positive professional relationship to ease the decision-making process in future cases. Consequently, judges may *suppress* their disagreement.

We test these expectations using all published U.S. Courts of Appeals search and seizure opinions issued from 1953 to 2010. We use three indicators of contact to examine how collegiality affects the expression of public disagreement: whether judges work in the same courthouse, the length of time two judges have served together on the court, and the probability that two judges will be assigned to hear a case together in the future. The empirical analysis supports both portions of our argument. First, conditional on a sufficiently high level of ideological distance between judges, each indicator of collegiality affects a judge's decision to write a dissenting opinion (but not a concurring opinion). Second, the effect of ideological distance on the decision to write a concurring or dissenting opinion vanishes among those judges who work in the same courthouse or who are likely to sit together on a panel soon.

In Chapter 5, we turn our attention to the U.S. Supreme Court. Historical and modern accounts of the Court indicate that collegiality plays a vital role in shaping the decisions that justices make. For example, the most famous period of collegial Supreme Court decision-making—Marshall's tenure as Chief Justice of the Supreme Court—was accompanied by a period of extreme frequency of contact: the justices lived together in a boardinghouse. We probe the importance of collegiality at the U.S. Supreme Court in recent decades using unique interview evidence from former U.S. Supreme Court clerks. We also estimate a statistical model of separate opinion writing in Supreme Court cases. The best measure of personal interaction available for Supreme Court justices is cotenure, the number of years two justices have sat together on the Court. The results demonstrate that increased time together on the bench significantly decreases the probability of dissent regardless of ideology and lowers the likelihood of concurrence for pairs of justices with divergent political preferences.

Having demonstrated the effects of collegiality *within* courts, we turn our attention in Chapter 6 outward to explain how collegiality affects the behavior of judges *across* courts. We examine the effects of collegiality on the propensity of U.S. Courts of Appeals judges to reverse the decisions made by their trial court colleagues. Because they have additional information about the case at hand, district judges are afforded some deference by appellate judges in both law and practice. We argue that the extent to which an appellate judge grants a district judge latitude is based on their assessment of the district judge in terms of both skill and ideological leanings and is conditioned by the appellate judge's personal interactions with the trial judge. Relying on a dataset of all published Fourth Amendment search and seizure decisions from 1953 to 2010, we find that when an appellate judge and a trial court judge have frequent interpersonal contact, the effect of ideology on the appellate judge's decision to reverse is essentially imperceptible.

In the next two chapters, we move beyond looking at votes to examine how collegiality can shape other types of judicial behavior. Chapter 7 explores the language of dissent. Although judges traditionally treat one another with great professional respect, disagreements over the law are sometimes expressed in the most vehement terms. Yet disagreement is not inevitably disagreeable. An opinion author can express their disagreement with the majority in benign legal terms, in starkly critical language, or anywhere in between. We expect that collegiality plays a role in this variation. Judges face a trade-off regarding the language that they use in a dissenting opinion; caustic phrasing may both negatively affect collegiality and increase the likelihood that the dissenting judge's policy position is publicized or influential in future cases (Bryan and Ringsmuth 2016; Hinkle and Nelson 2018a). We explore the language of dissent in both the U.S. Courts of Appeals and the Supreme Court. Our results indicate that

14 THE ELEVATOR EFFECT

collegiality can affect the expression of disagreement for all federal appellate judges. For example, circuit judges become substantially less likely to be rude when they expect to serve on more panels with the majority opinion author in the future.

The effects of collegiality likely exist across cases as well as within cases. In Chapter 8, we take up an examination of the broader impact of personal relationships by examining when judges cite one another's opinions. These citations are important because precedents are the building blocks of legal development. As a result, any link between personal relationships and citation behavior provides key insight into how the nature and extent of judges' interactions with one another shape legal development. We explore this dynamic in two contexts. First, we examine citations within each circuit using our search and seizure data described previously and citation information extracted directly from the opinions. Since all precedent from a circuit is binding on future cases within that jurisdiction, looking at in-circuit citations holds legal doctrine constant. This allows us to explore whether factors such as two colleagues having chambers in the same city, the length of time two judges have served together, and whether a precedent's author is no longer on the bench influence the probability a precedent is cited. We find evidence that circuit judges are more willing to cite a precedent when it is written by a colleague participating in the case or by a colleague they expect to work with quite a bit in the future. Serving with another judge in the same courthouse or for more years decreases the probability of citation, which is a bit puzzling. Second, we undertake a similar analysis of citation patterns among Supreme Court justices, relying on a dataset containing all citations from Supreme Court opinions from 1955 to 2009. In this context we are limited to exploring the effects of time on relationships since there is no variation in geographic proximity the way there is among circuit judges. Here, we find that justices are most likely to cite their current colleagues, but only if they are also ideological allies.

The final chapter of the book reviews our findings and discusses their implications for future scholarship and for policymakers in the United States and abroad. Overall, we find that increased collegiality may foster consensus, the effect of collegiality increases with greater ideological differences between judges, and collegiality dampens the effect of such ideological differences. We also discuss how collegiality flows both through persuasion and the suppression of disagreement (and other forward-looking behavior) and that institutional context matters. Our results help inform debates regarding many types of reforms, including those touching on institutional features, such as the optimal size of circuits and life tenure. Finally, we highlight avenues for future research, including the relationship between collegiality and judge characteristics and how collegiality works in other contexts.

2
Understanding Collegiality

Introduction

In the mid-1990s, many considered the powerful Court of Appeals for the District of Columbia Circuit to be dysfunctional due to infighting among the judges (Edwards 2004, 62 & 77). Harry T. Edwards[1] became the chief judge of the D.C. Circuit during this tumultuous time (see Federal Judicial Center 2022). As chief, Edwards instituted many "measures [that] were of a piece with, and were in service of, the broader object of promoting collegiality, which could be considered Judge Edwards's organizing principle of leadership," including a lunchtime speaker series, annual dinners, and handpicked birthday gifts (Srinivasan, Harris, and Renan 2021, 76). It is a task at which many say he succeeded, including Justice Ginsburg and Judge Sri Srinivasan (a subsequent chief judge of the D.C. Circuit) (see Srinivasan, Harris, and Renan 2021). Edwards himself became an outspoken advocate for the importance of collegiality in judicial decision-making (e.g., Edwards 1998; Edwards 2004).[2] He could also be a harsh critic of empirical work that he thought did not properly account for such interpersonal relationships (see Edwards 1998; Clermont and Eisenberg 2002).[3]

As Judge Edwards (2003, 1689) himself described:

> The D.C. Circuit has changed dramatically in the years that I have been on the bench. In that time, it has gone from an ideologically divided court to a collegial one in which the personal politics of the judges do not play a significant role in decision making. In reflecting on this over the years, I have come to understand that there are a number of factors that may affect appellate decision making, some that should and some that should not. Among these factors are the requirements of positive law, precedent, how a case is argued by the litigants, the effects of the confirmation process, the ideological

---

[1] Judge Edwards served on the D.C. Circuit from 1980 to 2005 and was the chief judge from 1994 to 2001 (Federal Judicial Center 2022).

[2] One court of appeals judge that we interviewed (J4) noted that in their clerkship experiences, Judge Edwards's efforts to change the culture of the D.C. Circuit came up often. Judge Edwards illustrated "ways in which one can consciously work on collegiality." This included "talking to people" and "inviting criticism."

[3] Clermont and Eisenberg (2002, 1275) had a more pointed interpretation: "Judge Harry Edwards dislikes empirical work that is not flattering to federal appellate judges." Furthermore, the targets of his ire often noted that his responses were not written with a civil tone (Revesz 1999; Clermont and Eisenberg 2002). For example, Revesz (1999) stated, "It is somewhat sobering when one of the Nation's leading federal appellate judges criticizes one's work with great vehemence." A former Supreme Court clerk (S5) discussed the "legend" of Judge Edwards's efforts to make the D.C. Circuit more collegial and enlisting Judge Laurence Silberman to help. They speculated that those strenuous efforts are why Judge Edwards's reactions to empirical work were "so powerful. I can imagine thinking 'I have worked so hard to create this environment [and then you] imply we are politicians in robes.'" They could see how it might have been "a threat to him" to have "professors saying it was just politics" and this might explain the "over the top response." Epstein, Landes, and Posner (2013, 53) described Edwards as "antirealism personified."

The Elevator Effect. Morgan L.W. Hazelton, Rachael K. Hinkle, and Michael J. Nelson, Oxford University Press.
© Oxford University Press 2023. DOI: 10.1093/oso/9780197625408.003.0002

16 THE ELEVATOR EFFECT

views of the judges, leadership, diversity on the bench, whether a court has a core group of smart, well-seasoned judges, whether the judges have worked together for a good period of time, and internal court rules. My contention is that decision making is substantially enhanced if these factors are "filtered" by collegiality. [...] In the end, collegiality mitigates judges' ideological preferences and enables us to find common ground and reach better decisions. In other words, the more collegial the court, the more likely it is that the cases that come before it will be determined on their legal merits.

Thus, it is clear that Judge Edwards considered collegiality to be an essential feature of judicial decision-making on panels.

One aim of this book is to provide empirical analyses that account for collegiality. In this chapter, we lay the groundwork for that and take the role of collegiality in judicial decision-making seriously in building our theory. In doing so, we seek to address Edwards (2003) and Epstein, Landes, and Posner (2013) and enrich our thinking regarding judicial behavior. We do so not with the aim of flattering or attacking federal judges, but rather better understanding judicial decision-making. We consider what collegiality is and why we should care about it. First, we define collegiality in terms of cooperative relationships among co-workers. Thus, we place collegiality in a general context that virtually everyone can relate to their own personal experiences. Second, we explain why these interpersonal relationships are important and deserve further attention. In doing so, we draw from existing work and new accounts regarding collegiality from original interviews with federal judges on the courts of appeals and former clerks from both the circuits and Supreme Court.[4] Third, we consider existing evidence regarding the effects of collegiality from a wide range of sources and disciplines. Fourth, we develop a theory of collegiality in judicial decision-making. We survey and integrate existing theories regarding collegiality in policymaking broadly speaking. Building on work in political psychology, small-group decision-making, and beyond, we assert that collegial interactions can lead to genuine persuasion through the deliberative process or the modification of behavior for purposes of strengthening relationships such as suppressing disagreement, disagreeing politely, or citing one another's work. Both processes are more likely to play a role when the relevant decision makers come into contact more frequently and spend more time with one another. Critically, the relative ideologies of the policymakers should play a key role in the influence of collegiality on policy outcomes.

For most types of judicial behavior, interpersonal relationships are unlikely to exert much influence in decision-making among policymakers who share similar ideological views (as they tend to agree from the beginning). For other behavior, specifically citation, collegiality should have the most impact where two judges tend to agree. In short, the effects of collegiality will depend upon whether two judges are ideological

---

[4] Saint Louis University IRS2 #31675; Approved 01-14-21; Board 1. All interviews were conducted and analyzed by Morgan Hazelton. Information regarding the interviews, including recruitment, participation, and format, are available in Appendix 2.A and 2.B. The interviews were anonymous and the interviewees are identified with the letter J is they were court of appeals judges, S if they were former Supreme Court clerks, and C for former court of appeals clerks. All interviewees are referred to using the pronoun "they" to increase anonymity.

allies or foes. Furthermore, collegiality should influence the effect of ideology. We hypothesize that higher levels of collegiality will dampen the effect of ideology on judicial behavior because when judges get to know each other better, they can rely on that deeper knowledge base rather than the blunter cue of ideology. Finally, we discuss how the varying institutional contexts between levels of the judiciary and types of judicial decision-making are likely to implicate collegiality and its relationship to ideology differently.

What Is Collegiality?

Commentators and scholars use the term collegiality in relation to co-worker interactions in many types of endeavors, including major industries (ten Brummelhuis, Haar, and van der Lippe 2010, 2813), academics (American Association of University Professors 2016), medicine (McDonald et al. 2009), politics (Lawless, Theriault, and Guthrie 2018), and law (Gorman 2004). As aptly described by Cross and Tiller (2007, 257), "[w]hile the merits of collegiality are often invoked, it is not a perfectly clear term." This lack of precision is likely a result of the term being used for both descriptive observations regarding encounters at work and normative statements about ideal conditions in employment.

The breadth of approaches to defining collegiality is seen both within and across disciplines and professions. In political science, the term has been used as meaning something akin to the "social glue" that holds elected officials together (Lawless, Theriault, and Guthrie 2018, 1270), broad interactions among colleagues (e.g., Maltzman, Spriggs, and Wahlbeck 2000), and "direct, personal interaction," "shared purpose among colleagues," and "professional respect" (Yalof, Mello, and Schmidt 2011, 4, emphasis removed). Within the legal realm, the term's meaning also varies. In one example, Cross and Tiller (2007, 257) believe that "interactions among members of [an organization]" form the basis of a definition of collegiality. Courts, when confronted with nailing down collegiality in a legal context, sometimes fail to provide a definition and instead list characteristics (Blankenship-Knox, Platt, and Read 2017, 39). When using the term regarding relationships among jurists, judges tend to offer more aspirational definitions. For example, Judge Harry T. Edwards (2004, 1644–45) stated:

> When I speak of a collegial court, I do not mean that all judges are friends. And I do not mean that the members of the court never disagree on substantive issues. That would not be collegiality, but homogeneity or conformity, which would make for a decidedly unhealthy judiciary. Instead, what I mean is that judges have a common interest, as members of the judiciary, in getting the law right, and that, as a result, we are willing to listen, persuade, and be persuaded, all in an atmosphere of civility and respect. Collegiality is a process that helps to create the conditions for principled agreement, by allowing all points of view to be aired and considered.

In contrast, in fields like organizational management and psychology, definitions tend toward a middle ground between merely describing communication among

18 THE ELEVATOR EFFECT

co-workers and more internal processes like respect and dedication to the law or other goals. For example, ten Brummelhuis, Haar, and van der Lippe (2010, 2813) define collegiality as "the social and communicative behavior of employees toward their co-workers, intended to contribute positively to team cooperation and the atmosphere at work." Thus, we see there is a spectrum of approaches to defining collegiality from concrete and simple to abstract and complex. The squishiness of the concept can cause researchers to speak past each other, so it is important to have a clear approach for our investigation.

In defining the phenomenon of collegiality, we take a middle path. We define collegiality as behavior by individuals that is intended to maintain relationships with colleagues. Collegiality, as we define it, does not require that co-workers to be friends or even like each other (though such bonds can't hurt). Rather, we are focused on actions intended to make interpersonal interactions better (see Collier 1992).

Collegiality Is Important

Regardless of how one defines collegiality, there is broad consensus that it is important. In surveying the importance of collegiality, we look to the world at large, courts in particular, and both popular and interview accounts. First, we discuss the central role of work and relationships in our daily lives. We then describe why relationships among colleagues are important in the work that judges do, drawing both on theoretical and firsthand accounts.

Collegiality in Our Everyday Lives

The sense that collegiality is important is unsurprising given the place of work in our lives. Most of us deal with issues of collegiality regularly, as we must interact with others to achieve goals. In the United States, individuals who work full-time tend to work around forty-seven hours a week (Saad 2014). Individuals between the ages of thirty and fifty-five interact with their co-workers approximately as much as they do with their partner (Ortiz-Ospina 2020). Those under the age of thirty actually spend more time with their co-workers. In fact, in those middle years, people are likely to only spend more time with their children than their colleagues.

With interactions at work being so common, it should be no surprise that society dedicates so much attention to them. Lists regarding how to get along with one's co-workers abound on the internet (e.g., Indeed 2022). Breakdowns in collegiality are the subject of public interest and commentary. For example, Cain (2016) collected office horror stories, including tales of co-workers undermining and attacking each other. In an instance from law practice, in summer of 2022, *Above the Law* reported on a scathing voicemail that a partner left for an associate (Patrice 2022). Additionally, efforts to increase collegiality in professions are apparent. Looking to examples in the medical and legal fields, we find movements toward greater contact to improve collegiality. In medicine, Rubin (2016) described efforts to allow medical personnel time to interact as they had in the past:

Those lounge and hallway conversations served more than social purposes. Clinicians learned and consulted with colleagues and the patients benefitted. Just as important are the benefits of the interactions in and of themselves. We, more than many other professions, have come to feel that only another physician can understand and empathize with what we are going through. These are our friends, and the benefits of seeing, talking and laughing with friends is obvious!

Similarly, in the legal context, Gorman (2004) reported on organizations that were formed and held events, such as meals and trivia, with the goal of increasing levels of collegiality among lawyers. At heart, these efforts look to strengthen bonds between individuals who must work together.

A growing body of evidence suggests that interventions like these are likely to be successful. In a study, ten Brummelhuis, Haar, and van der Lippe (2010) considered the role of contact in improving work conditions using survey data from over a thousand employees from Dutch firms across major industries. They tested, in part, a theory of social connections and collegiality. Ten Brummelhuis, Haar and van der Lippe (2010, 2842) found empirical support for "the idea that employees need time to interact in order to develop collegial relationships (Verbrugge 1977; McPherson et al. 2001)" based on decreased collegiality among colleagues using a flex-time system.[5] Thus, there are important reasons to promote collegiality in workplaces generally.

The Importance of Collegiality in Courts

Based on the importance of collegiality in the workplace generally, including within the legal profession, it is very likely that interpersonal relationships among judges matter in courts. Investigating the role of collegiality in judicial decision-making is important to a fuller understanding of the endeavor. We anticipate that it plays an essential role in shaping the work of judges. Within the study of law and courts, there are a number of reasons to expect that collegiality exerts a particularly powerful pull on judicial behavior, especially the extent to which panels reach consensual decisions. As aptly pointed out by Epstein, Landes, and Posner (2013), judges are people with human desires like leisure and good relationships. As a result, understanding the role that collegiality plays in judicial behavior—and, as Edwards (2003) suggests, its relationship to judicial ideology—is essential to our understanding of how judges decide cases. Collier (1992, 4 & 38), a psychologist, describes the importance of judges creating and maintaining such relationships to carry out the work of the judiciary: "[Collegiality's] absence clearly makes every judge's life much more difficult and isolated than it needs be. Lack of collegiality also can adversely affect the nature of the court system." In considering the extent to which interpersonal relationships matter, we consider the institutional features of courts that are likely to make interpersonal relationships especially important and what judges have said about collegiality, both in public statements and original interviews.

---

[5] Ten Brummelhuis, Haar, and van der Lippe (2010, 2842) did not find significant results regarding remote work.

Features of Courts that Make Interpersonal Relationships Important

Institutional features of appellate courts indicate that interpersonal relationships should be particularly important to their operations. First, compared to other types of policymakers, judges decide cases in small groups. Because larger groups encourage free riding and lessen the amount of effort an individual member needs to contribute to the group's output, the small-group nature of judicial panels heightens the importance of collegial relations (Atkins 1973; Martinek 2010). Such "[g]roups pursue [...] goals and functions by means of activities that entail ([a]) processing information and creating meaning, ([b]) managing group conflict and attaining consensus, and ([c]) motivating, regulating, and coordinating member behavior" (McGrath 1997, 18). All these types of behavior are present in judicial decision-making.

Second, judges often serve for long terms, making the long-run collegiality calculation especially important: two judges might serve together for decades and adapt their behavior to maintain positive relationships with their colleagues (see Maltzman, Spriggs, and Wahlbeck 2000). Supreme Court justices publicly acknowledge this fact (e.g., Mauro 2018). As do courts of appeals judges; cotenure on courts of appeals "ha[s] been analogized to arranged marriage with no divorce option" (Epstein, Landes, and Posner 2013, 32). Thus, the costs of burning bridges with colleagues are ones that appellate judges are likely to feel for many years into the future.

Third, judges have an interest in protecting the influence, prestige, and legitimacy of their court; maintaining at the least the appearance of collegiality might be one way to achieve those goals (see Atkins and Green 1976; Farhang and Wawro 2004; Ginsburg 1990; Hazelton and Hinkle 2022; Hettinger, Lindquist, and Martinek 2006; Kim 2009). For example, more consensual Supreme Court opinions enjoy more consistent enforcement (Black et al. 2016). Depending on the conditions (Salamone 2014, 2018), fewer dissenting justices can lead to greater acceptance from the public (Zink, Spriggs, and Scott 2009; Corley, Steigerwalt, and Ward 2013).[6] So unanimity can be a benefit to the institution from which judges draw their power.

Additionally, judges and justices act in ways that indicate that they think the legitimacy of the judiciary is influenced by how the public perceives relationships among them. For example, in January 2022, accounts regarding collegiality and the Supreme Court became controversial. Totenberg (2022a) reported on Justice Neil Gorsuch's decision not to wear a mask to oral arguments during the Omicron surge even though Justice Sonia Sotomayor has a heightened risk from COVID because she is diabetic. This was particularly notable because Totenberg reported that Chief Justice Roberts had "in some form asked the other justices to mask up." While the other eight justices attended oral argument in person, Justice Sotomayor attended the arguments remotely. In introducing the story, Steve Inskeep of NPR said: "Justices of the Supreme Court like to tell audiences how well they get along, even when they have profound legal disagreements. Some of that collegiality appears to be wearing thin now, and that has potential consequences" (NPR 2022). Within a day, Justices Sotomayor and Gorsuch had issued a joint statement: "Reporting that Justice Sotomayor asked Justice Gorsuch to wear a mask surprised us. It is false. While we may sometimes disagree

---

[6] Not all studies find that unanimity fosters acceptance (Gibson, Caldeira, and Spence 2005).

about the law, we are warm colleagues and friends" (Barnes 2022b). After commentators noted that the initial NPR report did not claim that Justice Sotomayor asked, Chief Justice Roberts issued a statement: "I did not request Justice Gorsuch or any other Justice to wear a mask on the bench." Totenberg (2022b) defended the initial report, while others criticized it (see, e.g., McBride 2022; see generally Dahlia Lithwick 2022). While we cannot determine what happened in this case, the rare public statements by three sitting justices highlight the extent to which members of the Court care about collegial they are perceived.

Thus, the characteristics of federal appellate courts indicate that relationships among judges are likely to be important. First, judges and justices make decisions about cases in small groups where they have a lot of direct interaction with each other. Second, the judges have life tenure and tend to serve together much longer than other types of co-workers. And, lastly, breakdowns in collegiality receive public attention and may influence the legitimacy of courts.

What Judges and Clerks Say about Collegiality in Public

Beyond institutional characteristics that enhance the importance of relationships on courts, we have reason to believe they matter because judges say they do. In public statements, judges often tout the role of collegiality in judicial decision-making. Judge Patricia Wald (1984, 11), of the D.C. Circuit, offered her perspective:

> After a few years, you learn your role on the court as a loner, an inveterate disagreer, an almost automatic agreer, or a conciliator able to influence rationales or even results by negotiation. [...] Decisions will be influenced a great deal by how much a judge accommodates colleagues or battles them, values the importance of the court's speaking with certainty, views a judge's role as a member of a group or as an individual.

Offering another perspective on the vital role of collegiality, Judge Harry T. Edwards (2003, 1645) has written that "collegiality plays an important part in *mitigating* the role of partisan politics and personal ideology by allowing judges of differing perspectives and philosophies to communicate with, listen to, and ultimately influence one another." Furthermore, judges also suggest the relationships among their colleagues are a consideration in how they decide to act. For example, Judge Diane Wood (2012, 1463), who sits on the Seventh Circuit Court of Appeals, said:

> [S]eparate opinions may create tension among the members of the court. Either side—the majority or the dissent—may feel personally attacked even if the other was striving to keep matters strictly professional. That risk may ebb if the dissenter becomes branded as a frequent complainer about one or more issues. But that raises a different problem: the dissenter will have lost credibility and may be disregarded altogether. Most judges will therefore think carefully before writing separately, even if they sincerely disagree with some or all of the proposed opinion.

Thus, we find that public statements by judges support the idea that collegiality is an important factor in judicial decision-making.

Table 2.1 Description of Interviewees and Identification Codes: This table contains the number and type of interviewees and the identification codes used to refer to them throughout the book.

Type	Number	Identification
Court of Appeals Judges	7	J1–J7
Former Supreme Court Clerks	5	S1–S5
Former Court of Appeals Clerks	4	C1–C4

What Judges and Clerks Say about Collegiality in Our Interviews

Beyond relying on public, nonsystematic, and attributed comments, we also sought out interviews with court of appeals judges and former circuit and Supreme Court clerks to help us learn about the issues. These interviews were carried out between February 2021 and April 2022. There were sixteen interviews in total, which are broken down by type and code in Table 2.1. Further details regarding the interviewees, including a general outline of the questions asked, are available in Appendix 2.A and 2.B.

The Importance of Collegiality and Fostering It

The judges we interviewed under conditions of anonymity repeatedly highlighted the central role of collegiality. Overwhelmingly, interviewees described collegiality as quite "important" (J1, J3, J4, and J7). Based on context and content, they tended to use the word collegiality as a shorthand for warm interpersonal relationships or respectful professional encounters.[7] When asked about the role of collegiality in their circuits, judges often described the values and norms of the circuit related to interpersonal and professional relationships. Furthermore, they tended to see their own circuits as quite collegial. To start, J1 said that collegiality was "very important" and that their circuit is "a very collegial circuit. We pride ourselves on being a collegial circuit." They noted that they don't have much of a point of comparison: "So perhaps we're a bit self-congratulatory, but I think we are and we try to be." They had heard "anecdotes about judges not getting along in other circuits." In the same vein, J4 stated that collegiality is "extremely important. We pride ourselves on it." Thus, overall, the court of appeals judges we interviewed touted the importance of interpersonal relationships among judges.

Furthermore, the judges described the ways in which collegiality is created or encouraged within their circuits. J2 spoke directly to the importance of norms within circuits and collegiality. First, they addressed different contexts in which it is obvious that culture is important. For example, the judge "loves football" and mentioned that "increasingly [sports] commentators talk about [team] culture [during games]." And, "in the corporate context, you hear a lot about culture." There is the "question of how to set the culture." J2 clarified that "culture is a subset of morality. It is the behavior

---

[7] Some judges specifically asked about the definition of collegiality. We described the broader meaning we employ but also invited them to share their thoughts as to collegiality as they understood it.

you expect and what is acceptable or not." When they came to their court, they learned other judges were "jealous regarding the reputation and culture of the circuit." Seasoned judges hosted the new circuit judge orientation. They would go around and talk to the new judges about where they were going. "[The seasoned judges] would say 'oh, you're going to the [X] circuit. I love it, they are so nice.' The senior judges didn't say this about the other circuits. I received consistent feedback about this from [the three judges.]" Internally, the judges have a proud nickname for the circuit.[8] "They discuss their culture in terms of that nickname." Thus, there is reason to believe that collegiality varies and can be influenced by institutional features.

Other judges spoke to intentionally promoting collegiality within their circuits. J3 had an "interesting experience" because they were "very short-handed and in a short period got many new judges. For a small organization, that is a lot of people. So, I spent a lot of time with them to make them feel welcomed and instill court values regarding how we try to achieve collegiality. It is very important and was successful." It involved "teaching and speaking about a commonality of purpose." "There is no one on the circuit that I would dread having dinner or a drink with. I have common ground with all other judges on the circuit" (J3). J7 saw themselves as "the right person to ask," as they have an administrative position designed to increase collegiality in the circuit. When they first came to the circuit, they learned that two judges already serving on the court did not speak with each other and a third party had to be brought to mediate between them when they had to talk to each other. It was the "worst example" of collegiality. The circuit was "lacking" in collegiality, and the chief judge charged the judge with encouraging it. "I have been quite successful. We have gone from [noticeably dysfunctional] to a model of collegiality. I know what it is like to be in a collegial circuit and what it is like to not be in a collegial circuit." The chief judge has been "thrilled with the results." Thus, collegiality is something that judges invest in through encouraging norms and values within their circuits.

The features that promote collegiality may encourage judges to think beyond their desired outcomes. Other judges have spoken about being oriented toward the court as a whole and subsuming individual preferences. J5 volunteered that when they write an opinion, "they are speaking as the Court. They are representative of the Court." In support of this idea, they noted that the "news often won't name the judge but instead [attributes the action to] the '[X]th Circuit.' So it is nice to get as much information as possible." When we asked J7 if they see themselves as speaking for the court in opinions, they said one "should speak for the court." They noted the use of the pronoun "we." One writes as "an individual only if dissenting." They noted that sometimes there are per curium opinions where not only one judge is writing. In their circuit, if they are "combining two drafts" it becomes a per curiam opinion. The interviewee also stated that these are not "unsigned" opinions as it sometimes is reported, but rather the more collective "opinion of the court." The "mindset is different when writing a majority opinion." This is true because of the other judges involved. There has to be "compromise" and you might not be able to go "as far as you want." With a dissent, "you can just write" and "don't have to deal with requests to cite this rationale, etc.,

---

[8] Omitted for anonymity.

24 THE ELEVATOR EFFECT

because other judges are not necessary." Thus, compromise and maintenance of relationships play a role in the work of courts.

Interestingly, the perceptions of high levels of collegiality within one's circuit did not always translate into a perception of collegiality throughout the courts of appeals.[9] Some judges spoke regarding other circuits. J3 thought their circuit was in the "top half" of circuits for collegiality. "There are famous incidents regarding breakdowns in collegiality. Assigning fault is unproductive. You need a restart. I watch [such instances] with sorrow and regret." In keeping with that theme, J4 said that there are "definitely circuits with pointed and harsher dissents and concurrences. There it spills out into the open and is very noticeable on the face of it." There is a "real danger if [you] engage in that [kind of approach]. It will spill out and damage [the relationship]. It is hard to take back nasty things [once they are] said, especially [when they are said] in public. [There is a] temptation to write sharp and sassy things. [They try to] leave it on the cutting room floor." They may write such things to "blow off steam," but then they edit it out. They do so because "they will work with these individuals for twenty to thirty years." J5 also said that collegiality varies across circuits. It depends on the "culture of the circuit. [In] some [circuits, the judges] don't like each other." When asked what they think affects such variation across circuits, they said "hot button issues." They gave the example of affirmative action cases. They noted that when judges attack each other's motives in separate opinions, "it doesn't help." These matters are "internal" and the elements of "public discussion" and "castigat[ion]" make it "tough to be together after that." J6 stated their experiences with gracious behavior after vote-switching is not assured: "Not every circuit is like that." They base this view on "anecdotes" related to "destroyed relationships." Thus, the judges have ideas about what types of behavior were likely to maintain interpersonal relationships.

Our original interviews with court of appeals judges reveal that they see collegiality as vital to their work and something that can be instilled and maintained. Thus, collegiality is not a given, but rather is a characteristic that varies. They also alluded to ways in which efforts to maintain interpersonal relationships with their colleagues shape how they approach their jobs and the opinions they produce, such as being careful regarding publicizing aspects of disagreements.

How Collegiality Manifests in Important Ways

Overall, the judges also spoke directly to how collegiality matters to the work of the courts and the opinions they write.[10] When asked how a culture of collegiality

---

[9] It should be noted that not all courts of appeals were represented in the interviews. J2 suggested that we should have asked about perceptions of collegiality in sister circuits. The interviewee anticipated that such inquiries could "glean more than gossip," and we might help learn "who has problems" or is "too big." They also suggested asking judges if they evaluate other circuits' collegiality in the same ways they think of their own. Additionally, J2 suggested asking if "substantive disagreement on topics creates sufficient discord to undermine collegiality. For instance, what are the hot button topics?" Examples they gave in response to this question were "voting, abortion, cases with the racial component, criminal sentencing, and discrimination." They also suggested "getting into a little more of the circuits with discord. Do they think they are being heard if they have a substantial minority view? Does it inhibit being heard? I don't mean black and white when I say minority, but rather ideological."

[10] J4 couldn't "remember [collegiality] mattering to outcomes per se."

manifests in discernible ways, J2 offered several examples. First, "there are no internal wars regarding Republican or Democrat or independent. When I first came on the court, I didn't think about who appointed whom." Now, the "politicization of the court of appeals and Supreme Court has increased, and I can't help but notice who was appointed by Trump." "There is the question of what does it mean regarding the culture? To work, it has to be self-policed by the people, the judges. It has to be self-policed by people on both sides of the aisle." When J2 was "new, there were many senior judges. They were very elderly and in their 80s or 90s. They were the keepers of the flame. From them, I learned that culture is very important to sustain how we work with each other, such as not making strident passing comments." Rather, one should make "substantive comments." The interviewee said they try to make comments in "a constructive manner, in a way that no one will think it's based on personal antipathy." Instead, they make it clear they "disagree about process" or the like. Thus, the types of disagreement that are publicized and the way in which they are expressed in writing likely vary based on features of interpersonal relationships.

The ultimate outcome of cases may change based on the ability of judges to work together productively according to the interview responses. J5 could think of multiple examples where they believed collegiality (seemingly in terms of having multiple colleagues you are willing to listen to) changed an outcome in terms of who won a case. First, they and another circuit judge were sitting with a district judge by designation. The district judge wanted oral arguments in the case. The other circuit judge said, "I don't get it," and the interviewee didn't either. Even after a discussion among the three judges, the circuit judges were "not sure, but we went for it." During oral arguments, both circuit judges "realized the district judge was right [to want oral arguments]." They noted that the panel ultimately didn't miss the important legal issue because they were "willing to listen to each other."

Next, the judge recalled being "on a panel with probably the most conservative member of the court" in a case involving an injured child. Due to procedural and jurisdiction complexities and potential errors by the attorney, the case was likely to be dismissed. The interviewee and a third judge on the panel didn't see a way around it. Based on prior experience, the very conservative judge was sympathetic to the difficulties that the attorney and, by extension, the client faced. The sympathetic judge asserted there was a path forward—"I can write it up." J5 described the ultimate opinion as "masterful." In another case, there were difficulties dealing with a case involving children with disabilities. It was a case where it was "hard to thread the needle." The attorney for the children made an impassioned plea to the panel—"this case is not going to the Supreme Court. It stops here. [These specific] children are depending on you for relief." The interviewee did not see a way to resolve the case in favor of the children. Here, a "tough" colleague who was not "touchy feely said, 'we can do something here!'" The tough judge "threaded the needle" and produced a "masterful" opinion. In yet another case, a panel member came up with a creative way to resolve a difficult discovery dispute in terms of remedies. "The group was headed one way and because of one judge we went another." Thus, at least one judge we spoke to remembered instances where they believe that acting in ways that gave other judges the benefit of the doubt and extending courtesy changed the way a case was decided.

26   THE ELEVATOR EFFECT

Judges also described ways in which collegiality influenced the ability to produce unanimous opinions.[11] When collegiality breaks down, J3 explained that "nothing gets done, [whether] in three-judge panels or en banc. Think about the Supreme Court and plurality opinions, 3–2–1,[12] etc. We have a responsibility to the bar and the public who follow our reasoning and explanation. It is not just affirm or reverse. There are no one-word decisions. We explain everything. [Without collegiality], there is a lower perception regarding the rule of law and confidence in the judiciary (which is already waning)." Similarly, J4 said that compromise in cases is "easier to do if you start from a place of collegiality. These discussions and compromises are lubricated by non-case interactions." Social interactions "bridge over what could have become divisions based on generation or partisanship or other divisions or differences. They counteract [such issues] with crosscutting bonds." J5 calls the idea of sharing perspectives on an issue "surrounding the idea." They might "look at it from the southwest, and [another judge] from the northeast, etc." Thus, the judges are "batting around the idea." One "may change [their] view," thereby "avoiding a concurrence." Thus, several interviewees indicated that strong interpersonal relationships allow the work of the courts to go forward in ways that reduce separate opinions.

Additionally, one judge spoke to the ways in which collegiality makes decision-making easier to bear and, thus, more productive. J6 described how these issues also make work less enjoyable while also echoing the issues regarding work product: "It is a difficult job in the best of circumstances. It is worse if you can't stand engaging with colleagues." It is "easier" and better for one's "physical and mental well-being" if judges are getting along. They said the topic of collegiality generally was "timely": "society is polarized" and the situation is "toxic." People "can't talk." "It is very unfortunate because you can accomplish more if you can sit down and talk without incrimination. So, it is even more important that judges don't retreat into ideological corners. Seeing things differently is okay." They noted all judges take an oath to uphold the law, which implicated their view of the law. "But you can do the work without ignoring each other or being uncivil." Again, insights we gleaned from the interviews indicate that collegiality is important to the efficiency of judges.

Similarly, one interviewee addressed the ability of interpersonal relationships to improve majority opinions. Specifically, J7 sees the benefits of collegiality as the reasoning and input of three judges. "You may think you are the smartest, but there are two other smart judges." The collective reasoning is "often better." The other judges' perspectives should be "taken to heart," and it is a "little humbling" how many "good ideas" the other judges have. In sum, judges we spoke to generally indicated collegiality likely increases the number of unanimous opinions.

---

[11] This idea was also addressed by one of the former Supreme Court clerks we interviewed. S5 described how collegiality might influence the drafting process specifically. They discussed how before authors circulate drafts of opinions there is "anticipatory" behavior. Justices will say things like "let's take out [this part] because it won't fly with [this person]." They speculated that these behaviors may vary based on collegiality "at the margins." Justices may be more inclined regarding concessions ("OK, I'll remove this sentence," etc.) based on personal relationships. While they did not have "specific examples," they found this account to be plausible based on their experiences.

[12] Here, the interviewee was making a shorthand reference to the small groupings of justices that can happen in plurality opinions, where no single approach garners a majority.

When judges explain why collegiality is important, they point to issues of productivity and unanimity. Stronger interpersonal relationships, in their estimations, can lead to the ability to compromise and reduce the number of opinions that are being produced. This was generally seen as promoting better decisions overall. Additionally, J3 noted that fractured opinions harm opinions of the court and the implementation of decisions. Thus, ties to other judges don't just make judges happier, they appear to make courts more effective. Thus, we find consistent assertions by federal judges that collegiality matters.

Existing Evidence on the Effects of Collegiality

We have many reasons to believe collegiality is important in judicial decision-making, including structural aspects of courts and statements by judges. Judges decide cases on small teams with long-term colleagues and a public that cares about how they decide cases. Furthermore, judges indicate that the extent to which a court speaks with one voice and with a clear, well-reasoned, convincing, and professional tone are influenced by the working relationships among judges. Despite these strong reasons to anticipate that collegiality matters, as we discussed in Chapter 1, tests of judicial collegiality have been scant. Still, others have theorized and tested the effects of collegiality in other policymaking contexts with a focus on contact among colleagues. We consider that body of work and what it can help us theorize regarding courts. We also investigate existing evidence from across many disciplines concerning the mechanisms by which relationships are likely to impact decision-making and how that relates to contact.

Studies of Collegiality in Policymaking and Contact

How do relationships among policymakers affect elite decision-making? This question has motivated generations of researchers seeking to explain how smoke-filled back rooms affect political phenomena as diverse as patronage and logrolling (e.g., Routt 1938; Young 1966). Prior work suggests that collegiality among policymakers is influential regarding the policies that they announce. For example, Matthews (1960) suggested that increased collegiality among members of the U.S. Senate translates to positive legislative results (see also Young 1966).

A recent resurgence of work regarding the influence of relationships among legislators and legislative outputs has reached mixed conclusions regarding the extent to which collegiality affects legislative behavior. Building on previous work regarding how sitting arrangements can influence legislators' voting behavior (Matthews and Stimson 1975), Masket (2008) analyzed the extent to which deskmates in the California Assembly were more likely to vote together and found a strong effect. Similarly, further considering prior work regarding the effects of shared boardinghouses in early America (Young 1966; Parigi and Bergemann 2016), Minozzi and Caldeira (2021) used weighting to account for the likelihood that legislators tended to gravitate toward the like-minded. Even with such adjustments, they continued to find a "boardinghouse effect," though it was not as large as prior studies. Additionally, Curry and Roberts (2022, 30) explored how congressional delegation (CODEL) travel, especially foreign travel, "helps members develop [...] positive and productive relationships, because of the bonds and mutual understanding that time together can foster." First, they conducted interviews with high-level congressional staff who overall indicated that positive relationships influence outcomes; travel is a "key venue for the formation of relationships" and the ability of relationships to help overcome political divides (Curry and Roberts 2022, 20). Building on the interviews, they analyzed an original dataset that included information regarding official foreign travel by members of the House between 1994 and 2020 and bill co-sponsorship. Their results indicate that "members who travel together even if they are from the opposite party are more likely to collaborate on legislation" (Curry and Roberts 2022, 30). These studies indicate that collegiality can influence the policies that legislators produce.

Not all recent studies have found such evidence. Rogowski and Sinclair (2012) used office locations in the House, which are randomly assigned, as an instrumental variable and found no evidence that proximity influenced roll call or cosponsorship behavior. Likewise, Lawless, Theriault, and Guthrie (2018) found evidence that women in Congress participate in more social engagement activities, such as softball games and gift exchanges, but did not find a relationship between gender and various legislative activities. Thus, while some studies suggest that interpersonal relationships among legislators affect their choices (e.g., Curry and Roberts 2022; Parigi and Bergemann 2016; Masket 2008), other studies find no evidence of an effect (e.g., Rogowski and Sinclair 2012; Lawless, Theriault, and Guthrie 2018). Therefore, while there are strong reasons to suspect interpersonal relationships affect policymaking, the evidence on this point is far from conclusive.

Notably, the importance of contact to collegiality is an implicit assumption in these studies; each study uses an indicator of interpersonal contact to measure the strength of a collegial relationship (Parigi and Bergemann 2016; Minozzi and Caldeira 2021; Masket 2008; Rogowski and Sinclair 2012; see also Bratton and Rouse 2011; Chown and Liu 2015). Building on Truman (1956), who noted that increased collegiality can be fostered both inside and outside of formal legislative activities, these studies consider both types of activities including legislators traveling together for official business (Curry and Roberts 2022) and the private act of living together (Young 1966; Parigi and Bergemann 2016; Minozzi and Caldeira 2021). So, in addition to having reasons to take the potential role of collegiality in policymaking seriously, we also have a rich intellectual history of tying relationships to contact, both personal and professional.

The Potential Mechanisms Tying Contact and Collegiality to Outcomes

In addition to the work on policymaking that suggests the importance of collegiality and its relationships to outcomes, there is a body of work spanning multiple disciplines that addresses the ways in which personal and professional relationships with colleagues are likely to have such an influence. This speaks to the importance of both more social and formal interactions among co-workers and the mechanisms by which collegiality shapes decisions. This rich literature points out several ways in which collegiality may matter: persuasion, which is linked to issues of trust and knowledge of another, and suppression, which reflects concerns about the quality of future interactions.

Persuasion

Some scholars assert that interpersonal relationships can shape the work of courts based on the ways they influence deliberation and subsequent persuasion (Caminker 1999; Edwards 1998; Edwards 2003; Hinkle, Nelson, and Hazelton 2020; Kim 2009; Spitzer and Talley 2013; Wald 1999). This perspective fits within approaching collegiality as "the constructive use of relationships with other professionals in the making of professional decisions" (Collier 1992, 4). Persuasion accounts of collegial judicial decision-making focus on sincere changes in opinion brought about by exchanges of perspective and information (Hinkle, Nelson, and Hazelton 2020) and "the careful consideration of the perspectives of other judges" (Yalof, Mello, and Schmidt 2011, 3). In such accounts, collegiality fosters such conversations by making them more likely and fruitful (Edwards 1998; Edwards 2003; Swalve 2022; Yalof, Mello, and Schmidt 2011; Wald 1999). Judge Patricia M. Wald (1984, 11) noted:

> Where you truly believe that you are right and colleagues wrong on the law or on fundamental concepts of justice, then surely you must be true to yourself. But in the majority of difficult cases, the law is not so clearly perceived. We are not infallible, and inevitably, what our respected colleagues, those with open and probing minds, think right, will influence our own thinking.

There is evidence that more cooperative teams produce better outcomes generally (e.g., Horowitz et al. 2019), though not always (Andrews, Boster, and Carpenter 2012). Under the umbrella of persuasion, scholars describe relationships mattering to outcomes based on elements of trust and knowledge of the other individual's perspective.

Trust

Interpersonal relationships in a work environment may lead to different outcomes based on the presence of trust. The importance of trust emerges from the interconnected nature of group work: "Working together often involves interdependence, and people must therefore depend on others in various ways to accomplish their personal and organizational goals" (Mayer, Davis, and Schoorman 1995, 710). Mayer, Davis, and Schoorman (1995, 728) described the "dynamic nature of trust" by which the outcomes of interactions inform such beliefs in future settings. Thus, interactions help build professional relationships by increasing faith in each other.

This relationship between knowing another person well and trust is supported by psychological research demonstrating that familiarity among group members mitigates problems with information processing that arise in groups (Janis 1972; Schulz-Hardt, Mojzisch, and Vogelgesang 2008). Group members who have worked together before experience less anxiety while completing tasks, which increases the fluency and flexibility of their thoughts, aiding in information processing (Goodman and Leyden 1991). Similarly, as Gruenfeld et al. (1996, 3) note, "familiar group members' knowledge about one another and what is or is not acceptable behavior in the group can inoculate them against the pressure to suppress unique information as a means of avoiding social ostracism." Groups composed of colleagues with positive relationships are better able to manage conflict than groups composed of strangers, further increasing information sharing and lessening the threat of social alienation (Valley, Neale, and Mannix 1995). Thus, both personal and professional encounters that help individuals become more familiar with each other and social norms are likely to result in groups having a greater ability to communicate and come to agreement.

Trust in another's intentions and abilities is important to being able to reach consensus. Mayer, Davis, and Schoorman (1995) described the element of risk that is inherent to situations in which trust is implicated. Specifically, "[t]he willingness of a party to be vulnerable to the actions of another party based on the expectation that the other will perform a particular action is important the trustor, irrespective of the ability to monitor or control that other party" (Mayer, Davis, and Schoorman 1995, 712). Furthermore, trust speaks to one's assessment of another's skill. Mayer, Davis, and Schoorman (1995) describe the importance of perceived ability in trust; previous interactions with an individual help inform these beliefs. In group decision-making situations, especially in ones where individuals have different stores of information and expertise, one can't fully monitor the extent to which another is correct and forthright (see Spitzer and Talley 2013). In the context of collegial decision-making, such risk and trust is involved in the act of persuasion as to legal outcomes and reasoning. Applying such ideas in the context of the German Federal Court of Justice, Swalve (2022) theorizes that trust is one mechanism by which familiarity may improve the work of judges.

Knowledge Regarding Another's Way of Thinking

Additionally, beyond trust, the more you know someone, the better you understand what types of arguments and evidence are most likely to persuade them. Facebook's business model of using personal data regarding individuals for marketing purpose is built upon this idea (Monnappa 2022). Swalve (2022, 225) speaks to the extent that familiarity can influence how judges coordinate, behave based on expectations of each other's behavior, and speak "a common language." Furthermore, research about persuasion indicates that you are more likely to bring someone to your way of thinking if you can "get your foot in the door" with a proposition that is likely to be accepted (Stanchi 2006). Prior knowledge of another person makes it more likely that you can make a tailored (nongeneral) opening argument to which the other person is likely to give credence. Therefore, collegiality bred out of interactions gives individuals insights into how to persuade each other.

Suppression
In considering how collegiality influences decision-making, scholars and commentators also point to instances in which individuals act based on concerns about future

ramifications, such as suppressing expressions of disagreement (Hinkle, Nelson, and Hazelton 2020). In such cases, apparent consensus on a point is the result of individuals opting not to publicize their reservations, counterpoints, or additional thoughts. For example, Patricia M. Wald (1984, 10–11) described decision-making on the courts of appeals:

> The dynamism of collegiality plays an important part in our decisionmaking. Very often a concurring judge will bend with the majority, thinking it better for a court to speak with one voice than several. I feel strongly that it is neither necessary nor advisable in every case that the judge voice his or her own special view because it does not coincide exactly with the other judges. Judges are human; they will accommodate those who do likewise. The lone dissenter plays to his own integrity, to history, perhaps to a higher authority, and very occasionally, one suspects, to the law reviews. If one becomes known as a perennial dissenter and a rare compromiser, his or her influence on the court may be discounted.

Similarly, as described earlier in this chapter, Wood (2012) suggested that judges do (and should) consider the effect of separate opinions on colleagues when deciding whether to issue one. Within and beyond the issuance of separate opinions, interpersonal relationships with fellow judges might induce behavior to maintain those relationships based on the costs of doing otherwise. While the most prominent example of such behavior is suppressing public disagreement, it can also operate in more subtle ways such as phrasing public disagreement in a polite and respectful manner or even making an effort to cite colleagues' opinions. There are a variety of ways in which judges may seek to preserve or improve their relationships with co-workers. For all of them, issues of costs, both personal and professional, weigh heavily.

Personal Costs

When judges weigh the costs and benefits of behavior that affects interpersonal relationships, they often confront a number of personal costs. Such costs generally involve issues of psychological pressures and enjoyment of work. As we explain in our discussion of whether behavior aimed at maintaining relationships with colleagues is inherently normatively good later in this chapter, working in groups creates pressures to conform (Asch 1955, 1956; Andrews, Boster, and Carpenter 2012; Kim 2009; Sunstein et al. 2006). In a pathbreaking study, Asch (1951) demonstrated that the pressure to conform to the stated beliefs of others can drive individuals to change their behavior, even when that behavior is obviously incorrect. A wealth of research has confirmed the phenomenon overall, while adding to our understanding of nuances regarding its effects (Cialdini and Goldstein 2004). Such pressures may lead a judge to not publicize disagreement (Atkins 1973; Sunstein et al. 2006). Additionally, many scholars point to the norms of consensus on the federal courts of appeals as a source of pressure to suppress separate opinions (e.g., Epstein, Landes, and Posner 2011; Fischman 2011; Goldman 1968; Hinkle, Nelson, and Hazelton 2020; Posner 2008). In this vein, humans generally care about maintaining good relationships with those around them. Conflict with others can lead to awkwardness in

32 THE ELEVATOR EFFECT

interactions. Clegg (2012) theorizes that psychological awkwardness in social interactions has the function of recentering individuals toward relationships. Thus, there are psychological mechanisms that would pull a judge, as with any human being, away from conflict with colleagues.

Professional Costs

For judges, being in the minority often involves increased costs (see Cameron, Segal, and Songer 2000; Caminker 1999; Carrubba and Clark 2012; Cross and Tiller 1998; Epstein, Landes, and Posner 2013; Howard 1981; Hinkle, Nelson, and Hazelton 2020; Kastellec 2007; Posner 2008). These costs include the time and effort of writing the dissent and strained relationships among judges within the panels (Cameron, Segal, and Songer 2000; Kastellec 2007). Conflict with colleagues may harm a judge's ability to compromise with them in the future. Maintaining relationships with fellow judges because you might need them in the future is a recurring theme in both public accounts of making decisions on panels (e.g., Stohr and Epstein 2018; Wald 1984) and in the interviews that we conducted and which are described throughout this book. For example, J5 told us that you might need another judge in the future though you disagree in the immediate case. Not making enemies is important because if one "thinks [the other judge] was a total idiot and [you] can't stand him[, you were] turned off and won't be able to come together." They believe that judges coming together is important even where they don't "fully agree." Similarly, J3 spoke to the fact that foes today may be potential allies in the future. Additionally, if a judge engages in whistle-blowing activity too often, their dissents become less effective as a signal (Beim, Hirsch, and Kastellec 2014).[13]

Furthermore, as we discussed regarding features of courts that make interpersonal relationships important, public disagreement may harm the legitimacy of courts and, thus, the power of judges. Issues of unanimity and legitimacy came up in the interviews. J3 said the circuits are "multi-membered courts getting things done." When acting as a "committee of the whole," they hope the votes don't always split on partisan lines. They seek "ways to find a middle ground," which sometimes involves producing less "ambitious" opinions. They noted that the Supreme Court had to operate as an evenly divided eight-person court after Scalia died, and "they did a fine job that year." There is a need for strong majorities and maybe unanimity on the court due to legitimacy concerns. In discussing the need for legitimacy to ensure enforcement, the interviewee referred to the incident in which Andrew Jackson is alleged to have responded to a Supreme Court ruling upholding treaties with the Cherokee in opposition to the state of Georgia by saying, "John Marshall has made his decision; now let him enforce it." They believe legitimacy helped ensure enforcement. Thus, at least one interviewee was concerned that public breaches of collegiality harm the legitimacy of the courts, which in turn harms the enforcement powers of the courts.

---

[13] The costliness of signals from separate opinions also makes them valuable to supervising courts (Beim, Hirsch, and Kastellec 2014; Epstein, Landes, and Posner 2011).

Is Collegiality Always Good?

We pause to consider whether behavior aimed at maintaining relationships with colleagues is inherently normatively good. There is evidence that groups tend to make better decisions than individuals (e.g., Horowitz et al. 2019). Scholars and judges often speak to the benefits of having multiple judges deciding appellate matters because it leads to better reasoned and informed decisions (e.g., Edwards 2003; Spitzer and Talley 2000). Additionally, judges we interviewed spoke to the benefits of being able to attack an issue from multiple perspectives (J5) and the ability of groups to rise above more individual views and concerns (J4). Thus, there are reasons to believe that collegiality likely enhances judicial decision-making.

It would be a mistake, however, to assume that it is inherently good or necessarily positive in all cases. Team interactions raise the potential for conformity effects (Asch 1955, 1956; Andrews, Boster, and Carpenter 2012) and groupthink (Janis 1982; Horowitz et al. 2019). For example, the use of collegiality as a standard for tenure in academia has been a matter of debate with some seeing it as posing "several dangers such as promoting homogeneity of thought, discouraging dissent, and acting as a cover for discrimination" with others asserting it has the "potential to improve the morale and job satisfaction of faculty while also increasing the overall effectiveness of the unit" (American Association of University Professors 2016). Thus, the influence of interpersonal relationships among judges who decide cases together is not necessarily a normatively desirable effect. Such influence might "represent psychological mechanisms—such as conformity pressures or group polarization—[that] may be operative, leading judges to change their minds when confronted with the opinions of their colleagues" (Kim 2009, citing Sunstein et al. 2006). Judges from underrepresented groups may be particularly susceptible "to conform to the dominant majority and to obtain legitimacy in the group" (Peresie 2005, fn.15 citing Kanter 1977). Failure to publicize disagreement with colleagues due to collegiality concerns might diminish the likelihood that the legislature or higher or future courts might correct a wrong decision (see Ginsburg 2010). Therefore, there are reasons to be concerned that collegiality might breed conformity instead of well-reasoned or justifiable consensus.

Concerns about the unwarranted suppression of opinions were reflected in the comments of interviewees. J4 described that there can be "trade-offs" where "collegiality is a club" and the older judges assume an "in my day" stance. Also, there are "real trade-offs with real differences and disagreements and the limits of collegiality. [You] have to be careful that collegiality is not being used to suppress vigorous debate." J4 said they "should point out that a fair-minded person could say that if [one is] too focused on collegiality as an end unto itself that it runs the risk of submerging real differences and not airing substantive disagreements." Another interviewee described more ideal forms of collegial interactions in comparison to repressing dissent. For example, J3 said, "disagreement is fine, but you need a reason to do so–not you just don't like it." With "friendly comments," one "usually can accommodate [the requests]." We have to have a "way of working through issues you can't talk about at Thanksgiving with Uncle [Frank]—gun control, death penalty, ... We have to talk about them. We don't have the privilege not to discuss them. [We] try to work through them in a non-confrontational and hopefully non-emotional way, and after working through them

34 THE ELEVATOR EFFECT

[we gain] camaraderie." "The nature of the job is that you have to disagree with your colleagues but you start with your position and work to compromise." Such compromise might take the form of "narrower common grounds." In these negotiations, disagreement is not "paper[ed] over" and they don't "make a hash out of compromise," instead it is "a principled resolution." Thus, even judges who see collegiality as important to judicial decision-making suggest it can also have negative consequences.

In our consideration of how collegiality influences judicial decision-making and why, we attempt to speak to these larger normative issues without assuming that the influence of collegiality is inherently positive in all cases. Rather, we seek to shed light on an understudied area to help us understand how judicial decision-making is operating in ways that we may not fully appreciate.

Our Theory

The existing evidence is helpful, but the judiciary is a unique animal. Thus, one must attend to the unusual aspects of courts and the nature of judging in crafting a theory of how judges' incentives to maintain relationships matter in judicial decision-making. We, like this existing literature, prioritize the importance of interpersonal contact to foster collegiality. In doing so, we look to both personal and professional interactions and the ways in which they can further both persuasion and suppression in decision-making. These two mechanisms are separate paths by which differences in contact among judges can yield varying levels of collegiality which, in turn, influence outcomes. We also focus on how collegiality and ideology influence decision-making and how the interplay of the two factors conditions their effects. Finally, we discuss how variation in types of courts and the decisions that judges make influence collegiality through its operating mechanisms and interactions with ideology.

Relationship of Collegiality to Contact

There are reasons to believe that relationships among judges are fostered by contact beyond just the evidence that it influences policymaking generally. For example, Judge Harry T. Edwards (2003) praised the practice of keeping judges in the same physical office space: "Having the entire circuit's chambers in the same building, as with the D.C. Circuit and the Federal Circuit, can also be immensely helpful. The ease of face-to-face interactions outside the context of hearings and conferences makes a difference" (1675). Under theories of persuasion and deliberation, the more contact judges have had with each other is likely to result in increased ability to reach consensus. Interactions among judges increase their knowledge of each other and also provide the potential to bolster trust. Edwards (2003, 1647) writes that familiarity is "one of the major components of collegiality." Judge Alvin B. Rubin (1976, 455), from the Eastern District of Louisiana argued:

> The judges of an appellate court ought to constitute a court, not congeries of judges who are drawn together in odd groups by chance. This might mean, if I may touch on

UNDERSTANDING COLLEGIALITY   35

a matter most sensitive, that they meet together more frequently, live closer to each other, and write their opinions in places where they can readily exchange views and drafts.

Fourth Circuit Judge J. Harvie Wilkinson (1994, 1173) asserted that "at heart the appellate process is a deliberative process, and that one engages in more fruitful interchanges with colleagues whom one deals with day after day than with judges who are simply faces in the crowd. Collegiality personalizes the judicial process." Contact should also increase the likelihood that judges will act in ways to preserve relationships, such as suppressing disagreement and using polite language. The more one anticipates future contact with someone, the higher the potential costs of harming that relationship. Enduring an awkward interaction once or twice a year is quite different than facing one daily in the cafeteria.

Our interviews with courts of appeals judges and clerks indicate that contact matters to collegiality.[14] When asked about ways that judges get to know each other and form relationships, judges tend to describe a range of types of interactions, most of which were face-to-face. For example, J3 cited multiple norms in the circuit that they think promote collegiality. These norms are often related to contact. First, they believe it helps to be relatively "geographically compact," and the panels are "constantly mixing up." Also, it is a "shadow of what it once was," but the judges used to "lunch together after sittings. Now, many judges want to head home directly after oral arguments. You know who is likely to want to join but send the emails and invite all. It is a relaxed and positive environment." When asked about formal and informal events both within the courthouse and outside of it, J1 said they were "rather infrequent" and "wish[ed] they were more frequent."[15] In-person contact, both formal and informal, was highlighted even by an interviewee who generally doesn't believe that it is important that judges office in the same location.[16] Certainly, judges we interviewed connected issues of contact to the formation of relationships among judges.

Judges described some more formal and professional encounters. Often these encounters were in small groups. J1 said that the "biggest way [of getting to know each other] is just sitting together on cases." J3 also mentioned sitting with other judges on panels. En banc hearings are another opportunity for the judges to come together (J1 and J2). Many judges also noted the importance of conferences. J1 noted that usually

---

[14] We return to this issue in Chapter 5, where former Supreme Court clerks also speak to the topic.

[15] It should be noted that the interviews took place during the COVID-19 pandemic.

[16] The principal manner of contact in J2's circuit is email, "so location is not important. There are plenty of opportunities for contact outside of oral argument, especially with those who are in the vicinage. Distance is not an impediment to opportunities for contact." An example they offered of such chances was the judicial conference where the judges come together, sometimes with lawyers included. When the interviewee is in the city where oral arguments are usually held, there is more "informal" contact with other judges as that city is "a hub." They run into other judges there. Occasionally, they also see judges in another city where the circuit sometimes hears cases. Additionally, there are a few scheduled en banc panels every year. As J2 explained, "we don't always hear en bancs when [they are] scheduled." Instead, they "attend to other duties," including "picking bankruptcy judges" and "other circuit-level decisions." When in the oral argument city, the judges "get together throughout the week." It is "an affable group." There is another judge who vacations in the same location and they "sometimes meet up" though it is "hard to coordinate." Court committees are another opportunity to interact with other judges—there is "serendipity there." J2 cites golf as "a great way to get together for those who play." Those judges who do play "get together on their own schedule and time."

36   THE ELEVATOR EFFECT

the judges meet once a year for a conference and that the conference dinner was a good way to get to know other judges. J6 also mentioned "administrative meetings as a source of contact." Additionally, there are "training sessions with the district judges." Thus, professional encounters contribute to collegiality.

However, personal interactions were a main focus of the interviewees' responses regarding how judges learn about each other. According to J4, the "bulk" of interactions are informal. One very common example was having lunch together (J3, J4, J5, J6, and J7) or dinner (J1, J3 and J5). J1 mentioned a ballgame with fondness. They believed that "the most important [events] are informal—'hey, let's get together and go to dinner.'" J1 said that such gatherings were "infrequent and important." They also received "phone calls with offers of assistance and help learning the job and settling in." The judge also referenced casual meetings during court week.[17] J3 also noted there are "get-togethers (though not in the last few years due to COVID)." They noted the importance of including partners and spouses in some events. J4 said that social interactions are "very important" and include "go[ing] out for drinks" and "joint trips with clerks." They also mentioned an upcoming judges retreat in their circuit where judges could bring spouses and children. There were plans for dinner and activities. Furthermore, J6 said that social events during court weeks are "one of the highlights of the year for judges and clerks" because they get to "informally interact." Thus, there are many less formal and more social opportunities for judges to learn about each other, which they seem to value.

The judges stressed the importance of such contact and the ability to bond. J4 described those types of events as "social glue." They continued:

> Judges come from a wide array of backgrounds. Some were state judges, district judges, partners in law firms, politicians, professors, [Department of Justice prosecutors], and public defenders. [They would] not have naturally known each other before [taking the bench]. They may have been picked by different administrations. They have different points of view, tendencies, ages, [etc.]. Sitting together and understanding each other is surprisingly important. It is like family, you don't pick [them]. You learn to get along with the different family members you have or [acquired by marriage].

An upcoming judge's retreat was also mentioned by J5, who said that the "issues [we address] may not be big but being together post-COVID is very important." It is important because you need to "know the people you are with on the court." This is especially true because you "often work with clerks in a sheltered existence." In the circuit, judges are "more apart. So, the more you can get together, the better. So you get to know [each other] on a personal level regarding [each other's] personal life. What affects them?" They were interested in learning about the viewpoints that other judges held. Thus, personal relationships were highlighted as important.

---

[17] As we explain in Chapter 3, many courts of appeals hold argument at a central location, often for a week at a time. "Court week" refers to the period when judges and clerks from a circuit come together to hear oral argument and hold initial deliberations on their cases.

UNDERSTANDING COLLEGIALITY 37

Encouraging contact and personal relationships were sometimes stated goals of having such events. The focus on in-person and more informal interactions also came up as part of J7's campaign to increase collegiality. Judges in J7's circuit have lunches together during sittings. On a specific day of the sitting week, all of the judges eat together. The night before they have a happy hour. Both events are held in a private space that was built for the judges. They also have special activities, including sporting events, outdoor outings, and special dinners and parties. They know from experience that everyone is "more collegial if you know each better." You are "less likely to attack another judge in an opinion if you know them, have a personal relationship with them, and are friendly."

During sittings in J7's circuit, the presiding judges "are encouraged but not required" to have dinner with their fellow panelists. "Almost all do, except a few judges who are not too social." The dinners "provide an opportunity to talk about cases informally." Unlike the rigid and seniority-based approach that is observed at the conferences, "dinner is less formal." It allows judges to "bounce off other ideas. You come to a consensus if you can. You try for unanimity." Because judges in J7's circuit are relatively spread out and isolated, they mostly see each other during court weeks and a few en banc panels. Thus, we see that at least some judges see connections between contact, collegiality, and the work courts produce.

There are also reasons to anticipate that interpersonal relationships among judges are not all the same. Some of the more informal contact is not equally distributed among judges within a circuit. J3 acknowledged that they socialize with "some judges but not others. I am not avoiding anyone. I am not as likely to see out-of-towners." Also, judges tend to be "at different stages of life—having kids in high school versus having grandkids. Some judges are doing other things." J4 did say that some judges interact with each other more than others:

It is easier in the same city. You see each other at the courthouse. You may have worked together before or be from the same place or generation. You may have kids of the same age. There are people who went through the confirmation process together. Geography and such features increase the likelihood of interactions. Judges also have different temperaments, outlooks, hobbies, religions, etc.—some things in common to start from [in forming relationships.]

Similarly, J5 said, "In a room, [some judges] gravitate together. Some more than others, [and you] don't always know why." They discussed being close to two other judges who were of a similar age and tenure. When asked if similar interests mattered to the amount of contact judges have with each other, J6 described judges who they know discuss baseball and college basketball—"I think it would matter." When asked if some judges are more likely to interact with each other, J7 attributed differences in interaction to personality: "Some judges are more outgoing versus introverted."[18] J6,

---

[18] They believe that former state court judges are "more outgoing" because they had to "run in elections in the states in the circuit." Thus, they tend to be "open and personable." They explicitly compare these formerly elected judges to circuit judges who came from "law firms and then were appointed by the president." J7 believes that "campaigns are humbling." J7 also described the issues with encouraging other judges to interact. Some judges are "introverted" and it requires more encouragement. There is one judge who is

38   THE ELEVATOR EFFECT

on the other hand, described themselves as "an equal opportunity abuser of time" and "think[s] most judges are." Thus, most judges believe there is variation in the extent to which judges have close relationships with each other.[19]

Thus, the extent of contact between judges tells us where we might look to find stronger or weaker collegial bonds. And it leads us to a central strategy in studying how variation in collegiality matters to judicial behavior. In decisions that involve publicizing disagreement, such as the issuance of a separate opinion or writing harshly about a colleague, increased contact should result in fewer instances of such behavior for reasons implicating both persuasion and suppression. In instances of desirable actions, such citing opinions written by other judges, increased contact should increase the frequency of such behavior either due to persuasion or because judges seek to flatter their colleagues to improve future working relationships.

The Role of Ideology

Collegiality doesn't happen in a vacuum: ideology also matters. Accounts of judicial decision-making suggest that the role of ideology is conditional on collegiality and that interpersonal relationships reduce the effects of personal beliefs (see Edwards 2003). Such effects were also suggested by interviewees. They reported that relationships among judges are often forming outside of partisan frameworks. For example, J5 noted that on the retreat there would likely "not be much if any discussion regarding political world views or political inclination." They would "talk about something else, like administrative issues or sports, but not debating politics!" They also described some informal interactions. There is one colleague with whom the interviewee discusses sports. They "call each other to see how [each other] are doing, especially if something personal [is happening]." If there is "a wedding of a child, you attend. We all like being together or don't dislike being together." J5 also reports that they get to know other judges at meals. They believe that "when [they are together] it is important to get to know [the other judges] as human beings." J7 said that the importance of having "events with all of the judges" is that otherwise the "tendency" is that judges socialize based on ideological differences. "We need to and wanted to mix it up so that we don't have factions." This "helps with unanimity." There is a "main goal" of having judges with "different philosophies" be "friendly and talk to each other." They don't

---

"very introverted," but this more insular judge "likes ribs." J7 can get the judge to come out if they go to the introverted judge's favorite rib place, but not for "a ball game or happy hour." Thus, they focus on drawing such individuals out based on their interests. In terms of why some judges may socialize more than others, J7 cited "geographic" factors. Some judges "are from the same city" and may have been "district judges together." There may be "long-term friendships." These individuals tend to "go out to dinner together." There is one judge who doesn't tend to participate in circuit social events but does go out with one another judge who is their "best buddy." The less-social judge "can be influenced by [their] close friend. [The best buddy] could say paragraph 25 in the opinion is a problem."

[19] We also include clerk perspectives on such interactions in Appendix 2.C.

want a "conservatives' dinner here and liberals' there." That is the "worst outcome" and would be the "tendency." There is "peer pressure" for all judges to attend together. Thus, there is indication that collegiality may operate in ways that can't be explained by partisanship.

Additionally, there is reason to believe that collegiality changes how ideology may matter. For example, in our interviews with judges, one participant spoke to the potential relationships between ideology and collegiality. To start, J5 described being close to another circuit judge down the hall from them who was appointed by a president of the other party than the one who nominated them. They said that they "wouldn't guess" regarding the other judge's ideological views on political topics. They further noted that not all cases have the same political salience: "Many cases are not political." They cited bankruptcy cases as an example. Though they also noted that there are "clearly issues that [judges of different ideologies] see differently." As an example, they described "the Federalist Society and American Constitution Society" as having clearly divergent views on some topics. Furthermore, they believe that "interpersonal relationships soften political divisions" or, at least, "may" do so. With an issue, you might not "look at something [in a certain way] or look hard [at the issue]." Another panel member may offer "another way to look at [it]." If one is "non-confrontational," they can generally "achieve consensus." Where someone is "confrontational, it is significantly negative" to coming together. Such accounts suggest that collegiality can diminish the link between ideological distance between judges and their decision-making, such as writing or joining separate opinions and including vitriolic prose in an opinion.

Additionally, there is reason to believe that judges' assessments of lower court judges may also be influenced by collegiality. Mayer, Davis, and Schoorman (1995, 721) theorize that trust is based on perceptions of "ability, benevolence, and integrity." In other words, the extent to which you are willing to rely on the opinions of another depends on your assessment of their skills in connection with the likelihood that the actor will behave in ways that benefit you. In the absence of information regarding another judge's capabilities, the first jurist must rely more heavily on other factors related to the likelihood they will agree with the decision. In the judicial decision-making context, ideology could be such a factor. Thus, collegiality may influence how ideology matters in judicial decision-making in multiple ways.

Therefore, we theorize that collegiality, as indicated by contact, operates to dampen the influence of ideology in situations where judges can harm their relationships with each other. The value of these relationships to judges will make them less likely to act on differences based on such concerns. We also anticipate that the presence of ideological differences among judges often heightens the importance of collegiality. Such differences make disagreement among judges more likely and create the potential for personal and professional costs. Therefore, collegiality typically has the largest effects where disagreements are most likely and large. However, this does not apply to behavior that colleagues would view positively, like citation. In that case, we anticipate that collegiality will have the largest impact among ideological allies.

40 THE ELEVATOR EFFECT

Institutional Differences in Balancing Ideology and Collegiality

There is also reason to expect that the influence of ideology and collegiality, both directly and conditionally, will vary by type of court and circumstance. Former clerks we interviewed spoke to the differences between the intermediate and highest appellate courts, with court of appeals judges tending to have more contact and interdependence with each other (see Chapter 5). In this vein, Harry T. Edwards (2003, 1644) declined to speak to collegiality and the Supreme Court in his investigation of courts of appeals "because I am inclined to believe that the differences between the Supreme Court and circuit courts may be too substantial to generalize from one to the other." He further elaborated:

> Most significantly, the Supreme Court's docket consists of many more very "hard cases" than do those of the lower appellate courts. The majority of the cases in the circuit courts admit of a right or a best answer and do not require the exercise of discretion. Lower appellate courts are thus constrained far more than the Supreme Court. As a result, in the eyes of the public, the media, judges, and the legal profession, the Supreme Court is seen as more of a "political" institution than are the lower appellate courts. The Supreme Court also faces the burden of having to sit en banc in every case. This may mean that collegiality on the Court operates very differently from the collegial process at work in the lower appellate courts, where judges only rarely sit en banc.

The potential differences between how collegiality operates on the courts of appeals and the Supreme Court was also articulated by Cross and Tiller (2007, 258–59). They observed, "[m]uch of the existing discussion of collegial courts has involved the circuit courts, and the Supreme Court may not be the situs of much collegiality of this type." They further elaborate (259, citing Greenhouse (2002)):

> Some features of the Supreme Court could encourage greater collegiality among the Justices than the level found in circuit courts. All the Justices sit together for each case, unlike circuit courts where panels vary widely. They all deliberate over the same cases, which they themselves have selected on certiorari. There is necessarily some collegial interaction on the Supreme Court, as "the justices are locked into intricate webs of interdependence where the impulse to speak in a personal voice must always be balanced against the need to act collectively in order to be effective."

Similarly, Nash (2022) offers evidence that Supreme Court justices exhibit more collegiality than court of appeals judges and attributes the differences to the fact that justices always sit and office together. So clerks, judges, commentators, and scholars indicate that one should be careful to consider context regarding courts, including issues related to the types of cases a court hears, issues of docket control, public attention, and institutional features.

Certainly, theories regarding collegial decision-making look quite different based on the nature of the court we are considering. There is evidence that the influence of trust in teamwork varies by context (Jarvenpaa, Shaw, and Staples 2004). Also, our understanding of how aspects of courts influence outcomes suggests that institutional context matters. For example, Martinek (2010) notes that "judges serving on appellate courts must interact on a regular basis to dispose of their caseloads." But those burdens look quite different at the circuit and Supreme Court levels of the federal judiciary. The Supreme Court resolves far fewer cases on the merits every year than the various circuit courts (see United States Courts 2022; Gou, Erskine, and Romoser 2022). There are approximately 170 active federal courts of appeals judges and collectively they resolved over 43,000 cases on the merits in the twelve-month period ending in March 2022 (United States Courts 2022). In comparison, the nine justices on the Supreme Court disposed of sixty-six cases in the 2021 term (Gou, Erskine, and Romoser 2022). While not a perfect comparison due to differences in panel sizes and the nature of cases and resolutions, courts of appeals judges resolved approximately thirty-five times more cases per judge than Supreme Court justices. Thus, we would anticipate that judges and justices have very different demands on their time. Judges are human and care about leisure time and will strive to be efficient (Epstein, Landes, and Posner 2013). Because justices have fewer demands, they have to rely on each other less.

The amount of information that justices are provided also may reduce their reliance on each other. Supreme Court justices generally enjoy more information in the cases they hear than courts of appeals judges do (see Hazelton and Hinkle 2022). The vast majority of cases that the Supreme Court hears have been litigated for years, often including at the federal courts of appeals level. Thus, justices have the benefit of additional judicial opinions and rounds of briefing when considering a case. Furthermore, individuals and interest groups provide a wealth of information to Supreme Court justices through amicus curiae briefs. Such briefs are filed in almost all cases before the Court (Collins 2007). In salient cases, the Court is likely to receive scores of such briefs: for example, in the *Dobbs* case, the Supreme Court received 140 amicus briefs (Erskine 2021). Such differences in external information again change the extent to which justices may have differing information by which they can persuade each other.

Additionally, the two levels of court deal with different types of audiences. At the court of appeals level, the panels may be reviewed by the full circuit en banc or the Supreme Court (e.g., Kim 2009) if there is an appeal. This has the potential to constrain the operation of ideology (e.g., Cameron, Segal, and Songer 2000) though it is a matter of scholarly debate if it does (see Bowie and Songer 2009; Klein and Hume 2003). The public is more dimly aware of the operations of circuit courts. At the Supreme Court level, the justices do not need to worry about review by another court (Segal and Spaeth 2002). Instead, any alterations in Supreme Court decisions would have to come through legislation passed by Congress for statutory matters or the arduous route of amending the Constitution in constitutional matters (Epstein and Knight 1998). The public, however, is paying much more attention to their decisions (Brudney and Baum 2016), especially the summer blockbusters. Thus, at the Supreme Court ideology is likely to have maximal effect and relationships may be sacrificed on the altar of public policy.

At the court of appeals level, there is often enough legal ambiguity for ideology to matter, but there are a multitude of reasons to worry about collegiality, such as the need to cooperate to contend with large workloads and the more limited sources of

42 THE ELEVATOR EFFECT

information. Based on the types and number of cases heard by the Supreme Court, justices experience different pressures. They are hearing many more cases where judges are likely to disagree (see Hall and Windett 2016; Wood 2012), and they are much more likely than court of appeals judges to be able to set their preferences as policy (see Epstein and Knight 1998). Therefore, we should not expect collegiality to look the same at those levels.

Collegiality and Different Types of Colleagues

Additionally, context should matter regarding differing types of relationships among judges. One's relationships with individuals beyond the judges in the conference room deciding the case as a panel may also matter to decision-making. In other words, judges' relationships with other colleagues in the circuit or with whom they served in the past may also matter in shaping their behavior. For example, past relationships might affect behavior in the present by making one more inclined to consult and adopt another judge's positions in the form of precedent (which we will discuss in Chapter 8). Additionally, past experiences regarding how interpersonal dynamics formed and mattered might influence how one approaches future ones (something we address in Chapter 5). For example, if you clerked during a dysfunctional period on the Supreme Court, you might be more wary of straining relationships with your fellow justices. However, there are reasons to anticipate that such effects will look different than those among panel members who meet in the same room and are interdependent as opposed to with more distant or past relationships. For example, L. Levy (1960) indicates that conformity effects operate differently when there are face-to-face interactions as opposed to more indirect ones. Because these varying situations implicate issues of persuasion and future-looking behavior differently, they offer an opportunity to disentangle which of these mechanisms best explain *why* collegiality shapes judicial behavior.

Conclusion

In this chapter, we have delved into several important aspects of collegiality—varying approaches to delineating it and our definition of it, its importance, what existing research can tell us about it, and previewing our theory regarding how it affects judicial behavior. In a world where the term collegiality is used to define everything from all interactions among co-workers to selfless and high-minded collective action, we define collegiality as behavior intended to maintain relationships with colleagues. The importance of our interactions in the workplace will come as no surprise to those who work with others. These relationships have a central place in our daily lives. Both research from psychology and organizational management reinforce these intuitions, as do the firsthand experiences of judges. Our original interviews with federal judges provided us with a multitude of examples about the importance of relationships among judges for the work they do. Furthermore, we see that these relationships are fostered in and out of the courtroom. Unfortunately, the role of collegiality in judicial decision-making has not received the attention it deserves. We build on existing research regarding interpersonal relationships and policymaking and related aspects of judicial behavior coupled with the perspectives of the judges with whom we spoke. In doing so, we focus on the role of contact in forming relationships. Additionally, we consider how these personal and professional relationships among judges likely influence behavior by facilitating persuasion through trust and knowledge and encouraging the suppression of disagreement based on its costs. All of these factors are pulled together for the articulation of our theory in the unique context of judicial decision-making.

We focus on the role of contact in forming the relationships that judges seek to maintain with their collegial behavior. Ultimately, we anticipate that greater collegial bonds, as indicated by increased contact, will result in judges behaving in ways that result in fewer expressions of disagreement and more frequent efforts to curry favor. We also recognize that ideology matters in judicial decision-making. However, we anticipate that the ways ideology shapes judicial behavior have been obscured by the lack of consideration existing scholarship has given to collegiality. We expect that heightened collegial concerns can reduce behavior motivated by ideological differences. Further, the influence of collegial concerns is accentuated by the presence of more fundamental ideological disagreements. Moreover, the direct and conditional effects of collegiality and ideology are further conditioned by the institutional context in which judges operate; the institutional context influences the extent to which judges interdependent or insular. With our theory in place, we spend the next six chapters investigating the role of collegiality in judicial behavior across a spectrum of settings and outcomes.

Appendix 2.A: Interview Methods

We sent recruitment letters to all active judges on one of the geographic courts of appeals based on the Federal Judicial Center (2022) on February 5, 2021, or February 28, 2022. The addresses were obtained from court websites. We sent out three waves: February 23, 2021 (60); October 18, 2021 (60); and March 1, 2022 (72). We interviewed seven courts of appeals judges overall.

We obtained the names of Supreme Court clerks from Wikipedia. For the clerks serving between 1999 and 2017, we located contact information for those former clerks from internet searches for publicly available information, including law firm and law school websites, and so forth. We sent out three waves of requests: February 24, 2021 (60); November 3, 2021 (60); and November 30, 2021 (60). We expanded the list of clerks to include all those who served from 1999 to 2022 but were no longer at the Court and sent out an additional set of requests on February 1, 2022 (116), for a total of 296 requests to randomly sampled former clerks. We ultimately interviewed five former clerks.

Court of appeals clerks were identified using the West Legal Directory on Westlaw on February 17, 2021. We searched for the word "clerk" within ten words of the term "U.S. Court of Appeals." We created a sampling frame from the first five hundred results and randomly sampled from it. We located contact information for those former clerks from internet searches for publicly available information, including law firm and law school websites, and so forth. The mailings went out in four rounds: February 24, 2021 (30); October 1, 2021 (30); November 3, 2021 (39); and January 7, 2022 (39). We interviewed four courts of appeals clerks using this method. It should also be noted that the former Supreme Court clerks also had experience clerking on the courts of appeals.

44   THE ELEVATOR EFFECT

Anonymity was promised to the interviewees. Specifically, the terms of the interviews were set that interviewees would not be identified other than based on the type of participant they were (e.g., former clerks). The interviews were anonymous, and efforts have been made to further obscure identities, including using the pronoun "they" for clerks and justices and not including details that might identify the participants, such as describing contemporary events or names of cases. Furthermore, to protect the interviewees and respect confidentiality, the participants were not asked about specific cases. The only recordings of the interviews were handwritten notes by the interviewer. Thus, the quoted material tends to include shorter quotes based on the limitations that such a system presents.

There was variation as to many of the demographic characteristics of the interviewees. The interviews were semi-structured, and examples of the types of questions that were asked are provided in the following appendix (2.B).

Appendix 2.B: Interview Questions

Court of Appeals Judges

General

- Please describe a typical day as a judge.

Judge-to-Judge

- How are panels assigned on your court?
- To what extent do judges (or their clerks) on the panel communicate about the case before oral argument? While drafting the opinion?
- Describe the process of oral argument in your circuit. Do you usually travel for oral argument?
- What are the office arrangements like for judges? Do you think these arrangements influenced relationships among judges? How?
- How important is collegiality among judges at the Court?
- How do the judges get to know each other, if at all?
- To what extent did you have contact with the other judges? Inside of the courthouse? Outside of the courthouse? Are there formal social events? What are they like? Informal social events? What are they like?
- Are some judges more likely to interact with each other than others? Why?
- Do the relationships among judges change the longer they know each other?
- Do you remember any examples of the importance of collegiality among judges from your time at the Court? What are they?
- Can you think of a time when collegiality among judges influenced the outcome of a case? The text of an opinion? How previous circuit precedents were handled? The text of a concurrence or dissent?
- How often do you come into contact with district court judges in your circuit? Under what circumstances? Locations? Events?
- How do you learn about the abilities of district court judges in your circuit? Their written opinions? Personal interactions with them? Descriptions of their reputation by others in your professional acquaintance? Other sources?

Clerk-to-Judge

- How do you get to know your clerks?
- Do you know if that looked different for other clerks and judges?

UNDERSTANDING COLLEGIALITY   45

- What types of contact do clerks have with judges? (In-person, electronic, formal, informal, etc.)
- How much contact was there between clerks and their judges generally?
- How much contact do you have with your clerks?
- To what extent did office arrangements influence how much contact you had with your clerks?

Supreme Court Clerks

General
- Please describe a typical day as a clerk at the Supreme Court.

Clerk-to-Clerk
- How did the clerks get to know each other, if at all?
- What are the office arrangements like for clerks? Do you think these arrangements influenced relationships among clerks? How?
- How important was collegiality among clerks at the Court?
- Do you remember any examples of the importance of collegiality among clerks from your time at the Court? What are they?
- Can you think of a time when collegiality among clerks influenced the outcome of a case? The text of an opinion?
- When would you work with other clerks? Describe those experiences. What made them better or worse?
- To what extent did you have contact with the other clerks? Inside of the courthouse? Outside of the courthouse? Were there formal social events? What were they like? Informal social events? What were they like?
- Were some clerks more likely to interact with each other than others? Why? (Personality, opinion assignments, physical location, etc.)
- Did the relationships among clerks change the longer they knew each other?

Clerk-to-Justice
- How did you get to know your justice?
- Do you know if that looked different for other clerks and justices?
- What types of contact do clerks have with justices? (In-person, electronic, formal, informal, etc.)
- How much contact was there between clerks and their justices generally?
- How much contact did you have with your justice?
- To what extent did office arrangements influence how much contact you had with your justice?

Justice-to-Justice
- What are the office arrangements like for justices? Do you think these arrangements influenced relationships among justices? How?
- How important was collegiality among justices at the Court?
- Do you remember any examples of the importance of collegiality among justices from your time at the Court? What are they?
- Can you think of a time when collegiality among justices influenced the outcome of a case? The text of an opinion?

46 THE ELEVATOR EFFECT

- In your experience, how much contact do justices have with each other? At the courthouse? Outside of the courthouse?
- Were some justices more likely to interact with each other than others? Why?
- Did the relationships among justices change the longer they knew each other?

Court of Appeals Clerks

General
- Please describe a typical day as a clerk.

Clerk-to-Clerk
- How did the clerks get to know each other, if at all?
- What are the office arrangements like for clerks? Do you think these arrangements influenced relationships among clerks? How?
- How important was collegiality among clerks at the Court?
- Do you remember any examples of the importance of collegiality among clerks from your time at the Court? What are they?
- Can you think of a time when collegiality among clerks influenced the outcome of a case? The text of an opinion?
- When would you work with other clerks? Describe those experiences. What made them better or worse?
- To what extent did you have contact with the other clerks? Inside of the courthouse? Outside of the courthouse? Were there formal social events? What were they like? Informal social events? What were they like?
- Were some clerks more likely to interact with each other than others? Why? (Personality, opinion assignments, physical location, etc.)
- Did the relationships among clerks change the longer they knew each other?

Clerk-to-Judge
- How did you get to know your judge?
- Do you know if that looked different for other clerks and judges?
- What types of contact do clerks have with judges? (In-person, electronic, formal, informal, etc.)
- How much contact was there between clerks and their judges generally?
- How much contact did you have with your judge?
- To what extent did office arrangements influence how much contact you had with your judge?

Judge-to-Judge
- How were panels assigned on your court?
- Describe the process of oral argument in your circuit. Did you travel for oral argument?
- To what extent did judges on the panel communicate about the case before oral argument? While drafting the opinion?
- What are the office arrangements like for judges? Do you think these arrangements influenced relationships among judges? How?
- How important was collegiality among judges at the Court?
- Do you remember any examples of the importance of collegiality among judges from your time at the Court? What are they?

- Can you think of a time when collegiality among judges influenced the outcome of a case? The text of an opinion?
- In your experience, how much contact do judges have with each other? At the courthouse? Outside of the courthouse?
- Were some judges more likely to interact with each other than others? Why?
- Did the relationships among judges change the longer they knew each other?

Appendix 2.C: Clerks' Perspectives on Collegiality

Former court of appeals clerks[20] also noted the importance of collegiality among judges and its relationship to contact. Outside of chambers, clerks had varying perspectives regarding relationships among circuit judges. Some of these differences appeared to be attributable to circumstances regarding office arrangements. C1, who was in a remote chamber, said, "They seemed to get along well." They also said they were "unsure." The judge "was easy to get along with. [They] liked everyone." In the same vein, C2 was not sure how much interaction their judge had with other judges. They don't remember the judge having meals with other judges and "was not privy to any calls [or other communications]." The chambers were "geographically isolated, so it might have been different [for other judges]." C2's judge "didn't speak ill of other judges" and "didn't speak regarding other judges in political terms." They "never witnessed a lack of collegiality causing problems."

On the other hand, C3, who was in a space with other circuit judges, said that their judge "got along reasonably well with [their] colleagues." There was "variation" in how "pairs of judges" interacted. Some were "very bitter" and it had "an impact on how things operated." There were "outliers" who functioned as "cautionary tales." The circuit as a whole and the judge within it "worked to build relationships and avoid [conflict]." C3's judge had been elevated from the district court and had an "existing reputation and knowledge" regarding the judges. The judge made "efforts to avoid riffs." The judges went to "lunch pretty regularly and sometimes dinner." Dinner was more likely with "judges from other courts." The judges "saw each other in the courthouse a lot. The clerk was aware of their judge going to the theater with other judges, and their judge would report back "about the plays to see." Similarly, C4's judge had lunch with other judges and acted as a mentor to a new judge. Sometimes the clerks were included in the lunches, but sometimes they were "closed-door and judges only." Also, other judges sometimes brought their clerks to the lunches. S1 "could tell the judges were friends." (This contrasted with the Supreme Court, where they were around the justices less.) S5 noted that they clerked for a conservative circuit judge whose "best [work] buddy was very liberal."

---

[20] Former clerks provide an important vantage point, as they worked closely with judges (e.g., Ward and Weiden 2006) and often act as conduits for communications among judges (see Appendix 2.C).

3
Interpersonal Contact and Publicizing Disagreement

Introduction

In the previous chapter, we argued that collegiality plays an important role in judicial politics. Especially on appellate courts, where judges decide cases in small groups, judges' interpersonal relationships might affect the tenor and quality of the opinion drafting process and, by extension, legal development. Drawing on interviews of federal circuit court judges and former clerks, we argued that collegiality has widespread consequences for the legal system.

In this chapter, we begin to put that theory to the test. We start by studying the behavior of judges on the U.S. Courts of Appeals, the middle rung of the U.S. federal judiciary. Judges on these courts decide most cases in rotating three-judge panels, providing variation in the amount of interpersonal contact between pairs of judges. We leverage this variation in interpersonal contact to assess the consequences of collegiality on the assumption that greater levels of interpersonal contact correspond to heightened collegial concerns. This conceptualization of collegiality echoes a sentiment expressed by Tenth Circuit Judge Michael R. Murphy (2000, 458–59): "Collegiality requires a familiarity with other judges, which occurs only with regular face-to-face contact.... On an appellate court, absence does not make the heart grow fonder, and familiarity does not breed contempt. Absence makes the heart unfamiliar, and it does not breed collegiality."

We test the effects of collegiality on the decisions of appellate judges to publicize their disagreement with their colleagues. Our empirical test relies upon a dataset comprising thousands of U.S. Courts of Appeals decisions on search and seizure cases and a unique measure of collegiality based on the physical proximity of a pair of judges. We use this data to test three hypotheses about the relationship between collegiality, ideology, and the likelihood that a judge chooses to release a concurring or dissenting opinion. First, we hypothesize that pairs of judges who interact more frequently, which we measure as whether two judges work day-to-day in the same courthouse, will vote together more frequently. Second, we expect that the effect of interpersonal contact increases with the level of ideological disagreement between a pair of judges: the effect of working in the same courthouse should be strongest for a judge-opinion author pairing with extreme ideological differences. Third, we hypothesize that collegiality dampens the effect of ideological disagreement on the probability of a dissenting or concurring vote; the effect of ideological disagreement should be smaller for pairs of judges who see each other frequently than for judges with low levels of interpersonal contact.

The Elevator Effect. Morgan L.W. Hazelton, Rachael K. Hinkle, and Michael J. Nelson, Oxford University Press.
© Oxford University Press 2023. DOI: 10.1093/oso/9780197625408.003.0003

50 THE ELEVATOR EFFECT

Our results provide initial support for the theory we described in Chapter 2. While shared office location has no direct effect on the probability of a dissent or concurrence, collegiality dampens the effects of ideology on judicial behavior. In fact, when two judges work together in the same courthouse, there is no statistically discernible effect of ideological disagreement on the likelihood that judge will dissent or concur. Moreover, at least for dissenting opinions, the effect of collegiality grows with the level of ideological distance between the judge and the majority opinion author. We conclude the chapter by discussing some implications of our findings and explaining how they set the stage for the rest of our empirical tests.

Collegiality and the Costs of Publicizing Disagreement

Appellate courts in the United States resolve cases by majority rule; legal doctrine is only binding in future cases when more than half of the judges agree on the case's outcome or disposition (which litigant is the winner) and rationale (the legal basis for the case's outcome) (Wahlbeck, Spriggs, and Maltzman 1999). An opinion that has the agreement of a majority of the judges about both the outcome and its rationale is the case's majority opinion.

What happens if a judge disagrees with their colleagues? They can write a separate opinion to explain their position.[1] These have two general forms. First, dissenting opinions indicate fundamental disagreement with both the panel's disposition and, inherently, the opinion's rationale (Blackstone and Collins 2014; Epstein, Landes, and Posner 2011).[2] Second, concurring opinions indicate that the judge agrees with the outcome but wants to make their own mark on the opinion: judges use concurrences to provide an alternative rationale for the outcome, narrow or broaden the scope of the majority opinion, or signal information to future litigants or other governmental actors (Corley 2010; Maveety, Turner, and Way 2010). In some cases, concurrences may represent serious disagreement; but, on average, they tend to indicate less disagreement with the majority than dissents (see Corley 2010; Epstein, Landes, and Posner 2011; Ginsburg 2010; Ray 1989; Scalia 1994; Turner, Way, and Maveety 2010; Wahlbeck, Spriggs, and Maltzman 1999). Importantly, in the U.S. Courts of Appeals, most cases are resolved without publicized disagreement. Epstein, Landes, and Posner (2011) report, based on Lexis and Westlaw data from 1990 to 2007, that less than 3 percent of cases terminated on the merits in the federal circuit courts include a dissenting opinion.

Drafting separate opinions is part of the larger process of opinion production on appellate courts. In virtually all such courts, judges collaborate on the creation of opinions. In circuit courts, one member of each three-judge panel is assigned (typically by the most senior active judge on the panel) to draft the majority opinion after

---

[1] Occasionally, judges will cast a dissenting or concurring vote but decline to write an opinion to explain their position. When discussing the U.S. Courts of Appeals, we treat votes to dissent or concur and the decision to write a dissenting or concurring opinion as synonymous.

[2] Sometimes a dissenter generally agrees with the majority regarding the applicable legal rule or rationale but disagrees with how it is being applied (Stephens 1952). This type of split still represents a disagreement over rationale regarding specific aspects of a case.

a conference discussion about the rationale and outcome. The votes at this conference are tentative, though (Maltzman and Wahlbeck 1996). The opinion author will circulate a draft to the panel, and fellow panel members can suggest revisions (Maltzman, Spriggs, and Wahlbeck 2000). During this period, judges who disagree with the panel majority will also circulate a draft dissenting or concurring opinion, providing the majority opinion author the opportunity to respond. The other panel member might find the dissent more compelling than the majority and switch their vote. In this way, an opinion that was originally drafted as a dissent may become the panel's majority opinion. Similarly, a rationale initially put forth in a concurrence may persuade another judge and become part of the final majority opinion. This bargaining process continues until all the judges on the panel have signed an opinion. At this point, the case is decided, and the opinions are released to the litigants and the public.

But not all separate opinions see the light of day. A judge can circulate a draft dissent or concurrence, extract concessions from the majority opinion author, and then "drop" their separate opinion to sign the now-satisfactory majority opinion (Maltzman, Spriggs, and Wahlbeck 2000). At other times, judges may join a majority opinion with which they disagree due to strategic or norms-based considerations (Epstein, Landes, and Posner 2013). For example, a judge might choose to join a less-than-ideal majority opinion in the hope of narrowing the opinion's holding to one that is more palatable than it would have been if the judge had dissented; likewise, some courts (like the early U.S. Supreme Court, discussed in detail in Chapter 5) have norms of consensus that prioritize the court's ability to speak as a unified voice over an individual judge's disagreement with the majority (Epstein, Segal, and Spaeth 2001). Disagreement is, therefore, made public only when a judge writes *and releases* a separate opinion.

Dissents and concurrences matter in many ways. They might affect the public's response to a decision, eventually altering public esteem for the judiciary. Judges may feel pressure to maintain institutional legitimacy and to increase the probability that their opinion is accepted by the public and properly implemented. Some studies show that unanimity can help judges achieve these goals (Zink, Spriggs, and Scott 2009; Corley, Steigerwalt, and Ward 2013; Salamone 2014). J6 and J7 echoed these concerns in our interviews. J7 was particularly clear on this point, saying that consensus "helps the institution of the court. It gives the court legitimacy, authority, and respect. [In] controversial cases, if judges from diverse approaches come together for the decision, there is a lot more respect and standing in the community." J7 contrasted the benefits of unanimity and a split decision where the divergent views of the judges are described: "So-and-so goes this way, so-and-so goes that way," implying that the message to the public is better when the court speaks with one voice.

The presence of separate opinions has important consequences for legal development. Unanimous decisions may enhance the clarity and stability of the law; when a court fails to speak with one voice, lower courts may either be unclear about the state of the law or might capitalize on the greater level of legal uncertainty to push the law in their own favored decision (see, e.g., Black et al. 2016; Corley 2010; Corley, Steigerwalt, and Ward 2013). Moreover, circuit rulings featuring dissent are more likely to be reviewed by the Supreme Court (Black and Owens 2009a). These considerations may often render separate opinions unpalatable.

52 THE ELEVATOR EFFECT

In addition to concerns regarding legal development, internal features of the circuit may also play a role. Separate opinions take time and energy to write; given the crushing workload many appellate court judges experience, the costs of dissenting or concurring might outweigh whatever expressive benefits they get from publicizing their disagreement with the majority (Epstein, Landes, and Posner 2011). Frequent expressions of disagreement could also run the risk of doing damage to relationships with colleagues. As Judge Jeffrey Sutton (2010, 870) has written:

> Most judges prefer to agree. Dissents and concurrences take time away from burgeoning dockets that already leave too little time. And dissents run the risk of straining collegiality. No appellate judge would last long who insisted on deciding every case just so.

As a result, Sutton suggests, judges may sign on to majority opinions they believe are imperfect, so long as their disagreements with that opinion are relatively minor. Were judges to insist on perfection in every opinion that crossed their desk, they would never be able to keep pace with the never-ending flow of cases for which they are responsible. This logic was echoed in our interviews. For example, J5 specifically cited Posner (2008) in their interview, saying that they thought research on the "social factors" matched their experience on the bench: "I have found it to be quite true over the years.... For example, if the opinion will be non-precedential and life goes on, I may not dissent."[3]

What can predict whether a judge declines to join the majority opinion? Time and again, scholars have found that the best predictor of a judge's willingness to dissent or concur is the level of ideological disagreement between that judge and the majority opinion author. Perhaps unsurprisingly, as two judges have different policy preferences, they are more likely to express those disagreements in writing (Epstein, Landes, and Posner 2011). Of course, pure attitudinal motives are not the sole cause of dissent; strategic considerations matter too (Hettinger, Lindquist, and Martinek 2004, 2006). Dissenting opinions can perform an important whistle-blowing function, alerting a higher court that a lower court has issued a questionable decision. However, judges must be careful to not whistle-blow too often lest they dilute the value of that signal and begin to sound like "the judge who cried wolf." To this end, even policy-minded judges must carefully weigh the pros and cons of publicizing their disagreement in each case (Beim, Hirsch, and Kastellec 2014, 2016).

While ideological disagreements among panel members provide one explanation for the presence of dissenting or concurring votes, personal characteristics of panel members also affect the likelihood that a judge will file a separate opinion. As discussed in Chapter 1, the most prominent arguments about the effects of group

---

[3] J5 went on to contrast Justices Brennan and Scalia's approach to judging as two models for how collegial concerns might affect a judge's legal legacy. J5 cited Justice Brennan as an example of a judge who "got his way [by] modifying his position." They noted that Brennan's clerks allegedly questioned the practice and Brennan "would hold up his hand and say 'tell me how to count to five.'" It was a matter of Brennan "getting more of what he wanted." By contrast, in J5's estimation, Scalia "stuck to his principles and was not terribly persuasive and didn't try to be." As a result, J5 told us, Brennan's legal legacy has been greater than Scalia's due to the former's willingness to compromise with his colleagues.

dynamics on judicial behavior have come from the well-noted tendency of appellate judges who sit on panels divided by political party, sex, or race to decide differently than when sitting on unified panels (Boyd, Epstein, and Martin 2010; Kastellec 2013). These patterns demonstrate that the decisions of collegial courts are affected not only by judges' policy preferences but also by the deliberative process in which they operate (Kim 2009; Edwards 2003). These studies illustrate how group dynamics might alter judicial behavior, in part, by affecting the occurrence of publicized disagreement on appellate courts.

In short, the literature and interview evidence, along with the theory we explained in the previous chapter, suggests an observable implication: *increased collegiality among federal judges should tend to make judges, on average, less likely to publicize disagreement with the panel's decision.* Our goal in this chapter is to provide a clear and simple test of the effects of collegiality on the presence of publicized disagreement in the U.S. Courts of Appeals. In the next chapter, we discuss (and test) different mechanisms that explain *why* collegiality might affect judicial behavior.

Collegiality and Ideological Disagreement

But, wait! We wrote earlier in this chapter that ideological disagreement among judges is an important predictor of whether a judge chooses to issue a dissenting or concurring opinion. Collegiality and ideology are not likely to operate independently of each other. Now we consider their intertwined effects. Because judges must balance their policy goals with their desire to maintain good working relationships with colleagues (Baum 1997; Epstein, Landes, and Posner 2013), we anticipate that the effects of collegiality and ideology are related. To preview, we anticipate that the effect of collegiality in reducing the appearance of a dissenting or concurring vote increases as the ideological distance between an opinion author and a panel member grows and that increased collegiality concerns dampen the effect of ideology disagreement on the decision to publicize their disagreement with the panel majority.

Why should the effect of collegiality vary according to the level of ideological disagreement between two judges? To begin, it is helpful to think about a judge's decision whether to write separately in an economic sense. The ideological distance between a judge and the opinion author affects the policy "loss" experienced if they support a majority opinion with which they are not completely satisfied (Epstein, Landes, and Posner 2011). As the expected policy loss increases, the likelihood of a dissenting or concurring vote also grows larger. Conversely, when two colleagues are ideologically compatible, there is typically little need for one to write separately. The judges are likely to agree on both the case's outcome and its rationale. If the majority opinion is written by an ideological ally, any disagreement is likely to be only at the margins, and the policy "loss" from signing onto that opinion is likely lower than the cost—in terms of time and effort beyond any collegiality cost—of publicizing their disagreement. In such circumstances, there is little opportunity for collegiality to matter simply because the baseline likelihood of dissenting or concurring is particularly low.

As the level of ideological disagreement increases, a judge's cost and benefit calculations change. When two judges have fundamentally different views of a case, they are

54 THE ELEVATOR EFFECT

unlikely to agree on the case's outcome or rationale. Choosing to sign on to an opinion with which a judge has grave policy disagreements can mean publicly signaling agreement with a decision that the judge believes is patently incorrect. Under these conditions, a judge has increased incentive to whistle-blow (Cross and Tiller 1998; Beim, Hirsch, and Kastellec 2014), signaling to others—be they higher courts, the public, or other branches of government—that the majority has reached a decision that needs to be rectified (see Urofsky 2017, 320–22). In these cases, the costs of publicizing one's disagreement can be outweighed by the policy loss of signing the majority opinion. This is an environment where there is room for collegiality to play a role: it may increase the costs of dissenting or concurring sufficiently to outweigh the benefits.

While judges with similar preferences are likely to agree on the outcome and rationale from the beginning, leaving little room for collegiality to matter, there could be countervailing forces in play as well. Collegiality might make it easier for disagreements to be publicized between ideologically similar judges because the costs of such publication would be minimal: the disagreements are likely to be rather small and the relationship may be strong enough to endure the airing of differences in perspective. When two judges have a strong relationship with one another, it is more likely to continue unaffected when they disagree in each case. But when two judges do not have a close bond, their disagreement in a particular case might be the dominant interaction between those two people.

Nevertheless, as the ideological differences between the opinion author and a judge increase, disagreement is more likely. Private disagreement is a necessary precondition for collegiality to prevent public disagreement. Consequently, relationships are most likely to ease conflict where differing viewpoints exist most frequently. In the face of such conflicts, judges who have long-standing relationships with each other may be able to capitalize on that increased familiarity to make effective private arguments, thereby making consensus more likely than it would have been if they did not know each other as well. Thus, we hypothesize that *the role collegiality plays in reducing the probability of dissent or concurrence increases with the level of ideological disagreement between a judge and the opinion author.*

We can also view the complex dynamic between preferences and relationships from the reverse perspective. Why might the effect of ideology vary according to the level of collegiality between two judges? We know that the ideological distance between two judges affects the probability of dissenting or concurring. However, as concerns about interpersonal relationships increase, the costs associated with publicizing disagreement similarly rise. As these costs become larger, they can begin to outweigh ideological considerations. A judge may be more likely to join a majority opinion when collegiality concerns are heightened because they have an increased desire to "keep the peace." Similarly, stronger collegial bonds mean an increased chance of persuasion: it is easier to extract concessions from someone you know well because you understand what sorts of arguments are likely to be effective. Regardless of the mechanism, when collegiality concerns render public disagreement very unlikely, there is little room left for ideology to affect that decision. We therefore also hypothesize that *higher levels of collegiality decrease the effect of ideological distance on the decision to dissent or concur.* In other words, collegiality dampens the effect of ideology on the decision to publicize disagreement.

The Differences Between Concurring and Dissenting

We expect the effects of collegiality and ideological disagreement differ according to the type of publicized disagreement. While both concurring and dissenting opinions constitute public disagreement, they indicate different types of divergence. A dissenting opinion represents a conflict with the way the panel majority has decided a case; a concurring opinion generally represents less severe criticism over the rationale for the panel's decision or a desire to add some information or perspective (see Corley 2010; Epstein, Landes, and Posner 2011; Ray 1989; Scalia 1994; Turner, Way, and Maveety 2010). Concurring opinions, by definition, indicate agreement with the outcome of a case. Dissenting opinions also tend to inspire sharper language and a more pointed exchange of ideas than concurring opinions. For these reasons, dissents pose a greater risk of alienating colleagues than concurrences, on average.

Additionally, as Corley (2010) explains, concurring opinions are heterogeneous. Some concurrences try to expand the reach of an opinion; others try to limit the opinion's implications; some concurrences enthusiastically endorse the court's holding, while others go to pains to explain why precedent compels a judge to join a majority opinion they dislike. Still other concurring opinions merely try to explain the majority's logic in alternative phrasing. In short, varying types of concurrences likely signal different levels of disagreement. Unlike Corley (2010), we are unable to differentiate among the types of concurring opinions in our dataset, and we acknowledge that—to the extent that we use the presence of a concurring opinion as an indicator of disagreement with the majority—judges sometimes write concurring opinions for reasons that are not strictly ideological, creating measurement error. This measurement error is likely to attenuate our findings with respect to concurring opinions. Thus, because (a) dissents generally signal a greater level of disagreement with the majority opinion than concurrences, and (b) concurring opinions are heterogeneous, we expect that *the effects of collegiality and ideology will be stronger for the decision to dissent than the decision to concur.*

Proximity and Collegiality

How can we determine the level of collegiality between a pair of judges? Unfortunately, courts do not generate any publicly available data describing which decisions are driven by collegiality and which are not. The most direct way to determine the level of collegiality among judges on the U.S. Courts of Appeal would be to survey them by asking a series of questions about every other judge on their circuit and then combining those survey responses into a measure of collegiality. Of course, most judges would not answer such a survey (but see Caldeira and Patterson 1987; Gibson 1977). And, even if they did, the answers are not likely to be valid: even in the face of promised anonymity, we expect many judges would be unwilling to indicate in writing that they dislike their colleagues. Even the burgeoning literature on judicial personality— a concept that psychologists have been able to measure with a series of well-vetted survey questions—does not rely on such evidence for its measures of judicial personality (e.g., Hall 2018; Black et al. 2019, 2021; Hall et al. 2021). Thus, we reject the possibility of measuring judicial collegiality with survey data.

Instead, we look for observable indicators of collegiality. The benefit of this approach is its reliability: we can derive discrete, transparent, and replicable measures of the level of collegiality between a pair of judges. The measures we employ in this book are easily applied to U.S. state courts and to other appellate courts around the world, enabling others to test the generalizability of our findings. However, we acknowledge that any indicators of this concept are subject to some degree of measurement error. We judge the benefits of these transparent measures to outweigh the costs and, where possible, supplement our analyses with the qualitative evidence we gathered from our interviews with judges and clerks to contextualize our findings.

We draw upon the often-recognized idea that the frequency of interaction between two people plays a fundamental role in collegiality. Despite the old adage that familiarity breeds contempt, studies in psychology suggest that "familiarity"—which is built through frequent interaction—is a key component of a collegial environment (e.g., Gruenfeld et al. 1996). This is the implicit assumption made in prior studies, discussed in Chapter 2, that use shared living space (Parigi and Bergemann 2016; Minozzi and Caldeira 2021), desk proximity (Masket 2008), and office proximity (Rogowski and Sinclair 2012) as measures of the strength of a collegial relationship (see also Bratton and Rouse 2011; Chown and Liu 2015).

In the judicial setting, scholars have long noted that close chambers locations foster frequent (and substantively important) collegial contact. Wasby's studies of judicial communication repeatedly make this point. For example, Wasby (1980, 590), studying the Eighth Circuit, reports that "[t]wo judges sitting in the same city tend to contact each other more frequently than judges who sit in different cities." Wasby (1987, 133), studying the geographically massive Ninth Circuit, writes that "[g]eography's principal negative effect was that face-to-face contact was more difficult." Further, a lack of face-to-face contact can be problematic because "something happens with physical contact that doesn't happen elsewhere" (133). Indeed, one judge stressed to Wasby (1987, 133) the need for such face-to-face contact "to take the sharp edges off communication," making it "less sarcastic and sharp."

More recent studies also note the relationship between physical proximity and collegiality. Lindquist (2006) suggests that greater interaction between judges results in increased consensus among appellate judges, and Epstein, Landes, and Posner (2011) find that smaller circuits, where judges interact more frequently, have lower dissent rates. In their study of the effects of gender and judging, Collins, Manning, and Carp (2010, 266) rely on the number of women judges in each federal district courthouse on the theory that inter-judge interaction "is more likely to occur when jurists are in close proximity with each other" (see also Harris 2021).

Judges also note the importance of physical proximity for collegiality. Cohen (2002, 156–57) quotes two Ninth Circuit judges discussing the effects of geography:

> I don't think there is any question that if all of us were in the same building, it would be, for many reasons, easier to get together on issues and talk about things.... It would [be advantageous] ... I think the process would be better served if we were all

in the same building.... From the very beginning, I could see the advantages of being in the same building.

I think that if you are in proximity to the other judges, I think it does encourage a bit more of an interaction ... I think, frankly, on working through a point, it is very helpful to sit down with the other judge, if there is a sticking point on a case—particularly if the difference is between two judges—to go into the other judge's chambers, sit down, and try to work through it. I think those are helpful sessions, but unfortunately, that is, I think, a weakness of the court in one respect is that there is less deliberation than if the court were a smaller court and sitting in one place.

Our interviews also indicate that proximity helps to build a collegial court. Several judges broached COVID-19 and social distancing in ways that highlighted their beliefs that personal interactions and contact are important. J1, discussing remote arrangements during the pandemic, felt that "being in-person is very important for collegiality." They highlighted the importance of "random interactions." For example, judges might see each other "in the hall" and "talk about a case." Being in-person allowed for "more communication between judges." While J1 reported that the shift to video arguments worked acceptably from a technical standpoint, "the problem is that it erodes collegiality because there are no informal interactions, only formal interactions and process."[4] Similarly, J4 cited the pandemic as changing the nature of the appellate process: judges were "isolated at home" in their "cocoons," "remote oral arguments are not the same. They are not as free-wheeling with the attorneys but also with the other judges," and "over lunch or a glass of wine."

Clerks also suggested that being together was important. C4 felt "collegiality was important" and almost "a given," in large part due to "the importance of being in the same place." C4 had also been a state court clerk and felt that collegiality was "stronger on the state court [for which they clerked] because the judges were in one place." That court had a "tradition to be unanimous if it could be." S4 had clerked on two courts of appeals before arriving at the Supreme Court. They believed that it mattered if circuit judges were spread out or in the same space—"when you see each other all the time, it is a big difference. It matters if you don't see each other all of the time." Unlike the Supreme Court, where clerks circulated across chambers very regularly, on the courts of appeals "you could call on the phone or by text but it is not the same." They also noted "generational differences" regarding comfort with modes of communication, particularly phone calls. While they conceded that "in the circuits the variety of representation of communities and geography is important, but there are real advantages to being together. It is suboptimal when [chambers] are apart."[5] S2 also clerked on the court of appeals and the U.S. Supreme Court. They reported that proximity "helps" relationships among judges. Specifically, being in the "same courthouse" can matter. However, they also noted historic examples where the judges were "contrarian." In

[4] J1 also noted another negative consequence: the "clerks never see the inside of a courtroom." J1 suspected "some attorneys like it better because it is less intimidating and they can have all sorts of notes and screens."

[5] Their account indicates that this was not just a matter of being isolated from others in a workspace: S4 had experiences both in office space that was shared with district judges and not. While sharing the space resulted in "seeing more people, it was not a huge difference" in terms of the experience.

58 THE ELEVATOR EFFECT

those cases, they noted, circuits made special efforts to improve collegiality. So "proximity won't solve everything."

Based on these studies, our interviews with judges and clerks, and judges' published accounts, we are confident in the validity of our conceptualization of collegiality: as two judges are more likely to encounter each other frequently, the level of collegial concern between those two judges increases.

A Measure of Collegiality: Same Courthouse

Given that familiarity should breed collegiality, how can we measure the level of collegiality between two judges? Here, we are helped by the institutional structure of the U.S. Courts of Appeals, in which judges on the numbered circuits are geographically dispersed across the circuit in which they work, though they often come together periodically for conferences and to hear oral argument. Circuit judges vary in the extent to which their chambers are in the same courthouse as other judges. Figure 3.1 shows the location of federal circuit judges' home chambers across the United States as well as the number of judges in each city in 2010. As the size of the dots on the map illustrates, some cities are home to multiple circuit judges while others have only one.

The location of a circuit judge's home chambers provides variation in the frequency of personal contact among judges. For judges whose chambers are in the same courthouse, frequency of contact is increased because they are more likely to see each other on a regular basis due to proximity. Reporting the results of his interviews with court

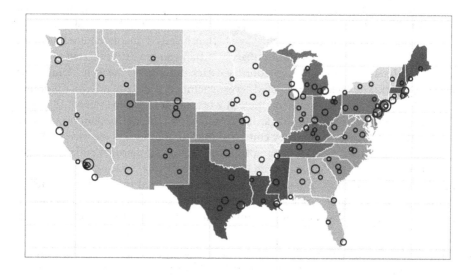

Figure 3.1 Location of Courts of Appeals Chambers in 2010

of appeals judges, Wasby (1987, 134) writes that "[j]udges in the same courthouse with others, in addition to having casual elevator or parking area encounters with their colleagues, found it 'much easier' to call and get together with another judge in the courthouse with their clerks present." When judges do not share a courthouse, they interact with each other less frequently, and the potential for unpleasant social interaction resulting from heated disagreement in a case declines.

Several of our judicial interviewees suggested that working in the same courthouse as one's colleagues facilitates a collegial environment.[6] J4, who works in a building with both trial and appellate court judges said they "think" office arrangements matter for decision-making: "It matters if they are around and can run into [each other] and there is a place for lunch. All of that helps." J6, who is the sole circuit judge in their courthouse, emphasized the importance of physical space for judicial behavior (and office politics), telling us, "The positive is that I am removed from courthouse politics and the negative is that I am removed from my colleagues." J6 talked about how the job "can be very isolating. I can't express how much you need to get out into or try to get out into the bar and community." Asked if they believed that location influenced how often judges interacted, J6 noted that judges "in some places are in the same courthouses. They are likely to spend time together."

We measure this concept with a dichotomous variable indicating whether two judges have their chambers in the same courthouse. We considered two alternative measures of collegiality: whether two judges have their chambers in the same state or same city. The first concept is simplest to measure since U.S. Court of Appeals seats are typically tied to particular states. Yet, for example, a judge in San Francisco and one in Los Angeles may not see each other frequently enough to satisfy the assumption in our theory: that geographic proximity breeds a need for increased collegiality. For this reason, we rejected this coarse measure.

A second measure of place-based collegiality we considered was whether two judges have their chambers in the same city. Of course, judges in the same city are usually in the same courthouse. However, some cities do have multiple federal courthouses, and the government has constructed and remodeled courthouses during the period we study. Our conceptualization of collegiality relies heavily on *frequent* contact between two judges, and those who work in the same building seem likely to us to, on average, see each other more often than two judges who work in a city large enough to demand two federal courthouses and who work in different courthouses. For this reason, we believe the validity of the Same Courthouse measure of collegiality is likely to be a bit better than the Same City variable, and we use that for our analyses. Happily, though, there is rarely—if ever—a noticeable difference in our results depending on whether we use Same City or Same Courthouse to measure collegiality.

---

[6] To be clear, some of our interviewees downplayed the importance of working in a courthouse with other circuit colleagues. For example, in J3's circuit, there is variation regarding the extent to which circuit judges have their chambers in the same courthouse. When asked if they thought being in the same courthouse mattered, J3 said, "Not very much." They "don't see other judges in the courthouse in person that much." Most communication was by "email or phone and now Zoom. It is easy to work remotely."

60   THE ELEVATOR EFFECT

Data and Research Design

Armed with our measure of collegiality—whether two judges have their chambers in the same courthouse—we now turn to the data we assembled to understand how collegiality and ideology together affect judges' decisions to dissent or concur. We study the numbered U.S. Courts of Appeals across several decades to ensure meaningful variation in collegiality. We exclude the D.C. Circuit from this analysis since its confined geographical reach and single courthouse substantially reduce variation in collegiality. Furthermore, the D.C. Circuit has an unusual mixture of cases compared to the other courts of appeals (Banks 1999; Roberts 2006), and judges on the D.C. Circuit have lower caseloads (see United States Courts 2022).

Federal intermediate appellate courts provide considerable variation in how judges interact. Most cases are initially resolved by a three-judge panel (Hinkle 2015); these panels frequently change, meaning that circuit judges must decide cases with constantly rotating combinations of colleagues. Even though panel assignment may not be entirely random (Chilton and Levy 2015), judges usually do not select the colleagues with whom they will serve.[7] Finally, unlike the Supreme Court or most state high courts, there is significant variation in where judges on the same court have their chambers, a necessary condition for our measurement strategy.

We utilize a database of all published Fourth Amendment search and seizure opinions from 1953 to 2010.[8] This topic incorporates a discrete set of legal issues that are routinely raised in litigation within the context of both civil and criminal cases. Moreover, search and seizure cases map well onto the traditional ideological spectrum. Decisions in favor of the government are conservative, while those in favor of individuals (often the criminally accused) are liberal. Perhaps most importantly, search and seizure is a legal topic with broad substantive importance. Every member of society is affected by how our legal system balances individual civil liberties against the need for effective law enforcement. Early in his career on the Supreme Court, then-Associate Justice Rehnquist highlighted this tension central to the Fourth Amendment in the following remarks: "The very strong core-area interest of the individual in not having private papers in his home searched and seized by the government may be overridden because of what is considered the even stronger societal interest in permitting police, upon a proper showing, to conduct a search in order to apprehend and convict a criminal" (Rehnquist 1974, 14).

Since the circuit courts decide a tremendous number of cases every year, we examine one issue area across a long time span rather than a broader range of cases over fewer years. Our decision to focus on a single issue was made for two major reasons. First, by focusing on one issue area, we avoid potential confounding that may occur across types of cases (see Friedman and Martin 2011). Second, a lengthy time span is essential to provide needed variation on our explanatory variables of interest. Our emphasis on time period over breadth of issue areas allows us to explore the effect of

---

[7] We discuss the interview evidence on this front in Appendix 3.C.

[8] Unpublished opinions are excluded because they typically involve clear-cut legal questions, rarely generate separate opinions, and are not readily available for the period of time we analyze (Sunstein et al. 2006). More information about the construction of the dataset is available in Appendix 3.B.

changes in circuit size, account for the changing interactions between pairs of judges over time, and examine each judge's behavior with a wider range of colleagues coming on and off the bench. In short, the decision to focus on a single issue area provides a number of positive research design characteristics.

At the same time, any single-issue study necessarily raises concerns, particularly those regarding generalizability. We selected search and seizure for several reasons. First, these disputes are considered bread-and-butter cases for court of appeals judges (see Klein 2002, 68); the widespread familiarity with search and seizure law helps reduce potential confounding factors related to specialized areas of law or unfamiliar issues. At the same time, this ubiquity reduces the amount of specialized expertise any panel member can bring to the table and therefore provides a level playing field among panel members upon which collegiality can do its work. Second, because search and seizure cases represent a sizable portion of federal courts of appeal dockets (Klein 2002, 68), they provide more statistical power than many other issue areas. Third, findings regarding search and seizure cases have been found to generalize well in many circumstances to other issue areas (see Segal 1984; Segal and Spaeth 2002; Bartels 2009; Wahlbeck 1997). Finally, Friedman and Martin (2011) theorize that precedent is more likely to be stable in criminal matters than in some other areas of law due to the need for notice to participants in the criminal justice system. Thus, search and seizure cases provide us with an issue area that represents everyday decisions by court of appeals judges in large enough numbers that we are able to explore the effects of collegiality.

Figure 3.2 provides a sense of the distribution of cases in our dataset by year (left-hand panel) and circuit (right-hand panel). Overall, there is a pronounced increase in the number of cases per year, which may reflect the increasing importance of federal criminal justice issues over time as well as the number of novel search and seizure issues that presented themselves with the rise of technology over the sixty-year period

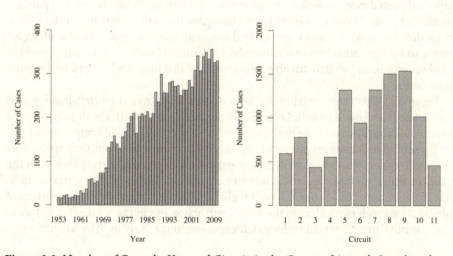

Figure 3.2 Number of Cases, by Year and Circuit, in the Courts of Appeals Search and Seizure Dataset

62   THE ELEVATOR EFFECT

we study. In terms of the number of cases per circuit in our dataset, we unsurprisingly see the highest number of cases from the largest circuits. The Fifth, Seventh, Eighth, and Ninth Circuits are well represented in our data, while the small Third Circuit and the Eleventh Circuit (which was created during the time period we study) are the circuits with the fewest cases in our data.

The behavior we are interested in explaining is the judge's vote, and it has three categories: (a) the judge signed the majority opinion, (b) the judge wrote a concurring opinion, or (c) the judge wrote a dissenting opinion.[9] The baseline category is signing the majority opinion and not noting a dissent or concurrence. Overall, most of the votes in our dataset (nearly 90 percent) were with the majority. Only 3.6 percent of votes were concurring, and 6.6 percent were dissenting.

Our major independent variable of interest is whether a judge has their home chambers in the same courthouse as the author of the majority opinion. This reflects variation in likely contact between the two judges in each case. To collect data on the chambers location of each circuit judge, we began with physical volumes of the *Federal Reporter*. These books contain the information on the city in which each judge has their chambers. Then, to find the cities with multiple federal courthouses, we relied upon the Federal Judicial Center's electronic database of Historic Federal Courthouses.[10] For those judges whose chambers were in a city that had multiple federal courthouses at some point during their tenure, we consulted a variety of judicial directories to find the mailing address for the judge's chambers. Here, we relied upon resources including the *Judicial Staff Directory* (published by Congressional Staff Directory, Ltd. in earlier years and CQ Staff Directories more recently), the *Judicial Yellow Book* (published by Leadership Directories), *BNA's Directory of State and Federal Courts, Judges, and Clerks* (published by the Bureau of National Affairs), and the *Federal-State Court Directory* (published by WANT Publishing Co.) as necessary. We also consulted publicly available information including court directories, judges' financial disclosure forms (available from Judicial Watch), obituaries of judges who had passed away, as well as other newspaper coverage. Where books and publicly available resources came up short (particularly for the earlier years in our data when print directories were scarce), we reached out to former law clerks, court staff, historians, and circuit librarians to obtain judges' chambers locations. Overall, 15 percent of observations in our data involve interactions of two judges who work in the same courthouse.

Figure 3.3 illustrates variation in Same Courthouse over time (left-hand panel) and space (right-hand panel). Overall, the percentage of our data with judges in the same courthouse peaks in the mid-1960s before beginning to equilibrate to about 15–20 percent of observations per year from the 1980s to the end of our time span. Note that the large amount of volatility in our data at the beginning corresponds with the years in which we have the fewest number of cases; as the time series starts to stabilize, the number of cases in our dataset is also increasing. Regarding the proportion of observations with two judges in the same courthouse, by circuit, we see that judges in the Seventh Circuit—which includes Chicago—are most likely to share a courthouse.

---

[9] A separate opinion that states a disagreement with any part of the case outcome is coded as a dissent.
[10] Available at https://www.fjc.gov/history/courthouses.

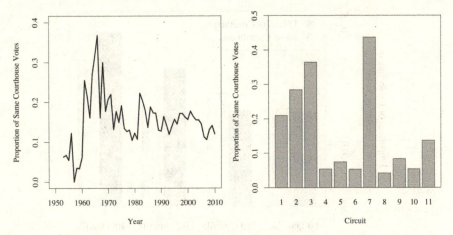

Figure 3.3 Summary of Same Courthouse Pairs: The distribution of opinion author-panel member pairs in the courts of appeals search and seizure dataset who have their chambers in the same courthouse by year (left-hand panel) and circuit (right-hand panel).

Judges in the northeastern U.S. (the First, Second, and Third Circuits) also sit together in 20 percent or more of our observations. On the other hand, judges in the Fourth, Sixth, Eighth, and Tenth Circuits are less likely to have their chambers in the same courthouse.

As discussed earlier, understanding the effect collegiality may have on the decision to write separately requires also accounting for how closely the ideology of the judge in question aligns with that of the opinion author. We use Judicial Common Space (JCS) scores to create the necessary variable.[11] Ideological Distance is the absolute value of the difference between the JCS scores of a judge and the majority opinion author in the relevant case. It has a theoretical range from zero to two and higher values indicate greater ideological disparity.

Descriptive Results

Armed with these three variables, we peek into the data to explore the relationship between whether two judges sit in the same courthouse, the ideological distance between them, and the likelihood that the non-majority author will decline to join the majority opinion. Recall that we expected that two judges who sit together in the same courthouse would be less likely to publicize their disagreement than two who work in different courthouses. In our data, judges who worked in the same courthouse as the opinion author concurred in 4 percent of cases and dissented in 7 percent of cases;

---

[11] JCS scores are based on the ideology of the political elites involved in the appointment of a judge and are located on a scale from −1 (liberal) to 1 (conservative) (Epstein et al. 2007; Giles, Hettinger, and Peppers 2001; Poole 1998).

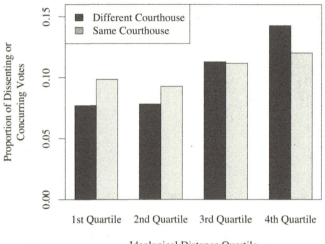

Figure 3.4 Distribution of Dissenting or Concurring Votes, by Ideological Distance Quartile

those who worked in different courthouses behaved *identically*: the judge concurred in 4 percent of cases and dissented in 7 percent of cases. This very basic look at the data suggests that there is no direct effect of collegiality on a judge's decision to publicize their disagreement.

Recall that our second and third hypotheses describe the conditional effects of collegiality and ideology. For simplicity, Figure 3.4 plots the proportion of observations in which the judge issued a concurring *or* dissenting opinion. There is one pair of bars for each quartile of ideological distance. The light bars show this quantity for pairs of judges who work in the same courthouse; the darker bars show the proportion for judges who work in different courthouses. For judges in the first quartile (those who are close ideologically), colleagues who work in the same courthouse decline to join the majority opinion slightly *more* than judges from different courthouses. As ideological distance increases to its maximum (the 4th quartile), the bars flip in size: two judges who work in different courthouses are more likely to publicly disagree than those who work in the same courthouse. This figure provides some evidence that—at least without accounting for other explanations of judicial behavior—the effect of collegiality differs according to the level of ideological disagreement between two judges.

Multivariate Analysis

Of course, this simple look at the data does not account for the myriad other factors that might affect a judge's decision to write a separate opinion. A multivariate regression model allows us to account for other factors that might influence the likelihood of dissent and concurrence as well as the level of interpersonal contact between two judges. To account for the possibility that factors will influence concurrence and dissent differently, we estimate a multinomial logit model with standard errors clustered on the case.

In addition to our measures of Same Courthouse and Ideological Distance, we control for judge characteristics, features of the case, hierarchical configuration, circuit caseload, and time. A judge's decision to write separately may be influenced by their own characteristics and those of the opinion author. For example, research showing that shared group membership can affect opinion assignment (Tillman and Hinkle 2018) and citation decisions (Hinkle and Nelson 2018b) suggests that judges who have demographic similarities with the opinion author may be less likely to dissent or concur. To account for this possibility, we control for whether the judge and majority opinion author are the same gender or the same race/ethnicity.

Next, we control for individual characteristics that might affect a judge's propensity to write separately. Studies of the U.S. Supreme Court have demonstrated that chief justices have additional reasons to avoid dissenting or concurring (Wahlbeck, Spriggs, and Maltzman 1999). A similar link between administrative leadership and enhanced concerns about collegiality may operate in circuit courts as well. Consequently, we control for whether a judge was serving as the chief judge of the circuit at the time of a particular case. Finally, we control for whether a judge has served less than two years on the court as well as their age because a judge's willingness to write separately may vary based on the stage of their career (Hettinger, Lindquist, and Martinek 2003).

We also consider the context of the case. Dissenting or concurring votes might be more common in more important cases, so we control for whether any amicus curiae briefs were filed in the case.[12] The type of litigation may shape incentives to write separately, so we control for whether the case is civil or a habeas petition; the baseline is a criminal case. Next, we look up the judicial hierarchy. A judge may be more likely to write separately when they are able to whistle-blow, that is, bring a perceived legal error to the attention of a reviewing court (Cross and Tiller 1998; Beim, Hirsch, and Kastellec 2014). Although the dynamics of whistle-blowing can be complex, in general the ideological distance between a judge and a potential reviewing court influences the whistle-blowing function of a separate opinion, especially a dissent. Circuit panel opinions can be reviewed by two sources, the Supreme Court or the full circuit rehearing a case en banc (Hinkle 2016). Consequently, we include controls for the distance between a judge and the Supreme Court median and the full-circuit median. These variables also utilize JCS scores. Finally, we include variables for caseload and the year of each case.[13] Caseload is the number of cases (in hundreds) terminated in the applicable circuit and year divided by the number of active circuit judges.

---

[12] This is a binary variable that equals one if the opinion mentioned participation by one or more amici and zero otherwise.

[13] J3 also suggested that differences in caseloads might decrease collegiality, suggesting that judges in circuits with higher caseloads have less time for interpersonal exchanges among judges.

66 THE ELEVATOR EFFECT

Summary statistics for all of the variables in the analysis are provided in Table 4.A.1 in the appendix to Chapter 4.

We examine the multivariate model in three steps. First, we test whether there is a direct effect of collegiality on the decision to write separately: all else equal, are judges who work in the same courthouse as the majority opinion author less likely to dissent or concur? Then, in the second and third steps of our analysis, we turn to the conditional effects of collegiality and ideological disagreement, testing whether the effect of collegiality on the decision to concur or dissent is magnified as ideological distance increases and whether the effect of ideology is dampened when two judges work in the same courthouse.

The Direct Effects of Collegiality

The descriptive results discussed in the previous section are useful to provide a simple look at the dynamics of collegiality, ideology, and publicized disagreement in our data. But our multivariate model provides a better test of our hypotheses because it can account for other explanations of dissenting or concurring behavior that might confound our results. The full results of our model are found in Table 3.A.1 in the chapter appendix. To keep the discussion focused on the effects of collegiality, we defer consideration of the control variables to the next chapter.

We begin by addressing the direct effect of collegiality, using the estimates from Model 1. Holding everything else—including ideology—constant, are judges who work together in the same courthouse less likely to write concurring or dissenting opinions from each other's decisions? Model 1 in Table 3.A.1 provides the multinomial logistic regression results for this analysis. Regarding concurrences, we find no evidence that judges who work in the same courthouse are less likely to issue a concurring opinion ($\hat{\beta} = 0.12$, $p = 0.32$). The predicted probability of a concurring opinion (holding all other variables at their median values) is 0.03 for pairs of judges who do not work in the same courthouse and also 0.03 for pairs of judges who work in the same courthouse.

Similarly, turning to dissenting opinions, we also have no evidence of a direct effect of collegiality ($\hat{\beta} = -0.07$, $p = 0.48$). When the two judges work in the same courthouse, the predicted probability of a dissent is 0.05. When the two judges work in different courthouses, the predicted probability is also 0.05. As such, we find no evidence that collegiality, by itself, diminishes the likelihood that a judge will choose to dissent or concur.

The Conditional Effect of Collegiality

Our second expectation was that collegiality among federal judges is most likely to have a notable impact on publicized disagreement when a judge is more ideologically distant from the majority opinion author. To test this hypothesis, we add a multiplicative interaction term between Same Courthouse and Ideological Distance to our model; the full regression results are provided in Model 2 in Table 3.A.1. For both the likelihood of concurrence and dissent, the interaction term in our multinomial logistic regression is statistically significant ($\hat{\beta} = -0.76$, $p = 0.02$ for concurrences and $\hat{\beta} = -0.63$, $p = 0.03$ for dissents). To visualize the effect of collegiality as

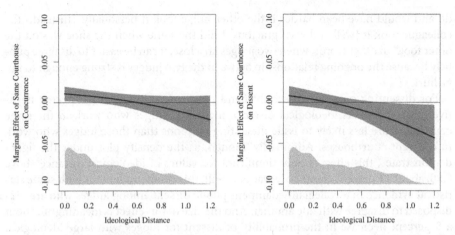

Figure 3.5 Effect of Same Courthouse on Concurring and Dissenting, Courts of Appeals: These plots show the marginal effect of Same Courthouse on concurrence (left-hand panel) and dissent (right-hand panel) over the entire range of Ideological Distance. Larger values of the x-axis indicate stronger ideological disagreements between two judges. The shaded regions depict the 95% confidence intervals. The density plots at the bottom of the figures show the distribution of Ideological Distance in the dataset.

ideological distance varies, Figure 3.5 plots the marginal effect of Same Courthouse, essentially the estimated difference between working in the same building rather than in a different courthouse, at each possible level of Ideological Distance. Positive values on this graph indicate that, for a given value of Ideological Distance, judges who work in the same courthouse are more likely to dissent or concur, compared to judges who work in different courthouse.

For both dissent and concurrence, we observe a gradual negative sloping line, as expected by our hypothesis. However, for concurrences (the left-hand panel), there is never a statistically significant negative effect of Same Courthouse, even among those judges who have the highest levels of Ideological Distance. Instead, for those judges who work in close proximity to one another, we observe a *positive* effect of working in the same courthouse. When two judges are ideologically congruent with one another, those who work together in the same building are slightly more likely to issue a concurring opinion than those who work in a different courthouse.

This is contrary to our expectations, though we interpret it as suggesting that judges with higher levels of familiarity are more willing to publish "friendly amendments"—in the form of concurrences—to their close colleagues' opinions. Indeed, some of our interview evidence suggested that publicized disagreement could be *more* likely when judges have close personal relationships. As J6, discussing how collegiality played a role on their court, reported: "It also happens that, when we took the vote, I was [voting] with a colleague but then switched. I already felt bad enough. It was hard to

68　THE ELEVATOR EFFECT

do and would have been harder if the other judge took it personally. [Instead,] the colleague took it [well and was] gracious. I did the same when the shoe was on the other foot." In other words, when two judges are close, it can be easier to disagree publicly because the ongoing relationship between the two judges is strong enough to not be hurt.

For dissenting opinions (the right-hand panel), we observe the expected negative relationship. As ideological distance increases, judges who work in the same courthouse are less likely to issue dissenting opinions than those judges who work in different courthouses. Admittedly, though, as the density plot under the figure demonstrates, this effect is only significant for values of ideological distance above 0.80, about 11 percent of our observations. Still, this result provides us with some statistical evidence that collegiality dampens public dissent among judges who are predisposed to disagree with one another. And the size of this effect is meaningful: about a 5 percent decrease in the probability of dissent for judges with large ideological disagreements.

The Conditional Effect of Ideology

Our final hypothesis concerned ideological dampening. We expected that the effect of ideological disagreement on the decision to concur or dissent would be smaller for judges who work in different courthouses than those who work in the same courthouse. Figure 3.6 shows the results of this analysis. Beginning with the solid lines in the left-hand panels of the figure, the strong positive slope suggests that concurrences and dissents become more likely as judges who work in different courthouses begin to have more pronounced ideological disagreements. Statistical evidence for this effect is shown in the left-hand point in the second panel for each row: a positive and statistically significant marginal effect for Ideological Distance when the judges work in different courthouses. Put differently, when interpersonal contact is low, greater levels of Ideological Distance are accompanied by a higher probability of dissent or concurrence, just as traditional theories of separate opinion writing predict.

But when we look at the effect for judges who work in the same courthouse (the dashed lines), we see a much weaker slope. In fact, this effect is not statistically significant for either dissents or concurrences. When two judges work together in the same courthouse, *there is no evidence that ideological distance with the opinion author is associated with the probability that they decline to join the panel majority.* Knowing whether two judges are ideologically similar or dissimilar enables someone to predict whether the other judge will dissent from the opinion author, but only if the two judges work in different courthouses. But when they are in the same courthouse on a regular basis, knowing the level of ideological disagreement between the two judges provides no information about whether a dissent or concurrence is likely.

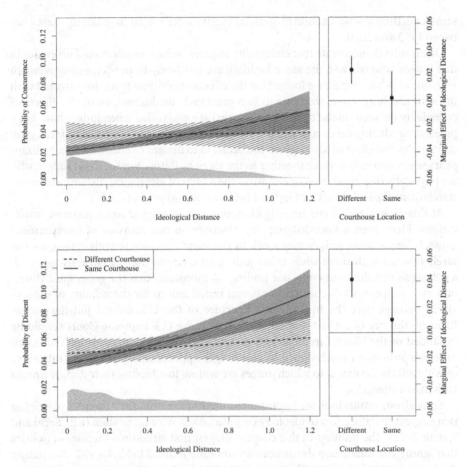

Figure 3.6 Conditional Effect of Ideological Distance on Concurring and Dissenting, Courts of Appeals: The left-hand plots show the predicted probability of concurrence (top row) and dissent (bottom row) as Ideological Distance varies. Larger values of the x-axis indicate stronger ideological disagreements between two judges. The density plots at the bottom of the left-hand panels show the distribution of Ideological Distance in the dataset. The right-hand panels show the marginal effect of Ideological Distance by the level of collegiality between the two judges. Shaded and cross-hatch regions and bars depict 95% confidence intervals.

Conclusions

Our goal in this chapter was to bring the theory of collegiality presented in Chapter 2 to the U.S. Courts of Appeals. Focusing on a judge's decision to publicize their disagreement with the panel's ruling through a dissenting or concurring opinion and using a novel measure of collegiality—whether two judges have their offices in the same courthouse—we examined judicial behavior in search and seizure cases between 1953 and 2010.

Our results demonstrate that collegiality matters. While we uncovered no evidence that judges who work in the same building are less likely to publicize disagreement with one another overall, we found that the effects of collegiality are intertwined with those of ideology. Here, we came to two principal conclusions. First, the effects of collegiality (at least on the decision to dissent) are magnified when judges have large preexisting ideological disagreements. Second, we uncovered evidence of *ideological dampening*: the effect of ideology on the decision to dissent or concur virtually disappears when two judges work together in the same building. But for those judges who are physically dispersed from one another, the effects of ideological distance are just as standard attitudinal theories of judicial behavior would predict.

At this early stage of our investigation, our results suggest some tentative implications. First, even acknowledging imperfections in our measure of interpersonal contact—since some judges may work in the same courthouse with colleagues but rarely interact with them while other judges on a circuit may be close friends with a colleague in a different city—our findings demonstrate that the geographic distribution of judges on a circuit has important ramifications for the stability of the law. While debates over the institutional structure of the U.S. federal judiciary often focus on the *size* of a court—whether the size of the U.S. Supreme Court should be expanded or the Ninth Circuit should be split—these results suggest that the extent to which judiciaries are designed to give judges opportunities to see each other frequently affects the extent to which judges are willing to advertise their disagreements with their colleagues.

Second, our results indicate important limitations to attitudinal theories of judging that suggest that the effect of ideology on judicial behavior is constant (e.g., Segal and Spaeth 2002). The findings in this chapter suggest that attitudinal theories of politics that ignore the intergroup dynamics that underlie judicial behavior risk overstating the importance of ideology. The findings in this chapter suggest that attitudinal theories of politics are most predictive in contexts where judges have low levels of collegiality. When judges' collegiality concerns are heightened, a desire to maintain strong interpersonal relationships can blunt the effect of ideology to the point where it is no longer predictive of a judge's decision to concur or dissent.

This analysis is just the first step in our attempt to untangle the effects of collegiality on judicial behavior. We have not sought to understand *why* interpersonal contact may blunt the effect of ideology nor have we examined the extent to which these results generalize to other courts or to other types of judicial behavior. Still, the analysis in this chapter provides a building block for our argument that judges' interpersonal relationships shape their behavior on the bench: even with a single, admittedly blunt measure of interpersonal contact, we see that collegial concerns can mitigate the effects of policy preferences.

Appendix 3.A: Regression Results

Table 3.A.1 Model Results: Multinomial logit regression estimates of the effect of Same Courthouse, Ideological Distance, their interaction, and a range of control variables on the likelihood of a concurring or dissenting vote. The reported standard errors are robust standard errors that are clustered on the case and * denotes a p-value less than 0.05.

	Model 1		Model 2	
	Coef.	S.E.	Coef.	S.E.
Concurrence				
Same Courthouse	0.118	(0.118)	0.452	(0.179)
Ideological Distance	0.682	(0.151)	0.836	(0.166)
Same Courthouse × Ideological Distance			−0.765	(0.326)
Same Gender	0.083	(0.116)	0.077	(0.116)
Same Race	−0.171	(0.117)	−0.161	(0.118)
Chief Judge	0.112	(0.159)	0.113	(0.159)
New Judge	−0.658	(0.267)	−0.657	(0.267)
Age	−0.027	(0.006)	−0.027	(0.006)
Amicus	0.982	(0.217)	0.979	(0.218)
Civil Rights	0.148	(0.106)	0.147	(0.106)
Habeas	0.062	(0.197)	0.065	(0.197)
ID Distance: Panel to Circuit	0.336	(0.223)	0.335	(0.223)
ID Distance: Panel to S.Ct.	0.308	(0.291)	0.320	(0.291)
Caseload/100	0.072	(0.053)	0.068	(0.053)
Year	−0.014	(0.005)	−0.014	(0.005)
Intercept	26.133	(10.245)	25.529	(10.264)
Dissent				
Same Courthouse	−0.067	(0.094)	0.218	(0.153)
Ideological Distance	0.729	(0.120)	0.842	(0.130)
Same Courthouse × Ideological Distance			−0.634	(0.283)
Same Gender	−0.134	(0.087)	−0.137	(0.087)
Same Race	−0.317	(0.084)	−0.309	(0.084)
Chief Judge	−0.403	(0.145)	−0.400	(0.145)
New Judge	−0.124	(0.171)	−0.124	(0.171)
Age	−0.007	(0.005)	−0.007	(0.005)
Amicus	0.552	(0.184)	0.550	(0.184)
Civil Rights	0.366	(0.076)	0.366	(0.076)
Habeas	0.061	(0.140)	0.062	(0.140)
ID Distance: Panel to Circuit	0.169	(0.173)	0.168	(0.173)
ID Distance: Panel to S.Ct.	0.582	(0.231)	0.589	(0.231)
Caseload/100	0.097	(0.035)	0.095	(0.035)

(continued)

72 THE ELEVATOR EFFECT

Table 3.A.1 Continued

	Model 1		Model 2	
	Coef.	S.E.	Coef.	S.E.
Year	−0.020	(0.004)	−0.019	(0.004)
Intercept	36.278	(7.262)	35.951	(7.272)
N	15,014		15,014	
AIC	11727.9		11722.9	
BIC	11956.4		11966.7	

Appendix 3.B: Detailed Data Collection Description

We identified relevant cases by using Lexis to locate all published opinions from the eleven numbered geographical circuits that cite the Fourth Amendment of the U.S. Constitution and use the word "search" or the word stem "seiz" at least once. The resulting dataset contains 10,461 authored opinions in panel cases. We exclude per curiam opinions since our research design requires being able to identify the opinion author. We exclude the small number of en banc opinions since a circuit sitting en banc performs a substantially different function within a qualitatively different institutional context.

There is an observation for each non-authoring active home-circuit judge in each case. There is no observation for the opinion author since they are not faced with making the decision to write a separate opinion. The responsibility of authoring an opinion is assigned by the most senior active judge on the panel (Bowie, Songer, and Szmer 2014; Tillman and Hinkle 2018). Although it is technically possible for the opinion author to also write separately, this is quite rare. We exclude these cases from our analysis. Furthermore, we exclude votes cast by judges from other courts sitting by designation to focus on the level of collegiality among the circuit judges who serve together on the same court. Finally, we exclude semi-retired judges who have taken senior status since that status both excludes them from the process of en banc decision-making and provides the opportunity to reduce one's caseload (Epstein, Landes, and Posner 2013). Since senior judges have spent an entire career in the circuit, their exclusion is a close call. However, including them in the model with a control variable to indicate senior status produces the same substantive conclusions.

Appendix 3.C: Interview Evidence on Panel Assignment

While circuit judges reported some variation in what panel assignments looked like in their circuits, they generally described systems based on random assignment with accommodations for generic workplace issues, like absences and vacations.

- In J1's circuit, the clerk's office in the main city for oral arguments randomly assigns panels: "The only exception is if a senior status judge wants to hear cases in their own city." In J1's circuit, panel assignments are made using a "combination" of factors including the availability of judges due to "vacations" and the like. So assignment is a function of the

INTERPERSONAL CONTACT AND PUBLICIZING DISAGREEMENT   73

calendar and the schedule set by the chief. There is no scheduling they are aware of "based on if there's a good match of judges." In other words, J1 was not aware of attempts to game the system to pair "Judge X with Morgan."

- J2 was also unaware of any instance in which a judge was selected for a panel based on "how they see things," saying that this type of selection "doesn't happen that I know of." As J2 put it: "The proof is in the pudding. Look at the assignments. [You will see] no chicanery."
- In J3's circuit, the chief judge's office assigns the panels "based on an algorithm." The panel is created for the day rather than the week. The goal is that everyone will sit with each judge "the same number of times." In the "short term," it tends not to be "equal because someone is ill, has commitments, or there is a recusal." However, in the long-term "it works quite well." When J3 was "new to the court, I loved it because in a short time I had sat with each of my colleagues a fair number of times and gotten to know them and how they approached things." J3 specifically noted that they were "glad" that we asked about panel assignment in "your circuit" due to variation.
- In J4's circuit, panel assignment has varied over time with a move to "straight random assignment." Their impression was "there is some preference for two active judges." This did not always happen because occasionally someone is sick or there is a new judge juggling cases. "Cases are generally assigned in the order they come in unless someone is recused or conflicted out. If so, then move on to the next panel." On J4's circuit, the panels are generally formed for the week but may be split in half to "balance workloads." For example, "if there is a visiting judge for a day or few days." Also, they described a reduced workload for senior judges.
- J5 reports that assignment in their circuit is "random but maybe not if there is an emergency motion. Then it would be in the order of seniority. Assignments just show up. I am unsure if it is done by a wheel or random generation. It is very unusual but if a case was one in a series of appeals in XYZ matter, it may go to [the panel that dealt with it before] because [they have] experience with the matter." They report that the panel lengths are "random" and the "chief judge selects." They "sit with different judges quite a bit from year to year. Some more than others." With six sittings a year, they usually sit with another judge "one to one and a half times." J5 did discuss some nonrandom assignments: each year, the judge requests to sit with two other judges with whom they are friends. This is done "a year in advance" and are "not special cases" but rather are "random cases." The judges are "close and want to sit together." The three judges are "around the same age and came onto the court around the same time."
- In J6's circuit, the assignment is "totally random." It is done using a "computer program taking into account recusals and conflicts such as vacations." The panels vary every day. There are usually three to four days of cases with four cases a day. There are five panels at a time.
- In J7's circuit, panel assignment is "random." There are four days of panels in a week and the panels change in the middle of the four-day period. Some senior judges "only come for the first half or second half of the week."

Clerks varied in their knowledge of how panels were assigned, but their descriptions generally matched the judges'. C2 was unsure how panels were scheduled and arranged generally. They never were part of en banc proceedings. In C3's circuit, the chief judge assigned the panels. There was "an opportunity for the judges to indicate their availability, such as trip schedules." As

74 THE ELEVATOR EFFECT

for the specifics of the assignment process, the clerk was "unsure because [they were] not privy to the procedure." There would be a "draft schedule," and judges "would identify conflicts." They did note that one specific courthouse "was very picturesque" and "great in fall" and that the chief judge seemed to often be "presiding there [...] especially when leaf-peeping season." They joked that it was "suspicious" and laughed. C4 noted that based on panel assignments, their judge sat with "almost everyone." They did note that their judge didn't overlap with another senior judge who had their home chambers in another state.

4
Why Does Collegiality Matter?

Introduction

In the previous chapter, we brought data to bear on our expectations about the effects of collegiality on judges' decisions to concur or dissent. Relying on a novel measure of collegiality—whether a pair of judges have their chambers in the same building—we found some evidence that (a) collegiality has its greatest effects among judges with the most severe ideological disagreements (at least for the decision to dissent), and (b) the effect of ideological disagreement on judges' decisions to dissent or concur is essentially nonexistent when there is a high level of collegiality.

Why does this happen? Our task in this chapter is to try to explain *why* collegiality affects judges' decisions to publicize their disagreement with the panel's decision. In the process, we make two major distinctions. First, collegiality might matter for *personal* and *professional* reasons. Consider two co-workers who also happen to be neighbors. Their interactions are likely based on a combination of personal ("I like talking to my co-worker about some television show over lunch and wouldn't want to mess that up by irritating them") or professional ("We have to finish a project together and it will be very difficult if we can't get along") considerations. Collegiality might affect a judge's decision to cast a dissenting or concurring vote out of a desire to preserve a personal relationship, a professional relationship, or both.

Second, two different interpersonal processes—persuasion and suppression— might explain the effects of collegiality. As J6 put it in their interview, "Collegiality matters because either [there was] compromise or I saw the merit of [the argument] and could live with the decisions." On the one hand, when two people know each other well, they can predict what sorts of points are likely to be effective in changing a colleague's mind. This familiarity, in turn, can improve the quality of deliberation and help two individuals see eye-to-eye. In this way, *persuasion* may lead to sincere consensus even in the face of a predisposition to disagree. On the other hand, some judges see each other often, socialize together, and have a desire to preserve that relationship. Under these circumstances, judges may *suppress* their disagreement, choosing to sign a majority opinion with which they have some quibbles and providing the illusion of consensus.

As we explained in the previous chapters, we expect that the need to maintain a collegial personal or professional relationship increases with the amount of contact between two judges. In this chapter, we use two additional indicators of contact to examine the interpersonal processes through which collegiality affects the presence and expression of public disagreement. First, we argue that *persuasion* is more likely as two judges have a higher level of past interactions, and we test the efficacy of this mechanism using the length of time two judges have served on the circuit court together (the level of cotenure). Second, we argue that *suppression* happens out of a desire to

The Elevator Effect. Morgan L.W. Hazelton, Rachael K. Hinkle, and Michael J. Nelson, Oxford University Press.
© Oxford University Press 2023. DOI: 10.1093/oso/9780197625408.003.0004

76 THE ELEVATOR EFFECT

avoid negative future interactions with panel members; we consider this factor using the probability that two judges will be randomly assigned to serve on a panel together. We estimate these effects alongside those of Same Courthouse, which we argue indicates the level of the personal relationship between two judges.

Armed with these new measures, we return to our search and seizure dataset to understand why collegiality affects the decision of a judge to publicize their disagreement with the panel majority. The results demonstrate that no single mechanism can account for the effects of collegiality. Judges with greater professional (but not necessarily personal) relationships with one another are, on average, less likely to dissent from each other's opinions. But our evidence suggests that ideological dampening happens as a result of a desire to suppress dissent in order to preserve personal relationships with colleagues.

Personal and Professional Relationships

We begin by distinguishing between personal and professional collegial relationships.[1] First, judges have some motivation to maintain a positive personal relationship with their colleagues. As Baum (2006, 60) argues, "[a] judge will be more open to influence from colleagues who are more relevant at a personal level." Judges who regularly see each other in the grocery store, at the country club, or at the local bar association dinner may be motivated by a desire to maintain a good relationship with each other; some of their professional behaviors could be tempered by a motivation to preserve a strong personal bond. In this way, relationships built outside of work might have consequences for judicial behavior.

Several of our interviewees explained how judges build strong personal relationships outside of the courthouse. J2 told us that shared interests and experiences help judges solidify personal bonds: "Do you golf? Do you have children the same age? Do you live within the same 20 miles? 40 miles?" Similarly, J4 noted that some judges golf together, and others "have shared joys and sorrows," inviting their judicial colleagues to their weddings or their children's religious celebrations. J4 recounted having encountered behavioral issues with their children, and another judge who had a similar experience "provided advice and resources." J4 told us that these interactions bring judges "deeper into each others' lives." It seems reasonable that these personal relationships outside of the courthouse might have consequences for judges' behaviors in chambers. In fact, J7 noted that judges often work for unanimity, and the importance of presenting a unified front grows with the strength of the judges' relationship: judges are more likely to "work to come together" where there is a "personal relationship."

Second, judges' *professional* relationships with their co-workers may also matter. As Wahlbeck, Spriggs, and Maltzman (1999, 496) argue, "[j]ustices are likely to reward colleagues who have cooperated with them in the past and punish those who

---

[1] We acknowledge some level of overlap between these two concepts. For example, judges who have worked together for long periods of time may develop strong personal ties even when they only interact professionally.

WHY DOES COLLEGIALITY MATTER? 77

have not." Strong professional relationships with colleagues may be instrumentally useful for policy-minded judges. Judges can harness their professional relationships not necessarily to logroll with one another, trading votes across cases, but rather to capitalize on the intensely personal nature of the process of bargaining and opinion writing to modify the language in draft opinions (and convince colleagues to sign them), helping judges bend the arc of the law toward their favored policy preferences in the long run.

Our interviewees also discussed the importance of professional relationships. J5 contrasted "a friend on another circuit who has a next-door neighbor who [they] can't stand" with his own experience. J5 told us that they have a friend on their courthouse floor with whom they are not politically aligned. But they are so close that the other judge on the floor is the only person J5 invited to a special event honoring J5. J5 said they "won't necessarily agree [with each other], but [they] will listen" to each other's positions. J5 suggested that their strong professional relationship with their colleague helped to make the process of judicial deliberations more free-flowing and open. As J5 summarized, "If someone likes you, then they may try to work to accommodate you. If not, they're not going to. No, thank you!" Similarly, C2 told us "collegiality matters. Those judges who are consistently disagreeing and must be heard are very annoying and disliked. The judge who can get along is more popular." Thus, professional relationships also affect judicial deliberations and case outcomes.

Persuasion and Suppression

Two interpersonal processes—persuasion and suppression—might explain how collegiality affects the decision to write separately. *Persuasion* happens when judges reach sincere consensus because of compromise among panel members. Collegiality eases the costs of compromise by providing judges with private information about their colleagues that they can use to make more effective arguments during the opinion drafting process. Judges who know each other well are therefore better able to "read" each other, tailoring arguments they make at conference and throughout the opinion-writing process toward ones that have the highest likelihood of swaying the colleague with whom they disagree. The exchange of effective private arguments can lead to alterations in the content of the majority opinion during the drafting process that negate the need to dissent or concur.[2]

In a rational choice framework, persuasion suggests that collegiality eases compromise, moving the location of the opinion in doctrinal space toward the potentially dissenting judge. Neither judge gets exactly the opinion that they prefer, but they agree to compromise. The potential dissenter (concurrer) succeeds in making the majority opinion a bit more preferable and saves herself the effort of dissenting (concurring). Likewise, by agreeing on the compromise location for the policy, the majority opinion

---

[2] Collegiality is not magic. To be clear, we do *not* suggest that higher levels of collegiality lead judges to dramatically reconsider their positions on most legal issues. As J6 told us, with regard to "civil, intelligent conversations that persuaded, I can count on one to two hands" the number of cases where a judge reconsidered their strongly held position as a result of a colleague's argument.

78 THE ELEVATOR EFFECT

author can achieve more support (perhaps staving off a higher probability of review). In short, this understanding of collegiality focuses on minimizing the amount of policy loss a judge suffers by signing a majority opinion (rather than changing the cost of dissenting or concurring). As this policy loss decreases, it becomes dwarfed by the costs of dissenting or concurring, making it better for the judge to simply sign the majority opinion than to publicize their disagreement.

Our interviewees provided us with some examples of how collegial concerns increase the ability of judges to persuade each other during the process of drafting opinions. J7 told us they will send the other judges the draft opinion, and if another judge "is not signing on," they ask the other judge "what can I do?" They are looking for changes that will make the other judge comfortable with joining the opinion. This can include changes in "tone" or "not [being] so broad" in the scope of the decision. "The goal is unanimity. If [the judges] are not talking and have no relationship, [the other judge] is more likely to write separately." When J5 drafts opinions, they "take into account others' concerns. I will avoid [X] because of [Judge Y]." Thus, they are "drafting with information from colleagues and their concerns at the time [of oral arguments]." Along similar lines, S5 described that when they clerked in the court of appeals, their boss would remove language that "[wouldn't] fly" with a colleague before circulating a draft opinion to that colleague.

The previous discussion suggests that persuasion is characterized by a free-flowing exchange of views facilitated by a strong interpersonal relationship. As Judge Harry T. Edwards (2003, 1645) has written, "In an uncollegial environment, divergent views among members of a court often end up as dissenting opinions. Why? Because judges tend to follow a 'party line' and adopt unalterable positions on the issues before them." In more collegial environments, Edwards suggests, judges are more willing to give and take during the opinion drafting process and to be open to influence from their colleagues' arguments.

Suppression represents a second process through which collegiality might affect judicial behavior. In contrast to persuasion, which is characterized by compromise and sincere consensus, suppression happens when a judge signs a majority opinion about which they have some quibbles. When judges suppress their disagreement, they provide an illusion of consensus to other courts and to the public even in the face of some level of policy disagreement.

Whereas collegiality might fuel persuasion by making judges more open to each other's arguments and providing them with the necessary knowledge to make the sort of arguments most likely to sway their colleagues, collegiality might bring about suppression by increasing the costs of dissent relative to the benefits. As Songer (1982, 226) suggests, judges might refrain from dissenting in order "to improve social relationships among the judges." When a judge does not interact with their co-workers very often, there are few ramifications for irritating them. However, as such interactions increase, the desire to maintain a pleasant working relationship (aided by not publicly deriding your colleagues) also grows. Given the high costs of dissenting— magnified under conditions of frequent contact—and the relatively low benefits, judges operating in collegial environments may conduct a simple cost-benefit analysis, deciding that paying the costs of writing and releasing the separate opinion just is not worth the time, effort, and unpleasantness. As members of a small group that will

WHY DOES COLLEGIALITY MATTER? 79

decide cases together for years to come, judges may choose to disagree silently rather than publicizing their disagreement and risking making an enemy of a colleague.

Our interviewees provided us with some examples of suppression. J2 said collegiality could matter if the case was "a close call [that] could go either way and you really respect the other judge," suggesting in those instances it might be better to sign that judge's majority opinion instead of writing one separately. S2 believes that "collegiality affects outcomes on the courts of appeals a lot more often than at the Supreme Court. There are judges that just go along because of the composition of the panel—who they serve with. They don't want to ruffle feathers or don't care or don't want to do the work. So they will go along with the two others and save conflict for important cases."[3]

Measuring the Mechanisms

Our next task is to explain the concepts we use to measure personal and professional relationships and to test for the effects of persuasion and suppression. In selecting these measures, we are again guided by the assumption that higher levels of collegiality are associated with more frequent interpersonal contact between judges. Our goal is to consider different types of interactions among judges and to make the case that these different types of contact serve as indicators for the mechanisms we seek to test.

Personal Relationships

To capture the effects of personal contact, we rely on our measure of Same Courthouse, introduced and discussed at length in the previous chapter. Judges who work together in the same courthouse are, on average, more likely to see each other frequently, to interact in nonjudicial settings, and therefore to develop strong interpersonal relationships with one another outside of the courthouse.

We are agnostic about which interpersonal process—persuasion or suppression (or both)—this indicator measures. On the one hand, people who see each other often might be more concerned about unpleasant personal interactions, suggesting that Same Courthouse measures the suppression mechanism. But a stronger personal relationship with another judge also provides access to a trove of personal information about that person's thoughts, likes, and dislikes that might make someone a persuasive colleague. Thus, we include Same Courthouse in our model to parse the distinction between the effect of personal and professional relationships, acknowledging that this indicator cannot differentiate between the two interpersonal processes—persuasion and suppression—we also seek to distinguish.

---

[3] S2 suggested that this is "enormously frustrating to advocates" who feel like they "didn't get a fair and full consideration" of the matter.

80 THE ELEVATOR EFFECT

Professional Relationships

Next, we need indicators of the level of professional contact between two judges. To distinguish between persuasion and suppression, we capitalize on the temporal component implicit in each mechanism. To preview, we argue that a greater level of past contact between two judges, which we measure through the length of their cotenure, should be associated with an increased ability for one judge to persuade another; a higher level of anticipated future contact, measured through the probability two judges will serve together on a future panel, should increase the likelihood that a judge will choose to suppress their disagreement to preserve that future working relationship.

Persuasion and Past Professional Contact

Persuasion is linked to the level of *past contact* between two judges: when two people have longer professional relationships with one another, they should acquire increasing levels of information about the sorts of arguments that the other person finds persuasive. For this reason, a judge should be better able to convince a colleague to find common ground when they have served together for a longer period than if they are hearing their first case together. As we noted in Chapter 1, former Third Circuit Judge Walter K. Stapleton (1995, 36–37) wrote eloquently about how a longer association between two judges is associated with a greater degree of collegiality. He writes:

> It is difficult to listen, much less give up something important to you in compromise, if you are dealing with strangers. It is only when you come to know a colleague in some depth as a human being that you accept without question his or her good faith. Only when the good faith of your colleagues is taken as a given is it possible to find wisdom in a thought of another in conflict with your own.

Thus, as two judges serve together, they should get to know each other and better understand each other's likes and dislikes. This information, in turn, should help judges *persuade* their colleagues.

The circuit judges we interviewed generally indicated that relationships change, usually for the better, with time.[4] J1 suggested that, with the passage of time, "you learn more about each judge. Are they particular regarding this issue but not particular regarding this one? Judges are different, and you learn from comments on drafts." J2 told us that time increased "opportunity and the outside exchange of ideas," which they related to increased levels of "getting along"; they suggested that getting

---

[4] Other judicial interviewees provided their perspectives on the relationship between time and collegiality. J4 explained (in an exaggerated condescending tone) that "at first [older judges present as] 'let me tell you how it is, how it works around here.'" However, as judges "work and share" they become "closer." J7 concurred and stated that prior professional contact matters because you may have "misimpressions" regarding another judge based on what you "heard or read" and "you learn more over time": "oh, [they are] actually brilliant!" On the other hand, J3 was more restrained in their view that years of service influenced the interpersonal relationships among judges. They believed that shared length of service "probably" matters "but also probably not that much." "Some people I already knew [in a different capacity] and now as a fellow judge. Others have come and you get to know them."

along was "directly proportional to how long you have been on the bench together." Moreover, relationships built through time can help to overcome lack of physical closeness: "Passage of time allows greater opportunity for contact with those farther away." J6 reported that longer periods of service with a colleague lead to more interpersonal contact, helping judges to get to know each other better: "It is hard to get to know [the other judges] at first. Court week is a short window."[5]

Two courts of appeals clerks indicated that cotenure affects interpersonal interactions among judges. C3 believed that relationships among judges changed the longer they knew each other, especially because judges will be colleagues "for so long." This has pros and cons: there is time for "idiosyncrasies to get under your skin," but it also meant that their judge "had a good sense of what other judges would ask" and could plan accordingly for argument and deliberations. Similarly, C4 noted that the judges on the circuit where they clerked had sat together for a long time, and their judge liked to regale clerks and new judges alike with lots of "war stories" about judicial deliberations. It was clear from these stories that the judge had built a strong relationship with these judges over time, with the other judges in the stories often realizing that their judge was correct. Further, C4's judge understood that they didn't know the newer judges as well and invited new judges to lunches and visits, as they were "invested in getting to know them."

In short, this interview evidence helps to validate our claim that, like most people, judges build stronger professional relationships through repeated interactions over time. Additionally, they may care more about, and therefore be less inclined to endanger, relationships they have had over many years. If collegiality leads to more fruitful bargaining environments or more valued relationships, judges' level of collegial concern should increase with cotenure, the number of years a pair of judges have served together. Therefore, we measure variation in past professional contact based on how long two judges have served together on the same court and use cotenure as an indicator of persuasion.

Suppression and Future Professional Contact

Judges know that they serve with each other for life, and they may want to adjust their behavior in the present in the hope of maintaining a positive working relationship into the future. It might be better in the long run to sign an opinion with which one has minor disagreements than to build a reputation for forcing one's colleagues to make a laundry list of small changes to an opinion or to refuse to sign on to an opinion with which one basically agrees because it has some small imperfections. This behavior—adjusting one's behavior in the present to preserve a relationship for the future—is the essence of *suppression*.

Our interviewees suggested that judges keep their future interactions with their colleagues in mind while deliberating in the present case. Judicial careers are long; as

---

[5] J6 also told us that, as time has passed, circuit norms have evolved to allow more face-to-face contact, which has increased collegiality on their court. They told us that "though you can talk over the phone, the circuit norm was dedicated to interacting over paper. [There is a] slow migration to less formal [interaction]." The letter-writing norm was so entrenched that judges would "send emails with the letters attached." "Ten years ago, it was verboten" to speak via telephone. The "younger folks chaffed against this." Norms have been changing, and the result has been "an almost universal growth in friendship."

82 THE ELEVATOR EFFECT

J5 suggested, "we disagree today, but I might need you in the future." As a result, in J2's words, there is "no gloating or being dispirited." Instead, "people are candid and don't pull punches, but also realize that tomorrow they can be on the other side." J6 said that judges do not always agree. "But, it is easier if the disagreement won't linger."

Judges' need to maintain a positive professional relationship with their colleagues should vary based on how often they are likely to serve on a panel together in the future. Variation in the number of judges across both circuits and time creates concomitant variation in the frequency with which a judge sits on a panel with each of their colleagues: the likelihood of future contact. In a large circuit, a judge may be less concerned about a dissent riling up a colleague since a relatively small percentage of their future panels will include that judge. Conversely, on a small circuit, the costs incurred by disagreeing might loom large in light of much greater certainty about shared panel service in the near future. If collegiality operates through suppression, we should observe the effects of collegiality most clearly when two judges are more likely to sit on a future panel together.

With this said, we now need to operationalize the likelihood that two judges will sit together on a panel in the future. The most obvious way we might turn this concept into data is to use the size of the circuit: as it increases, the likelihood that any two judges will sit together on a particular panel decreases (Epstein, Landes, and Posner 2011). And there is evidence that the size of the circuit affects the level of collegiality on a court. As Bowie, Songer, and Szmer (2014, 106–07) summarize their interviews with U.S. Courts of Appeals judges:

> While none of the judges we interviewed directly discussed the impact of circuit size on the efficiency of the opinion-writing process, there was frequent mention of the positive effect that high levels of collegiality and knowing the other judges on the panel had on the ability of a panel to quickly reach agreement on an opinion. Thus, as larger size would seem inevitably to reduce how well the judges know each other and is likely to reduce the extent of collegiality, circuit size may indirectly result in a less efficient opinion-writing process.

Or, consider this analogy by Gerald Bard Tjoflat (1993, 70), a judge on the Fifth (and then Eleventh) Circuit:

> In many ways, life as a judge on a jumbo court is comparable to life as a citizen in a big city–life on a smaller court to life in a small town. In a small town, folks have to get along with one another. In a big city, many people do not even know, much less understand, their neighbors. Similarly, judges in small circuits are able to interact with their colleagues in a more expedient and efficient manner than judges on jumbo courts.

Finally, Second Circuit Judge Jon O. Newman (1993, 188) provides a colorful illustration of the demands of judging on a large court: "It will not be a court; it will be a stable of judges, each one called upon to plow through the unrelenting volume, harnessed on any given day with two other judges who barely know each other." Thus, circuit size might reduce collegiality by reducing both the amount of past contact and

WHY DOES COLLEGIALITY MATTER? 83

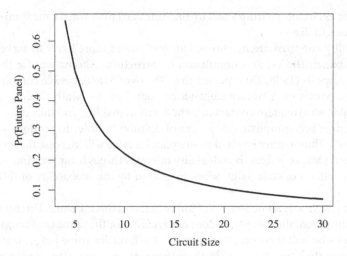

Figure 4.1 Relationship between Circuit Size and Probability of Future Panel Service

the anticipated frequency of future interactions (Cohen 2002; Epstein, Landes, and Posner 2011).

Circuit size has the benefit of being a simple measure of the future level of professional contact between two judges. But it has a major drawback: the difference in the probability that two judges serve together is not straightforwardly related to circuit size. As D.C. Circuit Judge J. Harvie Wilkinson (1994, 1175) has noted, "[s]imply as a matter of basic mathematics, the addition of each new judge creates many new possible panel combinations." Or, as U.S. District Court Judge Alvin B. Rubin (1976, 458), writing about the best size of a court, explains:

> Nine judges have often been referred to as the optimal number of judges for a circuit. I would opt for seven. This is in part based on experience, part on hunch. Seven judges can meet in a room that need not be an assembly hall, can get to know each other intimately, can dine together easily, and make only 35 possible combinations. Nine judges add only two more people but 49 more possible combinations. There is no empirical way to find a magic number, but large circuit courts present almost insuperable management and jurisprudential problems.

We quantify anticipated future interaction by calculating the probability that two judges will serve together on any given panel in each circuit and each year.[6] The relationship between circuit size and the probability of future panel service is illustrated in Figure 4.1. As a circuit gets bigger, the probability of any two judges sitting on a panel together decreases. But this relationship is not linear: the probability decreases

---

[6] Where N is the number of active judges: $Pr(Future\ Panel) = \frac{(N-2)}{\binom{N-1}{2}}$. The denominator of this fraction is the binomial coefficient.

84 THE ELEVATOR EFFECT

much faster as circuits go from small to medium sized than when a medium-sized circuit increases in size.[7]

Collegiality concerns are heightened among judges more likely to serve together soon on a panel. The White Commission on Structural Alternatives for the Federal Courts of Appeals (1998, 35) reported that "the over 3,000 possible combinations of three-judge panels on a twenty-eight-judge court" in the Ninth Circuit "precludes close, regular, and frequent contact in joint decision making, and thus the collegiality that lets judges accommodate differences of opinion in order to produce a coherent body of law."[8] Thus, higher levels of future panel service will increase the level of contact between pairs of judges. If collegiality operates through suppression, we should observe the effects of collegiality when measured by the probability of future panel service.

There are inevitably some sources of imprecision in this measure. This number may overstate the probability because it does not account for the number of senior and visiting judges who will serve on future panels. Additionally, some judges may be more likely to leave the court through death, retirement, or promotion, thus diminishing the future probability that their colleagues will serve with them. These elements all have a strong random component and are difficult to model.[9]

Moreover, our measure does not precisely describe the workload distribution since panel assignment is not *entirely* random (see, e.g., Atkins and Zavoina 1974; Brown and Lee 1999; Chilton and Levy 2015; and Appendix 3.C). Nonrandom assignment to panels can occur for various reasons. Atkins and Zavoina (1974) document nonrandom assignment in the Fifth Circuit in the early 1960s that had a direct impact on shaping federal law in race cases. While such extreme examples are uncommon today, there continue to be occasional accusations of using panel assignment to manipulate case outcomes (Brown and Lee 1999). More common reasons for deviating from random assignment relate to administrative housekeeping concerns such as efficiency and convenience (Brown and Lee 1999). Finally, assignment procedures may deviate from randomness to ensure a minimum level of interaction among all circuit judges. Levy (2017, 88) gathers extensive qualitative evidence about panel assignment and reports:

> All of the circuit courts surveyed here stated that they tried—in varying degrees—to take into account the number of times each judge had sat with every other judge when creating panels. Some of the circuits had precise rules about "co-sits"—that every judge must sit with every other judge at least some number of times, but no more than some other number of times. Other circuits had no precise rule about co-sits and simply tried to ensure that the judges were "mixed up" every so often.

---

[7] In our data, probability of future panel service correlates highly with circuit size: $r = -0.72$.

[8] The White Commission also notes objections that "collegiality is an elusive concept and that counting panel combinations cannot measure the ability of judges in the late twentieth century to fashion law" (35). As should be obvious at this point, we disagree!

[9] While we believe our measure represents an advance over using circuit size because it more precisely captures the possibility of sitting together, we acknowledge that circuit size is another plausible measure of this concept. When we have estimated the model with Circuit Size, rather than Pr(Future Panel), we reach similar conclusions.

The given rationale for attempting to equalize co-sits was consistent: doing so would enhance the court's collegiality.

Considering our larger project and overall theory, it is noteworthy that one of the reasons for departing from the general practice of random panel assignment is to improve collegiality by ensuring all circuit judges get to know one another.

For our purposes, nonrandom panel assignment only affects our estimates to the extent that it induces systematic bias in the likelihood that two judges sit together. That seems not to be the case. Levy's evidence suggests that, where panel assignment is not random, those making assignments actually do what they can to ensure regular rotation among judges and their colleagues. Appendix 3.C contains material from our interviews about panel assignment in the U.S. Courts of Appeals; our interviewees were clear that, in most cases, panels are assigned with little regard to the relationships of the judges on the panel; still, we acknowledge there may be a handful of cases where collegiality might affect panel assignment.

Empirical Strategy

Table 4.1 summarizes the interpersonal processes that might underlie the effects of collegiality on judicial behavior, how they relate to personal and professional interactions between judges, and the indicators that we use to test for the effects of each mechanism on judicial behavior.

We use the same data and multinomial logistic regression specification as Chapter 3.[10] The only additions to the model are our two additional measures of collegiality and their interaction with Ideological Distance. First, we measure cotenure: the number of years the judge and opinion author have served together. This variable ranges from 0 to 26 years, with an average value of 8.73 and a median of 8 years. Second, we measure the probability that a judge will be assigned to sit on any given panel with the opinion author in the applicable circuit and year. As a probability, this measure has a theoretical range of 0 to 1 and ranges from 0.08 to 1 in our dataset.[11] The variable has a mean of 0.22 and a median of 0.20.

Table 4.1 Indicators of Collegiality

Indicator	Concept	Mechanism
Same Courthouse	Regular Face-to-Face Contact	Personal
Cotenure	Past Contact	Professional: Persuasion
Future Panel Service	Anticipated Future Contact	Professional: Suppression

---

[10] Summary statistics for all of the variables in the analysis are provided in Table 4.A.1 in the chapter appendix.

[11] The very high values of this variable come in the beginning of the dataset when small circuit sizes and vacancies forced all the judges on a circuit to sit together.

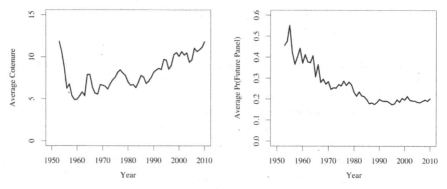

Figure 4.2 Trends in Collegiality Indicators over Time: The left-hand panel plots the average value of Cotenure in the courts of appeals search and seizure dataset over time; the right-hand panel plots the average value of the probability of future panel service in that same dataset. The correlation between these two variables is only $r = -0.01$.

To give a sense of each measure's central tendency and movement over time, Figure 4.2 plots the average value of cotenure (left-hand panel) and probability of future panel service (right-hand panel) over time. Here we see that the average cotenure between a pair of judges in our dataset steadily rises for the last 50 years in our dataset.[12] The opposite trend characterizes the relationship between time and the probability of future panel service: a gradual decline occurs as circuit sizes gradually increase, on average, throughout the period that we study.

These divergent trends raise the question of the relationship between the two variables. Here the central tendencies plotted in Figure 4.2 suggest that the relationship between the two variables is stronger in theory than it is in reality. In fact, there is little relationship among our key explanatory variables. The correlation between Pr(Future Panel) and Cotenure is $r = -0.01$. Those two variables each correlate with Ideological Distance at $r = -0.02$. The difference in average Cotenure among pairs of judges who work in the Same Courthouse and those who do not is less than one year; the difference in average Pr(Future Panel) for those two groups is less than 0.03 (on the 0–1 interval), and the average Ideological Distance differs by 0.05 (on a variable that ranges from 0 to 1.21).

Results

We analyze the model in five steps. First, we look for the direct effects of collegiality: Are judges less likely to dissent or concur when they have served together for a longer period of time or will probably serve again soon? Second, we examine the marginal effects of each indicator of collegiality over the range of Ideological Distance to determine if, as hypothesized, collegiality has the largest effect among judges who are

---

[12] Recall that we have few cases before 1960.

prone to disagree. Third, we change the perspective and consider the marginal effect of Ideological Distance as collegiality varies; here we posit that increased collegiality should dampen the effect of ideology on the decision to write separately. Fourth, we examine the cumulative effects of the three collegiality indicators by examining predicted probabilities of dissent and concurrence. Finally, we provide the full regression results and discuss the effects of the control variables.

The Direct Effects of Collegiality

We begin by examining the direct effects of collegiality: Are dissenting or concurring votes less likely when judges have a strong personal or professional relationship with one another than when they have a weaker relationship? The tabular results for this model are provided in Model 1 in Table 4.B.1 in the chapter appendix. The results for Same Courthouse mirror those we discussed in Chapter 3: there is no evidence of a direct effect ($\hat{\beta} = 0.13$, $p = 0.28$ for concurrences and $\hat{\beta} = -0.18$, $p = 0.85$ for dissent). The predicted probability of a concurrence remains 0.03 regardless of whether the pair of judges work in the same courthouse. Similarly, the predicted probability of a dissenting opinion is 0.05 regardless of whether the two judges work in the same courthouse or not.

The top row of Figure 4.3 shows the predicted probability of dissent and concurrence as cotenure varies. Were it the case that cotenure lowered the probability of a dissenting or concurring vote, we would see negative sloping lines in these panels. Beginning with the left-hand panel, we see that there is no statistically significant direct effect of cotenure on the likelihood of a concurrence ($\hat{\beta} = 0.004$, $p = 0.66$), but the likelihood of a dissenting opinion, shown in the right-hand panel, declines with cotenure ($\hat{\beta} = -0.02$, $p < 0.01$). Movement across the range of cotenure corresponds to a decrease in the probability of dissent of about 0.03. In short, we observe a direct effect of cotenure on the probability of dissent, but not on the likelihood of concurrence.

The same conclusion holds for the probability of future panel service. Once again, a direct effect of collegiality would manifest as a negative sloping line in each panel: the likelihood that a judge will publicize their disagreement should decrease as the probability of future panel service increases. Beginning with the left-hand panel, there is no direct effect of this indicator on the probability of concurrence ($\hat{\beta} = -0.45$, $p = 0.34$), but in the right-hand panel, we observe a larger and statistically significant effect for dissent ($\hat{\beta} = -1.65$, $p < 0.01$). A change across the range of future panel service is associated with a 0.06 decrease in the probability of dissent.

To summarize, we observe a direct effect of collegiality on the probability of a dissenting opinion for our two indicators of collegiality that respond to judges' professional relationships; for both Cotenure and Pr(Future Panel), our results suggest that higher levels of collegiality are associated in a decrease in the likelihood of dissent. However, as our indicator of judges' personal relationships—Same Courthouse— varies, we see no difference in the probability of a dissenting opinion. That we observe more consistent effects for the decision to dissent than the decision to concur further fits with the argument we made in the previous chapter.

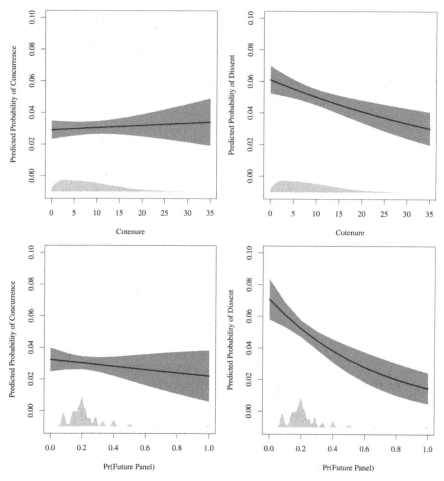

Figure 4.3 Direct Effects of Cotenure and Pr(Future Panel) on Concurring and Dissenting, Courts of Appeals: The top row plots the predicted probability of concurrence (left-hand panel) and dissent (right-hand panel) as Cotenure varies. The bottom row shows the analogous estimates over the range of Pr(Future Panel). The density plots at the bottom of each panel show the distribution of the relevant variable in the dataset. Shaded regions depict 95% confidence intervals.

The Conditional Effect of Collegiality

Recall that our second expectation related to the effect of collegiality as ideological distance varies. Specifically, we expected that the effects of collegiality would be strongest when the pair of judges had severe ideological disagreements with one another. To this end, we turn our attention to the results of Model 2, which includes multiplicative interactions between Ideological Distance and each of the three indicators of collegiality.

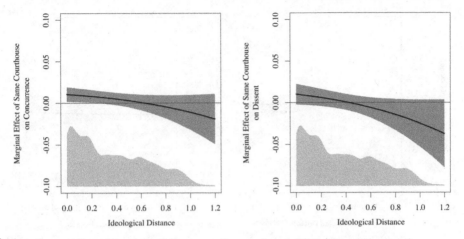

Figure 4.4 Effect of Same Courthouse on Concurring and Dissenting, Courts of Appeals: This figure shows the marginal effect of Same Courthouse on concurrence (left-hand panel) and dissent (right-hand panel) over the entire range of Ideological Distance. The shaded regions depict the 95% confidence intervals. The density plots show the distribution of Ideological Distance.

We begin by returning to the effects of Same Courthouse, albeit in a model that (unlike the results presented in Chapter 3) also includes two other indicators of collegiality. Figure 4.4 shows the marginal effect of two judges being in the same courthouse on concurring (left panel) and dissenting (right panel).[13] Here, after accounting for Cotenure and Pr(Future Panel), there are no values of Ideological Distance for which being in the same courthouse significantly decreases the probability of writing a concurring or dissenting opinion. However, as we also saw in Chapter 3, Figure 4.4 suggests that collegiality can foster environments where disagreement is *more* likely to be expressed (albeit only slightly): in cases where disagreements are unlikely to be severe and relationships are likely to be strong. Under these circumstances, the costs of dissenting or concurring are likely modest, and judges can publicize their disagreement without fear of harming an important interpersonal relationship.

We next turn our attention to our two indicators of judges' professional relationships. Figure 4.5 shows the marginal effect of Cotenure across the range of Ideological Distance. Beginning in the left-hand panel (the decision to concur), the confidence interval includes zero for the entire range of Ideological Distance. This illustrates that the number of years two judges have served together has no discernible impact on the decision to write a concurring opinion. This is borne out in the regression results, where the multiplicative interaction between cotenure and ideological distance is not statistically significant ($\hat{\beta} = -0.01$, $p = 0.79$).

---

[13] Both interaction terms are statistically significant: $\hat{\beta} = -0.71$, $p = 0.03$ for concurrences and $\hat{\beta} = -0.61$, $p = 0.04$ for dissents.

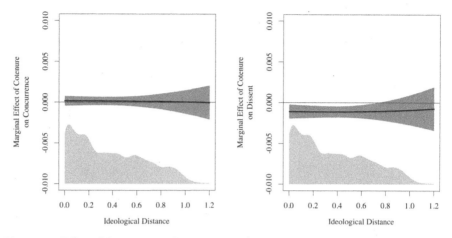

Figure 4.5 Effect of Cotenure on Concurring and Dissenting, Courts of Appeals: This figure shows the marginal effect of Cotenure on concurrence (left-hand panel) and dissent (right-hand panel) over the entire range of Ideological Distance. The shaded regions depict the 95% confidence intervals. The density plots show the distribution of Ideological Distance.

The right panel shows the results for a judge's decision to dissent. Here we see that increased Cotenure does very slightly reduce the probability of dissent. But the size of the marginal effect is almost constant across the range of Ideological Distance, and the effect is not statistically significant for estimates at the higher end of the range. Further, the interaction term in the multivariate regression model is not statistically significant ($\hat{\beta} = 0.02$, $p = 0.39$). In short, we do not find any evidence that the effect of Cotenure increases with ideological distance.

Third, we examine the effect of the probability of serving on the same panel in the future. Here Figure 4.6 shows the hypothesized pattern for both concurrences (left-hand panel) and dissents (right-hand panel). The effect is never statistically significant for concurrences, nor is the interaction term in the regression model statistically significant ($\hat{\beta} = -2.19$, $p = 0.08$). On the other hand, the marginal effect on dissent is not only significant for nearly the entire range of Ideological Distance, but that effect is also largest in size for judges who are ideologically furthest away from each other. The right-hand panel demonstrates that a higher probability of shared panel service translates into an even smaller probability of dissent when the judge is ideologically distant from the panel author than when they and the panel author are predisposed to agree. This multiplicative interaction term is statistically significant in the regression model ($\hat{\beta} = -2.52$, $p = 0.03$).

The results of this analysis suggest that judges' anticipated future interactions drive the direct effects of collegiality on judges' decisions to dissent. While we did not observe effects on judges' decisions to concur for any indicator, only Pr(Future Panel) is associated with a statistically significant interaction term in the model *and* a marginal effect that is statistically significant over the range of ideological distance. This result

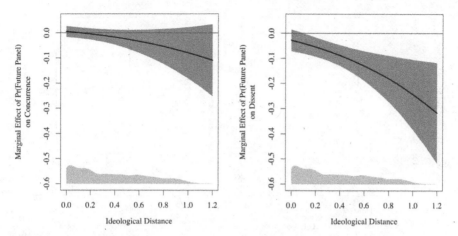

Figure 4.6 Effect of Pr(Future Panel) on Concurring and Dissenting, Courts of Appeals: This figure shows the marginal effect of Pr(Future Panel) on concurrence (left-hand panel) and dissent (right-hand panel) over the entire range of Ideological Distance. The shaded regions depict the 95% confidence intervals. The density plots show the distribution of Ideological Distance.

supports the contention that suppression, operating through judges' professional relationships, is a mechanism underlying the effect of collegiality.

The Conditional Effect of Ideology

In addition to examining the effect of collegiality as Ideological Distance varies, we also test for the effect of ideological dampening: our expectation that higher levels of collegiality increasingly diminish the effect of ideology on the decision to write separately. To this end, we consider the effect Ideological Distance has on the decisions to concur or dissent as the indicators of collegiality vary.

We begin by examining the effect of Ideological Distance as Same Courthouse varies, as shown in Figure 4.7. The effects on both concurrence and dissent follow an identical pattern: when a judge works in a different courthouse than the majority opinion author, the marginal effect of Ideological Distance is both positive and statistically significant. When they work in a different courthouse than the opinion author, a judge is significantly more likely to write separately as their ideological disagreement with the opinion author increases. However, when the two judges work in the same courthouse, the effect *disappears*: there is no evidence of a relationship between ideology and public disagreement. Moreover, under these conditions, the estimated effect sizes are close to zero, suggesting that this conclusion is not merely based on imprecision in the estimates.

Second, we turn to cotenure. Figure 4.8 plots the effect of Ideological Distance as cotenure varies. Were we to observe ideological dampening as hypothesized, we

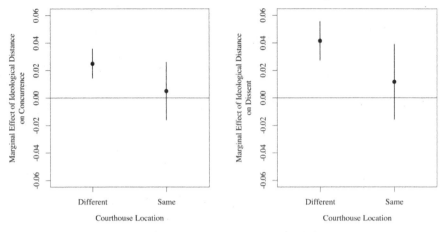

Figure 4.7 Effect of Ideological Distance, by Same Courthouse, on Concurring and Dissenting, Courts of Appeals: This figure shows the marginal effect of Ideological Distance on concurrence (left-hand panel) and dissent (right-hand panel) by Same Courthouse status. The lines depict the 95% confidence intervals. Fifteen percent of observations are judges who work in the same courthouse.

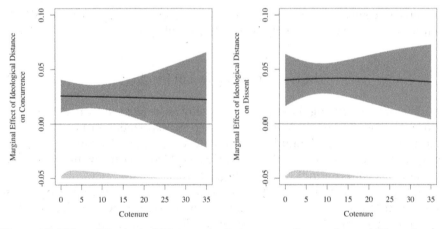

Figure 4.8 Effect of Ideological Distance, by Cotenure, on Concurring and Dissenting, Courts of Appeals: This figure shows the marginal effect of Ideological Distance on concurrence (left-hand panel) and dissent (right-hand panel) over the entire range of Cotenure. The shaded regions depict the 95% confidence intervals. The density plots show the distribution of Cotenure.

would expect to see a negative sloping line in each panel with a confidence band that encompasses the horizontal zero line at high values of cotenure. This is not what we observe. Instead, the effect of Ideological Distance is nearly consistent as Cotenure varies. Contrary to expectations, the effect of ideology on a judge's decision to dissent or concur does not diminish as years of shared service increases. While the confidence interval does cross zero in the right-hand side of the concurrence panel, this is most likely because of the scant number of judicial pairs who have worked together for more than two decades, not compelling evidence that higher degrees of cotenure diminish the effect of ideology on a judge's decision to write a concurring opinion.

Finally, Figure 4.9 illustrates the effect of Ideological Distance across the range of Pr(Future Panel). Again, were we to observe ideological dampening, we would expect to see a negative sloping line that begins above zero for low values of future panel service (suggesting that higher levels of ideological distance increase the probability of publicized disagreement for low levels of collegiality) and decreases to values that are statistically indistinguishable from zero for higher levels of collegiality. This is exactly the pattern we observe in both panels: when two judges have a relatively high level of collegiality, there is no evidence that ideology has any impact on their decision to write a concurring *or* a dissenting opinion. However, when a judge is unlikely to serve on a panel with the opinion author, they are more likely to write separately as their ideological disagreement with the opinion author increases.

The major conclusion we draw from this discussion is that collegiality plays an important dampening role on how ideology shapes the decision to write a concurring or dissenting opinion. For both Same Courthouse and Pr(Future Panel), the relationship between ideological disagreement and the decision to write either type of publicized disagreement disappears when two judges have higher levels of collegiality. Given the

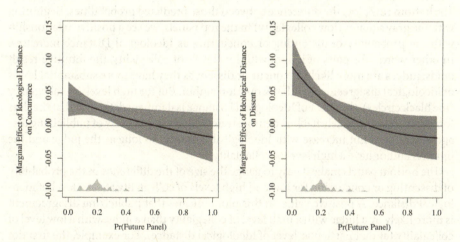

Figure 4.9 Effect of Ideological Distance, by Pr(Future Panel), on Concurring and Dissenting, Courts of Appeals: This figure shows the marginal effect of Ideological Distance on concurrence (left-hand panel) and dissent (right-hand panel) over the entire range of Pr(Future Panel). The shaded regions depict the 95% confidence intervals. The density plots show the distribution of Pr(Future Panel). The very high values of Pr(Future Panel) come from the (very small) First and Fourth Circuits in the very early years of our data.

94 THE ELEVATOR EFFECT

vital, and often central, role judicial ideology plays in explaining judicial behavior, it is important to understand the role collegiality plays in conditioning the effect of ideology. Evidently both personal relationships and future professional relationships play such a role.

The Cumulative Effect of Collegiality

To this point, we have discussed each of the collegiality indicators separately. But, though they each measure a slightly different type of collegiality, Same Courthouse, Cotenure, and Probability of Future Panel Service all measure the same concept. How important are the cumulative effects of collegiality, and how do they compare to the effect of ideological distance?

To answer these questions, we look to the predicted probability of dissent and concurrence. We rely on the model estimates from Model 2 in Table 4.B.1 in the chapter appendix, which includes multiplicative interaction terms between Ideological Distance and each of the three indicators of collegiality. Because the three collegiality indicators are measured on different scales, we use percentiles to combine the three indicators. We plot predicted probabilities at low (25th percentile or Different Courthouse) and high (75th percentile or Same Courthouse) values of collegiality and ideology respectively across the range of the other variable.

We begin by comparing the effect of collegiality, illustrated in Figure 4.10. The top row of the figure provides the predicted probability of concurrence (left panel) or dissent (right panel) for high (black circles) or low (gray squares) levels of collegiality. The bottom row plots the difference between those predicted probabilities. Beginning with the gray squares (low collegiality) in the top panels, we see a positive relationship with the probability of dissenting or concurring as Ideological Distance increases. In other words, for pairs of judges with low levels of collegiality, the intuitive result holds: judges are more likely to concur or dissent as they have more substantial levels of ideological disagreement with the opinion author. But for high levels of collegiality (the black circles), the effect of Ideological Distance is dampened: the fact that the dots form almost a completely flat line demonstrates that the probability of publicizing disagreement does not increase with Ideological Distance, so long as the judge and the opinion author have a high level of collegiality.

The bottom panels make it easy to gauge the size of the difference in the probability of dissenting or concurring for low and high levels of collegiality at each level of ideological distance. A positive value on this plot indicates that publicizing disagreement is more likely by a judge with a high level of collegiality than a judge with a low level of collegiality (at that particular level of ideological distance). For example, the first dot in the bottom-left panel shows that that a judge who is in maximum ideological agreement with the opinion author has a 0.017 higher likelihood of concurring if they have a high (75th percentile) level of collegiality than if they had a low (25th percentile) level of collegiality.

The most important conclusion from the left-hand panel is the persistence of our "friendly amendment" finding from our analysis of the individual indicators. Again

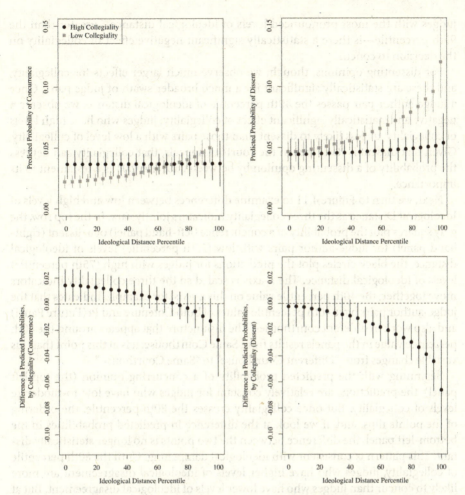

Figure 4.10 Cumulative Effects of Collegiality on Concurring and Dissenting, Courts of Appeals: The top panel of the figure shows the predicted probabilities of concurrence (left-hand panel) and dissent (right-hand panel) for low and high levels of collegiality as Ideological Distance varies. The black circles denote estimates at high values of the relevant variables (75th percentile or Same Courthouse), and the gray squares denote estimates at low values of the relevant variables (25th percentile or Different Courthouse). The bottom panel plots the difference in predicted probabilities between low and high levels of collegiality. The bars depict 95% confidence intervals.

we see that judges who are ideologically aligned are a bit *more* likely to write a concurring opinion if they have a high level of collegiality than if they have a low level of collegiality. However, once the ideological distance between a pair of judges passes the 40th percentile, the difference between the predicted probabilities is not statistically significance: there is no evidence of an effect of collegiality. Only for the

96 THE ELEVATOR EFFECT

judges with the most pronounced levels of ideological distance—greater than the 95th percentile—is there a statistically significant negative effect of collegiality on the decision to concur.

For dissenting opinions, though, we observe much larger effects for collegiality, and these are statistically significant for a much broader swath of judge pairs. Once a judge-author pair passes the 40th percentile of ideological distance, we observe a negative and statistically significant effect of collegiality: judges who have high levels of collegiality are less likely to dissent than those pairs with a low level of collegiality. Given that dissent is itself rare in the courts of appeals, that collegiality can depress the probability of a dissenting opinion by between 0.02 and 0.04 is a testament to its importance.

Next, we turn to Figure 4.11 to examine differences between low and high levels of Ideological Distance as the three collegiality indicators jointly vary. In the top row, the gray squares plot the probability of a concurrence (left-hand panel) or a dissent (right-hand panel) for judge-author pairs with low (25th percentile) levels of ideological distance; the black circles plot the predictions for judges with high (75th percentile) levels of ideological distance. The x-axis is scaled so the three collegiality indicators move together; the 40th percentile value on this x-axis, for example, indicates that the judge-author pairs have 40th percentile values of both Cotenure and Pr(Future Panel) and also work in different courthouses. The disjuncture that appears around the 80th percentile value in the panels results from Same Courthouse: it is at this point that this variable changes from "Different Courthouse" to "Same Courthouse."

Beginning with the predicted probability of a concurring opinion (the top-left panel), the predictions are relatively constant for judges who have low-to-moderate levels of collegiality. But once collegiality crosses the 80th percentile, the ordering of the points flips, and, if we look at the difference in predicted probabilities in the bottom-left panel, the difference between the two points is no longer statistically distant. This pattern is consistent with ideological dampening. Until the 80th percentile of collegiality, judges who have higher levels of ideological disagreement are more likely to concur than judges who have lower levels of ideological disagreement. But at high levels of collegiality, there is no relationship between ideological disagreement and the likelihood of a concurring opinion.

We observe an identical pattern for dissenting opinions, shown in the right-hand column of Figure 4.8. Until collegiality reaches its 80th percentile, the predicted probability of a dissent is higher for a judge who has a high level of ideological disagreement with the opinion author than one who does not. But as collegiality increases, these points gradually start to come closer together until, at the 80th percentile, the difference between them is no longer statistically significant (as shown in the bottom-right panel). Again, this is strong evidence that collegiality can dampen the effects of ideological distance.

How do the effects of collegiality and ideological distance compare? Table 4.2 displays changes in predicted probabilities of dissent and concurrence as Ideological Distance takes low (25th percentile), median, and high (75th percentile) values for changes in all combinations of the three collegiality indicators. When looking at Table 4.2, it is important to remember that both concurrence and dissent are relatively rare. The baseline rate of concurrence—with all variables held at their median values—is

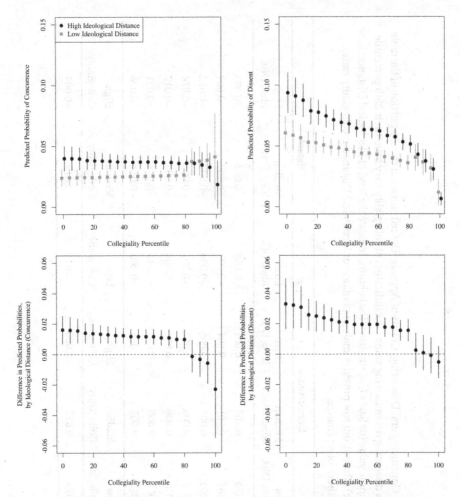

Figure 4.11 Conditional Effect of Ideological Distance on Concurring and Dissenting, Courts of Appeals: The top row of this figure shows the predicted probabilities of concurrence (left-hand panel) and dissent (right-hand panel) for low and high levels of Ideological Distance as collegiality varies. The black circles denote estimates at the 75th percentile of Ideological Distance, and the gray squares denote estimates at the 25th percentile of Ideological Distance. The bottom panel plots the difference in predicted probabilities between low and high levels of Ideological Distance. The bars depict 95% confidence intervals.

0.03; for dissents, the baseline rate is 0.05. Thus, absolute changes in predicted probabilities that seem small correspond to substantively meaningful relative changes in the probability of observing a concurring or dissenting opinion.

We draw three major conclusions from Table 4.2. First, as we have seen consistently, the effects of collegiality on dissent are greatest and most consistent under conditions of high Ideological Distance, but, contrary to our expectations, this is not

Table 4.2 The Combined Effects of Collegiality on Concurring and Dissenting, Courts of Appeals: The cell entries in the top portion of the table provide the change in the predicted probability of a dissenting or concurring vote as the indicators of collegiality vary from their 25th percentile value (or Different Courthouse) to their 75th percentile value (or Same Courthouse). The columns indicate the level of Ideological Distance: Low (25th percentile), Median, or High (75th percentile). The bottom row provides analogous values for Ideological Distance as collegiality varies. * denotes a p-value less than 0.05 against a null hypothesis of no change.

	Concurrence			Dissent		
	Low Ideo. Dist.	Median Ideo. Dist.	High Ideo. Dist.	Low Ideo. Dist.	Median Ideo. Dist.	High Ideo. Dist.
Same Courthouse	0.010	0.007	0.001	0.008	0.003	−0.005
Cotenure	0.001	0.001	0.001	−0.009	−0.009	−0.009
Pr(Same Panel)	0.000	−0.001	−0.003	−0.004	−0.007	−0.012
Same Courthouse + Cotenure	0.012	0.008	0.002	−0.001	−0.006	−0.014
Same Courthouse + Pr(Same Panel)	0.010	0.006	−0.002	0.004	−0.004	−0.017
Cotenure + Pr(Same Panel)	0.001	0.000	−0.002	−0.013	−0.016	−0.021
Same Courthouse + Cotenure + Pr(Same Panel)	0.012	0.007	−0.001	−0.006	−0.014	−0.026
	Low Collegiality	Median Collegiality	High Collegiality	Low Collegiality	Median Collegiality	High Collegiality
Ideological Distance	0.013	0.012	0.000	0.024	0.019	−0.004

WHY DOES COLLEGIALITY MATTER? 99

true for concurrences. Second, looking at the bottom row of the table, we see additional evidence that collegiality dampens the effect of ideological disagreement on the probability of dissenting or concurring. Whereas there is a statistically significant difference in predicted probabilities as ideological disagreement moves from a low to a high value under conditions of low or median collegiality, there is no analogous difference under conditions of high collegiality. Finally, we note that the size of the collegiality effect compares favorably to that of Ideological Distance. The maximum difference in the predicted probability of dissent as Ideological Distance varies (0.024, which comes under conditions of low collegiality) is *nearly the same* in magnitude as the maximum effect of collegiality: –0.026. This is over a 50 percent change from the baseline probability of dissent! For concurrences, the results are similar: the maximum effects of the two concepts differ by only 0.002 and correspond to about a 40 percent change from the baseline probability of a concurrence. Thus, *not only does collegiality have a substantively significant effect, but its effect rivals that of ideology under some conditions.*

Control Variables

The model also reveals some interesting results for the control variables. These can be seen in Figure 4.12, which presents changes in predicted probabilities for the entire model. Beginning with concurring opinions, judges in their first two years on the bench are less likely to issue concurring opinions, and older judges are also less likely to issue a concurring opinion; both effects correspond to a 2–3 percent decrease in the probability of a concurrence. On the other hand, judges in salient cases, measured by the presence of an amicus brief, are more likely to issue a concurring opinion; concurring opinions are about 4 percent more likely in these cases.

Turning to dissenting opinions, we find no analogous effect for a judge's age or time on the bench. However, the salience result also appears for dissenting opinions: judges are about 4 percent more likely to dissent in a salient case compared to one in which no amicus brief was filed. We see a 3 percent decrease in the probability of dissent when the judge and the majority opinion author are of the same race (though we do not find a similar result for gender). Dissenting opinions are slightly more likely when the judge is more ideologically distant from the U.S. Supreme Court and when the case is a civil rights (rather than a criminal) case.

Conclusions

Taken together, we conclude that collegiality-induced increases in the costs associated with publicizing disagreement result in more united opinions. We find these effects using multiple indicators of collegiality. First, when judges have a higher level of cotenure or are likely to serve again with the opinion author on a future panel, they are less likely to write a dissenting opinion. These two indicators are associated with

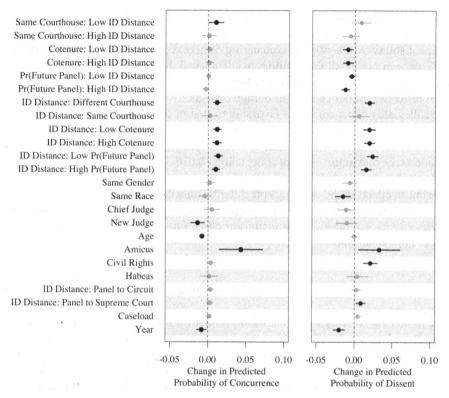

Figure 4.12 Changes in Predicted Probability of Concurring and Dissenting, Court of Appeals: Estimates (and associated 95% confidence intervals) of the change in the predicted probability of dissent and concurrence generated by moving each variable from a low to high value while holding other variables at their median. Changes produced by collegiality and ideology are presented at low and high values of the other to illustrate interactive effects. Low and high values are 25th and 75th percentile for continuous variables and zero and one for binary variables. Estimates and confidence intervals in gray (instead of black) indicate that the confidence interval includes zero. Full regression estimates for Model 2 are available in Table 4.B.1 in the chapter appendix.

judges' level of professional relationships with one another. We find no evidence—in this chapter or the previous one—that our indicator of two judges' personal relationships (working in the same courthouse) has a direct relationship to the likelihood of a concurrence or a dissent.

A major conclusion from Chapter 3 was that the effects of ideological disagreement on the probability of a separate opinion decrease as judges' collegial concerns increase. We tested this hypothesis again in this chapter, in a regression model that included all three indicators of interpersonal contact. We found robust evidence for this proposition for both dissenting and concurring opinions, especially for the Same Courthouse indicator. In a finding that echoes Chapter 3, our analysis

WHY DOES COLLEGIALITY MATTER? 101

demonstrated that there is no relationship between the level of ideological disagreement between a judge and a majority opinion author on the probability of dissent or concurrence when the two judges work in the same courthouse. Seeing each other often, it seems, goes a long way toward reducing the effects of policy considerations on judicial behavior. We found similar evidence for the probability of future panel service. In both cases, the impact of ideology both gets smaller as collegiality increases, and the effect is not statistically distinguishable from zero for judges with high levels of collegiality.

Our major aim in this chapter—and the reason we introduced two additional indicators of interpersonal contact—was to determine what mechanism best explains the effects of collegiality on a judge's decision to dissent or concur. We outlined two potential mechanisms, persuasion and suppression, and tested the mechanisms against each other with unique indicators of collegiality. It is clear from our analyses that no single indicator can explain the full effect of collegiality: all three of our indicators have some explanatory power. However, as Table 4.3 makes clear, future panel service has the most consistent effect. A greater level of anticipated future interaction between two judges is associated with both a decrease in the likelihood of a dissenting opinion and also conditions the effect of ideological disagreement between two judges such that there is no perceptible effect of ideological distance at high levels of Pr(Future Panel).

While we are cognizant of the limitations of our measures, our results help us to draw some preliminary conclusions about the mechanisms through which collegiality operates. In discussing mechanisms, we made two distinctions: (a) between personal and professional relationships, and (b) between persuasion and suppression. Our results leave us unable to eliminate any of these potential mechanisms, instead suggesting that collegiality might operate through each. Because Pr(Future Panel), which we use to measure the professional relationships-suppression mechanism, has the most consistent effect, we are most confident in our conclusion that one pathway through which collegiality operates is judges' desires to maintain a good working relationship with their colleagues. But we also find evidence in favor of the effects of personal relationships (measured with Same Courthouse) and the professional relationships-suppression mechanism. Thus, we view our results here as an initial step in unraveling the reasons why collegiality affects judicial behavior. As we continue through the book, we will look for evidence to distinguish these mechanisms at every turn, building on the results from these analyses.

Table 4.3 Summary of Results: A checkmark denotes a result that is statistically significant and in the direction we hypothesize.

Indicator	Direct Effect	Conditional Effect
Same Courthouse		✓
Cotenure	✓	
Pr(Future Panel)	✓	✓

102   THE ELEVATOR EFFECT

Further, we hope future work will employ other research designs to distinguish between persuasion and suppression. One possible way to disentangle these mechanisms would be to craft an experiment that manipulates levels of personal and professional contact, though implementation would be challenging due to difficulties with subject recruitment and manipulating the unique institutional setting of the federal judiciary. Another option might be to look to judges' papers. Maltzman, Spriggs, and Wahlbeck (2000) collected a wealth of data on the bargaining environment at the U.S. Supreme Court, and other scholars have analyzed the papers of lower court judges. The advantage to this sort of analysis would be its ability to track the processes of persuasion and suppression directly: In how many cases are there draft dissents or concurrences that were not published? Were judges who worked together more frequently more willing to accept each others' private arguments? How did the legal doctrine in an opinion change over time in response to the levels of collegiality and ideological disagreement between pairs of judges? These are all ripe for future investigations.

We close this chapter with some reflections on the substantive effects of collegiality and ideological disagreement. Our analysis in this chapter enables us to make two important conclusions. First, the effect of collegiality is substantively important. When judges work together, anticipate serving on future panels together, and have served on the same court for long periods of time, the effect of interpersonal contact on the likelihood of publicizing disagreement with the panel rivals some of the most prominent predictors of judicial behavior. In many cases, the effects of Ideological Disagreement and the combined effects of the collegiality indicators are statistically indistinguishable from one another.

Second, our results demonstrate that the effect of Ideological Distance on the decision to dissent or concur varies depending on the level of interpersonal contact between a judge and the majority opinion author. Again and again throughout the chapter we found evidence that judges preferences vary in their ability to predict whether a judge will issue a dissenting or concurring opinion, and that variation is related to the level of interpersonal contact between the two judges. Future work should continue to probe the varying effects of ideology on judicial behavior to understand when judges' preferences have more explanatory power and under what conditions judges' preferences are a poor predictor of observed behavior.

Appendix 4.A: Summary Statistics

Table 4.A.1 Summary Statistics for Courts of Appeals Search and Seizure Vote Dataset. Percentages may not add to 100% due to rounding.

Continuous Variables	Min.	25%	50%	75%	Max.
Ideological Distance	0.00	0.11	0.32	0.59	1.21
Cotenure	0	4	8	12	35
Pr(Future Panel)	0.07	0.15	0.20	0.25	1.00
Age	36	55	60	65	93
Distance to Circuit Median	0.00	0.08	0.21	0.42	1.00
Distance to S.Ct. Median	0.00	0.16	0.31	0.43	0.94
Caseload/100	0.20	2.04	2.74	3.37	7.40
Year	1953	1981	1992	2002	2010

Dichotomous Variables	0	1			
Same Courthouse	85%	15%			
Amicus	98%	2%			
Same Gender	21%	79%			
Same Race	17%	83%			
Chief Judge	92%	8%			
New Judge	96%	4%			
Civil Rights	76%	24%			
Habeas	94%	6%			

Categorical Variable	Percent				
Vote					
Joins Majority	90%				
Concurs	4%				
Dissents	7%				

104 THE ELEVATOR EFFECT

Appendix 4.B: Regression Results

Table 4.B.1 Model Results: Multinomial logit regression estimates of the effect of three indicators of collegiality, Ideological Distance, their interaction, and a range of control variables on the likelihood of a concurring or dissenting vote. The reported standard errors are robust standard errors that are clustered on the case, and * denotes a p-value less than 0.05.

	Model 1		Model 2	
	Coef.	S.E.	Coef.	S.E.
Concurrence				
Same Courthouse	0.127	(0.118)	0.444	(0.181)
Cotenure	0.004	(0.009)	0.006	(0.014)
Pr(Future Panel)	−0.454	(0.479)	0.206	(0.492)
Ideological Distance	0.686	(0.151)	1.351	(0.356)
Same Courthouse × Ideological Distance			−0.713	(0.330)
Cotenure × Ideological Distance			−0.006	(0.023)
Pr(Future Panel) × Ideological Distance			−2.190	(1.234)
Same Gender	0.089	(0.116)	0.081	(0.116)
Same Race	−0.169	(0.117)	−0.163	(0.118)
Chief Judge	0.138	(0.163)	0.145	(0.164)
New Judge	−0.642	(0.272)	−0.647	(0.272)
Age	−0.028	(0.006)	−0.028	(0.006)
Amicus	0.983	(0.217)	0.983	(0.217)
Civil Rights	0.147	(0.106)	0.145	(0.106)
Habeas	.0.059	(0.197)	0.065	(0.197)
ID Distance: Panel to Circuit	0.320	(0.224)	0.333	(0.225)
ID Distance: Panel to S.Ct.	0.334	(0.292)	0.346	(0.293)
Caseload/100	0.063	(0.054)	0.050	(0.054)
Year	−0.015	(0.005)	−0.015	(0.005)
Intercept	28.297	(10.500)	26.966	(10.574)
Dissent				
Same Courthouse	−0.018	(0.094)	0.263	(0.155)
Cotenure	−0.021	(0.007)	−0.028	(0.011)
Pr(Future Panel)	−1.647	(0.427)	−0.731	(0.571)
Ideological Distance	0.721	(0.121)	1.207	(0.314)
Same Courthouse × Ideological Distance			−0.607	(0.287)
Cotenure × Ideological Distance			0.017	(0.019)
Pr(Future Panel) × Ideological Distance			−2.529	(1.191)
Same Gender	−0.116	(0.085)	−0.121	(0.086)
Same Race	−0.289	(0.085)	−0.282	(0.085)

Table 4.B.1 Continued

	Model 1		Model 2	
	Coef.	S.E.	Coef.	S.E.
Chief Judge	−0.264	(0.146)	−0.252	(0.146)
New Judge	−0.245	(0.174)	−0.246	(0.175)
Age	−0.002	(0.005)	−0.002	(0.005)
Amicus	0.574	(0.184)	0.576	(0.184)
Civil Rights	0.366	(0.075)	0.366	(0.075)
Habeas	0.072	(0.140)	0.075	(0.140)
ID Distance: Panel to Circuit	0.157	(0.175)	0.172	(0.175)
ID Distance: Panel to S.Ct.	0.633	(0.233)	0.649	(0.234)
Caseload/100	0.080	(0.036)	0.072	(0.036)
Year	−0.020	(0.004)	−0.020	(0.004)
Intercept	37.898	(7.504)	36.865	(7.532)
N	15,014		15,014	
AIC	11701.89		11695.9	
BIC	11960.8		12000.6	

5

The Supreme Court: From the Boarding House to the Marble Temple

Introduction

U.S. Supreme Court justices have a number of unusual benefits to their positions, including lifetime tenure and the prestige, and power that come from sitting at the top of judicial apex. They also work in a unique environment: an unusually static group of coworkers working together over extended periods of time. Greenhouse (2002) described a time of unusual stability:

> Imagine going to work every day with the same eight people: laboring together on joint projects, eating together in a small private dining room, huddling together for hours every week behind a locked door that discourages all but the most urgent interruptions. The same eight colleagues. For nine years.

This arrangement stands in stark contrast to the courts of appeals, where judges are often not in the same courthouse and have variation in the colleagues with whom they serve on panels. Certainly, the unusual permanence of the position of being a Supreme Court justice and the ensuing relationships is a feature to which commentators and justices refer publicly. As Mauro (2018) noted, there is "the reality that justices are keenly aware of: They will be working with their colleagues for years or decades, so there is no profit in bearing grudges." Justice Kagan has articulated this way of thinking directly:

> [Justice Kagan] said the justices can't afford to hold grudges because they would lose the ability to persuade their colleagues in future cases. "We live in this world where it's just the nine of us," Kagan said. "We are the consummate repeat players." (Stohr and Epstein 2018)

In an example of perceptions regarding justices "moving past any differences," a lawyer who practices before the Court also noted that "[Kagan] is practical enough that she is going to put [the Kavanaugh nomination controversy] behind her and have the best relationship she can with someone she is going to have to put up with for 30 years" (Hurley and Chung 2018). Such views are consistent with what we saw in Chapter 4: long periods of cotenure implicate collegial concerns. Thus, there are reasons to anticipate that collegiality plays an important role in Supreme Court decision-making.

The Elevator Effect. Morgan L.W. Hazelton, Rachael K. Hinkle, and Michael J. Nelson, Oxford University Press.
© Oxford University Press 2023. DOI: 10.1093/oso/9780197625408.003.0005

108 THE ELEVATOR EFFECT

In the previous two chapters, we focused on the extent to which collegiality influences decision-making in the federal courts of appeals. In this chapter, we turn to consider the extent to which collegiality matters in a different institutional context, the highest court in the land. As we introduced in Chapter 2, there are important reasons to study collegiality in multiple institutional contexts. First, the importance of interpersonal work relationships will likely vary based on organizational features. Second, variation in such characteristics by level of court and nature of relationships allows for differing vantage points from which to test the influence of collegiality on decision-making. We highlight these differences before approaching if and how collegiality matters at the so-called Marble Palace.

In considering the extent to which interpersonal relationships influence the operation of the Supreme Court, we take a multifaceted approach by bringing qualitative and quantitative methods to bear on this question based on historical accounts, original interviews with former Supreme Court clerks, and empirical analysis. We use past and contemporary examples of the influence of collegiality on decision-making as an entry point into the effect of social interactions in important decisions and explain patterns in consensual decision-making on the U.S. Supreme Court over time. We also take the proposition that collegiality shapes unanimity at the Supreme Court to data, both qualitative and quantitative. We first probe the importance of collegiality at the Supreme Court in recent decades using unique interview evidence from former clerks. The accounts of the interviewees indicate that the Court values contact and positive relationships and suggest ways in which both may influence its work. We also estimate a statistical model of Supreme Court cases including the best measure of personal interaction available for justices: cotenure, the number of years two justices have sat together on the Court. Descriptive statistics support the idea that justices become more likely to agree with one another the longer they serve together. The pattern emerges in a multinomial logit model, even after controlling for other factors that influence the decision to dissent, including ideology. Increased time together on the bench significantly decreases the probability of dissent for pairs of justices with relatively similar political preferences and with fairly divergent views.

Collegiality and Institutional Context

Justices on the Supreme Court of the United States operate in a very different environment than judges on the federal courts of appeals. First, justices enjoy much greater resources in terms of support, time, and information. The Supreme Court deals with far fewer cases than the courts of appeals, giving the nine justices more time to devote to each matter. As an illustration, for the twelve-month period ending in March 2022, the First Circuit, which has six authorized seats, terminated 1,488 appeals with 1,119 resolved on the merits (United States Courts 2022). In the 2021 term, the Supreme Court, complete with nine justices, disposed of 66 cases and issued 58 decisions (Gou, Erskine, and Romoser 2022).[1] Additionally, with rare exception, the justices control

---

[1] It should be noted that the Supreme Court contends with thousands of cases in which review is sought via writs of certiorari. The majority of such cases receive only a cursory assessment of their suitability for Supreme Court review by clerks (see Epstein and Walker 2018, 13). Approximately 20–30 percent of such

THE SUPREME COURT   109

which cases they will hear each term (Songer and Sheehan 1992; Cross and Tiller 2007) and tend to select more salient and contentious cases (see Edwards 2003; Hall and Windett 2016). Appeals to the circuits, on the other hand, are generally done as a matter of right and the courts must resolve them (Giles, Walker, and Zorn 2006).

Supreme Court justices also reap the benefits of being at the apex of the judicial system: the cases that come to them tend to have been litigated for years and have a full record, multiple rounds of briefing and decisions, and robust amicus participation (Hazelton and Hinkle 2022). The courts of appeals usually hear cases in panels of three, while generally all nine justices are involved in each Supreme Court case. Thus, at the Supreme Court, there are more hands on deck to provide perspectives and information compared to circuit panels.

Justices also have much more attentive external audiences than judges on the courts of appeals (see, e.g., Bryan and Ringsmuth 2016).[2] While courts of appeals panel decisions are reviewable by both en banc panels and the Supreme Court, the Supreme Court generally has the final say with its decisions. While the Supreme Court's interpretations of statutes can be countered by congressional action, such a legislative response is unlikely, especially during times of divided government (Epstein and Knight 1998) and when the public's support for the Court is high (Nelson and Uribe-McGuire 2017). Additionally, constitutional interpretations can only be overturned formally by amendments to the Constitution, which are arduous to pass and exceedingly rare (Segal and Spaeth 2002).[3] Finally, unlike the courts of appeals, panels do not vary on the Supreme Court (Cross and Tiller 2007; Edwards 2003; Nash 2022; Posner 1990).

Thus, justices enjoy positions where their own views are most likely to become the law of the land and they don't need to coordinate with other judges to make reviewing bodies happy or deal with as arduous of workloads. Furthermore, they experience more external pressure and attention. We believe that these features reduce the likelihood of justices failing to publicize disagreement with each other in comparison with court of appeals judges. While the day-to-day desires to get along continue and interpersonal relationships are still important (perhaps even more so based on the lack of change across panels and courthouses (see Nash 2022)), the dependencies on each other are lessened while external forces are more pronounced. Specifically, with more time to dedicate to and information regarding cases, justices are more likely to be able to form independent assessments of cases or have resources to dedicate to separate opinions than court of appeals judges. Additionally, media coverage and attention from the government and interest groups is more pronounced for the justices. So, while collegiality is likely to still matter in the marble temple, its role may be more muted.

The Supreme Court context unfortunately also lacks the variation in institutional features that allows for better leverage on collegiality. For example, unlike the court

cases are discussed by the justices, with a much smaller group being considered on the merits (Epstein and Walker 2018, fig. 1.1).

[2] This point is further addressed in Chapter 7.
[3] That is not to say that Congress lacks the power to retaliate against the Court, but those actions, such as jurisdiction stripping or court-packing, require large majorities in Congress (see Epstein and Knight 1998).

110   THE ELEVATOR EFFECT

of appeals judges we considered in Chapters 3 and 4, the justices share a single office location and have minuscule variation regarding with whom they decide cases within short time frames.[4] In this chapter, we endeavor to find other means by which to investigate such nuance.

Historical Accounts Regarding the Operation and Importance of Collegiality

Both historical and contemporary accounts of the Supreme Court suggest that interpersonal relationships among justices matter regarding its work, though perhaps not to the same extent or in the same ways as in other judicial contexts. Many of these reports focus on interactions and relationships and public agreement and disagreement. To start, the most famous period of unanimity in the U.S. Supreme Court's history—the Marshall Court—is also the time in the Court's history when the justices lived, dined, and drank together in the same lodgings at the behest of the chief justice, all the while discussing and debating the issues before the Court. As White (1984, 40–41) explains:

> The boardinghouse provided not only an informal forum in which the justices could discuss issues until they were resolved but also a fraternal setting in which one justice might not want to disagree openly with another justice. Even justices who would have liked to disagree or to explain their reasoning were likely not to dissent to avoid discord among the Court's members.

In this way, familiarity led to consensus. Figure 5.1 suggests that Marshall's efforts may have been successful (Hinkle, Hazelton, and Nelson 2017). The boarding house years represent a period with a low number of dissents in the early years of the Court. However, this evidence is not particularly conclusive, due in part to the placement of the boarding house years near the start of both the Court and a growing trend of dissents.

Certainly, this potential connection made an impression on the justices: they often speak of Marshall and his ability to foster relationships. For example, former Chief Justice Rehnquist attributed part of Justice Marshall's success as a chief justice to his ability to make connections with colleagues (Rehnquist 2000). Chief Justice Roberts has similarly asserted that Marshall unified the Court through his relationships with the other justices (Rosen 2007).

The history of the Supreme Court also contains time periods in which justices had poor interpersonal relationships that affected the function and perceptions of the institution. For example, Frankfurter and Douglas famously grew to be rivals despite having been professors together and both appointed by Franklin Roosevelt (Urofsky 1988). As NPR reporter Nina Totenberg (2022a) recounts: "To cite just one example of how bad it was, Justice Felix Frankfurter called Justice William O. Douglas 'one

---

[4] Absent personnel change on the Court, the justices only experience small differences in who they decide cases with based on recusals (see Black and Epstein 2005).

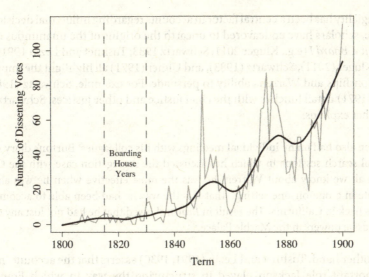

Figure 5.1 Dissent in the Early Years of the Supreme Court: The light gray line plots the number of dissenting votes per Supreme Court term. The black line plots a loess smoothed trend line.

of the completely evil men I have ever met.' And Douglas referred to the Austrian-born Frankfurter, who was Jewish, as 'Der Führer' and that was during World War II." Their growing differences in philosophy and animosity toward each other helped fuel a time in which separate opinions became much more frequent, "giving the Court the appearance of flying apart" (Urofsky 1988, 89). Feldman (2009) opines that historically "many of the greatest justices have been irascible, socially distant, personally isolated, arrogant or even downright mean." Evidence for this hypothesis included public and private behavior that strained interpersonal relationships within the Court. For example, "Douglas was an egotist who barely spoke to his colleagues, loved to vote alone, and once said that his law clerks were 'the lowest form of human life'" (Feldman 2009). Certainly, the Court is not always a bastion of collegiality.

As Posner (1990, 14) noted while praising Justice Brennan, for whom he clerked, as having been an unusually collegial member of the Court during that period:

> Justice Holmes described the Justices of the Supreme Court as nine scorpions in a bottle. The tensions within an appellate court in which all the judges sit en banc (rather than in rotating panels, the normal mode in the federal courts of appeals) are great; they are greatest in the Supreme Court. It is like an arranged marriage in a system with no divorce. The tensions fester, generating debilitating personal rivalries, resentments, apathy, burnout, idiosyncrasy, and a shrill and nasty rhetoric of invective.

Thus, the Supreme Court has generated famous examples of uncollegial behavior.

112 THE ELEVATOR EFFECT

Collegiality has been a central factor in accounts regarding influential decisions. For example, scholars have endeavored to unearth the origins of the unanimous opinion in *Brown v. Board I* (e.g., Kluger 2011; Schwartz 1983; Tushnet and Lezin 1991; Ulmer 1971). Kluger (2011), Schwartz (1983), and Ulmer (1971) all highlight the importance of relationships and Warren's ability to persuade. For example, Schwartz (1983) and Ulmer (1971) detail lunches with the chief justice and other justices. Schwartz (1983, 90) further explains:

> Warren also had many individual meetings with his colleagues. Burton's diary notes several search sessions in which he discussed the segregation case with the Chief. From all we know about Warren, he was the most effective when he was able to operate in a one-on-one setting. That was the way he had been able to accomplish things back in California. The result in *Brown* showed that he had not lost any of his persuasive powers in the Marble Palace.

On the other hand, Tushnet and Lezin (1991, 1930) asserts that the account "neglects the important role Jackson played in structuring the way in which Frankfurter thought about the problems of segregation and remedy." Thus, Tushnet and Lezin (1991) also highlight the role of interpersonal relationships among justices in shaping opinions.

Additionally, more recent accounts of the Supreme Court and decision-making often highlight the importance of these interpersonal relationships and how publicizing private processes may impact them. In early May 2022, an unknown source leaked a draft of the opinion in *Dobbs v. Jackson Women's Health Organization* (Barnes 2022a). At a conservative conference, Justice Thomas was reported as saying, "The leak of a draft opinion regarding abortion has turned the Supreme Court into a place 'where you look over your shoulder,' [...] and it may have irreparably sundered trust at the institution" (Barnes 2022a). He went on to say it "exposed the 'fragile, nature of the court.'" "This is not the court of [2000]. [...] We actually trusted each other. We may have been a dysfunctional family, but we were a family" (Liptak 2022).

An exchange between Justice Alito and an attendee at a public address which occurred shortly after the draft opinion was leaked further highlights the extent to which these relationships and contact among the justices are important to the Court and, also, the public:

> But [Alito] was a little stumped by the final audience question from a crowd at Antonin Scalia Law School at George Mason University: Are he and the other justices at a place where they could get a nice meal together?
>
> "I think it would just be really helpful for all of us to hear, personally, are you all doing okay in these very challenging times?" the questioner asked.
>
> The fact that Alito was speaking via closed circuit from a room at the Supreme Court seven miles away, rather than in person, was a sign these are not normal times.
>
> "This is a subject I told myself I wasn't going to talk about today regarding, you know—given all the circumstances," Alito replied.
>
> After a pause, he added: "The court right now, we had our conference this morning, we're doing our work. We're taking new cases, we're headed toward the end

of the term, which is always a frenetic time as we get our opinions out" (Barnes and Lumpkin 2022).

Historical and contemporary accounts of decision-making on the Court indicate that collegiality plays an important role in the work of the Court. Varying levels of collegiality influence the rate of separate opinions, as indicated by the accounts regarding Frankfurter and Douglas and *Brown v. Board*, and decision language, as suggested by Posner's account. It also matters to the public's perception of the Court, as illustrated by reports about the feud between Frankfurter and Douglas and the *Dobbs v. Jackson* leak. Thus, the influence of collegiality on the Supreme Court is an important phenomenon.

Interview Evidence Regarding the Operation and Importance of Collegiality

Beyond historical and popular accounts, we sought the perspective of individuals with a front-row view and active role in decision-making at the Supreme Court— former clerks. From original interviews with five former Supreme Court clerks (S1– S5) and comments included in an interview with a judge from the court of appeals who clerked with the Supreme Court (J3), a picture emerges of the potential importance of collegiality on the Court and the ways in which it might matter. First, we relay interviewees' perspectives regarding the extent to which collegiality might matter differently on the Supreme Court compared to the courts of appeals based on their experiences with both. We then offer the interviewees' comments on the culture of collegiality at the Supreme Court with regard to clerks generally. After that, we discuss the extent to which the former clerks had contact with justices and observed their interactions to provide a context for the clerks' observations. Next, we include clerk perspectives regarding aspects of collegiality and contact among the justices. Finally, the clerks' thoughts regarding the extent to which collegiality may influence outcomes and when such influence may be apparent are presented. Additionally, in Appendix 5.A, there is a wealth of information from clerks about the culture of collegiality and their experiences.

Institutional Differences

As is the case with most Supreme Court clerks, the former clerks we interviewed had also clerked for judges on one or more courts of appeals. Thus, they were able to speak to differences across those levels of court. S2 noted that the court of appeals judges are "not celebrities and don't draw a crowd and get recognized." The judges "live a more monastic life." They speculated that being a justice is first "being a celebrity" and you have life tenure and "are surrounded by sycophants and participate in tours of sycophants." "Does it make you more narcissistic? Or, more magnanimous and humbled?" S2 did state they thought collegiality was much more important for the outcomes of court of appeals cases. They were not alone in that assessment.

114 THE ELEVATOR EFFECT

J3 described that separate opinion writing differs between the courts of appeals and the Supreme Court. They also believe that dissents and concurrences in the courts of appeals are "understudied." At the courts of appeals, separate opinions are rare (only around 1 percent) and only in the "most important cases." This is stark in comparison to the Supreme Court, where they note "33% of cases had separate opinions because those cases are pre-selected to be the hardest and most difficult." They compared this to the courts of appeals with "mandatory jurisdiction. If you have $545, you can appeal. Yes, you have to pay some money, but it is very easy to file." They noted that there are many pro se cases in the courts of appeals.[5] These factors lead to "a separate opinion rate 1/10th of the Supreme Court." They noted that the rates of dissent in the courts of appeals tend to be around 3 percent based on research, including "published academic sources and own opinions." In "most of the cases, no matter who the other judges are, you will agree. The law is a constraint and is clear. Then there is the core of very different cases. This is why the presiding judge can assign even when in dissent." With this perspective and information in mind, we should anticipate that collegiality operates differently between these types of courts.

Thus, individuals with a firsthand view regarding judging at the court of appeals and Supreme Court levels indicate that collegiality is likely to operate differently at the high court as opposed to the circuit courts. The two interviewees highlighted differences in public attention and the nature of cases at the differing levels of the judiciary. This is in keeping with the theoretical accounts we note earlier in this chapter.

Clerk Professionalization and Socialization and the Importance of Collegiality

The importance of collegiality on the Court is illustrated by its culture and the extent to which clerks are encouraged to form relationships with each other. S5 said that high levels of collegiality among clerks were "overdetermined" by the examples set by the court of appeals judges and the justices. They think the clerks "noticed" friendships between justices across partisan divides and thought "if they can do it, then so can we." They did note that collegiality among the clerks was "not completely expected" because there had been problems among the clerks in the preceding term despite stable court personnel.

Clerks also described a general atmosphere centered on maintaining positive relationships, even where there were ideological divides. For example, S1 noted that there was certainly collegiality "within chambers and across clerks and their judges. At the time, it was less ideologically polarized. [Clerks took positions] across the ideological spectrum. [They were] not always aligned." S1 does not consider themselves to have been politically aligned with their justice, but was a "faithful agent that year."

---

[5] For example, approximately a quarter of the cases that the circuit courts hear involve pro se individuals (Hinkle 2023). The Supreme Court heard only four such cases between 2000 and 2018 and has never heard more than four in a year since 1945 (Robinson 2018).

THE SUPREME COURT 115

Generally, former clerks tended to describe stories about collegiality, including examples from prior courts or lower courts. For example, S5 discussed Harry Edwards's efforts to make the D.C. Circuit more collegial. Likewise, in describing modeling carried out by the justices, S5 noted the "famous" relationship between Scalia and Ginsburg: "They were buddy-buddy." These stories were seemingly important to their understanding of the Supreme Court. More detailed information regarding how interviewees described collegiality at the Court and relationships among clerks can be found in the Appendix 5.A.

Beyond illustrating a general culture in which collegiality is important, these relationships among clerks may serve substantial functions. S3 and S4 both noted that the only discussions regarding merits cases that occurred across chambers before oral arguments while they were there happened through clerks. Thus, the clerks may act as an important conduit of information regarding how the justices are thinking about cases before oral arguments (S3, S4). S1 described this type of activity generally among clerks (with some ambiguity regarding if they were describing the Supreme Court, as opposed to the courts of appeals). S4 explained that justices speaking directly to each other was "not historically the case" and that more direct pre-argument discussions in the past were "problematic" and caused tensions.

This is not to say that the former clerks were claiming a direct relationship between such work and outcomes, and so forth. In S2's estimation, collegiality among clerks "didn't matter much" regarding outcomes: "Some clerks might like to think it mattered. Justices have been there a long time and have consistent views. [...] We were like children to them. Our views weren't important. We were 'spear carriers' as we have been called." S5 shared similar sentiments (described in footnote 15).

Also, the experiences of clerks at the Supreme Court, many of whom go on to argue before and even sit on the Court, may help shape future behavior. The apparent focus on positive relationships may be in part based on fears regarding the costs of dysfunction. For example, S4 noted that many of the justices were clerks themselves: "There were periods where the Court was divisive—'nine scorpions in a bottle.' Many more justices are clerks now, and they saw the different ages of the Court." They believe there has been an "alteration regarding time." In their estimation, it is "really true since Rehnquist was chief justice that the justices try to be collegial. Many are personable. They have an interest [in getting] along [with colleagues they will serve with] for ten to forty years." When asked about the ideas that former clerkship experiences might influence justice behavior, S5 said they were "skeptical" that such attention to interpersonal relationships arose from the clerkship experience in and of itself but felt it might plausibly arise from having witnessed "earlier courts."

Overall, clerks paint a picture of an institution where collegiality is valued, encouraged, and modeled. With regard to clerks, this may be for good reason, as clerks are means of communication among most justices, though a few clerks downplayed the extent to which clerks influence outcomes. Finally, some former clerks discussed the possibility that Supreme Court justices who served as clerks at the Court may have been influenced by those experiences with regards to how they approach collegiality on the bench.

116   THE ELEVATOR EFFECT

Contact and Relationships among Clerks and Justices

There was variation in the extent to which clerks reported interactions with their justices. This information helps us understand the extent to which interviewees were able to observe how justices operated. S2 specifically noted that it was "different for other clerks and justices." S3 enjoyed being around their justice who was "very cool and professional." They "really liked" and "looked up to" their justice, with whom they had both "banter and serious conversations." They described regular conversations with their "boss" but noted "there were different senses of the warmth of the justices." Some were "intimidating and you don't want to disappoint. Others made clerks more confident [like their boss whom they appreciated.]" Other clerks described more formal relationships with their justices (S2, S5). S2 attended a dinner at the justice's house and approximately six lunches with them over the term. They did not report much close or warm contact with their justice. In another example, S5 said their justice was "personable," "warm," and "friendly" but also more formal than another judge for whom they clerked. They did "chat." S2 remembered one justice as having the "most personal involvement with [their clerks]" and another holding regular social events like "tennis and bridge."

Again, the work itself brought clerks together with their justices. S3 described their full chambers coming together to talk through cases, as did S5. The clerks would "get a debrief from the justice after the conference with a summary of the other justices' positions" (S2). S4 explained that before their time there was a "fishbowl" section of the cafeteria where justices and clerks interacted. Individuals "lost comfort" with the arrangement because they were "talking about privileged stuff." Instead, they described eating with their justice and other clerks in one of the series of courtyards on the grounds. S5 observed that relationships between justices and clerks were generally "friendly and amicable." They didn't observe clerks and justices "not seeing eye-to-eye." Though they had heard "stories of clerks getting dropped from opinions." So the possibility of a lack of strong relationships between clerks and justices was within the popular knowledge of the Court.

Additionally, there were events where clerks were encouraged to interact with other justices. For example, S1 described the clerks from chambers having lunch with each justice and also a Court-wide reception. S4 said that most justices "encouraged a lot of interactions among clerks and chambers." There were also "very elaborate [...] Christmas part[ies]" for the entire Court (S4). The infamous "highest court in the land"[6] also seems to have played a role. All the former clerk interviewees specifically mentioned basketball games as part of their interactions at the Court. S3 noted that they played in both the clerk and justice basketball games. As to the function of playing, S5 said that the basketball games were more "after you got to know each other more not before. They were to blow off steam." There were also casual "incidental interactions" (S5), such as in the hall (S1).[7]

---

[6] The basketball court on the top floor of the Supreme Court building (see Kay 2018).

[7] In response to the name of the project, S5 did say that for them interactions were "never [in] the elevator" due to it being cramped and the possibility of other people being there. As noted in other chapters, other interviewees did mention interactions in elevators.

THE SUPREME COURT   117

The former clerks described observing interactions with their justices, though there were differences in the extent to which the interviewees observed such interactions. These accounts help establish a basis for their observations and opinions about the Supreme Court and collegiality. They also allow transparency regarding such foundations and the extent to which they varied.

Observations about Justices, Their Interactions, and Collegiality

The interviewees also varied in the extent to which they recounted interactions among the justices. S3 stated there were a fair number of encounters both within and outside of the Courthouse. S5 described having observed regular conversations among the justices. In that vein, S4 said justices should be compared to members of Congress and implied that members of the Court have far more interactions with each other. They then noted the judges are "often in the same places and often with each other even though they travel a fair amount." Additionally, they stated that "justices have meals together" where they "don't talk regarding cases." S2 also mentioned justices eating communally after oral arguments and the conference in a private dining room. Likewise, S3 said that "justices ate together many days—after oral argument and more than that." They noted the justices ate "catered" meals with "white table cloths." S4 said some justices had "outside relationships." S1 noted that there were "formal conferences and informal interactions." But they don't recall much, though "justices talk and exchange drafts." There were "some phone calls and correspondence. Not a lot, but I may not have known. For example, [my justice] would say I'll call Justice [X] and see where [they are] at on this."

The former clerks gave a more mixed picture of justices having conversations in chambers. S4 said that the social behaviors of justices vary across individuals: "Some pop in all the time."[8] "Different justices engage differently." Additionally, S3 said that there was "some dropping by chambers" among the justices but that it was "unusual." S5 mentioned a specific justice who would come by their chambers. Instead, most of the work among the justices was done by letter (S3). S3 said there "may have been invisible conversations" but their "impression [was] that was not the case."[9] This was not because of "ill will" but rather "formality."

Interestingly, S2 said they were "surprised how often the justices are gone and not at the Supreme Court." They noted that justices are "celebrities" who spend a lot of time "speaking and at events." "They are not around each other that much except on argument days" (S2). Though they also noted that "it varied by justice." When it wasn't an argument day, they communicated by "calls and messengers with correspondence, which was antiquated at the time." They later reiterated that "justices are gone a

---

[8] Additionally, S4 noted the importance of spouses and "popular spouse[s]." "Spouses can play a key role in collegiality. They get together. They are key aspects of collegiality. For example, Justice Ginsburg's husband was [famously] very well-liked."

[9] Of course, justices may have interactions with each other that clerks do not know about. S1 specifically said they were unsure about the extent to which justices were interacting with each other.

118 THE ELEVATOR EFFECT

lot. When they are there, it is their work time." This time tends to be "busy and compressed." They felt they knew their justice much less than they knew their judge in a prior clerkship. S2 "never knew of visits to chambers [by other justices]."

The interviewees gave a general sense that the justices cared about interpersonal relationships. S3 described that collegiality was "very important" among justices. They felt that in their term "collegiality was very important to that Court. They have to work together in a sustainable way but with an older court it is less so." There were the "forms and reality of respect." When asked about the importance of collegiality on the Court, S1 said both that "collegiality is very important" and also that it was "an incredibly hard question because [they were] there for a short time period."[10] In S4's estimation, the justices "really, really try to be professional. They don't talk before oral arguments. They circulate to all nine justices all drafts." S4 "believe[d] they were trying to be collegial unlike with [earlier justices]." They pointed to the existence of "leaks" as some measure of noncollegial behavior in the past, while also acknowledging there have been "some leaks recently."[11]

S4 also described variation in how justices interpreted each other's behavior, some might be "put off by" a justice who wrote acerbic dissents or opinions, while "others were okay with [the justice] personally despite the writings." S3 also mentioned this interaction and that some saw the dissenting justice as a "scamp" with "sharp elbows." S5 said they "didn't detect any bad blood among the justices." They also surmised that this was "not true with previous generations."

The former clerks provided reports of the types of interactions they observed and their understanding of those encounters. As with accounts regarding interactions with their justices, the interviewees' reports about the extent to which they witnessed or were aware of interactions among the justices allow us to understand the basis for their responses and points of disagreement. Furthermore, they highlighted the extent to which the justices behaved in ways that indicated that collegiality and the maintenance of relationships were important to them, while suggesting that collegiality may vary on the Court over time.

Contact and Collegiality

In the interviews, we asked former clerks about the extent to which proximity and cotenure mattered to the relationships among the justices.[12] The responses help shed light both on the ways that contact is important to collegiality and aspects of the connection between interactions and relationships that are hard to observe from even a firsthand perspective.

---

[10] They also noted that there are "different types of collegiality." S3 similarly observed that collegiality can be defined in multiple ways. Clerks tended to use the term to mean warm relations as opposed to the more general definition of relationships among work colleagues that we employ.

[11] It should be noted that this was before the *Dobbs* leak.

[12] The interviews did not yield material directly related to our third indicator, probability of future panel, as that does not vary at the Supreme Court and is difficult to learn about over a single year of clerking.

Proximity

The interviewees were asked about the extent to which contact through proximity mattered to the relationships at the Court. Again, their prior experiences on courts of appeals provided some basis for comparison. Their observations reinforced the importance of shared space while also highlighting the extent to which there is little variation at the Court. S1 said that they "could not imagine what it is like with COVID and not being in the office together." "Office arrangements matter" (S1). The relative closeness of all of the offices and its importance was highlighted by S3: "Everyone in the building could walk to each others' offices within five to seven minutes." Relatedly, S4 discussed the differences between the arrangements at the Supreme Court with other courts on which they had clerked. They noted that the Supreme Court was "the first time [they had experienced all of the judges and clerks on the court] being in the same building." There is a "big difference" when court members "see each other all the time." They noted that on the courts of appeals one "could call on the phone or [email], but it was not the same." As evidence of the importance of the physical space, they noted that "even retired justices" are in the courthouse (generally in smaller offices). They recounted that this is true even though space is set aside for them in an administrative building near Union Station—"but they all stay in the Supreme Court. They want to be there." On the other hand, S5 thought courthouse arrangements matter "a bit" though the effects are likely "not detectable" using statistical means.

The importance of proximity seemed to be on the minds of justices regarding office arrangements. Certainly, the clerks relayed memories regarding the placement of offices. Several former clerks (S2, S3, S4, and S5) described the location of the justices' offices and whether all of a justice's clerks were on the floor with them. S4 described some justices moving offices to have their clerks together with them or making decisions to keep clerks together even though the quarters were cramped. Where clerks were split among floors, they switched mid-year (S2 and S5). S5 noted this was based on an understanding that clerks on another floor had less "incidental contact with the justice" and were "farther from the action." They did say it was "not huge" in terms of impact even when they were on the same floor as the justice. Either way, there was "lots of work."

S3 felt that the office arrangements mattered regarding relationships; they knew their officemate "much better and quicker" than the other clerks in the chambers but can't offer a "counterfactual." The two clerks would "throw a football and talk about cases." There were "no private phone calls" in their immediate office, and they heard conversations between the officemate and their significant other. Compared to other relationships with clerks, this relationship was "closer and with more sparks. [The interviewee and officemate also] butted heads more." All the clerks would gather for coffee in the area of the justice's office. They would "try to come down and see the boss." They said it was better when they officed near their justice.

Overall, the interviewees described the Supreme Court as a place where justices and clerks are physically close to each other. Furthermore, the behavior of justices in terms of arrangements with clerks and staying in the building after retirement indicates that justices see proximity as important to the operations of their chambers and attachment to the Court.

Cotenure

The former clerks also shared their views regarding whether the shared length of service between justices matters to their relationships. Regarding the length of cotenure, S1, while noting that they only clerked for the Court for one year, said they tended to think that "these are people who know how to interact with each other out of the gate." S4, on the other hand, believed that the length of service together likely mattered because it "takes a while to get comfortable on the job. One is anxious in the beginning. Thus, it is harder to develop friendships." S2 observed that difficult confirmations may affect this.

S2 thought that the length of service together "probably" mattered. They also noted that justices "generally have to move to start the job." Also, new justices tend to hire "Supreme Court clerks from the prior term and it helps with socialization." While "thinking out loud," they noted "the group had been together quite a while. They knew where [the others] were at" and were "not surprised." The justices were "used to disagreement." There were still "high levels of collegiality." Justices approached disagreement as "not personal, just what we do." They did suspect that based on length of service "there were fewer attempts to reach out to convince because either it was futile or [they] don't care." "Like any relationship, they get fixed over time." Based on observations of periods outside their term, they believe justices go through "a wooing process" with new colleagues. They mentioned Scalia and Kagan as an example. They also noted "some justices are gregarious and charming, some justices are introverted and loners. It depends."

Finally, S5 also noted the limited "viewpoint" from clerking of the effect of cotenure. They clerked during a time of relative stability regarding court personnel. They "couldn't differentiate who was newer or older." They were unable to tell the extent to which the justices were "predisposed to friendliness" or "friendliness developed with time." They would "conjecture" based on "introspection as a human" that "it would make sense" that it did matter positively, though it "can happen the opposite way and people despise each other over time." They did say the justices "knew of the preferences of each other." This was especially true within "coalitions" and how to "set up" opinions for other justices. Using a "public example," they said that if you were going to write something where you needed Scalia's vote and you used legislative history in the opinion, "it would need a specific setup." In S5's estimation, this was not "collegiality in the sense of getting along but knowing each other."

Generally, the former clerks reported that they were not in a good position to gauge how relationships among justices change over time due to their relatively short time with the Court (a year) and the fact that many clerks served with courts that had been together for a while. Several former clerks did find the idea that cotenure matters to be plausible, but they were speculating. These observations help highlight the need for a differing approach to consider the importance of cotenure.[13]

---

[13] We will address cotenure using quantitative methods. Another approach would be to ask Supreme Court justices. Such interviews are difficult to obtain. We did send recruitment letters to all sitting and retired justices on May 3, 2022. None opted to participate. Furthermore, to the extent scholars can interview justices, it is exceedingly unlikely that justices would be willing to describe negative feelings toward colleagues.

The Consequences of Collegiality

Finally, we turn to the former clerks' impressions regarding the influence of interpersonal relationships on outcomes. When asked about the extent to which collegiality affected aspects of decision-making at the Court, some of the former clerks noted the importance of confidentiality in terms of discussing details. Thus, the clerks spoke in general terms.[14] When asked about examples of collegiality mattering in cases before the Court, S1 said that while they had concerns regarding providing specifics due to issues of confidentiality, they "would just say that conversations between justices matter."[15] At the outset, S5 said that for the sake of the oaths of confidentiality they swore at both of their clerkships (both court of appeals and Supreme Court), they would not discuss details. However, they couldn't think of examples of collegiality mattering to the outcome of cases.

Some former clerks described their impressions regarding the extent to which collegiality influenced separate opinions and issues related to ideology and salience. When it came to "collegiality in terms of compromising of positions," S2 was "unsure if it was collegiality or game playing. Unsure of which bucket to put it in." The former clerk said they can "identify instances of justices taking positions that didn't align with their own to hold majorities or decide who would author." There are "those who engage" as "part of wooing justices" and are "willing to compromise to keep [another justice] with [them]." The former clerk could not think of any big firsthand examples.

Some responses suggested effects regarding separate opinions. S4 believed that "a reluctance to write a separate opinion out of respect varies. [One may have] separate thoughts but why detract from the chief opinion?" They did note the advent of "coalitions among the justices. Where there is a dissent, they try to have only one. Stevens started this, and it had an effect—the dissent as one voice. Fewer than accounts regarding the Warren Court." However, when we asked S4 if there is a culture of justices seeing their endeavors as being about the Court as opposed to the person, S4 noted that "courts are named after the chief justices or really the swing justice. (The justices hate the term swing.) There are some efforts regarding unanimity, but more in the past. Now, justices write so much more." There are more opinions now as evidenced by SCOTUSblog analysis (S4). "It is harder now with more writing." S3 offered that in their term when dealing with "big cases" there was a sense of "being in it together." Thus, there might be an effect with separate opinions.

Furthermore, S5 speculated that collegiality among justices might influence opinions through openness to change—they "could imagine" it might. Collegiality in terms of "intellectual respect" with "intellectual or ideological alignment" with a colleague might make a justice "reconsider" a position if a respected co-worker (justice, clerk,[16] etc.) disagreed. When asked if they could remember specific examples of effects on

---

[14] And, as noted in the Appendix 2.A of Chapter 2, the questions were not about specific cases but more general impressions.

[15] S1 started the interview by explaining that they were concerned about confidentiality and would speak in general terms.

[16] S5 wanted to make clear that while "some clerks will say I wrote that opinion or changed the justice's mind," they "didn't want to seem like that." They were much more circumspect regarding their potential impact.

decision-making, S3 said, "I actually can't" and if they could, they "probably shouldn't share." They went on to say, "Maybe one, but I can't really tell it." They clarified it was "not an explosive story" and was about the way something was written.

In considering the ways in which collegiality might matter at the high court, S1 offered that they believe collegiality can be a "huge help" in the work of the Court because it "blunts differences regarding politics." On the other hand, S5 thought collegiality was "more likely to matter" in cases that weren't "page one *New York Times* cases." Instead, collegiality likely "matters in legally hard cases but ones that don't activate previous political commitments." Likewise, S4 mentioned the theory that "in less high profile cases" collegiality matters more, and said it was "likely true."

While the interviewees were fairly sober in their assessments of the ways in which collegiality influences outcomes, some interviewees did identify ways in which it is likely to matter. Former clerks made references to conversations mattering and the potential for strategic behavior regarding authorship and coalition building. Furthermore, three participants described ways in which collegiality could matter to opinions, with two of the former clerks specifically speaking to variation in a willingness to write separately. Additionally, interviewees addressed the ways in which collegiality may lessen the impact of ideology or be conditional on the salience of a case.

Data and Research Design

The historic accounts and interviews indicate that the relationships among justices are important. Furthermore, they suggest that collegiality may influence the operation of ideology, as we have found regarding the courts of appeals in prior work (Hinkle, Nelson, and Hazelton 2020; Nelson, Hazelton, and Hinkle 2022) and in Chapters 3 and 4. Our quantitative analysis explores how broadly collegiality may affect the publicizing of disagreement throughout the judicial hierarchy (see Hinkle, Hazelton, and Nelson 2017). Here, we return to the decision to write separately but examine that decision in the context of the U.S. Supreme Court, a powerful collegial court.

In keeping with prior chapters, we anticipate that collegiality decreases the likelihood that a justice will dissent or concur. We also expect that ideological distance between a justice and an opinion author will make a concurrence or dissent more likely. Finally, in addition to these direct effects, we hypothesize that there will be a conditional effect by which the importance of collegiality will be more pronounced the larger the ideological distance between the two justices. Likewise, the influence of ideology should be lessened where there is a greater degree of collegiality.

Although the Supreme Court does not contain nearly the variation in collegial interaction evident in the circuit courts because the Court has long maintained its size and single location,[17] there is variation in how long two justices have served on the Court together. Therefore, our examination of the high court focuses on the effects of cotenure, the number of years that two justices have served together. As explained

---

[17] We do not include a measure for distance between offices at the Supreme Court, as we don't anticipate that such minor differences in distance should matter at the level of the justice (c.f. Harris 2021). As one interviewee pointed out, everyone is a short walk away from each other.

in the previous chapter, we believe that cotenure is linked to issues of persuasion. The longer justices serve together, the more likely they are to influence each other based on specific knowledge of each other and trust.

To provide information regarding cotenure's central tendency and movement over time for the Supreme Court, Figure 5.2 plots the average value of cotenure per year. Overall, cotenure among authors and other justices has a mean of 7.89, median of 7, and mode of 2. We see that the average cotenure between a pair of justices in our data has generally trended upward, with some periods of readjustment over the approximately five decades in our data. For example, in 2005, cotenure was at high point on the Court. This is unsurprising given that the last addition to the Court before 2005 was Stephen Breyer in 1994. Chief Justice Rehnquist died in September 2005 and was replaced by John Roberts. At the same time, Justices Stevens and O'Connor had been on the Court thirty and twenty-four years, respectively. We can compare that with the low point of 1972. In the previous five years, five justices left the bench: Clark, Fortas, Warren, Black, and Harlan II, with the last one (Harlan II) leaving near the end of 1971. The longest serving justice on the Supreme Court at the time was Black, who had served since 1937. He retired in September of that year along with Harlan II who had served sixteen years. The next longest serving justice on the Court was Douglas, who joined the Court two years after Black.

We also consider three experiential factors which may shape a justice's behavior once on the Court. In each instance, there is reason to believe that past encounters might influence the extent to which justices write separate opinions due to suppression of disagreement (see Liptak 2022). Clerkships occur very early in one's legal career and may have a strong impact on impressions regarding the extent to which interpersonal relationships are important. Based on the professionalization

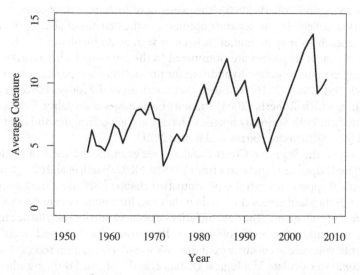

Figure 5.2 Trends in Cotenure over Time, Supreme Court: This figure plots the average value of cotenure in the Supreme Court over time.

and socialization that our interviewees described, it is reasonable to anticipate such clerkships might influence the operation of collegiality. Additionally, at least one interviewee anticipated that prior clerkship experience on the Supreme Court influenced a justice's approach toward interpersonal relationships. Another former clerk speculated that such experience might make a justice more interested in collegiality, not based on the nature of clerking specifically but due to situations they may have witnessed: particularly, former clerks may value the preservation of interpersonal relationships more based on past examples of how they can be helpful or their absence can be harmful. Thus, based on our interviews, we consider if such experience decreases separate opinions.

Other types of experience may matter regarding one's propensity toward writing or joining separate opinions: having served on the courts of appeals overall and on the D.C. Circuit specifically. Those justices who come from the courts of appeals likely bring some of those experiences with them. In fact, commentators have decried the norm of appointing justices with such experience based in part on the assumption that judges who served on federal courts of appeals behave differently than those who do not (e.g., Epstein et al. 2009). As we described in Chapter 4, there is evidence that collegiality allows for greater persuasion, but also more suppression of public expression of disagreement. Experiences based on both mechanisms may shape their habits and viewpoints regarding collegiality. Such practices and perspectives likely follow them to the highest court. Based on the evidence we have collected regarding how collegiality matters on the courts of appeals, we investigate if such experiences shape the behavior of justices and decreases the number of separate opinions they write.

Additionally, we consider if experience on the D.C. Court of Appeals matters differently than other circuit court tenures. It is unclear if such an effect would increase or decrease separate opinions. The D.C. Circuit is exceptional generally (Banks 1999). For example, its docket has far fewer criminal cases and more administrative law cases than other circuits (Roberts 2006). The presence of such important cases may reduce the effects of collegiality on separate opinions, as the benefits of airing grievances for external audiences may be higher. It is often seen as an incubator for the Supreme Court as many of its judges are nominated to the Supreme Court (Banks 1999, 4), which may encourage judges to audition for promotion via separate opinion writing (see Black and Owens 2016). On the other hand, all of the judges office in the same courthouse, which Roberts (2006) suggests encourages collegiality. Furthermore, it has a history of both famously hostile behavior among colleagues and efforts to correct that (e.g., Srinivasan, Harris, and Renan 2021).

Drawing on the Supreme Court Database, we examine the votes of justices in all orally argued Supreme Court cases from 1955 to 2009 (Spaeth et al. 2021). Continuing the empirical approach from the previous two chapters, we use a multinomial logit model (with standard errors clustered on the case) for a more systematic examination of the effect of collegiality. The data includes an observation for each justice in the case who did not author the majority opinion. Per curiam opinions and decisions with equally split votes are necessarily excluded. We use Martin-Quinn scores (Martin and Quinn 2002) to calculate Ideological Distance, and Cotenure is the number of years served on the Court together. We interact these two variables. The model also includes whether the justice clerked for the Supreme Court, was a federal court of appeals

THE SUPREME COURT   125

judge, or was on the D.C. Circuit (Epstein, Walker, and Roberts 2021). And we control for whether the justice is the chief, whether the justice has been on the Court less than two years, the justice's age (Epstein, Walker, and Roberts 2021), case salience (Clark, Lax, and Rice 2015), and the year of the decision. In addition, we include fixed effects for issue area with the modal area, Criminal Procedure, as the base category (Spaeth et al. 2021). Summary statistics for all variables are available in Appendix 5.A.

Results

Descriptive Statistics

Simple descriptive statistics provide some support for our theory. For example, Chief Justice Rehnquist and Justice Ginsburg sat together on the Court for a relatively short period—just over a decade. Yet their dissenting behavior toward one another changed substantially from the first two years they shared on the bench to their last two years serving together. In the early years, Rehnquist dissented from 47 percent of Ginsburg's majority opinions, and she dissented from 40 percent of his. In their final two years together, those numbers fell to 19 percent and 27 percent, respectively. The years did not erase their fundamental disagreements, but they do appear to have dampened their effect.

This trend does not apply to all pairings. As an example, Ginsburg dissented from opinions by her ideological foe but social friend, Scalia, a little under 18 percent of the time in their early years, with that percent more than doubling (44 percent) in their last years together on the Court. Scalia went from dissenting from Ginsburg's opinions 16 percent of the time in the beginning to a little over 23 percent of the time in their last two years of cotenure. Thus, a more robust assessment is called for in the form of multivariate analysis.

Multivariate Research

Figure 5.3 shows the regression results from the Supreme Court model. To start, we consider the direct influence of Cotenure and Ideological Distance and the interaction of the two. Figure 5.4 provides a more detailed look at how these factors influence separate opinions at the Supreme Court level. The left-hand panel of Figure 5.4 illustrates that Cotenure has a modest negative effect on concurrence, but it is only significant for higher values of Ideological Distance. However, for dissent, the impact of Cotenure is significant for both high and low values of Ideological Distance. Thus, overall, separate opinions are less likely the longer a justice has served with the author of the majority opinion.

Serving more years together on the Court dampens the probability of dissent a similar amount for both ideological allies and rivals. The size of the cotenure effect is somewhat modest. A justice who has served with the majority opinion author for thirty years is about 5 percent less likely to dissent than they would be in their first year of service with the majority opinion author. The effect of Cotenure, though limited,

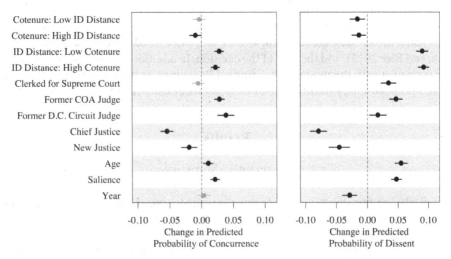

Figure 5.3 Changes in Predicted Probability of Concurring and Dissenting, Supreme Court: Estimates (and associated 95% confidence intervals) of the change in the predicted probability of concurrence or dissent generated by moving each variable from a low to high value while holding other variables at their median. Changes produced by collegiality and ideology are presented at low and high values of the other to illustrate interactive effects. Low and high values are 25th and 75th percentile for continuous variables and zero and one for binary variables. Estimates and confidence intervals in gray (instead of black) indicate that the confidence interval includes zero. Full regression estimates are available in the Tables 5.C.1 and 5.C.2 in the chapter appendix.

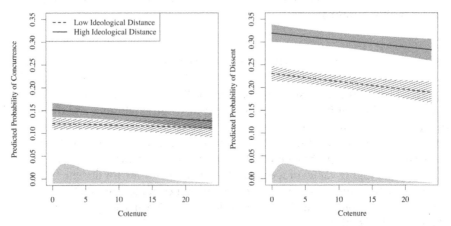

Figure 5.4 Effect of Cotenure on Concurring and Dissenting, Supreme Court: This figure shows the predicted probability of concurrence (left-hand panel) and dissent (right-hand panel) over the range of Cotenure while holding Ideological Distance at its 75th percentile value (solid lines) and 25th percentile value (dashed lines). The shaded and cross-hatch regions depict the 95% confidence intervals. The density plots show the distribution of Cotenure.

suggests the impact of collegiality even in an institutional context without a strong norm of consensus (see Walker, Epstein, and Dixon 1988; Caldeira and Zorn 1998).

Ideological distance is also a significant driver of separate opinions. As we would expect, where a justice is more likely to hold a different perspective than the opinion author, they are more likely to concur or dissent. Additionally, unsurprisingly, the influence of ideology is more pronounced in the decision to dissent as opposed to concur. We don't see evidence of an interactive effect between cotenure and ideological differences.

We anticipated that our two additional experiential factors, whether the justice clerked for the Supreme Court or served on a court of appeals, might lead a justice to be less prone to write separate opinions. We find the opposite. A justice is more likely to dissent if they served as a clerk to a Supreme Court justice ($\hat{\beta} = 0.18$, $p < 0.001$): there is a little over 3 percent increase in the likelihood of a dissent. The effect for concurrences is not significant. Also contrary to our expectations, both experience on the courts of appeals generally ($\hat{\beta} = 0.36$, $p < 0.001$ for concurrences and $\hat{\beta} = 0.32$, $p < 0.001$ for dissents) and the D.C. Circuit specifically ($\hat{\beta} = 0.40$, $p < 0.001$ for concurrences and $\hat{\beta} = 0.16$, $p < 0.001$ for dissents) result in an increase in both types of separate opinions. Where a justice has experience on the court of appeals, they are approximately 3 percent more likely to concur and 5 percent more likely to dissent. If that experience was on the D.C. Circuit, they are 4 percent more likely to concur and a bit under 2 percent more likely to dissent. In each case, the higher levels of separate opinions may be the result of greater skill or comfort with writing concurrences and dissents brought about by these experiences. We certainly do not find any indication that such experiences lead to more suppression of disagreement.

Multiple factors decrease the likelihood of separate opinions. Several control variables that operate in this way do so similarly and significantly regarding both concurrences and dissents. First, both chief justices and justices new to the Court are less likely to write separate opinions. Chief justices, who may be particularly invested in the Court as an institution, are around 5 percent less likely to concur and almost 8 percent less likely to dissent ($\hat{\beta} = -0.74$, $p < 0.001$ for concurrences and $\hat{\beta} = -0.57$, $p < 0.001$ for dissents). Similarly, in keeping with our expectations and prior work, new justices who are still finding their bearings are less likely to write a separate opinion ($\hat{\beta} = -0.26$, $p < 0.001$ for concurrences and $\hat{\beta} = -0.30$, $p < 0.001$ for dissents). Where a justice has less than two years of experience, the probability of writing separately or joining such an opinion is about 4 percent lower for concurrences and around 2 percent lower for dissents. The likelihood of dissents has decreased over time when accounting for the other factors in our model ($\hat{\beta} = -.01$, $p < 0.001$): moving from 1970 to 1991 results in the estimated probability of a dissent decreasing by a little under 3 percent. There is not a significant effect regarding concurrences.

On the other hand, separate opinions are more likely as judges age and in more salient cases. The increase in separate opinions from older judges (around 1 percent more likely to concur and 5 percent more likely to dissent moving from age 59 to 73), even while controlling for the so-called "freshman effect," suggests that justices are

128   THE ELEVATOR EFFECT

more likely to risk collegiality by writing separate opinions or joining them when their time horizons are shorter ($\beta = .01$, $p < 0.001$ for concurrences and $\beta = .02$, $p < 0.001$ for dissents). It may also be about experience. We also see indications that the decision to issue a separate opinion is influenced by the likelihood of a wider audience, the relative importance of the issues, or the more divisive nature of such cases ($\beta = 0.28$, $p < 0.001$ for concurrences and $\beta = 0.3$, $p < 0.001$ for dissents): when moving from the 25th percentile to 75th percentile for Salience, concurrences are 2 percent more likely, while dissents are almost 5 percent more likely.

Conclusions

In this chapter, we continued our exploration of the influence of collegiality on judicial decision-making, turning our attention to the Supreme Court. In many ways, the Supreme Court represents a hard test of the effects of collegiality for both theoretical reasons (discussed further in Chapter 2), including the relevant salience of cases, and methodological ones, such as the reduced variation across relationships. And yet, in keeping with accounts of the Supreme Court, our qualitative and quantitative analyses indicate that collegiality is important and has identifiable consequences. Our results suggest that scholars should be accounting for collegiality in their quantitative analyses, which rarely occurs.

Just as theory suggests, persuasion seems to be the driver. The longer justices serve together, the less likely they are to write or join separate opinions. Specifically, with greater Cotenure, they are less likely to concur when the majority opinion is written by a justice with whom they are ideologically distant and less likely to dissent regardless of ideological distance. While justices are overall more likely to concur or dissent the farther they are away from the author ideologically, the effect does not vary over years served together. We do not find similar effects with factors that could include suppression: experience as a clerk on the Supreme Court and service on a federal court of appeals. In fact, where we observe significant results related to these factors, they are in the opposite direction: concurring and dissenting votes are more likely.

We do find common threads between our investigations of collegiality at both the courts of appeals and Supreme Court: as in Chapter 4, we did find evidence of a direct, albeit modest, effect of Cotenure on the decision to dissent. As with Chapter 4, we do not find evidence that this effect is conditional on ideological distance. There are also notable differences regarding our investigations and results regarding the Supreme Court and the courts of appeals. We do not find that suppression operates at the Court, but we found that it has both a direct and conditional effect, as measured by the probability of future panel service, at the court of appeals.

We should note a few limitations with our analyses. First, assessment of the differences by level of court is difficult due to differences in the institutions. By necessity, we use different concepts to capture the concept of suppression. At the intermediate level, we can rely on differences in the likelihood someone will serve on a panel with a colleague, while at the Supreme Court we leveraged past service on a court of appeals or

THE SUPREME COURT   129

a Supreme Court clerkship. Furthermore, unlike with the courts of appeals, we were unable to assess the extent to which personal interactions, which we captured using same courthouse, influences the justices. We did find the effects of working in the same courthouse on the decision to dissent or concur varied according to ideological distance. We are unable to make a similar assessment regarding the Supreme Court. Ultimately, our results indicate the collegiality matters at the Supreme Court, but it is a relatively modest effect that suggests persuasion is increased as justices serve together. We continue our investigations in Chapter 6, where we look at the relationship between collegiality and how circuit judges determine whether to reverse the opinions of lower court judges.

Appendix 5.A: Interview Results

Collegiality among Clerks

The culture, norms, and traditions of the Supreme Court encouraged the clerks to get to know each other. There were many different types of events by which clerks came into contact with each other.[18] All of the former clerks described multiple interactions among the clerks (both within and across chambers) and the relationships that formed in part based on them. There were professional orientations at the outset (S2). S3 noted that the new clerks overlapped with the older clerks—so there was "some knowledge transfer." Some were more formal social outings including "both lunches and gatherings" (S1).

Other events appeared to be traditional or professional but less formal, such as annual parody shows and quiz bowl competitions where the teams were likely assigned[19] (S4). The traditional clerk happy hours, which are hosted by the chambers in rotation (see Nielson 2017), were discussed by several interviewees (S2, S3, S4, and S5). S5 noted that they "inculcated collegiality among the clerks." S4 described the happy hours as "very important" in that you would "see people weekly." "Everyone was invited though some might not be able to attend" (S4). S3 stated that clerks from all chambers went to the happy hours during their term. Additionally, there was a tutoring group (S3).

Other outings were more unstructured. According to S1, most interactions were informal. New clerks "wandered over to other chambers. It was not formal" (S1). There were also frequent lunches (S4). S2 reported that "more than half the time" the clerks ate lunch together in their separate dining room. Clerks would "get drinks and food together" (S2) and go out to "dinner and bars" (S3). S2 mentioned that sometimes clerks would "have dinner at a nearby restaurant," perhaps after basketball, and then work more. S3 described the outings as "standard 20s professional stuff." There were also clerk-hosted parties for special events, such as an inauguration party.

Many clerks are likely to get to know the other clerks before having significant interactions with their justices or the other justices at the Supreme Court because they start during the

---

[18] S3 did note that in their term one justice's clerks tended to stick to themselves. They attributed this to "justice preferences."

[19] The interviewee offered that the teams were assigned but wasn't entirely sure based on the passage of time.

130 THE ELEVATOR EFFECT

summer recess (S2, S4).[20] "There is a strange setup regarding Supreme Court clerks who start in June or July while the justices are traveling" (S4). For the first month or month and a half, S4 communicated with their justice "just on the phone [and the like] and hadn't seen the justice in a year since [they had] interviewed." Similarly, S2 remembered that their justice was traveling when they started: "[My justice] came back at some point and took us out to lunch and introduced [their] expectations for us." The clerk said "there were no icebreakers." S5 had a different experience. During their first week on the job, their justice invited the clerks out to eat ribs for lunch. The justice and clerks crowded into an "armored SUV," and a marshal drove them to the restaurant. There, they ate "out of styrofoam containers crowded around a table."

Of course, the work itself means that clerks spent "so much time together" (S1). S1 described endless hours spent working with other clerks in chambers on difficult legal issues. S2 described meetings "with each clerk assigned to the case at least early on." Furthermore, former clerks reported that these interactions helped them carry out their work. There were "thirty-six people" who were "very capable" (S2). S2 also said they were "getting the benefit of [the other clerks'] preparation. It could make up for a shortcoming. It could be used as a shortcut. [They] appreciated the help." S3 described daily discussions with other clerks within and outside of their chambers. S3 said that collegiality in terms of doing the work of the Court was very important: even when discussing very contentious issues, they "weren't at war with each other." Furthermore, S3 described meetings among the clerks to work through major and contentious issues. They think this resulted in "better work product." It helped them to "see things they wouldn't have" and "discuss when not" agreeing. It was helpful to have discussions when the views weren't "calcified." S4 noted that the social events ultimately allowed for "critical avenues for engagement" related to the work.

Descriptions of the interactions provide a nuanced picture of the extent to which ideological predispositions mattered. S4 noted things were "not collegial across the board. There were real tensions sometimes." Specifically, in that term they were dealing with very salient cases that were "very serious and divisive" and "set people up for tension." They also said this was likely "person-specific." S5 expressed uncertainty regarding the extent to which collegiality affected decision quality but said they would "guess so, especially in cases that were not ideologically or politically salient." They described that in more ideologically or politically salient cases that it was "not likely that unaligned clerks would work together. But, on complex technical issues, like in civil procedure or tax, you might." Then, the clerks generally "liked and respected each other [even if] they thought [the other had] wacky [ideas on certain topics]." They anticipated this would be "hard to pick up with traditional political science measures." S1 noted that clerks were aware of "who was likely to vote certain ways and gravitated to aligned clerks."

This was not the case for S3 who reported that groups of clerks "coalesced" across such divides. They noted that within the groups there was "initial shared background but [they] hung out with clerks from chambers ideologically far away more than close." Furthermore, S3 mentioned that collegiality was very important in their year due to social upheaval and contentious cases. Likewise, S5 noted that the relationships among the clerks, in part based on prior ties, "straddled" ideological divisions and allowed for "cross-cutting" relationships.

---

[20] According to all the interviewees, Supreme Court clerks also tend to arrive at the Supreme Court knowing many other clerks from law school or prior clerkships or having friends in common. S5 noted that the clerks tend to come from a small number of law schools and that two law schools were very well represented during their term, including the school they attended. S4 said they were "one person removed from almost all other clerks" that term. Dating also occurred (S1). S2 noted that they prepared for their clerkship in part by speaking with former clerks and, thus, "knew pretty well what to expect" based on those discussions along with their interview. S3 noted that there was a lot of circulation early on among clerks who tended to be in their "mid-20s." They stated they already knew some and got to know the others. They also admitted they "already didn't like one person from before" the clerkship.

THE SUPREME COURT 131

Efforts to promote interactions and positive relationships among clerks appear to generally be successful. S3 said that collegiality was "very important" to the clerks during their term. They "lived it to a degree not always the case. It can vary by year."[21] According to S3, the clerks "liked each other." They "valued that year. Even more now. It was not a mellow or happy year [due to external factors]. [They were] not angry that year." S3 sees collegiality in terms of "good feelings and solidarity" are "glue" and "predicate conditions" to the work of the Court. In their year, S4 reported that "everyone could work together with varying levels of friendliness." S5 stated it was a "highly collegial" environment that improved quality of life, including "talking to others" and a "pleasant" workplace. Relatedly, S2 said that clerking duties "were a lot more pleasant if people were collegial." The long-term ramifications of such interactions were highlighted by J3, who discussed that they attend horizontal clerk reunions for the period in which they clerked rather than ones arranged by justice.

Clerks as Conduits

S1 described collegiality mattering in terms of "needing to draft an opinion and make sure it is consonant with the other judges' understandings of the case." There were "informal conversations" with other judges' clerks to help make sure that happened, though "some more sensitive matters were discussed in-chambers only." "Most cases are non-controversial." Where a case is "technical" and you "need to figure out complex issues to make sure you are not missing things," checking with others was important. Discussion of cases, at least in some instances, seemed to have been so commonplace that not being able to talk about cases kept clerks from talking to each other at all. Specifically, S5 interacted with most other judges' clerks. One judge's clerks couldn't talk about cases with other clerks. "The judge disallowed it." So S5 didn't talk to them much because it was too difficult when you have to avoid talking about the cases. Additionally, tensions in relationships among judges could foreclose relationships among clerks: C2 "didn't talk to the clerks of one of the other judges. The [two] judges didn't get along, and [C2's judge] suggested that [their clerks] stay away." C2 did say the conversations with clerks outside of the chambers consisted mostly of "chit chat and not much substance." They went to dinner with their judges when they were traveling. They did discuss politics in the office—"it was a heady time."

[21] S5 also noted differences across years of clerkship, saying they heard there were divisions in the prior term.

Appendix 5.B: Summary Statistics

Table 5.B.1 Summary Statistics for Supreme Court Vote Dataset. Percentages may not add to 100% due to rounding.

Continuous Variables	Min.	25%	50%	75%	Max.
Cotenure	0	3	7	12	32
Ideological Distance	0.001	1.04	2.20	3.85	12.28
Age	43	59	66	73	89
Salience	−1.32	−0.56	−0.27	0.43	3.44
Year	1955	1970	1981	1991	2009
Dichotomous Variables	**0**	**1**			
Clerked for Supreme Court	75%	25%			
Former COA Judge	48%	52%			
Former D.C. Circuit Judge	86%	14%			
Chief Justice	89%	11%			
New Justice	89%	11%			
Categorical Variables	**Percent**				
Vote					
Joins Majority	69%				
Concurs	10%				
Dissents	21%				
Issue Area					
Criminal Procedure	22%				
Civil Rights	17%				
First Amendment	8%				
Due Process	4%				
Privacy	1%				
Attorneys	1%				
Unions	5%				
Economic Activity	21%				
Judicial Power	11%				
Federalism	5%				
Interstate Relations	1%				
Federal Taxation	4%				
Miscellaneous	0.3%				

Appendix 5.C: Regression Results

Table 5.C.1 Model Results: Multinomial logit regression estimates of the effect of Cotenure, Ideological Distance, their interaction, and a range of control variables on the likelihood of a concurring or dissenting vote (base category—majority vote). The reported standard errors are robust standard errors that are clustered on the case and * denotes a p-value less than 0.05.

	Coef.	S.E.
Concurrence		
Cotenure	−0.005	(0.007)
Ideological Distance	0.151	(0.013)
Cotenure × Ideological Distance	−0.002	(0.001)
Clerked for Supreme Court	0.006	(0.044)
Former COA Judge	0.361	(0.039)
Former D.C. Circuit Judge	0.405	(0.056)
Chief Justice	−0.738	(0.065)
New Justice	−0.265	(0.064)
Age	0.013	(0.002)
Salience	0.275	(0.032)
Year	−0.001	(0.002)
Civil Rights	−0.304	(0.072)
First Amendment	0.321	(0.081)
Due Process	−0.184	(0.120)
Privacy	0.219	(0.157)
Attorneys	−0.399	(0.202)
Unions	−0.549	(0.132)
Economic Activity	−0.765	(0.077)
Judicial Power	−0.410	(0.091)
Federalism	−0.685	(0.122)
Interstate Relations	−0.515	(0.395)
Federal Taxation	−1.080	(0.174)
Miscellaneous	−0.212	(0.417)
Intercept	−1.709	(3.964)

(continued)

134 THE ELEVATOR EFFECT

Table 5.C.1 Continued

	Coef.	S.E.
Dissent		
Cotenure	−0.012	(0.005)
Ideological Distance	0.188	(0.011)
Cotenure × Ideological Distance	0.001	(0.001)
Clerked for Supreme Court	0.175	(0.032)
Former COA Judge	0.317	(0.030)
Former D.C. Circuit Judge	0.162	(0.041)
Chief Justice	−0.567	(0.046)
New Justice	−0.298	(0.051)
Age	0.023	(0.002)
Salience	0.296	(0.022)
Year	−0.007	(0.001)
Civil Rights	−0.343	(0.051)
First Amendment	−0.028	(0.061)
Due Process	−0.339	(0.087)
Privacy	−0.276	(0.143)
Attorneys	−0.383	(0.148)
Unions	−0.488	(0.087)
Economic Activity	−0.586	(0.051)
Judicial Power	−0.637	(0.067)
Federalism	−0.504	(0.084)
Interstate Relations	−0.646	(0.235)
Federal Taxation	−0.600	(0.095)
Miscellaneous	−0.497	(0.274)
Intercept	11.622	(2.880)
N	43,934	
AIC	68031.04	
BIC	68448.18	

Table 5.C.2 Model Results: Multinomial regression estimates of the effect of Cotenure, Ideological Distance, their interaction, and a range of control variables on the likelihood of a dissenting vote (base category—concurring vote). The reported standard errors are robust standard errors that are clustered on the case and * denotes a p-value less than 0.05.

	Coef.	S.E.
Dissent		
Cotenure	−0.008	(0.007)
Ideological Distance	0.037	(0.014)
Cotenure × Ideological Distance	0.003	(0.001)
Clerked for Supreme Court	0.169	(0.049)
Former COA Judge	−0.044	(0.044)
Former D.C. Circuit Judge	−0.243	(0.063)
Chief Justice	0.170	(0.073)
New Justice	−0.033	(0.074)
Age	0.010	(0.003)
Salience	0.021	(0.035)
Year	−0.007	(0.002)
Civil Rights	−0.039	(0.080)
First Amendment	−0.349	(0.094)
Due Process	−0.155	(0.139)
Privacy	−0.495	(0.167)
Attorneys	0.016	(0.231)
Unions	0.061	(0.151)
Economic Activity	0.179	(0.086)
Judicial Power	−0.227	(0.106)
Federalism	0.181	(0.134)
Interstate Relations	−0.131	(0.447)
Federal Taxation	0.480	(0.189)
Miscellaneous	−0.285	(0.424)
Intercept	13.330	(4.453)
N	43,934	
AIC	68031.04	
BIC	68448.18	

6
The Lunchroom Politics
of Intercourt Relations

Introduction

So far, we have focused on the effect of collegiality *within* courts. We have learned that increased levels of contact between judges can dampen the effect of ideology and are also associated with more consensual decision-making. But these analyses have been limited in two ways: they focus on the internal operations of a single court and one type of judicial behavior (the decision to publicize disagreement). However, as we discussed in Chapter 2, collegiality might affect other types of judicial behaviors, such as an appellate judge's decision to reverse a lower court or the language judges use to express themselves. Thus, this chapter marks a pivot in our analysis as we broaden our approach to unravel the relationship between collegiality and a variety of other judicial behaviors.

In this chapter, we suggest that the effects of collegiality might also extend to intercourt relations, especially as judges on one court have personal or professional relationships with those on another court. Consider the recollections of U.S. Supreme Court Justice John Roberts (2006, 376), who served as a judge on the D.C. Circuit before his elevation to the nation's highest court. Roberts notes that the D.C. Circuit's appellate and trial judges work in the same courthouse and frequently dine together, a social interaction that emphasized the importance of collegial relationships among judges:[1] "[A]ll the D.C. Circuit judges are in the same building, along with all the district court judges. This allows the circuit judges the unique opportunity of sitting down to lunch right next to a judge who, moments before, they had announced was guilty of abuse of discretion or clear error. It can make for a very short lunch."

We follow Roberts's lead, focusing on the decision of an appellate court judge to vote to reverse a lower court judge. Appellate judges are supposed to conduct a careful evaluation of each case, relying only on the record before them, the arguments made by the parties in their briefs, and, if applicable, oral argument. But appellate dockets are unrelenting, limiting the time and effort that can be devoted to any given case. And a trial record is the product of myriad decisions made by the lower court judge. For these reasons, appellate judges might vary in the scrutiny they give to the decisions of their trial court colleagues based on their prior assessments of that judge.

---

[1] The caricature of legal realism is that "law is only a matter of what the judge had for breakfast" (Dworkin 1986, 36; see also Kozinski 1993) (though we note that some have presented empirical evidence on this front, e.g., Danziger, Levav, and Avnaim-Pesso (2011)). We suggest, in analogous fashion, that the outcomes of appeals may be based, in part, on with whom a judge eats lunch. We argue that interpersonal contact, such as lunchroom conversations, affects the credibility of the lower court judge's decision, which, in turn, affects the likelihood of appellate reversal.

The Elevator Effect. Morgan L.W. Hazelton, Rachael K. Hinkle, and Michael J. Nelson, Oxford University Press.
© Oxford University Press 2023. DOI: 10.1093/oso/9780197625408.003.0006

138   THE ELEVATOR EFFECT

To understand the importance of these assessments, we turn to principal-agent theory (Miller 2005).[2] We view appellate review as an instance of principal-agent monitoring with asymmetric information.[3] Because trial judges have more information regarding the facts of the case than their counterparts at the appellate level, there is a risk that trial judges will "shirk" and decide cases in ways that don't comply with the wishes of appellate judges (Haire, Lindquist, and Songer 2003). Such shirking could take the form of not exerting the proper amount of effort, deciding a case based on the trial judge's ideological preferences rather than the legal standard, or deciding a case against the ideological leanings of the higher courts. At the same time, reviewing the decisions of an agent (the lower court) takes time, energy, and effort. Principals usually want to conduct oversight with as little effort as possible (Epstein, Landes, and Posner 2013), and there is no reason to expend a lot of effort to carefully review a decision that one believes is probably correct.

To this end, rational appellate judges rely on heuristics about the case and the lower court proceedings to determine which appeals deserve scrutiny and which deserve only fleeting attention. One important heuristic that appellate judges use is the identity of the trial judge. When a principal holds an agent in high regard, they may accept the agent's suggestion without pause; the ideas of an agent who the principal holds in low esteem may receive additional scrutiny by the principal. In this way, appellate court judges are more likely to defer to the decisions of trial judges who they believe are likely to have reached the correct decision on their original review.

How do judges develop assessments about the quality of lower court judges' decisions? We begin by turning to the literature on source credibility, which notes that two factors—skills and shared interests—condition the power of a cue (Lupia and McCubbins 1998; Druckman 2001b). Many studies have shown that judges' shared interests—measured through the level of ideological alignment between the appellate court judges and the trial judge—are a powerful predictor of reversal (e.g., Haire, Lindquist, and Songer 2003; Sunstein et al. 2006). However, studies are mixed about whether judges' skills—most often measured through the lower court judge's formal qualifications—similarly predict the likelihood of reversal (c.f. de Rohan Barondes

---

[2] For more on principal-agent relationships between courts, see, e.g., Clark (2009), Giles et al. (2007), Lindquist and Solberg (2007), and Songer, Segal, and Cameron (1994). For a dissenting view, see Kim (2011).

[3] Of course, the analogy is not perfect. Unlike traditional principal-agent relationships, appellate judges neither hire nor fire trial judges. But, as Boyd (2015b, 155) points out, "many of the characteristics native to [principal-agent] theory, such as effective monitoring, tools of punishment, and incentivized agents, are present between the hierarchically situated federal courts." For example, appellate judges' decisions do potentially affect a trial judge's reputation and chances of promotion (Haire, Lindquist, and Songer 2003). An important line of research has examined the extent to which fear of reversal motivates lower court judges. Caminker (1994), for example, suggests that judges dislike reversal because it harms their reputation and promotion prospects, and Smith (2006, 30) claims that reversals "may cause the lower-court judge to perceive that he has lost some of the respect of the legal community" (see also Klein and Hume 2003). Indeed, Smith (2006) shows that judges change their behavior in response to reversals. We acknowledge that trial court judges may adjust their behavior in this vein (e.g., Randazzo 2008), though our focus is on the appellate court's decision to reverse, not the trial court judge's strategic decision to preemptively decide a case in a way they believe is preferable to the eventual reviewing court. After all, a trial court judge does not know which appellate panel will review their opinion (Hinkle et al. 2012).

2010; Haire 2001; Sen 2014). In this chapter, we expand the conceptualization of skills beyond formal qualifications to include the ideological character of the lower court judge's decision as well as firsthand judgments of skill based on frequent contact. Further, we consider the conditional effect of skills, testing whether each of these three assessment tools can dampen the effect of ideological alignment on the appellate court judge's decision to reverse.

Using a dataset of all published Fourth Amendment search and seizure decisions from 1953 to 2010 which appeal the decision of an identifiable U.S. District Court judge, we examine how collegiality, compared to other indicators of a trial judge's skills, affects the likelihood an appellate judge votes to reverse. Further, we examine the extent to which each of three assessment tools—formal qualifications, ideological congruence, and first-person contact—condition the effect of shared interests on the appellate judge's reversal decision. We find no relationship between any of the indicators of a trial judge's skills and the probability of reversal. However, unlike either of the other assessment tools, increased levels of interpersonal contact dampen the effect of ideological disagreement. The role of ideology is substantially reduced when the trial and appellate judges have frequent interpersonal contact, which we measure by them having offices in the same courthouse. Under these conditions, the effect of ideology on the probability of reversal is essentially imperceptible.

Reversal and Reputation

Appellate court judges are limited—both legally and practically—in their ability to survey the evidence in a case. The legal system allows trial judges to make factual determinations while appellate courts review lower court decisions to determine whether they comply with existing law. Standards of review generally dictate that appellate judges show deference regarding factual matters (*Fed. R. Civ. P. 52(a)*). At the trial, the judge has access to a plethora of additional, contextual information not available to their appellate reviewers: they usually interact with the parties before the ruling or verdict that forms the basis of the appeal, observe witnesses in person, and dedicate more resources to assessing testimony and evidence. Further, they curate the record through their evidentiary and procedural rulings. Appellate judges, on the other hand, are typically limited to the briefs and the record in a case during their review.

As principals tasked with conducting oversight of their agents on lower courts, appellate court judges need both to be effective—keeping trial judges in line—and savvy, giving their limited time and energy where it is most useful. It makes little sense for an appellate judge to devote a lot of time to a lower court opinion they believe to be correct; instead, their time and attention should go where it is most likely to be needed. In this way, appellate court judges are on the hunt for heuristics they can use to help them conduct oversight as efficiently as possible.

The identity of a judge provides a powerful cue that appellate court judges can use to triage their limited resources. For decades, advocates have been instructed that the identity of the lower court judge matters on appeal. As Davis (1940, 896) notes, judges have "a certain curiosity to know just whose judicial work it is that the court is called

140 THE ELEVATOR EFFECT

upon to review. For judges, like humbler men, judge each other as well as the law." Or, as an article written for appellate attorneys suggests:

> Recognize that the identity of the judge whose decision is being appealed may well influence an appellate court. Appellate judges who have been on the bench awhile develop a keen sense of the quality of the work done by many of the trial judges in their jurisdiction. In most appellate jurisdictions, there are a few trial judges whose rulings come to the appellate court almost with a presumption of error, and a larger number whose decisions are very difficult to overturn because of a well-deserved assessment of excellence. If your particular appeal comes from a judge who falls into either category, that fact is likely to make a difference in your approach (Schroeder and Dow Jr. 1999, 41).

Sherry (2006, 137) notes the same phenomenon:

> Over time, as individual trial judges develop a reputation for using wisely or poorly whatever discretion they are given, the appellate court can take that into account when it reviews the decisions of those judges. So the appellate court might grant broad discretion, but scrutinize the decisions of particular judges with more care; or it might grant little discretion, but exercise little oversight over the decisions of the judges thought to be most trustworthy.

Thus, an appellate court judge's assessment of a lower court judge might very well affect the amount of scrutiny the lower court judge's decision receives.

Case law provides a legal basis for appellate judges incorporating their assessment of a trial judge into their decisions. The Seventh Circuit has suggested that "the reputation of the district judge for care and skill in resolving factual disputes and making the many discretionary determinations confided to trial judges" may be helpful when resolving cases (*FMC Corp. v. Glouster Engineering Co.*, 830 F.2d 770, 772; 7th Cir. (1987)).[4] On this point, the U.S. Supreme Court has weighed in, noting that deference to an experienced trial court judge does not allow appellate judges the ability to abandon their independent responsibility to review the facts and law of a case, even on technical issues of state law when the district court judge had previously been a distinguished state court judge (*Salve Regina College v. Russell*, 499 U.S. 225 (1991)). Still, the identity of the judge may be an important complement to that review.

Our interviewees spoke to the importance of reputation. As J2 described: "Everyone has a reputation! You want a good one. You test if your reputation is good when you go up for circuit judge. You find out. Someone can sink you." Similarly, J4 said, "There is some gossip. There is a long-term awareness based on repeated interactions." J6 also mentioned district judges' "reputations from cases," saying they "get a reputation—this guy is thorough and conscientious versus this guy is sloppy and not detailed." C3 said "collegiality with district judges mattered." The "identity of the district judge [who authored the lower-court decision]

---

[4] For Judge Richard Posner's summary of the reaction to the Seventh Circuit noting that it considers the identity of the lower court judge when making its determination, see Patry (2005).

would be discussed within the chambers." It could "color [perceptions of] how well-considered the district court opinion was." District judges had reputations as to "factors regarding honing" and "how thorough and thoughtful" they were with respect to "considering cases and drafting decisions."

When the courts of appeals judges were asked how they learned about district judges, they cited varying sources. Asked if they learned through written work, reputation, or interactions, J1 said "all of the above, but mostly written opinions."[5] J2 described in more detail that, when reviewing a lower court judge's opinions, you see "what they did with the record and how they write opinions."[6] In federal judgeships, "everyone is smart. [The decisions] tell you about their judgment versus so-called smarts."

To summarize, principal-agent theory suggests that judges will want to exercise oversight with minimal effort. Over time, appellate judges build assessments of the quality of lower court judges. Appellate judges then use their assessment of the trial judge as a heuristic to determine the level of effort they need to expend to review that judge's decision.

Building Assessments

The idea that appellate judges will use their assessment of a lower court judge as a heuristic to determine the appropriate level of effort to apply to their review an appeal requires that lower court judges vary in the quality of the signals their decisions send to the higher court. Luckily, a well-tilled concept in social psychology and political communication—source credibility—provides us with a theoretical framework we can employ to determine which lower court judges send high-quality signals and which do not. Dating back to at least Hovland and Weiss (1951), scholars have found that communications from actors who the receiver perceives as more credible receive more weight in the receiver's decision-making process (Druckman 2001a; Mondak 1990).[7] As they decide cases over time, trial court judges, like all agents, vary in their level of credibility.

But on what dimensions does an appellate judge build their assessment of the quality of a trial judge's decision? Here, we draw upon the work of Lupia and McCubbins (1998), who demonstrate that "an individual considers a source credible and follows the source's advice *if* the individual believes that the source shares the individual's interests and possesses knowledge about the decision". (Druckman 2001b, 65). Thus, assessments of lower court decision *quality* and the deciding judge's *interests* influence

---

[5] When asked about other possible avenues to learn, J2 mentioned bar surveys, though J2 said they "didn't think [the surveys] were great but you can learn from them."

[6] They were also sympathetic: "District judges have to judge right then. Three circuit judges are reviewing it a year later and have to think about 'what if I was in that circumstance?'" And those circuit judges are in a different position: "District judges have a substantially different job. The law is not different but the circumstances of the decisionmaking are different. Circuit judges can be deliberate. A district judge can't deliberate. Something happens, a plea, etc., and a decision needs to be made instantaneously or relatively quickly."

[7] For a critical review of the literature on source credibility, see Pornpitakpan (2004).

142   THE ELEVATOR EFFECT

the level of credibility their decisions signal to the appellate court judge. As a result, we expect that decisions of trial court judges of high quality and those whose interests are aligned with the appellate court judge should receive more deference.

That shared interests would affect the decision to reverse is not surprising. Just as ideological disagreement between panel members is the preeminent predictor of a judge's decision to issue a dissenting opinion, the extent of ideological congruence between the higher and lower court judges is an important predictor of the appellate judge's reversal decision (e.g., Haire, Lindquist, and Songer 2003; Sunstein et al. 2006). Lupia and McCubbins (1998) suggest that sources who share the receiver's interests are more likely to be followed. Applied to appellate review, when the trial and appellate judge are predisposed to agree in a case, that appellate court judge may be particularly likely to defer to the trial judge's opinion and affirm the ruling below. But the identity of the judge may have the opposite effect when the two judges have starkly different ideological proclivities: that an ideologically distant trial court judge heard the case initially may lead to a presumption of reversal.

But how does an appellate judge assess the quality of the decision they are reviewing? A first way for a judge to assess the quality of the decision is to evaluate the deciding judge's formal qualifications. Judges may believe trial court judges with more formal credentials are "better" jurists who are less likely to make mistakes. In turn, appellate judges might view the decisions of lower court judges with superior credentials as higher quality, becoming less likely to scrutinize (and, hence, less likely to reverse) those judges' decisions (Haire 2001). As a result, more qualified judges should be more credible sources, and their decisions should be reversed less often.

Perhaps surprisingly, however, this proposition has received only sporadic support. Haire (2001) finds that more qualified judges—those with higher American Bar Association (ABA) ratings—are less likely to be reversed, de Rohan Barondes (2010) reports that more qualified judges are *more* likely to be reversed, and Sen (2014) finds no relationship between the ABA measure of quality and reversal. Furthermore, use of ABA ratings as measures of judicial quality have come under scrutiny, given evidence by Sen (2014) and others that ABA ratings are not objective indicators of judicial quality. Scholars have used measures of credentials, such as the ranking of a judge's law school or their prior judicial experience as alternative measures of quality. Here, Sen (2015, 208) finds sporadic correlations writing that "relatively few of the educational measures and professional experiences predict reversal." In short, existing studies provide only piecemeal evidence of a relationship between quality and reversal.

A second way to examine the quality of a lower court decision is to assess the likelihood that it is legally correct. All else equal, judges prefer to affirm lower court decisions that align with their policy preferences and reverse those that do not. But judges are bound by legal principles, especially at lower levels of the judicial hierarchy (Zorn and Bowie 2010). In some cases, the law is determinate, and the lower court judge has little recourse but to rule in a way that is not aligned with their preferences. Those trial court decisions that are based on strong, determinate legal foundations should be more likely to withstand appellate review. However, assessing whether a given ruling is legally correct can require substantial investment by an appellate judge beyond just reading the lower court opinion.

THE LUNCHROOM POLITICS OF INTERCOURT RELATIONS   143

To this end, the appellate court judge can use the policy preferences of the trial judge and the outcome of the lower court case together to gauge the strength of the legal merits of the decision. If an appellate judge knows the ideological preferences of the lower court judge, they can identify rulings that are particularly likely to be legally correct and therefore deserve deference: lower court decisions that are contrary to the trial judge's preferences. Many studies have demonstrated that decisions made by sources that appear contrary to their interest are particularly credible. For example, Calvert (1985) shows that information from an ideologically biased source can be particularly informative to a decision maker; if the source decides contrary to expectations, that action is likely to be particularly influential to the receiver of that message (see also Berinsky 2015; Slothuus and de Vreese 2010). Thus, when a liberal trial judge hands down a conservative ruling (or vice versa), reversal should be less likely than when the ruling is consistent with the trial judge's ideology.

Third, a judge's assessment of the quality of the lower court decision may come from their personal experiences with that trial judge. Some information about one's colleagues is widely available, such as where they went to law school or which president nominated them to office. Other information about one's co-workers is best determined in person through repeated interactions. Some people have a sterling resume but a poor work ethic. Both characteristics relate to the quality of one's work product. While the former is easily learned from a judge's biography, the latter is best picked up through repeated interpersonal interactions. Appellate judges learn about the skills of trial judges through their interactions with them. Through these experiences, an appellate judge can learn about various traits of a trial judge, such as intelligence, technical expertise, work ethic, and carefulness. All of these pieces of information can help appellate judges form opinions regarding how closely they need to check the trial judge's work.

Our interviewees discussed learning (and using) this information during the process of appellate review. J3 described having views of lower court judges, like "Judge X is fantastic" and their opinions are "well reasoned." For "a few" the response to seeing their names was, "oh no, so-and-so, let's see how they did this time." According to J4, there is a "long-term awareness" from trial judges' opinions regarding "how careful they are." J4 related that when they see they are reviewing some district judges' work, they think "oh, him" (using a tone that expressed trepidation). J5 said they learn if district judges are "careful or do they go from first to third [base] without touching second?" They have an openness to district judges in the beginning, regardless of "political or social view," which can change with information. They may begin to think the district judge is "not a goodie, not careful." While if it is "someone who is careful regarding analysis, I will respect their decisions and find in favor [of their position] if it is plausibly supported." It could matter if they "get an opinion" from such a judge and it is a case where the outcome is unclear: "Am I going to reverse? If it is tough and I don't know," it might matter. Thus, these reputations color how a lower court judge's case is considered.

While we have clear expectations about the effects of formal qualifications and the ideological character of the lower court decision on the probability of reversal, we are less sure about the direct effect of interpersonal contact on an appellate judge's reversal decision. The information that comes from interpersonal interactions is

144 THE ELEVATOR EFFECT

heterogeneous, sometimes suggesting a presumption of reversal and other times a likely affirmance. For this reason, we do not expect that interpersonal contact has a direct effect on the decision of an appellate judge to reverse a lower court judge. Instead, as we discuss next, we expect that interpersonal contact—continuing a theme from the previous chapters—affects appellate review by conditioning the role of ideology. Thus, we now turn to the relationship between judgments of quality and shared interests.

Assessments, Collegiality, and Ideology

We expect that the real power of these three assessment-building tools comes in their ability to interrupt the effect of ideological alignment on the decision to reverse the lower court judge. Beginning with formal qualifications, as a judge's credentials increase, their decisions should be entitled to more deference on appeal. Empirically, this greater level of deference means that the appellate judge's ideology should weaken as a predictor of reversal as the trial court judge's level of qualifications increases.

Regarding the ideological congruence of the lower court judge and their opinion, we expect a similar dynamic. When the lower court judge and their decision are ideologically congruent, we expect canonical ideological decision-making at the appellate court: greater alignment between the two judges will be associated with a lower probability of reversal. But when the trial judge and their decision are ideologically at odds, this incongruence should send a strong signal to the appellate judge about the strength of the decision, weakening the ability of ideology to predict the appellate judge's vote.

Finally, frequent interpersonal contact can provide an appellate judge with a rich store of private information. Through this contact, the appellate judge may learn that a trial judge is lower quality than their credentials indicate or that the trial judge performs their job with a great deal of care. To the extent that this private information suggests that the trial court judge has decided the case correctly, the appellate judge treat the lower court decision with deference even when ideological considerations would suggest otherwise. When interpersonal contact suggests that a judge is not very good at their job, the appellate judge should be *more* likely to reverse, even when the decision might initially appear to be aligned with their ideological preferences. After all, because their decisions are subject to further review, intermediate appellate court judges care about the legal correctness of a decision as well as its ideological implications (Bowie, Songer, and Szmer 2014).

Thus, private information, formed from interpersonal contact, provides judges with a variety of information they can bring to bear when reviewing a decision. Given this data, the appellate judge, acting as a principal, can overcome some of the challenges associated with information asymmetries due to information regarding the agent's (trial judge's) quality. Sometimes those factors will suggest reversal when ideological considerations align; other times, the converse will be true. In all cases, these details will help the appellate judge's decision calculus alongside knowledge of the trial judge's ideology. We expect this private information to take precedence over judgments of ideological alignment or, at the very least, to cloud the impact of shared

THE LUNCHROOM POLITICS OF INTERCOURT RELATIONS 145

interests. On balance, the introduction of private information should dilute the effect of ideology on the decision to reverse. Therefore, when two judges have frequent interpersonal contact, the relationship between the appellate judge's ideological alignment with the lower court decision and reversal should be dampened.

Measuring Hierarchical Collegiality

Having explained why interpersonal contact between trial and appellate court judges should condition the role of ideological disagreement on votes to reverse, we now turn to the issue of measurement. As we did in Chapters 3 and 4, we utilize an observable indicator of frequency of interaction: whether the appellate court judge and lower court judge have their home chambers in the same courthouse. Most appellate judges have their primary office space in the same building as U.S. District Court judges—some of whom have recently issued a decision they must review. Judges who work in the same courthouse are more likely to see each other on a frequent basis, professionally and/or socially. In short, such judges have more frequent interpersonal interactions.

Our interview data help us validate this assumption as it pertains to cross-court relationships. For example, J2 reported "seeing [district judges] in the building all the time" but not those in "other vicinages." Otherwise, they see district judges at conferences, "which are often great opportunities for exchange." Based on their own experience as a district judge, they know that when such judges get "the slip opinion [they are] looking for the A-word." In other words, they are looking to see if they were affirmed by the circuit panel. The interviewee noted that it was "infrequent that it wasn't there for me. If not, I would not have my job now." "As a district judge, I thought of the circuit judge as an uncle who talks to your dad at Christmas but not you," though they principally felt this about circuit "judges from other vicinages." They noted that they knew a Supreme Court justice from their time on the circuit and another prior job and that the relationship hadn't become distant or a cause for concern. They also noted that they had voted for many of the magistrate judges when they were a district judge. "I've known them all for years. There is no distance."

The judges we interviewed generally reported having more contact with the judges who work in the same cities and courthouses.[8] J4 also listed several ways they have

---

[8] Our interviewees also mentioned two other ways that judges might build assessments of their lower court colleagues. First, J3 mentioned that many appellate court judges were promoted from a lower court and may have a sense of those judges' capabilities from that prior service; trial judges who are promoted to the court of appeals often keep their chambers in the same courthouse, helping cement their collegial ties with others in that courthouse. Second, J3, J5, J6, and J7 all indicated that they learned about district court judges when they sat by designation on appellate panels. For example, J5 described that circuit judges can learn about district judges by sitting in that position by designation. This is important because "once again if you know who someone is, it is tough to be nasty." It "let the district judges see it from the view of a [circuit judge] and what we are looking for in an opinion." When serving with district judges, J3 got to know them. J6 also noted that the hierarchical relationship inherent in the appellate-trial judge relationship also plays an important role, and it is incumbent on appellate court judges to respect their peers on trial courts. They think "it is a problem if courts of appeals judges act like they are better than district judges. We are all just judges. Wait ten years, and no one will remember you." In describing the fleeting nature of judge importance, they noted that there are former Supreme Court justices who never wrote a "significant opinion."

146 THE ELEVATOR EFFECT

contact with district judges. First, they mentioned seeing the district judges "in passing in the judges' gym." "Pre-COVID, once a month I would go and have lunch with the district judges. That is not usual for [circuit judges]." They also mentioned in "the elevator," "in the garage," and at events "[such as] the Christmas party and investitures." They learn about the ability of district judges in part based on their knowledge of an individual before becoming a judge; there is "some sense pre-bench how they were." J6 said they "know the district judges in [their] city." They have had dinners with district judges. They see them at "monthly [...] committee meetings and other events occasionally." J6 encountered district judges at "conferences," "in the hall," and at "federal bar lunches." "Unfortunately, there is not a lot of interaction [with the district judges] but it is helpful when we have it." J3 was an outlier; when asked if they interact with the district judges in their circuit, J3 said, "Other than in the elevator? Not much."

Scholars of U.S. District Courts have come to similar conclusions about the importance of geographic location for frequency of contact. Carp and Wheeler (1972, 377) note increased prevalence of interaction among district court judges who office in the same city, quoting one judge who told them, "'I had the help I needed right down here in the corner of this building on this floor,' pointing in the general direction of another judge's chambers." More generally, Carp (1972, 413), summarizing interviews with federal district judges, argued that "informal social contact among district judges is a current and ever-increasing phenomenon among judges within the same circuit." Carp (1972, 414) goes on to note that this contact was particularly important for judges who worked in the same city:

> Because Judge Riley [a judge in the Southern District of Iowa] presided over his own separate judicial district he very rarely enjoyed daily personal contact with other federal district judges. Nevertheless, this was a privilege experienced by a number of district judges within the Eighth Circuit who resided in states where the judges sat at large and where they often had joint offices with other judges in the same city. Such was the case, for example, in the state of Minnesota, where several district judges held court jointly in Minneapolis, and in the state of Missouri, where several such judges operated out of St. Louis. Therefore a third of the Eighth Circuit trial judges were able to see one another on almost a day-to-day basis and were thus able to exchange information and advice with considerable ease.

Recognizing the positive benefits of this close proximity, Carp (1972, 414) notes that Judge Riley was "env[ious] of those Eighth Circuit judges who could enjoy daily contact with one another."

Thus, information about a trial court judge's reputation is more easily gathered through frequent interpersonal contact. As a judge gets to know a lower court colleague, they gather independent information about that judge's ability to ferret out

---

"You are important to the persons before you." For example, a judge is important "to the attorneys. You are not going to write *Brown v. Board* and be remembered a hundred years from now."

the important facts of the case, make sure that those facts appear on the record, and write an opinion that summarizes the important facts and applies the law correctly. Similarly, when the two judges know each other personally, the appellate judge can gain an opinion about the extent to which the lower court judge is likely to reveal any potential weaknesses in their conclusion or whether that decision needs to be held to a higher degree of scrutiny to ensure it is correct.

In possibly the most well-known study of this phenomenon, Epstein et al. (2009) find that U.S. Supreme Court justices with prior federal appellate experience tend to favor the circuit from which they came. In fact, they find that some justices are twice as likely to rule in favor of their home circuit as they are the other federal courts of appeals. In this way, personal experiences with the reviewing court might magnify the credibility of the lower court's decision. If an appellate judge has good personal reason to believe that the lower court judge is a "good judge," they might be even more likely to defer to the lower court judge's ruling.

There are good reasons to believe that being in the same courthouse can help a circuit judge get to know district judges better, but how frequently does that opportunity arise? To get a sense of the distribution of same courthouse pairs across circuits, Table 6.1 provides information about the distribution of judges. The Third, Seventh, and Ninth Circuits have the highest number of district judges per federal courthouse with at least one circuit judge; the Second, Fourth, and Tenth Circuits have the lowest number.

Table 6.1 Distribution of District Judges: The average number of district court judges per courthouse with at least one circuit judge, by circuit, in 2010.

Circuit	Number of Courthouses with a Circuit Judge	Average Number of District Judges per Courthouse
First	6	4.8
Second	7	2.3
Third	8	8.5
Fourth	10	2.1
Fifth	8	5.1
Sixth	16	4.3
Seventh	6	6.8
Eighth	11	4.1
Ninth	19	5.1
Tenth	10	2.8
Eleventh	8	4.9
Total	109	4.5

148   THE ELEVATOR EFFECT

Data and Research Design

To examine the dynamics of collegiality and reversal, we again return to our dataset of all published Fourth Amendment search and seizure decisions made by the numbered U.S. Courts of Appeals from 1953 to 2010.[9] After excluding all opinions that did not address the merits, resulted in a split decision (e.g., affirmed in part and reversed in part), were en banc, or were not appealed from an identifiable district judge, the resulting dataset contains 11,734 opinions. The unit of analysis is the judge-vote. The outcome variable indicates whether the appellate judge voted to reverse the lower court ruling; 26 percent of votes in the dataset were to reverse.[10] We estimate a probit model with circuit fixed effects (to account for differential reversal rates by circuit) and standard errors clustered on the case.

We have four main explanatory variables. First, we measure the ideological preferences of the appellate judge using Judicial Common Space (JCS) scores (Boyd 2015a; Giles, Hettinger, and Peppers 2001; Epstein et al. 2007), which range from −1 (liberal) to 1 (conservative). When the lower court ruling is conservative, the appellate judge's JCS score reflects how well they are aligned with the ruling below. When the lower court ruling is liberal, we multiply the appellate judge's JCS score by −1. Therefore, this variable measures how well the appellate judge is aligned with the lower court ruling. The variable has a median of 0.03.[11]

Second, we measure the qualifications of the lower court judge. We account for the trial judge's credentials by summing binary variables indicating whether they graduated from a top-14 law school (Sen 2015); clerked for a judge; or had prior experience as a prosecutor, public defender, attorney general, solicitor general, professor, or judge before ascending to the federal bench.[12] This variable ranges from 0 to 6 with a mean of 1.95, a median of 2, and a standard deviation of 1.23. Eleven percent of observations include a lower court judge who had none of these credentials; another 11 percent include a judge with four or more of them.

Third, the ideological preferences of the trial judge help appellate judges interpret their ruling (Black and Owens 2012; Cameron, Segal, and Songer 2000). Counterideological lower court decisions might be particularly strong signals of a quality fact pattern or determinate precedent (Black and Owens 2012; Calvert 1985; Cameron, Segal, and Songer 2000), so we account for whether the trial judge decided the case in line with their ideological preferences. When a district judge who was appointed by a Republican president decides a case in favor of the prosecution in a criminal case or the defendant in a civil case, Ideological Lower Court Ruling equals one. The same is true when a district judge appointed by a Democratic president rules in favor of the defendant in a criminal case or the plaintiff in a civil case.[13] Because many

---

[9] Unpublished opinions are excluded because they are not readily available for the timespan covered here (Sunstein et al. 2006). We again exclude the D.C. Circuit from this analysis since the confined geographical reach of that circuit eliminates variation in chambers location.

[10] A dissent in a case that affirmed the lower court ruling is coded as a vote to reverse (and vice versa).

[11] Summary statistics, including information on the distribution of Aligned, are available in Table 6.A.1 in the chapter appendix.

[12] Prosecutorial and public defender experience indicate subject expertise in the search and seizure cases.

[13] We use party of the appointing president because JCS scores are not available for some of the district judges in the early years of our dataset.

THE LUNCHROOM POLITICS OF INTERCOURT RELATIONS   149

of the features of the Supreme Court that are thought to allow justices to make ideological decisions are not present in the district courts (Segal and Spaeth 2002), ideology should play a less important role in district court decision-making (Zorn and Bowie 2010). This expectation is borne out in the distribution of this variable: the percentage of ideologically congruent lower court decisions is only 54 percent.

Finally, to measure the level of interpersonal contact between the pair of judges, we include an indicator variable for whether they have their home chambers in the same courthouse. We followed the same procedure to code this variable as we outlined in Chapter 3. Same Courthouse equals one if the appellate and trial judge have their chambers in the same courthouse and zero otherwise; 10 percent of votes in our dataset were cast by an appellate judge reviewing a trial judge with chambers in the same building. Table 6.2 shows the distribution of observations across circuits, as well as some information about how Same Courthouse varies across circuits.

We further control for factors that may influence reversal and our primary explanatory variables. A substantial literature on circuit court decision-making shows the persistent effect of panel composition on an individual judge's votes (Sunstein et al. 2006); these panel effects might complicate the influence of the appellate judge's private information. We therefore control for the panel type, using the party of the appointing president to classify each judge vote as occurring in one of three situations: on a unified panel, on a split panel where the judge is in the majority, or on a split panel where the judge is in the minority. We also control for whether the appellate and trial judges have a shared legal education background. We further account for if the appellate judge sits on the panel by designation and if they had judicial experience before their current job. Finally, we control for case type, trial judge demographics (to account for differential reversal rates (Sen 2015)), salience (the presence of an amicus

Table 6.2 Distribution of Votes and Same Courthouse Pairs, by Circuit

Circuit	Number of Votes	Percent Same Courthouse Pairs
First	2,039	27%
Second	2,544	20%
Third	1,346	18%
Fourth	1,686	7%
Fifth	4,763	5%
Sixth	3,165	5%
Seventh	4,245	20%
Eighth	5,237	8%
Ninth	5,162	6%
Tenth	3,263	5%
Eleventh	1,725	3%
Total	35,175	10%

150   THE ELEVATOR EFFECT

brief), caseload, and year. Caseload is the number of cases (in 100s) terminated in the circuit-year divided by the number of active circuit judges that year.

Results

We analyze the results of our multivariate probit model in two steps. First, we examine the direct effects of the three indicators of judicial reputation to learn if appellate judges are less likely to vote to reverse lower court judges who are more highly qualified, who issue ideologically incongruent rulings, or who work in the same courthouse. Second, we examine whether these three factors attenuate the effect of ideological disagreement on the decision to reverse. Table 6.B.1 in the chapter appendix provides all regression results.

Direct Effects of Reputation

We begin by examining Model 1, which includes no interaction terms, for evidence that judicial qualifications, ideologically congruent rulings, or the credentials of the trial judge affect the probability that an appellate judge will vote to reverse the trial court decision. Recall that we hypothesized that circuit judges should be less likely to vote to reverse district judges who are more qualified and whose decisions are incongruent with their own ideologies. We did not have a clear hypothesis for the direct effect of interpersonal contact (Same Courthouse). Figure 6.1 shows the predicted probability of a vote to reverse as each of the assessment tools varies.

The results do not support our hypotheses. In fact, the direction of the estimated effects for both qualifications and an ideological lower court decision are contrary to expectations: more qualified judges are more likely to be overturned, and ideologically congruent lower court rulings are less likely to be reversed than those that defy ideological expectations. However, neither qualifications ($p = 0.06$) nor the ideological congruence of the trial court judge and their decision ($p = 0.82$) nor interpersonal contact ($p = 0.56$) has a statistically significant relationship with the probability of reversal. From these results, we conclude that none of these three assessment tools has a direct relationship with the probability an appellate court judge votes to reverse.

What, then, explains the likelihood of a vote to reverse? As existing studies would predict, we find a strong effect of ideological alignment between the two judges on the probability of reversal, as shown in Figure 6.2. The size of this effect is quite large: a difference in probabilities of about 0.20 between judges whose ideological differences are imperceptible to those whose differences are the largest we observe.

Conditional Effect of Ideology by Assessments

Having seen that ideological alignment is a strong predictor of an appellate court judge's decision to reverse, we next examine whether the determinants of assessment

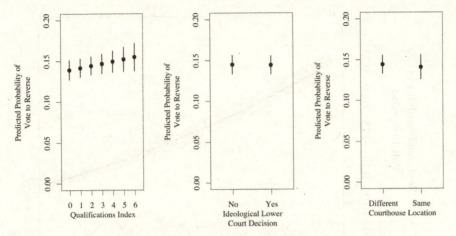

Figure 6.1 Predicted Probability of Vote to Reverse for Each Determinant of Assessment: This figure shows the predicted probability of a vote to reverse at each value of each of our variables that reflect an appellate judge's ability to assess the lower court ruling. Higher values of the y-axis indicate that the judge is more likely to vote to reverse. The lines are 95% confidence intervals. Model estimates come from Model 1 in Table 6.B.1 in the chapter appendix.

condition the effect of ideological alignment. Figure 6.3 illustrates the results from our regression model.[14] The left-hand column shows the predicted probability of reversal as ideological alignment varies. The two lines in each figure show the 25th and 75th percentile value of each assessment variable.

The general negative slope of these lines mirrors the pattern from Figure 6.2: as two judges have smaller ideological differences, the probability of reversal decreases. In the top two rows, the fact that the two lines in each panel are nearly identical is evidence that neither qualifications nor an ideological lower court decision condition the effects of ideological alignment. Indeed, in the regression model, neither interaction term is statistically significant. And when we look at the right-hand column, we see that the marginal effect of ideology for both variables remains constant for each value of the assessment variable.

These findings fit well with the evidence presented by Sen (2014, 2015), whose data suggested no strong relationship between measures related to trial court judicial quality and appellate court decisions to reverse. Coupled with our initial ideological finding, discussed earlier, we conclude that appellate court judges, perhaps unsurprisingly, appear to prioritize their own ideological wants over any weak constraint

---

[14] We use a model that includes all three interactions at once. The results are the same if we estimate three separate models, each with one interaction term. Further, if we add Same Courthouse to the other two interactions, the three-way interaction is not statistically significant: we find no evidence that the effects of Qualifications or Ideological Lower Court Decision on Alignment vary according to Same Courthouse status.

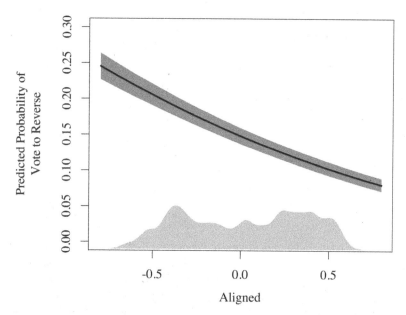

Figure 6.2 Predicted Probability of Vote to Reverse over Range of Aligned: This plot shows the predicted probability of a vote to reverse the lower court across the range of circuit judges' ideological alignment with the lower court judge. Higher values of the y-axis indicate that the judge is more likely to vote to reverse. The shaded region depicts the 95% confidence interval. The density plot shows the distribution of Aligned in the dataset. Model estimates come from Model 1 in Table 6.B.1 in the chapter appendix.

that a trial court judge's credentials might have on the appellate court judge's ability to pursue their own policy goals.

However, when we look to the bottom row of Figure 6.3, we see that the effect of ideology is conditional. When two judges do not work in the same courthouse (the dashed line in the left-hand panel), more ideological congruence is associated with a lower probability of reversal: the standard attitudinal expectations hold. However, when the two judges work in the same courthouse (the solid line), there is *no effect of ideology*. Just as we saw in Chapter 3 regarding interpersonal interactions and the decision to dissent, working in the same courthouse dampens the effect of ideology on the decision to reverse such that it is imperceptible. Indeed, when we look at the size of the effects in the right-hand panel, we see that not only is there a large difference in the effect of ideology between judges who work in the same courthouse and those that do not, but the estimated effect of ideology when the two judges work in the same courthouse is almost exactly zero.

From these findings, we conclude that assessments of trial court judges do condition the effect of ideological alignment on the probability of a vote to reverse. But contrary to traditional theories of source credibility which prioritize formal qualifications or the lower court judge's interests, we find that the level of face-to-face contact, measured here as two judges working in the same courthouse, is the primary mechanism

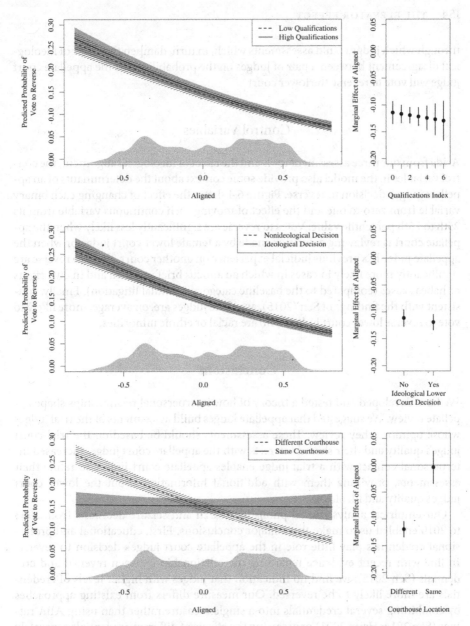

Figure 6.3 Conditional Effect of Each Determinant of Assessment on the Probability of a Vote to Reverse: The left-hand column shows the predicted probability of a vote to reverse, for each determinant of assessment as ideological alignment varies. "Low" and "High" qualifications correspond to the 25th (one qualification) and 75th (three qualifications) percentile of that variable. Higher values of the y-axis indicate that the judge is more likely to vote to reverse. The bands are 95% confidence intervals. The density plots show the distribution of Aligned. The right-hand column shows the marginal effect of ideology for each assessment variable category. The lines are 95% confidence intervals. Model estimates come from Model 2 in Table 6.B.1 in the chapter appendix.

154 THE ELEVATOR EFFECT

through which judges build assessments which, in turn, dampen the effect of ideological disagreement between a pair of judges on the probability that the appellate court judge will vote to reverse the lower court.

Control Variables

Aside from our three assessment tools and the effect of ideological alignment, the control variables in the model also provide some context about the determinants of an appellate judge's decision to reverse. Figure 6.4 shows the effect of changing each binary variable from zero to one and the effect of moving each continuous variable from its 25th to 75th percentile value. Votes to reverse are significantly less likely when the appellate court is reviewing a decision made by a female lower court judge or when the appellate judge has previous judicial experience on another court. Votes to reverse are significantly more likely in cases in which an amicus brief was filed and in civil rights or habeas cases (compared to the baseline category, criminal litigation). Finally, consistent with the findings of Sen (2015), appellate judges are, on average, more likely to vote to reverse lower court judges who are racial or ethnic minorities.

Conclusions

We have developed and tested a theory of how interpersonal relationships shape appellate review. We suggested that appellate judges build assessments of the trial judges whose opinions they review. These assessments should be based on the trial court judge's quality and their shared interests with the appellate court judge. Increased interpersonal contact with a trial judge enables appellate court judges to refine their assessments, providing them with additional information about the lower court judge's quality and ideology.

Our empirical analysis of all published search and seizure decisions from 1953 to 2010 enabled us to make three major conclusions. First, educational and professional credentials play little role in the appellate court judge's decision to reverse. In line with recent evidence regarding the relationship between reversal and credentials (Sen 2015), we find no indication that judges with higher levels of credentials are more likely to be reversed. Our measure differs from existing approaches by combining several credentials into a single measure rather than using ABA ratings (Sen 2014; Haire 2001) or assessing the effects of different credentials separately (Sen 2015).

Second, examining the relationship between ideology and reversal, we conclude that the appellate court judge's ideological alignment with the lower court ruling is the predominant factor in the reversal decision when the trial and appellate court judge do not have frequent contact. In many ways, this finding is rote: ideology drives appellate review, just as many existing studies (e.g., Sunstein et al. 2006) have demonstrated. Still, that more extreme judges are particularly likely to reverse provides additional evidence in favor of the importance of acknowledging the variation in appellate court judicial ideology.

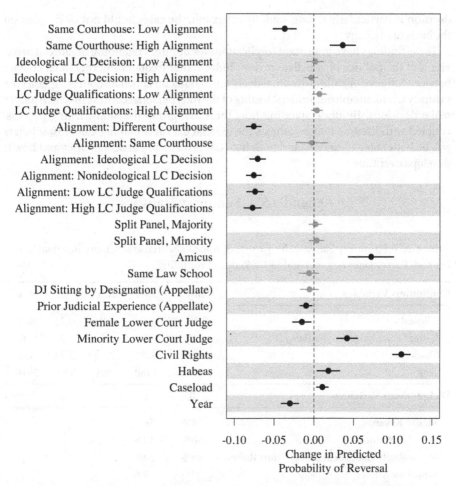

Figure 6.4 Changes in Predicted Probability of a Vote to Reverse: Estimates (and associated 95% confidence intervals) of the change in the predicted probability that a circuit judge votes to reverse the lower court generated by moving each variable from a low to high value while holding other variables at their median. Changes produced by collegiality and ideology are presented at low and high values of the other to illustrate interactive effects. Low and high values are 25th and 75th percentile for continuous variables and zero and one for binary variables. Estimates and confidence intervals in gray (instead of black) indicate that the confidence interval includes zero. Full regression estimates are available in Model 2 in Table 6.B.1 in the chapter appendix.

Finally, and most importantly, when trial and appellate court judges have frequent contact, there is no relationship between ideology and the decision to reverse by the appellate court judge. Though we are unable to test this mechanism directly, we expect this relationship exists because more frequent contact with a trial court judge enables an appellate court judge to better identify those decisions where a trial court judge has decided a case contrary to their ideology, thereby signaling that the legal basis for the

156 THE ELEVATOR EFFECT

decision is particularly strong, and, by extension, the case should not be decided on the basis of ideology.

These findings have important implications for our understanding of judicial behavior and the politics of appellate review. Indeed, that frequent interpersonal contact between judges can stifle attitudinal decision-making on appellate courts suggests the primacy of enhancing our understanding of the interpersonal context in which judges make decisions. By understanding how the small-group decision-making process, coupled with lifetime tenure, adjusts the judicial decision-making calculus, scholars will be better able to understand both how law is made in particular cases and how it develops over time.

Appendix 6.A: Summary Statistics

Table 6.A.1 Summary Statistics for Courts of Appeals Search and Seizure Reversal Vote Dataset. Percentages may not add to 100% due to rounding.

Continuous Variables	Min.	25%	50%	75%	Max.
Aligned	−0.80	−0.30	0.03	0.33	0.80
Lower Court Judge Credentials	0	1	2	3	6
Caseload	0.31	1.98	2.64	3.33	7.40
Year	1953	1980	1991	2001	2010
Dichotomous Variables	**0**	**1**			
Vote to Reverse	74%	26%			
Same Courthouse	90%	10%			
Ideologically Congruent Lower Court Ruling	46%	54%			
Same Law School	92%	8%			
DJ Sitting by Designation (Appellate)	91%	9%			
Prior Judicial Experience (Appellate)	74%	26%			
Amicus	98%	2%			
Civil Rights	75%	25%			
Habeas	93%	7%			
Female Lower Ct. Judge	92%	9%			
Minority Lower Ct. Judge	90%	10%			
Categorical Variable	**Percent**				
Split Panel					
Unified	30%				
Majority	47%				
Minority	23%				

Appendix 6.B: Regression Results

Table 6.B.1 Model Results: Logistic regression estimates of the effect of three assessment tools, ideological alignment, their interaction, and a range of control variables on the likelihood a court of appeals judge votes to reverse the lower court judge. The models include circuit fixed effects and * denotes a p-value less than 0.05.

	Model 1		Model 2	
	Coef.	S.E.	Coef.	S.E.
Same Courthouse	−0.015	(0.025)	0.009	(0.025)
Ideologically Congruent Lower Court Ruling	−0.003	(0.015)	−0.004	(0.015)
Lower Court Judge Credentials	0.012	(0.006)	0.012	(0.006)
Aligned	−0.446	(0.022)	−0.475	(0.047)
Aligned × Same Courthouse			0.505	(0.067)
Aligned × Ideologically Congruent Lower Court Ruling			−0.036	(0.043)
Aligned × Lower Court Judge Credentials			−0.005	(0.018)
Split Panel, Majority	0.009	(0.018)	0.008	(0.018)
Split Panel, Minority	0.015	(0.020)	0.014	(0.021)
Amicus	0.278	(0.049)	0.277	(0.050)
Same Law School	−0.020	(0.029)	−0.027	(0.029)
DJ Sitting by Designation (Appellate)	−0.022	(0.025)	−0.024	(0.025)
Prior Judicial Experience (Appellate)	−0.044	(0.017)	−0.044	(0.017)
Female Lower Court Judge	−0.068	(0.027)	−0.068	(0.027)
Minority Lower Court Judge	0.171	(0.024)	0.169	(0.024)
Civil Rights	0.404	(0.017)	0.402	(0.017)
Habeas	0.078	(0.030)	0.078	(0.030)
Caseload	0.035	(0.012)	0.035	(0.012)
Year	−0.006	(0.001)	−0.006	(0.001)
Intercept	11.133	(2.215)	11.384	(2.217)
N	35,175		35,175	
AIC	38640.6		38589.1	
BIC	38869.2		38843.1	

7
Collegiality and the Language of Dissent

Introduction

After examining the impact of judicial relationships across hierarchical boundaries, we return to considering how judges interact with those on their own court. As we have shown throughout this book, appellate judges are only human. They are subject to the same concerns and considerations as anyone in a professional environment composed of people who anticipate working closely with one another over a long period. Federal appellate judges serve life terms and can only shape policy with the cooperation of their colleagues. They spend a significant amount of time in one another's company. This environment incentivizes judges to manage their relationships with an eye to both substantive cooperation and general harmony. As a result, it is unsurprising that in previous chapters we have found that judges who spend more time with each other can be less likely to publicly dissent from each other's opinions. Armed with evidence that collegiality can motivate a judge's *vote*, we now explore if collegiality can shift the *content* of a judge's dissenting opinion.

Dissenting opinions are not necessarily a negative feature of an appellate court system. Although there can be good reasons to limit the extent of public disagreement, the public may well benefit from hearing minority views. Throughout history there have been examples of ringing dissents that ultimately became the conscience of future generations. Among the most prominent examples is in Justice Harlan's dissent in *Plessy v. Ferguson*, with well-known phrases such as "There is no caste here" (Tushnet 2008). While dissents in the courts of appeals are both less likely and receive little public attention, they can play an important role too. For example, the well-respected Judge Henry Friendly, who served on the Second Circuit from 1959 to 1986, solidified his reputation through producing more than one hundred high-quality dissents during his career (Boudin 2011). One of his dissents was even directly incorporated by a Supreme Court opinion that stated, upon review, "We agree with the dissent" (Boudin 2011, 893).[1]

The presence of public disagreement is not the only factor that determines whether the impact of a dissent, internally and externally, is predominantly negative or positive. Even once a judge decides to make their minority views available to the public, the effect of such a decision will depend on how those views are expressed. Disagreement is not inevitably disagreeable. A dissenter can express her divergence from the majority opinion in an apologetic tone, benign legal terms, or starkly critical language. Judges traditionally treat one another with considerable professional respect, but they can express disagreements over the law in vehement terms.

---

[1] The case was *Schweiker v. Hansen*, 450 U.S. 785, 788 (1981).

The Elevator Effect. Morgan L.W. Hazelton, Rachael K. Hinkle, and Michael J. Nelson, Oxford University Press.
© Oxford University Press 2023. DOI: 10.1093/oso/9780197625408.003.0007

160   THE ELEVATOR EFFECT

We posit that the collegial relationships among appellate judges play a role in this variation. They face a trade-off regarding the language that they use in a dissenting opinion: starkly hostile or caustic language may negatively affect collegiality and increase the likelihood that the dissenting judge's policy position is publicized or influential in future cases (Bryan and Ringsmuth 2016; Hinkle and Nelson 2018a). Thus, the language judges use reflects a policy-collegiality trade-off. We theorize that collegiality affects the level of politeness and rudeness they use to express disagreement. Once a judge decides to publish a dissent, both extensive service with the majority opinion author and the anticipation of many future interactions should lead to dissenting language that is more polite and less rude. Such collegial contacts should also dampen the effect that ideology has on the tone of dissents.

We test these hypotheses using dissenting opinions in the U.S. Courts of Appeals and the Supreme Court. We use our search and seizure database that includes every published circuit opinion citing the Fourth Amendment of the U.S. Constitution from 1953 to 2010. Although dissents are relatively rare at the circuit level, this large dataset includes 1,012 dissenting opinions. We also examine the 3,627 dissents in Supreme Court cases with oral arguments from 1955 to 2009. Our results indicate that collegiality concerns affect the expression of disagreement among federal appellate judges both directly and indirectly. For circuit judges, we find that having chambers in the same city and a higher probability of future interactions with the majority opinion author lead a dissenter to frame a dissent in ways that are more conducive to future healthy relationships. Moreover, as we anticipate, there is also evidence that collegial concerns can dampen the effect of ideological distance on the language of dissent. There is less evidence in the Supreme Court context. Justices can actually become less polite and more rude to each other as they serve together longer. However, they are less confrontational with long-term colleagues, at least when those colleagues have similar ideological leanings.

The Context and Complexity of Dissent

Judges on appellate courts resolve cases based on majority rule. In the United States, judges have the opportunity to publicize their disagreement with the majority's decision in a separate opinion.[2] As discussed in Chapters 3 and 4, there are three major types of separate opinions: a dissenting opinion, in which a judge disagrees with the outcome; a concurring opinion, in which the judge disagrees with the rationale (but agrees with the outcome); and a hybrid that is part dissent and part concurrence (Corley 2010). We focus on pure dissents in this chapter because they signal a greater level of disagreement. Reaching different conclusions about who should win or lose a case presents the greatest potential strain on relationships among judges. As a result, it provides an opportunity to consider the effects of collegial considerations where they are most likely to matter.

---

[2] This practice varies around the world. Some courts universally present a united front to the public (Ginsburg 2010).

COLLEGIALITY AND THE LANGUAGE OF DISSENT   161

Judges write dissents in a complex institutional context. That background is important to understand when examining the linguistic choices dissenters make. A fundamental consideration when examining any text is the author's audience, as the targeted readers may well affect the judge's language choices (Krewson 2019). As is often the case, dissents have multiple audiences (Goźdź-Roszkowski 2020; Krewson 2019; Vass 2017; Varsava 2021; Zilis and Wedeking 2020). A dissenter's first key audience is their own colleagues (Corley and Ward 2020; Goźdź-Roszkowski 2020; Vass 2017). The goal at this stage is not persuasion. The fact that a judge is publishing a dissenting opinion means that persuasion is no longer possible (in either direction): the judge has already lost (Corley and Ward 2020; Vass 2017).

To date, the scholarship that considers the relationship between separate opinions and the majority opinion in the same case focuses primarily on how drafts of the dissent can influence the majority opinion (Corley and Ward 2020) or coalition (Zilis and Wedeking 2020). Judges themselves often cite dissents' tendency to push majority opinion authors to make their own opinions clearer and better as a benefit of such writings (see, e.g., Ginsburg 2010). Corley and Ward (2020) explore how variation in the language of dissents can generate direct references in the majority opinion. They find that majorities are more likely to explicitly reference dissents with a more negative emotional tone, reflecting the potential impact of such separate opinions (Corley and Ward 2020).

Although scholars have explored many facets of dissent influence (at least in the Supreme Court), their impact on the relationships among justices remains largely unexamined. We do not propose to examine that dynamic directly, as it is impractical to measure the ebb and flow of relationships among judges. However, we can observe whether they act in a manner consistent with keeping collegiality concerns in mind when crafting the parameters of public disagreement. There is good reason to expect appellate judges to do exactly that. A judge's relationships with her colleagues affect their ability to collaborate and communicate in future cases as well as general quality of life. The existence of such collegial relationships increases the costs of publicizing disagreements with fellow judges (see Epstein, Segal, and Spaeth 2001; Goelzhauser 2015). In short, "repeated negative dissenting opinions could decrease other justices' respect for and willingness to compromise with the offending justice in future opinion negotiations" (Bryan and Ringsmuth 2016, 167). Additionally, such behavior may endanger social relationships among judges. The desire to avoid such negative consequences may affect how they frame their disagreement in a particular case.

Certainly, judges who repeatedly write acerbic opinions draw the attention, and often criticism, of the legal world and beyond. In just one example, Judge Lawrence VanDyke of the Ninth Circuit has issued a series of opinions that have raised eyebrows among judges and journalists (e.g., Ford 2002). As The Recorder (2021) noted in an article about a particularly "fiery dissent": "Since taking the bench in January 2020, VanDyke has not held back from lambasting his Ninth Circuit colleagues, accusing majorities of making a 'blatantly inappropriate power grab' in one matter and engaging 'in mischief' and 'some good old-fashioned judge-jitsu' in others." In another case, Judge VanDyke included a concurrence that was a draft of an opinion that the full circuit might issue to reverse the decision of the panel. It was also widely seen as being rude and unprofessional (e.g., Alder 2022). A former court of appeals clerk we interviewed (C4) described it as "fucking crazy." It made them concerned that "collegiality is tanking." Summarizing reporting on a biting dissent from Judge VanDyke that came out more recently, Bashman (2022) wrote: "Circuit Judge Lawrence VanDyke continues his campaign to win the Ninth Circuit's Mr. Congeniality award." The attention that rude dissents and other opinions receive indicates that there is a perception that such behavior is harmful and should be avoided.

There is evidence from our interviews that collegiality may influence opinion language in this way. For example, as part of the "unwritten rules" in J1's circuit, there is "no direct criticism regarding reasoning and logic but one can present their own interpretation and different logic." They noted that "collegiality affects how to write a dissent," specifically that dissents should be written "respectfully." J2 noted that one can "disagree in an agreeable manner" which is "better off for all." "We won't always agree." But it is important there is "mutual respect and no singling out regarding a judge with an unpopular view or a view associated with one side or another." J4 thought relationships mattered to "how [opinions] are written. People keep a careful eye on the rhetoric." This results in "fewer dissents and separate opinions and they are narrow. Any suggestion of impropriety gets a chilly reception." They noted that they are "careful and sparing with a disagreeable tone." In their circuit, the norm was that separate opinions should be kept "in terms of merits and facts and not allegations of ill motives." J5 believes that disagreement on panels is generally "amicable in ways that are vastly different than what you see on MSNBC or Fox News."

Other sources also provide indications that judges care about how their language affects each other. Judges can directly consult each other to help moderate the tone of their opinions. Rice (2021) reported that "[w]hen John Roberts was a judge on the appeals court, he and Garland implemented a process called 'de-snarking.' The liberal and the conservative read over each other's opinions to make sure neither said anything too heated." Garland was quoted as saying, "The idea is that these sort of clever negative cuts toward judges on the other side are both unnecessary and unhelpful.... Judges are human beings, and they don't like to be attacked in that sort of snarky way either, however thick-skinned you think we are" (Rice 2021). Occasionally, judges' dislike of such attacks makes its way into opinions. Judge Kevin Newsom once noted of an Eleventh Circuit colleague's dissent, "spicy rhetoric doesn't enhance its argument— but rather pretty severely diminishes it, to my mind—it does, I fear, corrode the collegiality that has historically characterized this great Court" (McDonald 2020).

However, while collegiality can motivate dissenters to choose phrases calculated to mollify their colleagues, other audiences may push the language of dissent in the opposite direction. Although majority opinions shape policy, dissents have the potential to influence as well. One of the classic purposes scholars and commentators cite for why judges invest effort in crafting separate opinions is to influence future jurists (Bryan and Ringsmuth 2016; Corley and Ward 2020; Ginsburg 2010; Zilis and Wedeking 2020). Anecdotes and pithy quotes abound to describe how future judges are an important audience for dissents (Corley and Ward 2020; Ginsburg 2010; Hinkle and Nelson 2018a). For example, Chief Justice Hughes described a dissent as "an appeal to the brooding spirit of the law, to the intelligence of a future day" (Hughes 1928, 67–68). Language choice is one factor among many that can shape which dissents have future impact. Hinkle and Nelson (2018a) show that dissenting opinions with more memorable language, including negative emotional appeals, are more likely to be cited by the U.S. Supreme Court in future majority opinions.

In addition to future judicial audiences, dissenting judges can also craft their message with external audiences in mind. For example, language may be directed to elected officials to plea for legislation to overturn the effects of a majority's ruling (Bryan and Ringsmuth 2016; Ginsburg 2010). Circuit court judges may write dissents to maximize the possibility of review either by the full circuit en banc or by the Supreme Court (Hinkle, Nelson, and Hazelton 2020). It is also possible that dissenters appeal to the public, typically via the media (Bryan and Ringsmuth 2016; Denison, Wedeking, and Zilis 2020; Krewson 2019). Additionally, judges may seek to persuade litigants and lawyers to continue to bring future cases to courts (Bryan and Ringsmuth 2016).

To get the attention of these external audiences, judges have a linguistic tool at hand—using a distinctly negative tone. Research finds that such negativity is more successful at generating news coverage but notes that there is likely a limit to how negative a dissent can be without risking collegial relations with one's colleagues (Bryan and Ringsmuth 2016; Zilis and Wedeking 2020). Furthermore, negativity in majority opinions can lead to media coverage that is more negative in tone, which may undermine the Court's legitimacy (Denison, Wedeking, and Zilis 2020). This is likely why majority opinions use less disagreeable rhetoric in cases where the public is likely to pay attention and disagree with the Court (Wedeking and Zilis 2018). It is similarly possible that negativity in dissents might also contribute to more critical media coverage. Consequently, it is unsurprising that scholars have speculated that harsh phrasing in dissents might harm the Court's legitimacy (Hume 2019; Zilis and Wedeking 2020) while respectful language could conversely bolster legitimacy (Cross and Pennebaker 2014; Note 2011).

In our interviews, J6 voiced similar concerns, stating that when separate opinions suggest positive interpersonal relationships, it "reflects better on the judiciary. It is important for institutional reputation." They noted that "aside from moral authority," the judiciary famously has "no standing army" and "needs other branches to enforce" their edicts. The "more we tear each other apart, the more others ignore our opinions and thumb their noses at them. The institution benefits as a whole from [more civil opinions]."

When drafting a dissent, a judge's many audiences create a multitude of considerations to juggle. As discussed previously, scholars have provided intriguing evidence regarding how many of these considerations might shape the language of dissent. Here, we extend that important work by considering how the collegial concerns generated by a small group environment play a role in how judges choose to express their disagreements publicly.

The Impact of Language on Relationships

There is considerable scholarly work devoted to understanding how people strategically use language to navigate and construct relationships with one another. While the context of discourse matters a great deal, certain broad principles are helpful in understanding the specific context of appellate legal discourse. P. Brown and Levinson

164   THE ELEVATOR EFFECT

(1987) pioneered an extensive field of research into the role of politeness in language. The multiple lines of inquiry their work spawned provide key insights for our understanding of dissenting opinions. While language is complex and nuanced (perhaps especially so in the legal context), we focus our theoretical approach by considering two types of linguistic techniques: those calculated to preserve or enhance interpersonal relationships and those likely to damage relationships (but potentially useful to accomplish other goals such as communicating with future or external audiences).

First, dissenters may seek to preserve relationships by using politeness (Breeze 2012; Harris 2001; Lakoff 1989). Just because the fundamental reason for a dissent is an underlying disagreement, that does not mean that a judge cannot also seek to reduce the potential negative effect of that dispute. In fact, Breeze (2012, 153) theorizes that dissenters "may choose to take special care in the way this criticism is expressed, with a view to long-term network issues." Scholars who study the important role of face in communications frequently point out that when a speaker engages in a "face-threatening act" (FTA), they often seek to mitigate the very threat they are making (Archer 2011; Breeze 2012; Harris 2001). This can occur in various ways, including hedging criticisms, expressing respect, emphasizing agreement, or using an indirect style (Archer 2011; Breeze 2012; Danescu-Niculescu-Mizil et al. 2013; Kurzon 2001).[3]

A dissent is a classic example of an FTA (since it necessarily argues that the majority is wrong). Therefore, dissent is a context that is ripe to observe the kinds of politeness techniques that a speaker can deploy to mitigate such FTAs (Breeze 2012). In other words, while a dissent may seem like a strange place to look for polite behavior, its very confrontational nature is what creates the societal pressure for politeness. One rarely uses the phrase "with all due respect" before paying someone a compliment. It is invariably a negative comment, combined with a desire to limit damage to a personal relationship, that generates the need for such a preface.[4]

As Yalof, Mello, and Schmidt (2011, 3) observe, "[d]issent does not have to be non-collegial, so long as disagreements are handled in a professional and respectful manner." Examples of politeness techniques from actual dissenting opinions are useful to illustrate these concepts. One method is to hedge criticism. Here are examples from excerpts of dissents, with the hedging language in italics:

(A) "But the habeas process the Court mandates will *most likely* end up looking a lot like the DTA system it replaces." –Justice John Roberts[5]

(B) "Moreover, the majority *seems* to work under the *perhaps* erroneous conclusion that it was solely Agent Arwine's evidence that was presented to the grand jury...." –Judge Gerald Bard Tjoflat, Fifth Circuit[6]

A second method is to express respect, deference, or constraint.

---

[3] While it is plausible that excessive politeness can go too far and generate negative reactions such as annoyance, we expect that the countervailing concerns in the context of dissenting opinions are likely to keep this extreme from occurring.

[4] This is taking aside the issue of sarcasm or irony. While these are difficult to detect, they tend to accompany more overt and readily observable rudeness (Yalof, Mello, and Schmidt 2011).

[5] *Boumediene v. Bush*, 553 U.S. 723, 802 (2008).

[6] *Rodriguez v. Ritchey*, 539 F.2d 394, 402 (1976).

COLLEGIALITY AND THE LANGUAGE OF DISSENT   165

(C) "Hence, with all respect for the strength of the opposed view, I dissent." –Justice William O. Douglas[7]

(D) "With due respect to the majority, I dissent from this radical departure from American traditions." –Justice William O. Douglas[8]

This particular politeness technique has not gone unnoticed by the legal world. Scholars have frequently noted that Supreme Court justices routinely express respect while saying they dissent (Denison, Wedeking, and Zilis 2020; Hinkle and Nelson 2018a; Hume 2019; Note 2011). Circuit judges also use this technique.

(E) "I therefore must and do respectfully dissent." –Judge Kermit E. Bye, Eighth Circuit[9]

(F) "With deference, I think both the Ninth Circuit and the majority have stood the Act on its head." –Judge Julia Smith Gibbons, Sixth Circuit[10]

(G) "Respectful of the views of my colleagues who join in the majority opinion, I am constrained to record my dissent." –Judge Clifford O'Sullivan, Sixth Circuit[11]

Finally, dissenters can mitigate the FTA inherent in a dissent by emphasizing agreement (to the extent possible).

(H) "Thus, although I agree with most of the Court's reasoning and specifically with its jurisdictional holdings, I respectfully dissent from its conclusion concerning the enforceability of the arbitration agreement." –Justice John Paul Stevens[12]

(I) "And while I also agree with much of the Court's reasoning in Parts I and II of its opinion, I believe the Court goes too far in commenting on issues that are not directly before us and that have not been fully briefed." –Justice John Paul Stevens[13]

(J) "Although I agree with much in the majority opinion, I respectfully dissent because I see no basis for Murphy's malicious prosecution claim under the Fourth Amendment." –Judge Dennis Jacobs, Second Circuit[14]

(K) "[M]y colleagues [in the majority] make several other suggestions for improving the accuracy and fairness of the FBI criminal data collection and dissemination, most of which appear worthy of serious consideration." –Judge Malcolm R. Wilkey, D.C. Circuit[15]

Second, there are a variety of reasons dissenters may choose to be rude despite the potential damage to collegiality. According to Finegan (2020, 68), "the justices' words

---

[7] *H. K. Porter Co. v. NLRB*, 397 U.S. 99, 111 (1970).
[8] *Johnson v. Louisiana*, 406 U.S. 356, 381 (1972).
[9] *United States v. Coleman*, 603 F.3d 496, 503 (2010).
[10] *NLRB v. Pincus Brothers, Inc.*, 620 F.2d 367, 398 (1980).
[11] *United States v. Sanchez*, 509 F.2d 886, 890 (1975).
[12] *Southland Corp. v. Keating*, 465 U.S. 1, 21 (1984).
[13] *Gonzalez v. Crosby*, 545 U.S. 524, 539–40 (2005).
[14] *Murphy v. Lynn*, 118 F.3d 938, 953 (1997).
[15] *Tarlton v. Saxbe*, 507 F.2d 1116, 1142 (1974).

166 THE ELEVATOR EFFECT

have teeth—and can bite." As Locher and Watts (2005, 11) point out, "[i]mpolitic behavior is thus just as significant in defining relationships as appropriate/politic or polite behavior." Like politeness, the use of impolite or rude language is also an element of "relational work" or "facework" (Bousfield 2008; Dynel 2015). One of the elements of research on the topic of impoliteness that is particularly intriguing in relation to dissents is that the expectations within a community of practice are critical to whether a particular choice of words is rude (Harris 2001; Kurzon 2001; Tracy 2011). As Locher and Watts (2005, 29) put it, "politeness, like beauty, is in the eye of the beholder." For example, in the context of appellate oral arguments, judges do not need to refrain from interruptions as a matter of politeness because it is not expected (Tracy 2011). However, a failure to use a politeness technique expected within the context of a particular type of discourse is rude and can be interpreted as an intentional effort to exacerbate conflict (Dynel 2015; García 2014; Harris 2001; Lakoff 1989). When judges conclude their dissent with a summary statement, that sign-off is expected to have a politeness technique such as "I respectfully dissent." Simply saying "I dissent" is seen as rude (Denison, Wedeking, and Zilis 2020; Hinkle and Nelson 2018a; Hume 2019; Note 2011). One of the Supreme Court clerks we interviewed (S4) also noted this difference between "I dissent vs. I respectfully dissent." Here are some examples.

(L) "From this misguided effort, I dissent." –Justice Byron White[16]
(M) "On this ground, I dissent." –Judge Nathaniel R. Jones, Sixth Circuit[17]

A person can also use language that is explicitly rude by directly addressing critiques to a specific source or by using intensifying words such as "very" to increase or boost the aggressiveness of language (Dynel 2015; García 2014; Harris 2001). Consider the following progression: "The strict scrutiny standard should not be applied"; "The majority was wrong to apply the strict scrutiny standard"; "The majority was completely wrong to apply the strict scrutiny standard." Both directness and intensifiers can be used, either independently or in conjunction, to make a rhetorical blow land with greater force. The following excerpts illustrate each technique in turn and then a combination of both. Intensifiers are in italics and direct references are in bold.

Directness:

(N) "Today **the Court** launches a missile to kill a mouse." –Justice Harry Blackmun[18]

Intensifiers:

(O) "The suggestion is *plainly* wrong" –Justice William J. Brennan Jr.[19]

Directness + Intensifiers:

---

[16] *Bowen v. American Hospital Association,* 476 U.S. 610, 665 (1986).
[17] *United States v. Savoca,* 761 F.2d 292, 302 (1985).
[18] *Lucas v. South Carolina Coastal Council,* 505 U.S. 1003, 1036 (1992).
[19] *U.S. Industries/Federal Sheet Metal, Inc. v. Director, Office of Workers' Compensation Programs,* 455 U.S. 608, 619 (1982).

(P) "*Truly*, the Court giveth, and the Court taketh away." –Justice William J. Brennan Jr.[20]

(Q) "[T]he majority fails to consider these *clearly* relevant factors." –Judge Stephen Reinhardt, Ninth Circuit[21]

In summary, a variety of linguistic techniques can be used to enhance or harm the relationships between two people. On one hand, politeness techniques such as hedging criticism, expressing respect, and emphasizing agreement where possible can shore up good feeling even in the face of disagreement. On the other hand, rude approaches including withholding expected politeness techniques, direct address, and intensifying criticism may risk damaging personal relationships.

Collegiality and the Language of Dissent

When two people are engaged in a single-shot relationship, they don't need to care about collegiality. While basic politeness may well be observed as a matter of social convention, such a speaker is not motivated to use politeness and avoid rudeness as strategies to enhance or preserve the interpersonal relationship for future interactions. In the judicial context, Kurzon (2001) posits that appellate judges have little reason to use politeness strategies in the opinion language they direct toward lower court judges they are reversing.[22] Conversely, two people who see each other frequently over many years face heightened collegiality concerns. For this reason, Kurzon (2001) further theorizes that appellate judges will be polite when addressing dissenting colleagues. Collegiality concerns are particularly strong in small groups—when co-workers cannot escape each other—and in situations where colleagues will work together for long periods. This precisely describes the context of federal appellate courts. After all, as Cross and Pennebaker (2014, 877) state, "[e]ven dissents may be influenced by collegiality."

Our interviews also indicate that collegiality matters to opinion language. J7 believed that positive interpersonal relationships reduce "personal attacks regarding character, intelligence, and motives" in opinions that are "very harmful" in their view. When such language appears in a draft, the chief judge will intervene and ask that such language is removed. Other judges in the circuit will alert the chief judge and ask them to intervene. The chief judge will ask the author to "tone down" the language. "If that doesn't work, the chief judge contacts a colleague who is close to the [author]." The chief judge will ask the author's close colleague to intercede and ask the author to change the language. "It hasn't happened recently, but in the past and when it fails, it is in the headlines." That is what they are "trying to avoid." S4 noted that collegiality caused "different tacks in writing. There was variation, many justices won't criticize

---

[20] *United States v. Valenzuela-Bernal*, 458 U.S. 858, 880 (1982).

[21] *United States v. Hudson*, 100 F.3d 1409, 1424 (1996).

[22] We do not examine the effect of collegiality on the language directed to lower court judges, but it is an intriguing area for future study, especially in light of our findings in the previous chapter that the frequency of interaction can affect reversal behavior.

168   THE ELEVATOR EFFECT

other justices in decisions." They attributed care regarding language to justices "trying to learn the lessons of history."

Yet working in a small group does not always lead to careful and respectful phrasing. S1 noted that there is more "vehemence" in "today's opinions and dissents. At the time [they clerked], it was not so [vehement]." They "hope and think maybe [the justices] are still friends." When asked if negativity in opinions mattered, S1 said, "Yes, it is fair to say it mattered regarding justice interactions." Relatedly, J6 reported that "there have been some spicy opinions in the last few terms that tested bounds. [...] Some judges like colorful language." When asked what makes spicy or colorful language more likely, J6 replied that "contentious issues" increase both, while "very technical issues" tend not to do so. "Some judges (generally not my colleagues) enjoy a turn of a phrase" and the public reception of the phrase. Overall, we expect dissenting judges to employ both politeness and rudeness in light of the relational costs and benefits each provides.

Archer (2011, 14) points out that "managing relationships is a primary concern within every arena of human interaction ... legal and otherwise." Relationships between people shape their communication strategies (García 2014; Locher and Watts 2005). We theorize that interpersonal relationships among judges can potentially shape the language of dissent. Both past contact and anticipated future interactions can play a role in how judges craft their dissents. First, we consider the impact of past relationships. The more extensively two judges have interacted, the greater opportunity they have to get to know each other well and build respect and camaraderie.[23] Greater respect may lead to more extensive use of politeness as a method of demonstrating that respect, even, or especially, in the face of disagreement.

However, there is also theory to suggest that perhaps the opposite effect might emerge. P. Brown and Levinson (1987) point to social distance between speaker and hearer as one of the factors that conditions how people use politeness techniques. Specifically, as social distance shrinks and individuals become increasingly familiar with one another, the need for politeness techniques is reduced and they become less worried about threatening a colleague's face (P. Brown and Levinson 1987; Keltner et al. 2001). For example, one study of basketball campers found that the participants heckled each other in more hostile terms later in the camp than they did on the first day (Keltner et al. 2001). Consequently, it may also be possible that more extensive past relationships lead to judges being less polite and more rude.

Second, we turn to forward-looking language choices. When a dissenting judge knows that they will be interacting with the author of the majority opinion extensively in the future, the dissenter will have increased concerns about collegiality compared to when they are unlikely to interact with the majority opinion writer much going forward. For example, in the U.S. Courts of Appeals, a dissenter would have little reason to worry about future relationship dynamics when the majority opinion is written by a judge from another court sitting by designation. Conversely, that same dissenter may be very concerned about how their dissent will be received if the majority opinion is written by a colleague with chambers down the hall. Politeness can

---

[23] Considerable time spent in close professional contact will not inevitably generate respect, but we anticipate that these tend to be correlated in a formal, professional legal setting.

enhance or preserve relationships, and rudeness can damage relationships. Therefore, we hypothesize that *both more extensive past contacts as well as an expectation of more future interactions with the majority opinion author will lead a dissenter to use more politeness and less rudeness in their dissent.*

Next, as discussed in previous chapters, we also expect collegiality and ideological disagreement to each condition the effect the other has on dissenting language. Scholars have theorized that dissents may contain more caustic and harsh rhetoric when the ideological distance between the dissenter and majority opinion writer is greater. In this vein, Krewson (2019) finds that greater distance is associated with more "sensational" language in dissents. This finding makes sense as judges are more likely to express fundamental disagreements in more emphatic terms. Suppose a dissenter has a relatively mild divergence. In that case, the impact of collegiality on rude language might be minimal simply because the dissenter does not have much incentive to use rudeness strategies in the first place. However, when the disagreement is more extreme, a dissenter may use more extensively rude language. As a result, this is where collegiality has the greatest potential to dampen and tone down dissenting language. In short, *collegiality should have the greater impact when the distance between the dissenter and the majority opinion author is greatest.*

Finally we consider how the effect of ideological distance might be conditional on collegiality. The role of ideology on language choice in dissents is substantially different from the role of ideology on the decision to dissent. A liberal judge is more likely to dissent from a conservative colleague than from a similarly minded colleague. But conditional on the decision to dissent, the role of ideology is less straightforward. It is not necessarily the case that a judge will feel more strongly about a disagreement with an ideological opponent than an ally. Hume (2019) finds that although there is some indication that harshness in Supreme Court dissents is associated with ideological distance in the 1980s, more recent data reveal the opposite effect, with justices directing more caustic language toward their ideological allies. Hume (2019) theorizes that his findings reflect a shaming mechanism whereby caustic language is used to impose substantial costs on disagreement to incentive a plausible ally (i.e., ideologically similar judge) to agree with one in the future. To the extent this is the case, concerns about relationships with one's colleagues should reduce the use of such a heavy-handed approach which is likely to have deleterious consequences for interpersonal relationships. Therefore, we hypothesize that *the effect of the ideological distance between a dissenter and the majority opinion author on dissenting language will be dampened under circumstances of more extensive past relationships or more frequent anticipated future interactions.*

Measuring Politeness and Rudeness

Our approach to quantifying politeness and rudeness in judicial opinions is to measure objective linguistic elements that are associated with these concepts. The primary benefits of this approach are that our measures are objective and scalable. The complexity of language poses difficulties for constructing largely automated computational methods for capturing politeness and rudeness strategies in language

170 THE ELEVATOR EFFECT

(Danescu-Niculescu-Mizil et al. 2013). However, we can isolate three aspects of language that provide key insights into the relational effects of language in a dissent: the emotional tone, the nature of the summary declaration of dissent, and the extent to which the dissent addresses the majority's arguments directly or indirectly. We now proceed to discuss each of these factors in turn.

The first linguistic element is the amount and direction of emotional language in dissenting opinions. This is a common focus of research on judicial opinions (Black et al. 2016; Corley and Ward 2020; Hume 2019). Some scholars look at overall tone on a scale from negative to positive (Corley and Ward 2020; Hume 2019), while others look at negative and positive terms separately (Hinkle and Nelson 2018a). Words with positive emotional affect are associated with a more polite tone and can generally be expected to mollify, or at least not antagonize, one's audience (Breeze 2012; Danescu-Niculescu-Mizil et al. 2013). Using negative emotional words, on the other hand, indicates rudeness. Such language may well irritate the judge toward whom it is directed (Corley and Ward 2020; Hume 2019).[24]

We examine the usage of different kinds of emotional language separately. If we used a single measure of tone, a dissent with 50 positive and 50 negative words would look the same as a dissent with 10 of each. By using separate measures, we can explore the quantity as well as direction of such language. This measurement approach also reflects the expectation from linguistic theory that politeness and rudeness strategies are separate processes that may be driven by different considerations (Bousfield 2008; Dynel 2015). We use the positive and negative emotion categories from the Linguistic Inquiry Word Count (LIWC) software (Pennebaker, Booth, and Francis 2007) to calculate the number of positive and negative words in each dissent. These LIWC variables have been shown to be valid measures of expressions of emotion (Kahn et al. 2007) and useful as applied to legal writing (Black et al. 2016; Bryan and Ringsmuth 2016; Corley and Ward 2020; Cross and Pennebaker 2014; Denison, Wedeking, and Zilis 2020; Wedeking and Zilis 2018; Zilis and Wedeking 2020).[25] Circuit dissents contain an average of 57 positive and also 57 negative words while Supreme Court dissents have an average of 49 positive and 37 negative words.[26]

For our second measure of politeness and rudeness, we focus on the succinct summary that usually concludes (and occasionally leads off) a dissenting opinion (Goźdź-Roszkowski 2020). As mentioned previously, legal scholars have frequently noted that a Supreme Court justice using the bare phrase "I dissent" is expressing a particularly high level of pique (Denison, Wedeking, and Zilis 2020; Hinkle and Nelson 2018a; Hume 2019; Note 2011). This often-observed nuance of legal language is a specific example of the broader phenomenon that one technique for being rude is to withhold expected measures of politeness (Dynel 2015; García 2014; Harris 2001; Lakoff 1989). One of the informal conventions that has developed in the Supreme Court over the past few decades is the practice of expressing respect alongside a statement of dissent.

---

[24] There is also evidence that using negative emotional language in legal argumentation can reduce credibility (Black et al. 2016). This possibility would pose an additional reason for judges to minimize such language.

[25] We have modified these dictionaries slightly where the legal context requires some modification because a handful of legal terms of art fail to retain the emotional content present in a more general context.

[26] The datasets from which these, and other, summaries are calculated are described below.

COLLEGIALITY AND THE LANGUAGE OF DISSENT   171

As a result, some version of "I respectfully dissent" is the typical, polite, mode of address. Kurzon (2001) also notes that expressions of regret can be used in judicial opinions to mitigate face threatening acts. Although the "respectful" dissent gets the most attention in legal circles, expressions of regret are fairly common in dissents as well, and they serve the same function. Along similar lines, the statement of dissent can also be mitigated by citing legal compulsion or some other indication of reluctance such as "I am constrained to dissent."

In light of the expectation that justices dissent politely, stating disagreement without a politeness technique is viewed as rude. However, polite and rude are not the only two options. Historically, an overt statement of dissent was not always employed (Note 2011). More neutral forms such as "I would affirm" or "I would reverse" were often used (Note 2011). These forms are still fairly common.[27] We have automatically extracted all first-person statements of dissent and then hand-coded them into one of two categories. Each summary dissent statement is classified as polite if there is an expression of respect, regret, or compulsion and rude if there is a bare "I dissent" statement with no politeness technique. We code all remaining dissenting opinions that contain a different linguistic formulation that avoids this dynamic of explicit dissent as neither polite nor rude, but neutral. This approach develops the previously employed technique in this literature of simply using a binary variable that indicates whether a dissent used a bare "I dissent" without an expression of respect (Hinkle and Nelson 2018a; Hume 2019). The results of our more extensive coding efforts are quite interesting. The rate of rude dissents is the same in circuit and Supreme Court dissents: 21 percent. However, the picture is quite different for polite dissents. Circuit judges use an expressly respectful polite form of dissent 53 percent of the time, while justices do so only 31 percent of the time. Figure 7.1 shows how usage of these forms has changed over time.

Our third and final metric of how judges can use language to shape their relationships with their colleagues is the extent to which they directly engage the majority opinion author. Indirectly stating a disagreement is a classic politeness technique used to mitigate face threatening acts in a variety of contexts (Breeze 2012; Danescu-Niculescu-Mizil et al. 2013), including appellate opinions (Kurzon 2001). Conversely, directly addressing the object of disagreement raises the stakes and makes an attack more personal. In fact, many examples of the most caustic rhetoric seen in dissenting opinions contain language that directly references the majority. The examples provided earlier, especially quotes (N) and (Q), illustrate this technique. To capture the extent of direct address to the majority, we utilized a combination of automated and human coding. First, we used Python code to extract every sentence that contained the phrase "the Court," "the majority," or, for circuit cases, "the panel." Next, we read each sentence to eliminate those that refer to a precedent, the lower court, or otherwise did not reference the majority in the case at hand.[28] We create a variable, Number

---

[27] While the conventions related to expression of respect in dissents has not been discussed or explored in the context of circuit courts, we anticipate that the expression of respect, and lack thereof, should operate in a similar way as it does in the Supreme Court.

[28] This second step was necessary as 19% of the references extracted by Python in circuit dissents and 29% of them in Supreme Court dissents did not actually reference the majority opinion.

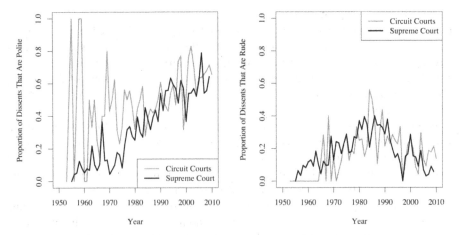

Figure 7.1 Tone of Dissents over Time: The proportion of dissents with an explicitly polite (left-hand panel) or rude (right-hand panel) sign-off by year. The gray lines show the data for circuit court dissents and the black lines show the Supreme Court data.

of Direct Sentences, that is a count of all sentences in each dissenting opinion that include a direct reference to the majority. Such references appear an average of 4.5 times per circuit dissent and 6.7 times per Supreme Court dissent.

Our measures provide a variety of different ways to test our hypotheses. The examination of positive and negative emotion separately allows us to observe whether politeness and rudeness might be affected by different factors. While we expect collegiality concerns to increase politeness and decrease rudeness, they may not necessarily operate to the same extent. Moreover, other factors such as the length of the opinion or passage of time may be associated with an increase of both polite and rude language. The way we categorize a summary dissent statement (i.e., "sign-off") as polite, neutral, or rude allows us to explore what factors push judges to behave in non-neutral ways. This is important as we do not want to assume polite behavior is the norm, but rather measure whether, and to what extent, it is. Our continuous measure of direct address is less flexible as it assumes politeness and rudeness are complements of each other. Nevertheless, it is valuable as an additional way to quantify the language of dissent.

Data and Methods

We explore the relationship between collegiality and dissenting language in both the U.S. Courts of Appeals and the Supreme Court. Studying the circuit courts is useful both because we know little about what shapes the content of dissenting opinions at that level and because it allows us to take advantage of the considerable variation in interpersonal contacts between judges across time and circuits. This enables us to test whether variation in collegial relationships has an effect on how judges dissent. Once again, we utilize our database of all published search and seizure opinions from

COLLEGIALITY AND THE LANGUAGE OF DISSENT   173

1953 to 2010, which includes 1,012 dissenting opinions in panel cases.[29] Although the Surpreme Court does not contain nearly the variation in collegial interaction evident in the circuit courts, there are differences in how long two justices have served together. Moreover, dissent is considerably more frequent, providing a rich assortment of dissenting opinions to analyze. Consequently, we also explore the relationship between collegiality and dissenting language in this context. Drawing on the Supreme Court Database[30] we use all orally argued Supreme Court cases from 1955 to 2009, which includes 3,627 dissents. While our hypotheses apply to both contexts, we do note that, as we discuss in Chapter 5, collegiality might well operate in a more restricted way at the Supreme Court level than for circuit judges.

For both the circuit and Supreme Court models, the unit of analysis is the dissenting opinion.[31] A key advantage of looking at language in this particular type of opinion is that the author can choose their own language largely free from the influence of their colleagues (Bryan and Ringsmuth 2016; Cross and Pennebaker 2014; Yalof, Mello, and Schmidt 2011; Zilis and Wedeking 2020). This also came up in our interviews. J7 informed us that a judge's "mindset is different when writing a majority opinion" than a dissenting opinion. This is true because of the other judges involved. When writing a majority opinion, J7 informed us, there has to be "compromise" and you might not be able to go "as far as you want." With a dissent, "you can just write" and "don't have to deal with requests to cite this rationale, etc., because other judges are not necessary." As a result, the language of a dissenting opinion is likely to be influenced primarily by the relationships of the dissenter.

We estimate a series of models of different types as appropriate for the various measures of polite and rude language discussed in the previous section. First, we use negative binomial regression to model both the number of positive and negative words and the number of sentences directly addressing the majority since these are all overdispersed count variables. Next, we deploy a multinomial logit model to examine how collegiality influences how a judge signs off in a dissent.[32] A neutral conclusion to a dissent is the baseline. For the Supreme Court models, standard errors are clustered on the case level since a case can have more than one dissenting opinion.

Our primary explanatory variables measure the level of interpersonal contact between each dissenter and the author of the majority opinion in a given case the same way we measure contact in Chapters 3 through 6. The first measure of interpersonal contact is whether two circuit judges have their home chambers in the same courthouse. Such colleagues should come into contact considerably more frequently than those in different courthouses, which typically also means in separate cities and even

---

[29] We exclude the small number of en banc opinions since cost-benefit analyses concerning dissents are likely to be substantially different in those particularly important and salient cases.

[30] Available at https://www.scdb.wustl.edu (Spaeth et al. 2021).

[31] We do not include opinions that are dissenting in part and concurring in part. Such opinions are likely to utilize different types of language simply because they are expressing partial, rather than full, disagreement.

[32] We use a multinomial logit rather than an ordered logit because there is reason to believe some variables, e.g., salience, might make both rude and polite sign-offs more likely than neutral ones.

174   THE ELEVATOR EFFECT

states.[33] Next, we count the years the judge and opinion author have served together at the time of the relevant case. This measure of Cotenure reflects the extent of past interactions between two judges and can easily be calculated for both circuit judges and Supreme Court justices. Finally, we measure the probability that a circuit judge will be assigned to sit on another panel with the opinion author. While this calculation is linked to circuit size, there is not a linear relationship between the number of judges in a circuit and the probability of serving together on a future panel. Therefore, we calculate the probability that the judge in question will serve on another panel with the author using the number of other active judges in each circuit and each year. This will overstate the probability somewhat because it does not account for the number of senior and visiting judges who will serve on future panels, but it is a better measure than simply using the number of judges on the circuit.

As we discussed earlier, understanding the impact collegiality may have on the content of dissents requires accounting for how similar the ideology of the dissenter is to the ideology of the opinion author. To create the necessary variables, we use Judicial Common Space (JCS) scores.[34] Ideological Distance is the absolute value of the difference between the JCS scores of the author of a dissent and the majority opinion author. Higher values indicate greater ideological disparity. Ideological Distance is interacted with Same Courthouse, Pr(Future Panel), and Cotenure, in turn, in the empirical models.

Finally, we control for features of the dissent, dissenter, case, the hierarchical configuration of courts, and time. As we discussed in Chapter 5, justices who previously clerked for the Supreme Court, served on a court of appeals, or served on the D.C. Circuit specifically may lean on those experiences to inform their perception of the importance of interpersonal relationships. This could easily affect dissenting language as well. Therefore, we control for these experiences in the Supreme Court models. The circuit courts have enough demographic diversity that in those models we can account for whether the dissenter is the same race or gender as the majority opinion author to see if these impact the content of a dissent. In all models, we control for whether the dissenter is either the chief or is new to the court. Dissenters who have less than two full years under their belt may be more hesitant or careful in their language, or they may not yet have learned the informal expectations of the institutions.

Features of the case and institutional context may also shape dissent. Salience is an important consideration. In the circuit court models we use amicus participation as a pre-decision proxy for salience. In this context such third-party advocacy is quite rare, so we create a binary indicator that equals one if there was any amicus participation

---

[33] We expect increased contact from working in the same courthouse to increase politeness and decrease rudeness. One of our interviewees speculated that it could have this effect. C4 described being in the same space as important so you can put "a face to the name" if you might say a "nasty thing about them on the page." They could think of no example of such nasty language, which they attributed to being "with them every day in the same building." They did note there were "not many contentious cases. It was not abortions and guns every day."

[34] For circuit judges, JCS scores are based on the ideology of the political elites who appointed a judge and are located on a scale from −1 (liberal) to 1 (conservative) (Epstein et al. 2007; Giles, Hettinger, and Peppers 2001; Poole 1998). Supreme Court JCS scores are on the same scale but are derived from justices' voting patterns (Epstein et al. 2007; Martin and Quinn 2002).

and zero otherwise. For the Supreme Court, we use Clark, Lax, and Rice's (2015) measure of pre-decision salience. The subject matter of the case might also affect language choices. Although our circuit data contain only search and seizure cases, we control for whether the case is civil rights, habeas, or criminal (the baseline category). For the Supreme Court data, we include issue fixed effects (Spaeth et al. 2021). Our circuit court models account for the possibility of review within the judicial hierarchy. A dissenter who is ideologically aligned with the full circuit or the Supreme Court may use linguistic techniques calculated to garner the attention of those bodies, even at the potential expense of collegiality. As a result, we control for the distance between the dissenter and the median of the full circuit and the median of the Supreme Court. Next, we control for the logged word count of the dissent as the amount of polite and rude language is almost certainly correlated with the total amount of language in an opinion. Finally, we control for the year of the dissent to allow for variation in linguistic use or informal expectations over time. Summary statistics for all variables in both datasets are available in Tables 7.A.1 and 7.A.2 in the chapter appendix.

Results: U.S. Courts of Appeals

We first examine whether there is evidence of collegiality shaping the language of dissent in the circuit courts. The regression results for all of these analyses are presented in Tables 7.B.1–7.B.3 in the chapter appendix. Figure 7.2 presents the effect of changing each variable from a low to high value[35] on the predicted number of positive and negative emotional words in a dissent. Since we expect our collegiality variables to interact with the ideological distance between a dissenter and majority opinion author, we present each of these variables at both a low and high value of each other.[36] All other variables are held at their median. Recall that we hypothesize that collegiality will affect language both directly and indirectly. First, we expect it to directly increase politeness and decrease rudeness. Consequently, we anticipate that all three collegiality variables will have a positive effect on the number of positive emotion words used and a negative effect on the number of negative emotion words employed. Furthermore, our direct effect hypotheses states that such patterns will emerge regardless of the ideological compatibility of the dissenter and majority opinion author. Figure 7.2 reveals that we do not find any evidence consistent with our direct effect hypothesis for either type of emotional language.

However, there is some evidence that supports our conditional collegiality hypothesis with respect to the use of negative emotion words. Throughout the book we have noted that collegiality might not have much "elbow room" to operate between like-minded judges who are predisposed to agree based on ideological similarity. Therefore, our conditional collegiality hypothesis is that the effects of frequent contact

[35] Throughout our discussion, a "low" level of a variable means zero for binary variables and the 25th percentile for continuous variables. A "high" level refers to one for a binary variable and the 75th percentile for a continuous variable.

[36] We present the results in this format to permit a more intuitive assessment of the interactive effects as well as provide a visual representation of the substantive size of effects.

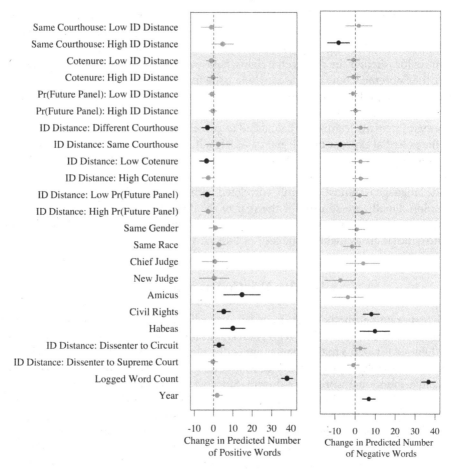

Figure 7.2 Changes in Predicted Number of Positive and Negative Emotion Words, Courts of Appeals: Estimates (and associated 95% confidence intervals) of the change in the predicted number of positive and negative emotion words generated by moving each variable from a low to high value while holding other variables at their median. Changes produced by collegiality and ideology are presented at low and high values of the other to illustrate interactive effects. Low and high values are 25th and 75th percentile for continuous variables and zero and one for binary variables. Estimates and confidence intervals in gray (instead of black) indicate that the confidence interval includes zero. Full regression estimates are available in Table 7.B.1 in the chapter appendix.

might only emerge at higher levels of ideological disagreement. We see such a pattern with respect to the effect of serving in the same courthouse on the use of negative emotional words ($\hat{\beta} = -0.43$, $p = 0.01$). Dissenters who are ideologically distant from the majority opinion author are less likely to use such negative words in their dissent when the two judges have chambers in the same courthouse compared to when they do not. We show this conditional relationship in greater detail in Figure 7.3, which

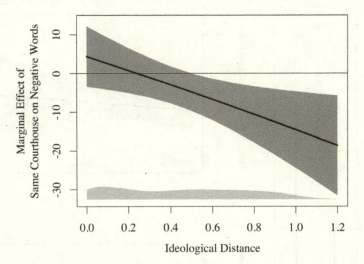

Figure 7.3 Effect of Same Courthouse on Negative Emotional Language, Courts of Appeals: This figure shows the marginal effect of Same Courthouse on the number of negative emotional words in a dissenting opinion over the entire range of Ideological Distance. The shaded region depicts the 95% confidence interval. The density plot shows the distribution of Ideological Distance in the dataset.

presents the marginal effect of Same Courthouse on negative emotion words across all values of Ideological Distance. This marginal effect is only statistically significant when Ideological Distance is 0.5 or larger. This finding is consistent with the idea that a dissenter might not be as motivated to use harsh language in the first place when dissenting from an ideological ally. When Ideological Distance is at its 75th percentile, a dissenter uses 8.3 fewer negative words when addressing a majority opinion written by a colleague housed in the same building compared to one who works elsewhere. The median number of such words used in a dissent is 41, so the change brought about by being in the same courthouse as an ideological foe is one-fifth of the total. Residing in the same courthouse is the only indicator of collegiality that shapes the amount of emotional language circuit judges use.

We also hypothesize that frequent interpersonal contacts should operate indirectly to dampen the effects of ideology. In this context we generally expect ideological disagreement to reduce the amount of positive language and increase the amount of negative language. Our conditional ideology hypothesis posits that such effects will be indistinguishable from zero at higher levels of our collegiality variables. There is consistent evidence of such a pattern in the model of positive emotional language. When two judges are in the same courthouse, have served together for a substantial number of years, or anticipate a high probability of serving together in the future, the effect of Ideological Distance on positive emotional language is not statistically significant. Conversely, Ideological Distance has a significant negative effect at low values of all three collegiality measures. Under those conditions, a circuit judge uses less positive emotional language when they are more ideologically distant from the

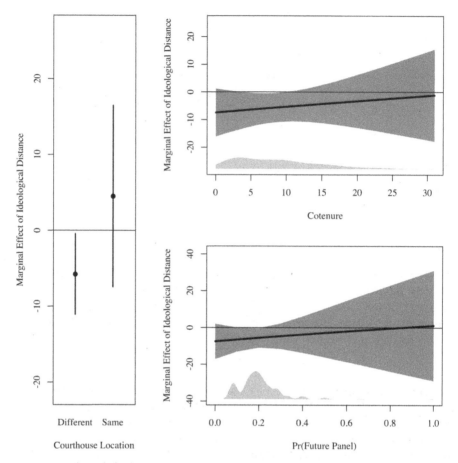

Figure 7.4 Effect of Ideology on Positive Emotional Language, Courts of Appeals: This figure shows the marginal effect of Ideological Distance on the number of positive emotional words in a dissenting opinion over the entire range of each collegiality variable. The shaded regions and bars depict the 95% confidence intervals. The density plots show the distribution of each collegiality variable.

majority opinion author. We provide greater detail in Figure 7.4 by showing the marginal effect of ideology for all values of the collegiality variables. These plots indicate a fair amount of imprecision in our estimates and warrant some caution in drawing conclusions. The left panel shows that the marginal effect of ideology is significant for different courthouse but not for same courthouse. But the difference between those two estimates is not statistically significant because of the uncertainty surrounding the estimate for same courthouse. Both of the figures on the right show that ideology is negative for low levels of Cotenure and Pr(Future Panel) and reaches nearly zero at high values of each. While this is precisely the pattern anticipated by our conditional ideology hypothesis, the fairly wide confidence intervals indicate imprecision in these estimates as well. There are some values of each collegiality variable on the right for which the marginal effect of ideology is statistically significant, but those values are quite limited.

While the positive emotion model provides some cautious support for our ideological dampening hypotheses, the results in the negative emotion model do not provide any such evidence. The only circumstance where ideology significantly predicts negative wording is when the two judges are from the same courthouse. If frequent contact dampens the effect of ideology, we would expect it to be significant for those in different courthouses only, yet we see the opposite. However, the direction of the effect of ideology for judges in the same courthouse is not the direction we would expect. Typically, one would anticipate that greater ideological distance would lead to *more* usage of negative emotional terminology. Yet when two judges are in the same courthouse, the opposite actually occurs. The dissenter uses less negative language the farther they are from the majority opinion author. Therefore, while this pattern does not fall squarely within our hypotheses, it is suggestive of collegial behavior.

Next, we turn to examine a circuit dissenter's decision to sign off their opinion with a polite, neutral, or rude summary of their disagreement from the majority. The baseline category for our multinomial logit model is a neutral approach that avoids a first-person statement of dissent. Figure 7.5 presents the results from our model by showing the changes in the predicted probability of a polite or rude dissent when moving variables from a low to high level. While Same Courthouse was the only collegiality variable to affect emotional language (at least for sufficiently high levels of Ideological Distance), we find that Cotenure and Pr(Future Panel) have an impact on the nature of a dissenter's summary conclusion. Cotenure only has a significant impact on polite sign-offs among ideological allies, which is contrary to our conditional collegiality hypothesis. Furthermore, when such allies serve together longer, they actually become *less* likely to dissent politely. Although this is contrary to what we would expect, it may reflect that strong relationships that have been forged among like-minded people over many years render linguistic politeness techniques less necessary. Unlike past contacts, anticipated future contacts operate as we hypothesize. Judges who expect a higher probability of serving with the majority opinion author in future cases are less likely to use a rude sign-off ($\hat{\beta} = -6.99$, $p = 0.001$). This effect persists regardless of the ideological distance between the two judges, which makes it consistent with our direct effect hypothesis. Figure 7.6 illustrates this effect in more detail. As dissenters anticipate a greater frequency of future contact with the majority opinion author, they become dramatically less likely to use a rude form of dissent that withholds the expected politeness techniques. When Pr(Future Panel) is set at its 25th percentile (0.15), a dissenter uses a rude tone in 23 percent of dissents compared to only 16 percent when Pr(Future Panel) is at the 75th percentile (0.25).

As with emotional language, we also find some evidence that collegiality conditions the way ideology affects the decision with respect to how to draw a dissenting opinion to a close. In fact, there are considerable similarities between our findings. There is evidence of ideological dampening for polite dissents, but not rude dissents. This

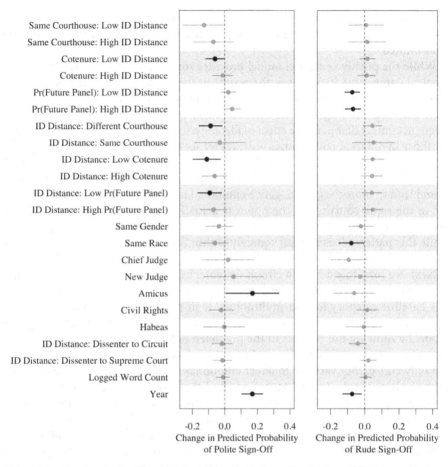

Figure 7.5 Changes in Predicted Probability of a Polite or Rude Sign-Off, Courts of Appeals: Estimates (and associated 95% confidence intervals) of the change in the predicted probability of a polite or rude sign-off generated by moving each variable from a low to high value while holding other variables at their median. Changes produced by collegiality and ideology are presented at low and high values of the other to illustrate interactive effects. Low and high values are 25th and 75th percentile for continuous variables and zero and one for binary variables. Estimates and confidence intervals in gray (instead of black) indicate that the confidence interval includes zero. Full regression estimates are available in Table 7.B.2 in the chapter appendix.

parallels our findings about positive emotional language, but not negative. The patterns we show in Figure 7.7 also echo those in Figure 7.4 to some extent. Once again, the marginal effect of ideology on polite sign-offs is significant for different courthouses only, but the difference between different and same courthouses is not significant ($\hat{\beta} = 0.10$, $p = 0.51$). The effects of ideology are not quite as imprecisely estimated for Cotenure as we saw previously. Ideological Distance has a significant negative

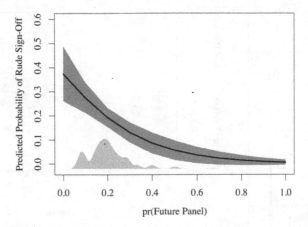

Figure 7.6 Direct Effect of Pr(Future Panel) on Rude Sign-Offs, Courts of Appeals: This figure shows the predicted probability of a rude sign-off as Pr(Future Panel) varies. The shaded region depicts the 95% confidence intervals. The density plot shows the distribution of Pr(Future Panel).

impact on the use of polite dissents if two judges have served together less than ten years. The marginal effect of ideology on the likelihood of a polite dissent ranges from −0.23 when Cotenure is only one year to −0.13 when two judges have served together for ten years. The estimates for Pr(Future Panel) are somewhat imprecise, although the range where ideological distance significantly decreases the probability of a polite dissent does contain a nontrivial portion of the data, as reflected in the density plot.

Our last model of circuit court dissenting behavior is shown in Figure 7.8, which presents the results from our model of how many times a dissenting circuit judge directly references the majority opinion. There is no evidence that either collegiality or ideology play a role in this particular linguistic choice. However, the control variables do reveal some interesting patterns. Chief judges are less likely than other judges to directly engage the majority in their dissenting opinions ($\beta = -0.35$, $p = 0.065$). This may reflect the chief's institutional commitment to harmony among colleagues. We also find more direct reference in salient cases ($\beta = 0.54$, $p = 0.005$), which may reflect that judges are more willing to risk interpersonal relationships in cases with higher stakes. Finally, we also observe that direct references to the majority have been increasing over time.

Results: Supreme Court

Next, we turn to examine the context where dissenting language has been studied previously: the Supreme Court. Although the Supreme Court does not contain nearly the variation in collegial interaction evident in the circuit courts because the Court has long maintained its size and single location, there is variation in how long two justices have served on the Court together. Therefore, our examination of the high

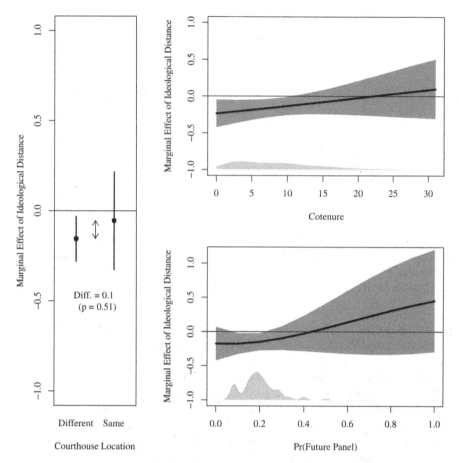

Figure 7.7 Effect of Ideology on Polite Sign-Offs, Courts of Appeals: This figure shows the marginal effect of Ideological Distance on the probability of a polite sign-off in a dissenting opinion over the entire range of each collegiality variable. The shaded regions and bars depict the 95% confidence intervals. The density plots show the distribution of each collegiality variable.

court focuses on the effects of Cotenure. Using this measure, we once again look for evidence of our three hypotheses: that collegiality directly affects dissenting language, that collegiality affects dissenting language conditional on ideological distance, and that ideology has an effect that is conditional on low levels of collegiality. The models results for our Supreme Court analyses are available in Tables 7.B.4–7.B.6 in the chapter appendix.

Figure 7.9 shows the determinants of emotional language at the Supreme Court level. As with the circuit court models, we present the effect of changing each variable from a low to high value on the predicted outcome. There is no evidence of Cotenure affecting emotional language either directly or indirectly. Nor is there any indication of ideology shaping the decision to use positive or negative words. However, there is

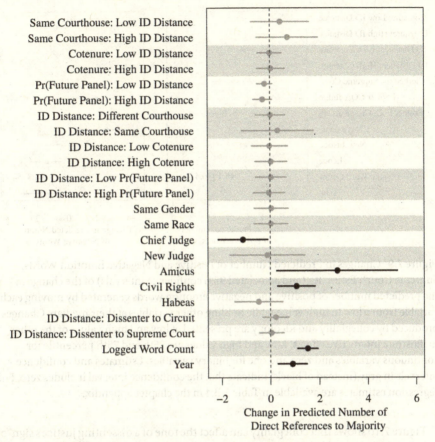

Figure 7.8 Changes in Predicted Number of Direct References to Majority, Courts of Appeals: Estimates (and associated 95% confidence intervals) of the change in the predicted number of sentences with direct references to the majority generated by moving each variable from a low to high value while holding other variables at their median. Changes produced by collegiality and ideology are presented at low and high values of the other to illustrate interactive effects. Low and high values are 25th and 75th percentile for continuous variables and zero and one for binary variables. Estimates and confidence intervals in gray (instead of black) indicate that the confidence interval includes zero. Full regression estimates are available in Table 7.B.3 in the chapter appendix.

one finding that might suggest that courts of appeals judges who are elevated to the Supreme Court might bear in mind their lower court experiences regarding the importance of collegial relationships. Such justices use fewer negative emotional words in their dissents than their peers who did not previously serve on the circuit courts ($\hat{\beta} = -0.05$, $p = 0.02$). Chief justices also use less of this type of language ($\hat{\beta} = -0.07$, $p = 0.02$). These effects are not substantially large though. The median dissent includes 23 negative emotion words and former circuit judges use only 1.8 fewer such words, while chief justices use 2.4 fewer.

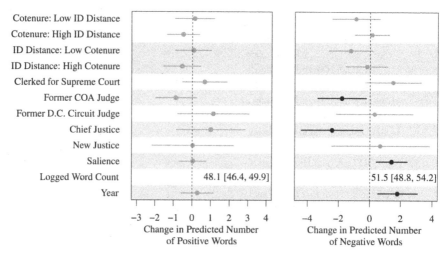

Figure 7.9 Changes in Predicted Number of Positive and Negative Emotion Words, Supreme Court: Estimates (and associated 95% confidence intervals) of the change in the predicted number of positive and negative emotion words generated by moving each variable from a low to high value while holding other variables at their median. Changes produced by collegiality and ideology are presented at low and high values of the other to illustrate interactive effects. Low and high values are 25th and 75th percentile for continuous variables and zero and one for binary variables. Estimates and confidence intervals in gray (instead of black) indicate that the confidence interval includes zero. Full regression estimates are available in Table 7.B.4 in the chapter appendix.

Figure 7.10 shows that collegiality can affect the tone of a dissenting justice's sign-off at least to some extent. When a dissenting justice has served longer with the majority opinion author, the dissenter is both less likely to use a polite sign-off ($\hat{\beta} = -0.03$, $p = 0.13$) and more likely to conclude their opinion with a caustic "I dissent" ($\hat{\beta} = 0.02$, $p = 0.17$). Not only are these findings in the opposite direction from what we expect, they are both only statistically significant at low levels of Ideological Distance, which is at odds with our conditional collegiality hypothesis. Figure 7.11 provides greater detail by displaying the marginal effect of Cotenure on both polite and rude dissents over the entire range of Ideological Distance. Cotenure significantly decreases the likelihood of a polite dissent when Ideological Distance is less than 0.71, and it significantly increases the usage of rude dissents when such distance is less than 0.84. The substantive size of these effects appear rather small, but it is important to bear in mind that these are the effects generated by a one-unit increase in Cotenure, a variable that ranges from 0 to 32. Consider two judges with the same ideology. In the first year they sit on the Court together, our model predicts they would use a polite form 46 percent of the times they dissented from the other and would use a rude sign-off in 20 percent of such dissents. Fifteen years later, those estimates would shift to 33 percent polite and 30 percent rude. It is worth noting that we found the same pattern with respect to polite sign-offs in the equivalent circuit court model. This consistency across different institutional contexts suggests that strong relationships don't always lead to

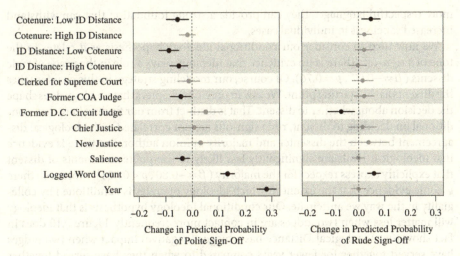

Figure 7.10 Changes in Predicted Probability of a Polite or Rude Sign-Off, Supreme Court: Estimates (and associated 95% confidence intervals) of the change in the predicted probability of a polite or rude sign-off generated by moving each variable from a low to high value while holding other variables at their median. Changes produced by collegiality and ideology are presented at low and high values of the other to illustrate interactive effects. Low and high values are 25th and 75th percentile for continuous variables and zero and one for binary variables. Estimates and confidence intervals in gray (instead of black) indicate that the confidence interval includes zero. Full regression estimates are available in Table 7.B.5 in the chapter appendix.

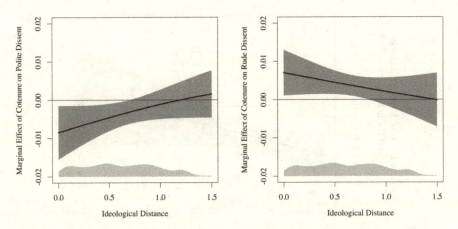

Figure 7.11 Conditional Effect of Cotenure on Polite and Rude Sign-Offs, Supreme Court: This figure shows the marginal effect of Cotenure on the probability of a polite (left-hand panel) or rude (right-hand panel) sign-off in a dissenting opinion over the entire range of Ideological Distance. The shaded regions depict the 95% confidence intervals. The density plot shows the distribution of Ideological Distance.

more respectful language. They can provide a strong foundation that can withstand increased sauciness in individual cases.

We now turn to consider our conditional ideology hypothesis as it relates to the tone of a sign-off. There is no evidence that ideology plays a role in the usage of rude dissents ($\beta = -0.07$, $p = 0.76$). Of course, our modeling strategy in this chapter takes the dissents as the starting point. We saw in previous chapters that ideology does shape the decision about whether to dissent. That is distinct from our finding here that, conditional on deciding to dissent, rude sign-offs are not correlated with ideological disagreement between the dissenter and majority opinion author. But there is evidence that ideological rivals are significantly less likely to use polite statements of dissent that explicitly express respect for the majority ($\beta = -0.80$, $p < 0.001$). Moreover, there is some evidence that the extent to which ideology operates is conditioned by collegiality in the way we anticipate. Our conditional ideology hypothesis is that ideology will matter less when two judges are in contact more frequently. Figure 7.10 does in fact show that Ideological Distance has a bigger (negative) impact when two judges have served together for fewer years compared to when they have served together for more years. That figure shows the comparison between Cotenure being held at its 25th and 75th percentile values. At those values, the difference in the marginal effect of ideology is -0.07 with a p-value of 0.15. When we hold Cotenure at its 5th and 95th percentile values (0 and 20), the difference in the marginal effect of Ideological Distance is -0.14 with a p-value of 0.04. In other words, the effect of ideology does vary based on collegiality, but that difference is only statistically significant when cotenure is varied quite substantially. Figure 7.12 shows how the effect of ideology varies over the range of Cotenure. It is helpful to compare this effect size to that of Cotenure. Consider another example in which two pairs of judges are in their first year serving

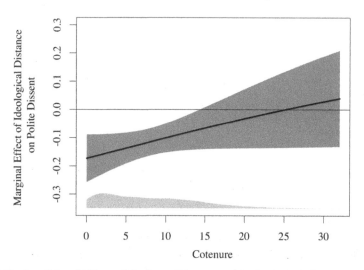

Figure 7.12 Conditional Effect of Ideological Distance on Polite Sign-Offs, Supreme Court: This figure shows the marginal effect of Ideological Distance on the probability of a polite sign-off in a dissenting opinion over the entire range of Cotenure. The shaded region depicts the 95% confidence interval. The density plot shows the distribution of Cotenure.

together. The first two judges have the same ideology score, while the second pair are as far apart from each other as it is possible to be. The first pair will use polite dissents 46 percent of the time when dissenting from each other, and the second pair will use polite dissents 22 percent of the time. This difference of 24 percent is almost the same as the difference in polite dissents generated by moving Cotenure from its minimum to maximum values (while holding Ideological Distance constant at 0).

Lastly, with Figure 7.13 we explore how collegiality affects the number of sentences with a direct references to the majority opinion. Unlike the corresponding circuit court model, we find that in the Supreme Court, both collegiality and ideology play a role for this linguistic feature. Cotenure decreases how frequently a dissenter directly addresses the majority, but only when the opinion author is ideologically proximate. The direction of this effect is what we expect, but the conditions under which it occurs defy our expectations. We expected that collegiality would operate most between rivals rather than allies. However, there is evidence of ideology being conditional on cotenure that does conform with our expectations. Namely, ideology is only significant when two justices have the fewer interpersonal contacts that come with not having served together very long. The direction of the effect is not what anticipated though. Greater ideological distance decreases the direct references to the majority.

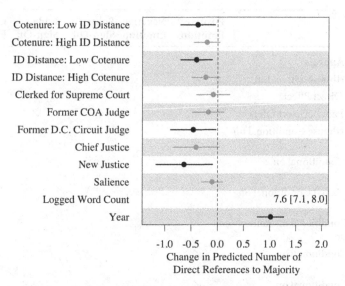

Figure 7.13 Changes in Predicted Number of Direct References to Majority, Supreme Court: Estimates (and associated 95% confidence intervals) of the change in the predicted number of sentences with direct references to the majority generated by moving each variable from a low to high value while holding other variables at their median. Changes produced by collegiality and ideology are presented at low and high values of the other to illustrate interactive effects. Low and high values are 25th and 75th percentile for continuous variables and zero and one for binary variables. Estimates and confidence intervals in gray (instead of black) indicate that the confidence interval includes zero. Full regression estimates are available Table 7.B.6 in the chapter appendix.

Conclusions

"Style may be critical to the power and influence of a dissenting opinion" (Cross and Pennebaker 2014, 876). There are, however, both costs and benefits to using disagreeable rhetoric, so judges are likely to save it for situations where it is especially needed (Zilis and Wedeking 2020). We show that this expectation is borne out, at least to some extent, in the empirical realities of decades of dissenting opinions from both the U.S. Courts of Appeals and the Supreme Court. Table 7.1 provides an overview of where we found evidence for our three hypotheses and where the results shed surprising light that can inform future theoretical developments in new directions.

Our first hypothesis is that increased collegiality directly increases politeness techniques and reduces rudeness in the language of dissent. There is only limited evidence that such is the case. However, it does emerge strongly in one context. When circuit judges anticipate working together more frequently in the future they are less likely to use the bare "I dissent" that is viewed as quite rude in judicial circles. Second, we

Table 7.1 Summary of Results, Dissenting Language: A checkmark denotes a result that is statistically significant and in the direction we hypothesize. An "x" denotes a result that is significant, but in the opposite of the hypothesized direction.

	Positive Emotion	Negative Emotion	Polite Sign-Off	Rude Sign-Off	Direct References
Courts of Appeals					
Same Courthouse, Direct Effect					
Cotenure, Direct Effect					
Pr(Future Panel), Direct Effect				✓	
Same Courthouse Conditional on Ideology		✓			
Cotenure Conditional on Ideology			x		
Pr(Future Panel) Conditional on Ideology					
Ideology Conditional on Same Courthouse	✓	x	✓		
Ideology Conditional on Cotenure	✓		✓		
Ideology Conditional on Pr(Future Panel)	✓		✓		
Supreme Court					
Cotenure, Direct Effect					
Cotenure Conditional on Ideology			x	x	
Ideology Conditional on Cotenure			✓		

hypothesized that any effect collegiality might have on the language of dissent could be moderated by ideological distance and only appear when a dissenter was sufficiently far ideologically from the majority opinion author. Such evidence also only appeared in one context. When two circuit judges have their home chambers in the same courthouse and are ideologically distant, the dissenter uses fewer negative emotional words. However, when two judges are ideological allies, being in the same courthouse is not a significant predictor of such language use.

Same Courthouse and Pr(Future Panel) were not statistically significant in several models, but they are never significant in the opposite direction from what we hypothesize. The same cannot be said for Cotenure. In fact, where Cotenure is statistically significant, it is always in the opposite direction from what we expect. When the dissenter and majority author are ideological allies, both circuit and Supreme Court dissenters who have served longer with the majority opinion author are less likely to sign off in a polite manner. Moreover, Supreme Court justices are also more likely to use a rude sign-off as Cotenure increases.

Our third hypothesis is that collegiality can indirectly impact the language of dissent by dampening the effect of Ideological Distance when the dissenter anticipates frequent interactions will lend greater importance to their interpersonal relationship with the majority opinion author. This hypothesis receives the most support in our models, although the picture that emerges is complex. We see the hypothesized ideological dampening for positive emotional words and polite sign-offs in circuit dissents and for polite sign-offs in the Supreme Court. In the first two instances, Ideological Distance is statistically significant for low levels of collegiality, and not statistically significant for high levels of collegiality. For polite dissents in the Supreme Court, ideology has a significant effect for both low and high levels of Cotenure, but the effect is more pronounced when two judges have served together for fewer years. However, in the Supreme Court, the opposite pattern is present for rude sign-offs. In that instance, Ideological Distance is significant for high levels of collegiality, but not low levels.

Language is complex, and judges have nearly infinite options available for arranging their thoughts in an opinion. Moreover, the many audiences and purposes present in the context of dissent create a potentially bewildering array of concerns and countervailing considerations that may affect linguistic choices. Nevertheless, we can delve into the content of dissenting opinions to provide evidence that collegiality concerns do color the expression of dissent on appellate courts. This is in keeping with findings that judges care about such things when they decide whether to disagree publicly in the first place. Our work here shows the business of maintaining relationships does not end when judges find themselves unable to reach a compromise. Instead, it continues to shape their behavior even as they take up the pen to explain their substantive disagreements to the world.

Our results have important ramifications for ideological accounts of judicial behavior. The fact that our analyses reveal an important conditional relationship between collegiality and the nature of a dissent suggests an important limitation to these accounts: ideology plays an important role, but the personal and professional relationships among judges condition its reach. When judges have incentives to maintain good personal and professional working relationships, they are more likely to utilize techniques linguists have long recognized help relationships.

Appendix 7.A: Summary Statistics

Table 7.A.1 Summary Statistics for Courts of Appeals Search and Seizure Dissenting Opinion Dataset. Percentages may not add to 100% due to rounding.

	Min.	25%	50%	75%	Max.
Continuous Variables					
Number of Positive Emotion Words	0	23	42	70	452
Number of Negative Emotion Words	0	22	41	74	555
Number of Direct Sentences	0	1	3	6	133
Cotenure	0	4	8	12	31
Pr(Future Panel)	0.07	0.15	0.18	0.25	1
ID Distance: Maj. Opin Au. to Dissenter	0	0.15	0.44	0.71	1.14
ID Distance: Dissenter to Circuit	0	0.12	0.30	0.49	0.98
ID Distance: Dissenter to Supreme Court	0	0.20	0.35	0.47	0.88
Logged Word Count	3.95	7.75	8.17	8.56	10.2
Year	1953	1981	1991	2002	2010
Dichotomous Variables	**0**	**1**			
Same Courthouse	87%	13%			
Same Gender	21%	79%			
Same Race	20%	80%			
Chief Judge	95%	5%			
New Judge	97%	3%			
Amicus	96%	4%			
Civil Rights	71%	29%			
Habeas	93%	7%			
Categorical Variable	**Percent**				
Tone of Sign-Off					
Polite	53%				
Neutral	26%				
Rude	21%				

COLLEGIALITY AND THE LANGUAGE OF DISSENT 191

Table 7.A.2 Summary Statistics for Supreme Court Dissenting Opinion Dataset. Percentages may not add to 100% due to rounding.

	Min.	25%	50%	75%	Max.
Continuous Variables					
Number of Positive Emotion Words	0	14	34	66	539
Number of Negative Emotion Words	0	9	23	49	575
Number of Direct Sentences	0	1	4	9	94
Cotenure	0	3	7	12	32
ID Distance: Maj. Opin Au. to Dissenter	0	0.32	0.59	0.89	1.45
Salience	−1.32	−0.49	−0.24	0.65	3.44
Logged Word Count	2.83	6.85	7.72	8.32	10.37
Year	1955	1971	1981	1991	2009
Dichotomous Variables	**0**	**1**			
Clerked for Supreme Court	73%	27%			
Former COA Judge	52%	48%			
Former D.C. Circuit Judge	87%	13%			
Chief Justice	89%	11%			
New Justice	94%	6%			
Categorical Variables	**Percent**				
Tone of Sign-Off					
Polite	31%				
Neutral	48%				
Rude	21%				
Issue Area					
Criminal Procedure	28%				
Civil Rights	18%				
First Amendment	11%				
Due Process	4%				
Privacy	2%				
Attorneys	1%				
Unions	4%				
Economic Activity	17%				
Judicial Power	8%				
Federalism	4%				
Interstate Relations	0.4%				
Federal Taxation	3%				
Miscellaneous	0.3%				

Appendix 7.B: Regression Results

Table 7.B.1 Emotional Language Model, Courts of Appeals: Negative binomial regression estimates of the effect of personal and professional contacts, Ideological Distance, their interaction, and a range of control variables on the number of words in a dissenting opinion that have positive or negative emotional content. * denotes a p-value less than 0.05.

	Positive Emotion		Negative Emotion	
	Coef.	S.E.	Coef.	S.E.
Same Courthouse	−0.060	(0.079)	0.102	(0.093)
ID Distance: Maj. Opin Au. to Dissenter	−0.203	(0.135)	0.002	(0.163)
Same Courthouse × ID Distance	0.231	(0.143)	−0.427	(0.168)
Cotenure	−0.004	(0.004)	−0.003	(0.005)
Cotenure × ID Distance	0.004	(0.009)	0.000	(0.010)
Pr(Future Panel)	−0.239	(0.235)	−0.361	(0.288)
Pr(Future Panel) × ID Distance	0.195	(0.481)	0.535	(0.590)
Same Gender	0.021	(0.041)	0.016	(0.047)
Same Race	0.062	(0.040)	−0.035	(0.047)
Chief Judge	0.013	(0.076)	0.085	(0.089)
New Judge	0.007	(0.090)	−0.186	(0.105)
Amicus	0.291	(0.084)	−0.088	(0.098)
Civil Rights	0.114	(0.037)	0.167	(0.042)
Habeas	0.207	(0.062)	0.201	(0.073)
ID Distance: Dissenter to Circuit	0.174	(0.083)	0.154	(0.097)
ID Distance: Dissenter to Supreme Court	−0.029	(0.103)	−0.077	(0.121)
Logged Word Count	1.063	(0.027)	1.027	(0.032)
Year	0.002	(0.002)	0.007	(0.002)
Intercept	−8.900	(3.005)	−19.098	(3.515)
N	1,012		1,012	
AIC	9097.7		9315.7	
BIC	9196.1		9414.1	

Table 7.B.2 Sign-Off Model, Courts of Appeals: Multinomial logit regression estimates of the effect of personal and professional contacts, Ideological Distance, their interaction, and a range of control variables on whether a dissenter signs off with a rude, neutral, or polite tone. * denotes a p-value less than 0.05.

	Polite		Rude	
	Coef.	S.E.	Coef.	S.E.
Same Courthouse	−0.749	(0.380)	−0.447	(0.473)
ID Distance: Maj. Opin Au. to Dissenter	−1.666	(0.750)	−0.981	(0.930)
Same Courthouse × ID Distance	0.585	(0.697)	0.462	(0.840)
Cotenure	−0.046	(0.023)	−0.020	(0.028)
Cotenure × ID Distance	0.060	(0.046)	0.036	(0.054)
Pr(Future Panel)	−2.206	(1.211)	−6.990	(2.095)
Pr(Future Panel) × ID Distance	3.243	(2.545)	4.240	(3.695)
Same Gender	−0.318	(0.224)	−0.352	(0.262)
Same Race	−0.851	(0.250)	−1.051	(0.278)
Chief Judge	−0.208	(0.353)	−0.822	(0.532)
New Judge	0.206	(0.470)	−0.026	(0.592)
Amicus	0.805	(0.514)	0.185	(0.632)
Civil Rights	−0.073	(0.190)	0.037	(0.228)
Habeas	−0.040	(0.305)	−0.060	(0.372)
ID Distance: Dissenter to Circuit	−0.665	(0.425)	−1.094	(0.514)
ID Distance: Dissenter to Supreme Court	−0.001	(0.522)	0.472	(0.628)
Logged Word Count	−0.058	(0.130)	−0.008	(0.156)
Year	0.033	(0.008)	0.001	(0.010)
Intercept	−61.460	(15.174)	1.790	(18.892)
N			1,012	
AIC			1998.7	
BIC			2185.6	

194 THE ELEVATOR EFFECT

Table 7.B.3 Direct Address Model, Courts of Appeals: Negative binomial regression estimates of the effect of personal and professional contacts, Ideological Distance, their interaction, and a range of control variables on the number of sentences in a dissent that directly address the majority opinion. * denotes a p-value less than 0.05.

	Coef.	S.E.
Same Courthouse	0.085	(0.181)
ID Distance: Maj. Opin Au. to Dissenter	0.048	(0.321)
Same Courthouse × ID Distance	0.121	(0.331)
Pr(Future Panel)	−0.535	(0.534)
Cotenure	−0.001	(0.011)
Cotenure × ID Distance	0.003	(0.021)
Pr(Future Panel) × ID Distance	−0.398	(1.122)
Same Gender	0.012	(0.094)
Same Race	0.007	(0.094)
Chief Judge	−0.351	(0.190)
New Judge	−0.034	(0.213)
Amicus	0.542	(0.193)
Civil Rights	0.246	(0.085)
Habeas	−0.135	(0.149)
ID Distance: Dissenter to Circuit	0.158	(0.194)
ID Distance: Dissenter to Supreme Court	0.046	(0.248)
Logged Word Count	0.494	(0.059)
Year	0.011	(0.004)
Intercept	−24.843	(7.162)
N	1,012	
AIC	5112.3	
BIC	5210.7	

Table 7.B.4 Emotional Language Model, Supreme Court: Negative binomial regression estimates of the effect of personal and professional contacts, Ideological Distance, their interaction, and a range of control variables on the number of words in a dissenting opinion that have positive or negative emotional content. The reported standard errors are robust standard errors that are clustered on the case and * denotes a p-value less than 0.05.

	Positive Emotion		Negative Emotion	
	Coef.	S.E.	Coef.	S.E.
Cotenure	0.002	(0.003)	−0.005	(0.004)
ID Distance: Maj. Opin Au. to Dissenter	0.014	(0.034)	−0.078	(0.045)
Cotenure × ID Distance	−0.004	(0.004)	0.006	(0.005)
Clerked for Supreme Court	0.020	(0.018)	0.042	(0.025)
Former COA Judge	−0.027	(0.017)	−0.052	(0.023)
Former D.C. Circuit Judge	0.033	(0.028)	0.009	(0.035)
Chief Justice	0.029	(0.027)	−0.072	(0.031)
New Justice	0.001	(0.033)	0.019	(0.045)
Salience	0.001	(0.010)	0.035	(0.013)
Logged Word Count	1.024	(0.008)	1.040	(0.010)
Year	0.000	(0.001)	0.003	(0.001)
Civil Rights	0.098	(0.025)	−0.384	(0.029)
First Amendment	0.256	(0.024)	−0.254	(0.030)
Due Process	0.236	(0.035)	−0.105	(0.050)
Privacy	0.150	(0.049)	−0.265	(0.077)
Attorneys	0.340	(0.050)	−0.468	(0.092)
Unions	0.233	(0.040)	−0.344	(0.054)
Economic Activity	0.073	(0.022)	−0.331	(0.032)
Judicial Power	0.155	(0.026)	−0.446	(0.041)
Federalism	0.019	(0.045)	−0.469	(0.050)
Interstate Relations	0.312	(0.108)	−0.650	(0.129)
Federal Taxation	0.147	(0.048)	−0.462	(0.080)
Miscellaneous	−0.221	(0.071)	−0.648	(0.100)
Intercept	−5.233	(1.292)	−9.451	(1.769)
N	3,627		3,627	
AIC	27817.2		27149.8	
BIC	27972.1		27304.7	

196 THE ELEVATOR EFFECT

Table 7.B.5 Sign-Off Model, Supreme Court: Multinomial logit regression estimates of the effect of personal and professional contacts, Ideological Distance, their interaction, and a range of control variables on whether a dissenter signs off with a rude, neutral, or polite tone. The reported standard errors are robust standard errors that are clustered on the case and * denotes a p-value less than 0.05.

	Polite		Rude	
	Coef.	S.E.	Coef.	S.E.
Cotenure	−0.026	(0.017)	0.024	(0.018)
ID Distance: Maj. Opin Au. to Dissenter	−0.796	(0.208)	−0.066	(0.217)
Cotenure × ID Distance	0.024	(0.022)	−0.014	(0.023)
Clerked for Supreme Court	−0.032	(0.113)	0.068	(0.120)
Former COA Judge	−0.190	(0.105)	0.031	(0.111)
Former D.C. Circuit Judge	0.107	(0.168)	−0.343	(0.196)
Chief Justice	0.076	(0.157)	0.114	(0.156)
New Justice Salience	0.279	(0.218)	0.324	(0.214)
Logged Word Count	−0.184	(0.066)	−0.088	(0.063)
Year	0.598	(0.042)	0.466	(0.046)
	0.079	(0.005)	0.034	(0.004)
Civil Rights	−0.038	(0.137)	−0.124	(0.140)
First Amendment	−0.332	(0.168)	−0.017	(0.157)
Due Process	−0.113	(0.228)	0.001	(0.212)
Privacy	−0.169	(0.421)	0.143	1.124
Attorneys	0.146	(0.443)	(0.310)	(0.418)
Unions	0.429	(0.229)	−0.128	(0.252)
Economic Activity	0.028	(0.136)	−0.511	(0.152)
Judicial Power	−0.117	(0.185)	−0.354	(0.200)
Federalism	−0.013	(0.222)	−0.663	(0.266)
Interstate Relations	−0.665	(0.456)	−0.216	(0.668)
Federal Taxation	0.611	(0.265)	−0.131	(0.340)
Miscellaneous	0.763	(1.224)	0.885	(1.240)
Intercept	−160.870	(8.922)	−71.956	(8.365)
N		3,627		
AIC		6614.2		
BIC		6911.6		

Table 7.B.6 Direct Address Model, Supreme Court: Negative binomial regression estimates of the effect of personal and professional contacts, Ideological Distance, their interaction, and a range of control variables on the number of sentences in a dissent that directly address the majority opinion. The reported standard errors are robust standard errors that are clustered on the case and * denotes a p-value less than 0.05.

	Coef.	S.E.
Cotenure	−0.009	(0.005)
ID Distance: Maj. Opin Au. to Dissenter	−0.137	(0.059)
Cotenure × ID Distance	0.005	(0.006)
Clerked for Supreme Court	−0.015	(0.028)
Former COA Judge	−0.031	(0.027)
Former D.C. Circuit Judge	−0.084	(0.041)
Chief Justice	−0.074	(0.042)
New Justice	−0.117	(0.053)
Salience	−0.016	(0.016)
Logged Word Count	0.941	(0.014)
Year	0.009	(0.001)
Civil Rights	−0.018	(0.035)
First Amendment	−0.047	(0.043)
Due Process	0.013	(0.063)
Privacy	0.146	(0.087)
Attorneys	0.019	(0.099)
Unions	−0.082	(0.072)
Economic Activity	−0.079	(0.035)
Judicial Power	−0.057	(0.043)
Federalism	−0.140	(0.065)
Interstate Relations	−0.493	(0.219)
Federal Taxation	−0.150	(0.084)
Miscellaneous	−0.148	(0.165)
Intercept	−22.883	(2.064)
N	3,627	
AIC	17761.1	
BIC	17916.0	

8
The Impact of Relationships on the Use of Precedent

Introduction

As the previous chapter illustrates, there is a lot more to a case than just how the judges vote. Not only is the content of judicial opinions important, but how they are referred to in the future also matters (Kassow, Songer, and Fix 2012; Niblett and Yoon 2015). Citation decisions are undoubtedly largely driven by which precedents are similar to the case at hand. But other considerations may still affect the way judges select which relevant cases to cite. Opinion authors may gravitate toward precedents written by past colleagues whom they respect, those with whom they have solid relationships, or even those with whom they would like to be on good footing going forward. Such motivations are rarely explicitly discussed by judges, but there are exceptions. While writing an opinion in the Eighth Circuit, Judge Edward Dumbauld included the following: "The writer of this opinion cites with pride this timely and pertinent decision of a former colleague as District Judge in the Western District of Pennsylvania, now a Senior Circuit Judge, who recently served as chairman of the Federal Courts Study Committee appointed by the Chief Justice"[1] (Klein and Morrisroe 1999). The opinion he is referring to was written by Judge Joseph F. Weis, Jr. Judge Dumbauld clearly had a high opinion of Judge Weis as well the precedent he had written. And that high opinion was informed by the three years the two spent as colleagues on the same court.

Citations can provide key insight for a variety of reasons. As Walsh (1997, 338) explains, "citations potentially open a window to better understanding of judicial decisionmaking, the development of the law, use of precedent, intercourt communication, and the structuring of relations between courts." Precedents are the building blocks of legal development (Cross et al. 2010). When a judge pens an opinion, the reach and significance of that document can vary widely (Nelson and Hinkle 2018). The number of subsequent citations is a classic way to quantify that significance (Cross et al. 2010).

Judges have relatively little constraint on the number of citations they include in their opinions; they can proliferate references to case law as much as they want (Landes, Lessig, and Solimine 1998). While appellate judging is a group activity, an opinion author has considerable discretion regarding which cases they choose to cite

---

[1] In re *Da-Sota Elevator Co.*, 939 F.2d 654 (8th Cir. 1991).

The Elevator Effect. Morgan L.W. Hazelton, Rachael K. Hinkle, and Michael J. Nelson, Oxford University Press.
© Oxford University Press 2023. DOI: 10.1093/oso/9780197625408.003.0008

in their opinions (Hinkle 2015; Niblett and Yoon 2015; Pryor 2017). This creates an opportunity for the personal dynamic between two judges—the opinion author and a precedent author—to play a role in citation.[2] As a result of these dynamics, there is considerable variation in how much judges cite each other (Nagel 1962). This variation facilitates exploration of judicial behavior.

In this chapter, we take up an examination of the broader impact of judicial relationships across time by examining when judges cite one another's majority opinions. We theorize that relationships like the one between Judge Dumbauld and Judge Weis can impact such decisions. The effects of collegiality might exist both across cases as well as within cases. Even when judges are not sitting together in a room discussing a specific case, they can be influenced by their interactions from the past and the opinions that were generated as a result. And, if two judges are both participating in the same case, then their personal and professional relationships are even more likely to shape citation decisions. We examine four reasons why an opinion author's relationship with the author of a precedent might affect citation. First, past interactions may have led the opinion author to gain knowledge about and respect for the precedent author that increases how persuasive they find that judge's precedents. This dynamic can operate even if two judges are no longer serving together. The second reason relationships can impact citation applies only if two judges are both participating in a case. Under those circumstances, the opinion author may cite a precedent by a colleague to persuade them to join the majority. The third reason also only pertains when there is joint participation in a case. It is possible that during deliberations the precedent author will persuade the opinion author to cite an opinion they have written. Finally, if two judges are still currently serving on the same court, the opinion author may be motivated to cite a colleague as a form of flattery to enhance or preserve a good working relationship going forward.

Our analysis of citation behavior extends the theoretical development from the previous chapters in two important ways. First, since judges necessarily consider precedents from the past, examining citation decisions allows us to compare the relative effect of relationships with past colleagues and current colleagues. Second, we can compare the effect of relationships with colleagues participating in a case to members of the same circuit who are not on a given panel. In this way, we can look beyond the effects of collegiality when two judges are in the same room (at least for cases that involve in-person conferences) to see if relationships continue to shape judicial behavior when there is no mandated consultation regarding a specific case. These extensions of our previous analyses are useful because they permit us to test what effect collegiality has under increasingly difficult conditions for our theory. Even if relationships shape how two judges interact in a case, that may not extend to when they are not on the same case, or it may not extend to when one of the two judges is no longer on the court.

Like the analysis of dissenting opinions in the previous chapter, we test our hypotheses in both circuit courts and the Supreme Court. For courts of appeals, we explore citations within our search and seizure data (1953 to 2010) from one majority opinion

---

[2] While it is possible that other judges on the respective panels have an impact on citation as well, we focus on the authors and leave the topic of non-authoring judges' influence for future research.

to another within the same circuit. Since all precedent from a circuit is binding on future cases within that circuit, looking at in-circuit citations holds legal doctrine constant (Hinkle 2015). For the Supreme Court, we look at all majority-to-majority citations within orally argued cases from 1955 to 2009. We find evidence that circuit judges are more likely to cite precedent written by an author who is participating in the current case and by a colleague with whom they anticipate a higher probability of serving in the future. However, we were puzzled to find that circuit judges are less likely to cite colleagues with whom they have served longer or who have chambers in the same courthouse. Supreme Court justices are more likely to cite precedent written by their current colleagues compared to past colleagues or justices with whom they never overlapped, but only when the current colleague is an ideological ally.

The previous chapters have revealed interesting features about votes and the text of dissenting opinions. This chapter builds on those findings by using a different type of judicial behavior—citation practices—to evaluate the difference between how collegiality affects judicial behavior when two judges are in the same room compared to when they are at arm's length. Understanding how collegiality operates over time and between colleagues not sitting on the same case is fundamental to understanding the extent to which collegiality can affect judicial behavior. Our findings indicate that while the effect of interpersonal contact does lessen when two judges are not sitting on the same panel, it does not necessarily disappear. The benefits gained when judges get to know each other better can have wide-reaching consequences. However, we do not find any evidence that such benefits last beyond the point where one of the judges has left the court.

The Importance of Studying Citations

Beyond the tone of an opinion, discussed in the previous chapter, the contents of judicial rulings also deserve study. As Friedman et al. (1981, 773) point out, these opinions are "crucial documents for any study of judicial culture." An important component of those opinions is what cases they cite (Kassow, Songer, and Fix 2012; Niblett and Yoon 2015). Common law courts operate by using analogical reasoning to draw parallels between the case at bar and previous similar cases (Aldisert 1989). Consequently, appellate judges routinely "explain case outcomes with references to precedents that are factually similar" (Solberg, Emrey, and Haire 2006, 277). These citations from one case to another can provide several useful types of insight.

First, citations are useful for examining how law develops because they "set forth the authority on which a case rests" (Friedman et al. 1981, 794). Appellate judges cite precedent as part of the norm of stare decisis, the legal doctrine that judges should resolve cases by drawing analogies to previous disputes with similar facts (Solberg, Emrey, and Haire 2006). As Friedman et al. (1981, 793) point out: "It would, for example, be wrong for a judge to let a case turn on a coin toss." Instead, judges are expected to reference previous rulings on the same topic and these references are embodied in citations (Smyth and Mishra 2011). Each opinion, in turn, becomes part of the body of case law available for citation in future cases. The result is a system of law that while providing uniformity of rules is also flexible. "The law, and the legal

202 THE ELEVATOR EFFECT

rules that comprise it, change in part as precedents are cited in court opinions. Judges' choices to reduce or eliminate citations to cases ... can thus influence the shape the law takes" (Black and Spriggs 2013, 355). As a result, studying the citations within opinions is a window to understanding legal development.

Second, citations constitute patterns of communication. In fact, the communicative element of citation is a feature of citations broadly and is not limited to courts. For example, Balkin and Levinson (1995, 845) posit that "citation practices are a sort of economy of communication and exchange between academics." They evoke a colorful metaphor by proposing that examining citations is like studying a people or culture by means of examining their garbage. "Both citations and thrown-away objects provide entryways into people's lives and the larger culture in which they live and by which they are shaped" (Balkin and Levinson 1995, 843). In the legal context, studies have leveraged citations between state high courts to examine how legal policies and approaches are communicated across jurisdictional boundaries (Caldeira 1985; Harris 1982, 1985; Hinkle and Nelson 2016; Smyth and Mishra 2011). Harris (1982, 201) notes that "[t]his use of each others' decisions and opinions as authorities amounts to the communication of precedent among the courts."

Third, citations reflect influence (Hinkle and Nelson 2018a; Nelson and Hinkle 2018). As Kosma (1998, 338) describes, "[a]uthored opinions represent the primary work product of members of the Court, and the frequency with which a particular opinion has been cited generally indicates how often it has influenced the resolution of subsequent cases." Opinions are a way for judges to exercise influence and persuade future jurists to take a similar approach (Niblett and Yoon 2015). Therefore, citations to an opinion indicate that it had such an influential or persuasive effect.

In summary, citations provide insight into legal development, communication, and influence. By exploring how collegiality impacts citation, we can shed important light on these processes.

Reasons to Cite a Precedent

Understanding any behavior requires unpacking the motivations that underlay it. Citation decisions are no different. Therefore, we begin our exploration by considering a range of possible motivations that contribute to judges' decisions to cite (or not) any given precedent. These factors include features of the precedent, similarities between two cases or courts, and relationships between judges.

Several features of a precedent itself shape how much it is cited. The first is whether it is binding under the doctrine of stare decisis. Binding precedents include those from a directly supervising court as well as a court's own previous rulings (Hinkle 2015). As we would expect, most citation studies focused on a particular court find that the court cites its own previous cases more than any other sources. This is true for apex courts throughout the United States (Friedman et al. 1981; Manz 2001; Merryman 1977), as well as the High Court of Australia (Smyth and Nielsen 2019). Second, even when a precedent is not binding, a judge may choose to cite ones that they find particularly persuasive and influential (Walsh 1997). A precedent may be in a stronger position to influence future judges when it is issued by a particularly prestigious court

THE IMPACT OF RELATIONSHIPS ON THE USE OF PRECEDENT   203

or author (Caldeira 1985; Hinkle and Nelson 2016). For example, circuit judges who went to more prestigious law schools are cited more frequently (Szmer, Christensen, and Grubbs 2020). Third, scholars have proposed that judges may selectively cite (i.e., cherry-pick) precedents that shore up or strengthen the arguments the judge wants to make (Denniston 2014; Niblett 2010; Walsh 1997). However, the empirical evidence on this point is mixed (cf. Niblett 2010; Walsh 1997). The fourth and final feature of a precedent that affects its citation is age. Studies have repeatedly found that precedents are cited much less as time goes by (Black and Spriggs 2013; Landes, Lessig, and Solimine 1998; Manz 2001; Merryman 1977).

Scholars have also examined how the similarity between two cases or courts can affect citation. Since factual relevance is part and parcel of analogical reasoning, it is unsurprising that precedents with more similar underlying disputes are more likely to be cited (see, e.g., Hinkle 2015). Caldeira (1985) theorized that citation behavior might also be influenced by the similarity between two courts. After all, "[h]umans tend to seek out information that fits their preexisting schemes ... viewing information that accords with prior opinions as stronger evidence" (Hinkle and Nelson 2016, 6, citing Braman and Nelson 2007; Taber and Lodge 2006). Cross et al. (2010, 501) find that "[j]ustices who are ideologically distant from a precedent are less likely to cite it." There is evidence that both federal circuit courts and state high courts are more likely to cite Supreme Court precedents that are more closely aligned to their own ideology (Niblett and Yoon 2015; Kassow, Songer, and Fix 2012). Moreover, shared policy preferences are not the only type of similarity that can impact citations. Pryor (2017) shows that Supreme Court justices more frequently cite the separate opinions of colleagues with whom they have more life experiences in common.

The recent citation literature has begun to look beyond the features of a precedent and the similarity between cases or courts to examine how the relationships between individuals can impact citation decisions. In the context of academic citations, Balkin and Levinson (1995) note that friendship can play a role in citation, including a norm of reciprocity. While judges don't necessarily directly cajole each other to increase their citation counts,[3] Niblett and Yoon (2015) argue that "[i]n much the same way that one might gravitate toward friends when entering a party, judges gravitate toward friendly precedent when writing judicial opinions" (1795–96). Szmer, Christensen, and Grubbs (2020) point out that judges know their colleagues from their own court much better than those from other circuits and conclude that judicial characteristics should have a bigger effect on citation when the judge in question is well known. They find evidence to support this theory; a circuit opinion is cited more frequently when the author is from the same court (i.e., not a judge sitting by designation) (Szmer, Christensen, and Grubbs 2020). Pryor (2017) points out that there are multiple ways relationships can shape how much justices influence one another. Specifically, he argues that serving together for a longer period and having served with someone in the past should increase how much a justice cites a colleague's separate opinions (Pryor 2017). He finds evidence for both patterns, including that moving the length of time two judges served together from one term to twenty-nine (the maximum in the

---

[3] Consider yourself cajoled to cite this book.

204 THE ELEVATOR EFFECT

data) increased the predicted number of citations from one justice to another from 1.3 to 1.7 citations per year (Pryor 2017).

The Impact of Collegial Relationships on Citation

The literature on citation behavior sheds light on a multitude of factors that can affect the way a judge goes about deciding which precedents to include in an opinion. However, only a few scholars have addressed the question of how relationships between judges might affect citation. This oversight is unfortunate, but we are in an excellent position to remedy it. Our theory of collegiality as developed throughout this book is perfectly poised to further our understanding of the role of relationships in legal development. Pryor (2017) has laid groundwork by examining how some features of relationships impact whether Supreme Court justices cite each other's separate opinions. As he cogently observes, "[j]ustices develop interpersonal relationships and intellectual respect with their colleagues. This respect is evident in and can be measured by their citation practices" (Pryor 2017, 380). Since we are interested in how collegial relationships shape the development of law, we focus on citations between majority opinions.

There is an enormous amount of case law available for citation. How do judges decide which to discuss or ignore? More importantly, how do relationships factor into that decision? As a metaphor to think about citation decisions, Niblett and Yoon (2015, 1792) pose the following: "Imagine that you are invited to a party. Upon entering a crowded room, you see people that you know and like, those you know but dislike, and still others whom you do not even know. To whom do you gravitate? Do you converse with your existing circle of friends? Do you exchange pleasantries with your adversaries? Do you strike up conversation with strangers?" As anyone who has attended a cocktail party for work can attest, two people who are more familiar with one another will interact differently in social situations than two strangers. This is a useful way to conceptualize how interpersonal relationships between judges can influence citation.

When a judge is faced with a multitude of precedents, stronger bonds with the people who wrote some of them may increase the probability that such cases are selected for discussion. However, judges themselves do not necessarily discuss citation in these terms. For example, in our interviews, J5 opined that collegiality does not affect citations, stating the following: "I don't really care who wrote the opinion. It's not like, 'oh, I don't like Joe Schmo, so nah.'" But it is possible that relationships matter in subtle and subconscious ways. In fact, developing our broader theory of collegiality to apply to the specific context of citation decisions leads us to expect not only that interpersonal contact matters but that different types of relationships affect citation for particular reasons and under specific circumstances.

Deciding whether to cite a case has two major distinctions from the other types of judicial behavior we have explored in this book. Chapters 3 through 6 examined how judges vote. Whether one looks at that from the perspective of voting to join a majority or write separately or from the perspective of whether a vote is to reverse or affirm, every judge must cast a vote in every case. Similarly, once a judge has chosen to

THE IMPACT OF RELATIONSHIPS ON THE USE OF PRECEDENT   205

issue a dissenting opinion, as we discussed in Chapter 7, that dissent will have a tone of some kind. Citation is different: choosing to cite a particular case is the exception. Any given majority opinion cites only a sliver of the available case law. As a result, citing precedent offers opportunities to strengthen relationships without (for the most part) posing a serious threat of harming them.[4] Unlike dissenting votes or opinions, there is no conflict of confrontation inherent in not citing a particular precedent.[5] The inaction of ignoring a precedent is not necessarily viewed in a negative light, and it may often not be noticed at all. Thus, there is little to no downside to inaction, but citing a precedent may potentially strengthen a relationship.

The second unique feature of the context in which citation decisions are made is that they involve interactions across time. Of course, the author of a majority opinion makes decisions about what to include in the draft within a similar time frame as the other types of judicial decision-making we have studied. But a citation decision is made about something that is a product of another time. That time may be decades before or only a week before. This creates interesting and useful variation in relationships. As we build a theory about how interpersonal contacts between an opinion author and a precedent author can impact citation decisions, we consider how the passage of time gives rise to different types of collegial contacts. We organize our theory by discussing relationships with former and current colleagues in turn.

Relationships with Former Colleagues

First, we consider how personal interactions from the past might affect citation decisions. Our analyses in previous chapters necessarily focused on relationships between current colleagues. We elaborated on two explanations for how collegiality can influence judicial behavior: persuasion and suppression. When it comes to citation, the corollary to suppressing a dissenting vote for the sake of future peaceful interactions is choosing to cite a colleague to build goodwill for that same purpose. Therefore, in this chapter we will discuss the two mechanisms of collegiality in terms of persuasion and flattery.[6] One of those mechanisms does not automatically evaporate when a colleague leaves the bench. While there is no longer a need for flattery, collegiality can lead to greater persuasive ability because getting to know someone well can lead to increased understanding and respect for alternative views. That may well continue to shape a judge's thinking when considering a precedent written by a former colleague. The citation literature tends to discuss such a dynamic in terms of influence, but it is closely related to our idea of persuasion. As Pryor (2017, 372) notes, "If, however, justices are more likely to cite the opinions of former colleagues than they are to cite the opinions of justices with whom they never served, it would indicate that there must

[4] While it is possible for a judge to disparage a precedent in a way that might rile up its author, such negative treatments are not common.

[5] There is a chance that a judge might notice a precedent of theirs was overlooked, but they would have to read the opinion and recall their own previous efforts on the same topic without prompting.

[6] Suppression and flattery are essentially context-specific versions of forward-looking strategic relationship management.

206   THE ELEVATOR EFFECT

have been some interpersonal element that draws the citing justice to the views of the cited justice."

Comparing citation behavior with respect to non-colleagues and former colleagues does require care. Older precedents are both less likely to be cited and more likely to be written by judges with whom an opinion author has never served. However, it is possible to compare precedents of the same age written by both types of judges because of variation in when they leave and join courts. Holding the age of precedent constant, the presence or absence of a professional relationship on the court provides an excellent test of the effect of collegiality. When a judge considers a precedent written by someone with whom they have served, they have the personal knowledge that flows from that relationship. *We hypothesize that in the aggregate this will lead to a higher probability of citing a precedent written by a judge with whom one has served in the past compared to a judge who was never a colleague.*

As in previous chapters, we also anticipate that the effect of relationships might by conditioned by the effect of ideology. However, our expectation for when collegiality is most likely to matter with respect to citation is not the same as it was for votes. This difference is generated by the fact that citing a precedent is not expected and inaction is often perfectly normal. As a result, a judge can usually ignore a precedent written by someone who has a vastly different ideology without fearing repercussions. This may mean that the presence of a previous professional relationship will not have much of an impact when the ideological distance between two judges is larger because citation itself is less likely. Conversely, when an author is ideologically proximate to the precedent author, having served with them in the past may well increase the author's underlying inclination to cite. In sum, *we expect the effect of past relationships to have a larger effect on citation when the opinion and precedent author are more closely aligned ideologically.*

Next, we shift perspective and consider how the effect of ideology might be conditioned by whether two judges have served together in that past. The effect of knowledge and respect built in past relationships may potentially dampen the effect of ideology on citation decisions. In Chapter 6, we established that when circuit court judges work in the same building as district court judges, thereby likely possessing more detailed information about them, the effect of ideology on the decision to reverse disappears entirely. In a similar fashion, when a judge has had the opportunity to get to know the author of a precedent through serving at the same time, that knowledge may well take the place of the blunter cue of ideology. As a result, *we hypothesize that ideological distance will have less of an impact on the decision to cite a former colleague than it will on the decision to cite someone with whom they have never served.*

A discussion of former colleagues is not complete without pointing out the opportunity this examination affords. Understanding the role of collegiality in judicial decision-making means seeking answers to not just the questions of *if* or *when* it matters but also *why* it matters. The "why" question is particularly tricky because both persuasion and flattery are plausible mechanisms that may be in play. By examining the effect of past relationships, we can shed light on this difficult question of mechanism because only one of the two options is available. The heart of flattery as a mechanism is concern about current and future professional interactions. Comparing past colleagues to non-colleagues takes these concerns out of the equation. As a result, to the extent we see past relationships affect citation (either directly, conditionally, or through ideological dampening), that is evidence of persuasion exclusively. Furthermore, it is an indication of a very specific type of persuasion where the opinion author's knowledge of a person increased receptivity to their ideas even when that person was not in the same room or even on the same court.

Relationships with Current Colleagues

We now turn to considering how interpersonal contacts with current colleagues may influence citation. When the opinion and precedent authors are contemporaneously serving on the same court, collegiality may affect citation through the mechanisms of either persuasion or flattery. Furthermore, there are two additional types of persuasion in play in addition to the one discussed in the previous section. Not only may an author be persuaded by knowledge of, and respect for, a colleague based on their shared service to date, they may also be personally persuaded to cite a case by the precedent author, or they may choose to cite a precedent in order to persuade its author to sign on to the opinion. In other words, persuasion can manifest as influence, lobbying, or wooing.

First, as with former colleagues, a strong interpersonal relationship based on past professional contacts can lead a precedent author to have influence over how an opinion author selects precedent. Most of the theory from the previous section applies here as well. The one distinction is in how we think about the extent of past relationships. For current colleagues, we expect that the amount of influence a precedent author will have should be related to how extensive their collegial contacts with the opinion author have been. The passage of time and accumulation of contacts is needed to gain the knowledge of each other that can ripen into influence.

Second, we turn to a combined discussion of lobbying and wooing. The reason we combine these concepts is that there is no way to distinguish between them empirically. When both judges are participating in the same case, the precedent author may take advantage of either in-person discussions or written communications to lobby the opinion author to cite their precedents. But it is also possible that the opinion author may cite a colleague's past opinions unprompted to persuade them to sign the opinion (and not write separately). While these two mechanisms cannot be easily disentangled, they can be isolated as a pair, at least in the circuit courts. For these explanations to be in play, the precedent author must be participating in the immediate case. At the Supreme Court level, this includes virtually all cases with current colleagues. At the circuit level this only occurs when the precedent author is one of the other two judges on the panel. To the extent that lobbying, wooing, or both are operating, *we expect an opinion author to be more likely to cite a precedent written by a current colleague who is participating in the case compared to one who is not.*

Finally, judges may also engage in forward-looking behavior when making citation decisions. Citing a current colleague's precedent may have a beneficial effect on future interactions. After all, who doesn't like to be cited? Citations are widely regarded as a sign of status (Balkin and Levinson 1995). There is at least some reason to believe that judges might care. Szmer, Christensen, and Grubbs (2020) find that an opinion gets significantly more citations from within its own circuit when the author has been on the court less time. While perhaps puzzling at first glance, there are potential explanations. Newer judges may be more representative of the current political environment. More importantly for our purposes, this finding is consistent with the idea that a newer author is also, by definition, someone with whom other judges generally anticipate having to work for many years to come. As a result, judges may be seeking to "butter up" a newer judge to create a positive working environment for years to come. The longer an opinion author anticipates serving with a precedent author, the more they have to gain from using citation as a form of flattery. Consequently, *we hypothesize that judges who expect to work with a colleague more in the future will be more likely to cite that colleague compared to when there is a lower (or no) chance of shared future service.* For ease of reference, the circumstances under which each collegiality mechanism should operate are summarized in Table 8.1.

So far, we have discussed our expectations regarding how features of collegial relationships with current colleagues can directly affect citation. However, our expectations do not end there. We also examine how the effects of collegiality and ideology may interact. We begin by considering how the effects of collegiality might be conditional on ideology. Citation of any given precedent is exceedingly rare. Under conditions where a judge is especially unlikely to cite a precedent, there is little opportunity for collegiality to play a role. Therefore, as we discussed previously with respect to former colleagues and the influence they can exert, we expect collegiality to have the most impact under circumstances where citation is more likely, that is, when two judges are closer ideologically. The same logic applies to the other two types of persuasion that are in play for current colleagues who are serving in the same case. An opinion author may make little effort to woo the vote of an ideologically distant judge, giving them up as a lost cause. A precedent author may not try to lobby for inclusion of their precedent in the opinion for similar reasons. The situation is not quite as clear if citation is being used for purposes of flattery. One might argue that ideological foes are the colleagues most in need of such attention. However, the very ideological distance between two judges might make any appeal to ego through citation ring a bit false. Even with these misgivings with respect to one possible mechanism, our conditional collegiality hypothesis is that *interpersonal contacts will matter most between ideological allies.*

Table 8.1 Summary of Collegiality Mechanisms for Citation

Mechanism	Former Colleague	Current Colleague	Current Colleague, Same Case
Types of Persuasion			
Influence	✓	✓	✓
Wooing			✓
Lobbying			✓
Flattery		✓	✓

Next, we turn to considering how the effect of ideology might vary based on collegiality. It is possible that when current colleagues interact in terms of citing one another's precedents, concerns about working together as a group may sometimes be more important than differences of ideology. These concerns should be highest when judges come into contact frequently and anticipate doing so in the future too. For example, the interpersonal dynamic between two judges on the same panel who know each other well and see each other frequently will be informed by the more in-depth knowledge of each other that such contacts create. That more nuanced picture of each other may lead to wooing and lobbying behavior that is less shaped by ideology. When two judges know each other less, they may be more likely to fall back on the cue of ideology to decide whether attempts to woo or lobby are even worth the effort. Consequently, as we have throughout the book, we hypothesize that *high levels of collegiality will dampen the effect of ideological distance.*

Research Design

Like our analysis of dissenting opinions in the previous chapter, we examine citation practices in both the federal circuit courts and the Supreme Court. Once again, studying the circuit courts is particularly useful because we can take advantage of the rich variation in interpersonal contacts between judges. The fact that circuit judges only hear a fraction of cases with their current colleagues provides an additional type of variation in relationships that helps us understand how collegiality affects citation. Looking at the Supreme Court as well gives us insight into different institutional contexts and provides a way to look at virtually unconstrained citation behavior. While circuit courts are bound by their own horizontal precedent, there is a higher level of precedent, from the Supreme Court, that may bear on how they treat circuit precedent. The Supreme Court has no such considerations, nor is their horizontal precedent quite so binding since they can disregard their previous work with little outside interference, at least from the judiciary. Justices being less constrained when it comes to their citation decisions might mean there is more opportunity for collegial considerations to come into play. Interestingly, this is the opposite from what we expect with respect to concurring and dissenting. As we discuss in Chapter 5, in that context we expect collegiality to matter most in the courts of appeals and have less impact in the Supreme Court.

The unit of analysis is an opinion-precedent dyad, and the outcome we are modeling is whether the opinion cites the precedent. Throughout the analyses we exclusively use "precedent" to refer to the past case that may or may not be cited and "opinion" to refer to the current ruling in which a judge may or may not choose to cite a precedent. We construct dyadic data structures by creating a dyad for every opinion paired with each previously issued opinion. In other words, we are specifically studying the decision to cite precedents within each of our datasets.

Figuring out which majority opinions cite each other required us to go beyond the existing data and mine the actual content of majority opinions. For every case, we obtained the text of the ruling, extracted the majority opinion, and used the lexNLP package in Python to extract all citations within the majority opinion (Hinkle 2022).

210 THE ELEVATOR EFFECT

Next, we processed all the extracted citations to exclude any citation to a dissent or concurrence. Finally, we matched the cited cases to those within our datasets. The resulting data allows us to model whether each majority opinion cited each previous one in the dataset.

There are several additional important features of our empirical analyses. First, we limit our focus to decisions to cite precedent from the same court to control for the doctrinal status of precedent. This is primarily important in the circuit court model. Precedents from other circuits are not legally binding and are also less likely to be influenced by close personal relationships (Szmer, Christensen, and Grubbs 2020). For these reasons, citations to someone in your own circuit are not the same as those to a judge in a different circuit (Landes, Lessig, and Solimine 1998). Consequently, we only examine opinion-precedent pairs from the same circuit.

Another key decision is our focus on majority opinions. Although one similar previous study has examined citations within separate opinions to isolate a justice's influence (Pryor 2017), we use majority opinions because we are interested in the effect of collegiality on future legal policy. As a practical matter, it is also useful that there are considerably more citations in majority opinions compared to dissents or concurrences (Merryman 1977). Third, we look only at the decision of whether to cite a case and do not further investigate how cited cases are treated.[7] This approach is common in citation studies (Friedman et al. 1981; Landes, Lessig, and Solimine 1998; Pryor 2017; Smyth and Nielsen 2019; Szmer, Christensen, and Grubbs 2020), although some look at both stages (Hinkle 2015; Masood, Kassow, and Songer 2017). Examining the binary decision of whether to cite a precedent provides some parsimony in an already complex analysis. Future research may fruitfully investigate further nuance in how cited precedents are treated.

One final concern for setting up the kind of dyadic citation study we use here is how to deal with the huge number of dyads, many of which are not actually realistic candidates for citation. As noted earlier, we begin by pairing every opinion with each previous precedent in our data. But many of these will simply not be similar enough to merit serious consideration (Fowler et al. 2007). To solve the fundamental problem of identifying those precedents (among thousands of cases) that are so dissimilar from an opinion that citation is exceedingly unlikely, we follow previous research by utilizing a tool from the field of machine learning (Hinkle 2015; Hazelton and Hinkle 2022). Specifically, we use cosine similarity scores to calculate how similar every opinion is to each precedent. This is a standard scoring method for comparing the text of two documents (Manning, Raghavan, and Schütze 2008).[8] For the sake of computational efficiency, the scoring does not take the order of words into account. Similarity is assessed based on the number and importance of words that occur in both opinions (Hinkle 2015). Words that appear in fewer cases within the entire data set are given a higher weight since they carry more information (Hazelton and Hinkle

---

[7] A necessary aspect of this approach is that we are treating negative citations that criticize, limit, or overturn a precedent the same as all other citations. However, these types of treatments are fairly rare. For example, in our circuit dataset only 6 percent of all citations are negative in nature.

[8] Cosine scores were calculated using the text of the majority opinion in each case after removing citations, words shorter than three letters, and stop words (commonly used words such as "a," "and," and "the").

2022). For example, the appearance of the word "curtilage" in two cases would increase the similarity score more than the appearance of the word "defendant" in both. Two cases that discuss curtilage are more likely to be similar than two cases that mention a defendant.

This method provides a feasible way to objectively assess a large body of case law involving millions of pairwise combinations and narrow down the choice set in a principled way. We follow Hinkle (2015) and posit that the potential precedents ranked in the bottom half in terms of similarity to an opinion are not viable candidates for citation. The data bear this out. In the circuit data, 93 percent of all citations are to precedents in the top 50th percentile of similarity. In the Supreme Court data, 97 percent of citations are from the top half. Therefore, our empirical analyses include only opinion-precedent dyads for which the cosine similarity between the two documents is in the top 50th percentile for the relevant dataset.[9]

Collegiality and Citation in the Circuit Courts

Data

For the circuit court analysis, we use our search and seizure dataset described in preceding chapters that covers all published Fourth Amendment opinions from 1953 to 2010. Since the outcome variable is binary (whether a precedent is cited or not), we estimate a probit model. Because each opinion is in the dataset multiple times, paired with many potential precedents, we cluster on the opinion.

Our primary explanatory variables capture multiple elements of the relationship between an opinion author and the judge who wrote the precedent. At one extreme, the two judges have never been colleagues; at the other, the two judges are current colleagues and are both participating in the current case. We begin with a pair of binary variables that equal one if the opinion and precedent authors were former colleagues or are present colleagues, in turn. When the two judges never served together, both variables equal zero. Next, we look at the number of years two judges have served together (or did serve together in the past) to capture past professional relationships. We also examine the effect of having chambers in the same courthouse to account for personal relationships between judges. If the precedent author is still on the court, it is important to account for whether that judge is sitting on the panel in the current case. We use a binary variable that equals one when this is the case and zero otherwise. To examine the effect of future professional relationships, we use our calculation of the probability any two judges in a circuit will sit together on a future panel. Finally, as in previous chapters, we interact our collegiality variables with ideology. In this context the variable Ideological Distance is the absolute value of the

---

[9] We err on the side of retaining many dyads because using the text of an opinion to calculate similarity means that there may be some endogeneity in this measure. While it would be preferable to use text generated prior to the citation decision (e.g., the district court ruling being appealed or legal briefs submitted by the parties), this type of information is not readily available (Hinkle 2015).

212 THE ELEVATOR EFFECT

difference between the Judicial Common Space (JCS) scores of the opinion author and precedent author.

We control for a variety of factors that reflect aspects of the relationship between the opinion and precedent, as well as aspects of each individually, that make citation more likely. In order to take into account the very important matter of legal relevance, we use the cosine similarity measure described previously to control for how similar an opinion and precedent are (Hinkle 2015).[10] If the opinion author participated in the precedent-making case themselves, citation may also be more likely as the opinion author is more likely to be aware of, and familiar with, the precedent. We break this participation down into two types. First, we control for whether the opinion author wrote the precedent in question. Self-citation is often more frequent than citing others (Hinkle 2015; Landes, Lessig, and Solimine 1998). Second, we account for whether the opinion author participated in the precedent case in a non-authoring capacity. The circuit courts have enough demographic diversity that we also control for whether the opinion and precedent authors were the same gender or race. We also control for whether the opinion author is the chief judge or new to the court and their age.

Next, features of the opinion and precedent separately can make citation more likely. Any feature of a case that makes more extensive citation probable also increases the chance of any given citation. For example, particularly important cases can generate more extensive discussion and citations. To capture this, we control for whether there was amicus participation and for the nature of the case in which the opinion was written. All of these cases are classified as criminal, civil rights, or habeas. We include indicator variables for the latter two, with criminal cases being the baseline. We also control for the length of the opinion as longer opinions generally contain more citations. Features of the precedent can also shape citation. Amicus participation in the precedent can indicate the type of case importance that may make later citation more likely (Szmer, Christensen, and Grubbs 2020). A precedent being decided unanimously may indicate the kind of particularly strong legal arguments that will be cited more frequently down the road. The length of the precedent may matter as well. More extensive legal analysis in a precedent provides more opportunity for things to cite. Research has also shown that the age of a precedent plays an important role in citation patterns, and we follow that research by including both age and age squared in the models (Black and Spriggs 2013; Landes, Lessig, and Solimine 1998; Manz 2001; Merryman 1977). Finally, we control for the year of the opinion to account for any changes in citation usage over time (Fowler et al. 2007). Summary statistics for all variables are available in Table 8.A.1 in the chapter appendix.

Results

We now turn to look for evidence of our hypotheses in the circuit courts. Figure 8.1 illustrates our results by showing the predicted change in probability of citation when moving a variable from a low to a high value (from its 25th to 75th percentile or from

---

[10] We scale cosine similarity scores so that they range from zero to one hundred; higher scores indicate greater similarity.

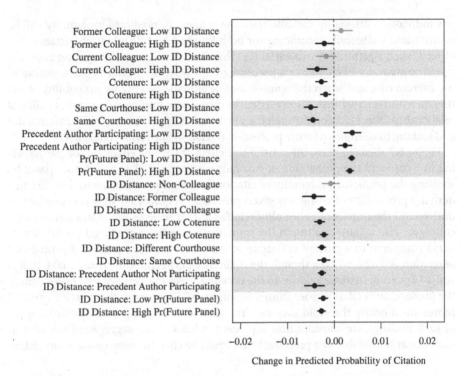

Figure 8.1 Changes in Predicted Probability of Citation, Courts of Appeals, Main Explanatory Variables: Estimates (and associated 95% confidence intervals) of the change in the predicted probability a majority opinion cites a precedent by moving each variable from a low to high value while holding other variables at their median conditional on citation. Changes produced by collegiality and ideology are presented at low and high values of the other to illustrate interactive effects. Low and high values are 25th and 75th percentile conditional on citation for continuous variables and zero and one for binary variables. Estimates and confidence intervals in gray (instead of black) indicate that the confidence interval includes zero. Full regression estimates are available in Table 8.B.1 in the chapter appendix.

zero to one) and holding control variables at their median value conditional on citation.[11] The full regression results are available in Table 8.B.1. Because we interact our collegiality variables with Ideological Distance, we show the changes in predicted probability for each collegiality variable at low and high values of Ideological Distance and the changes for a corresponding shift in Ideological Distance at low and high values of each collegiality variable.[12] First, we look at whether there is evidence that collegiality directly increases the probability of citation. If this is true for

---

[11] All discussion of predicted probabilities and marginal effects in this chapter hold all other variables in the relevant model at their median value conditional on citation. This is an approach used in citation analyses to put the results on a more relevant scale (Hinkle 2015).

[12] Due to the size of this model, we present the results for the control variables below in Figure 8.3.

any individual collegiality variable, then the changes in predicted probability will be positive and statistically significant for both low and high Ideological Distance. We observe such a pattern for two variables. There is evidence that the opinion author is significantly more likely to cite a precedent both when its author is participating in the current case and when the opinion author anticipates a higher probability of sitting on a future panel with the precedent author. These findings suggest that collegial relationships affect citation through the mechanisms of persuasion in the case at hand and seeking to strengthen future professional relationships with colleagues.

Figure 8.2 sheds light on the substantive effect of the precedent author participating in a case and the probability of two judges sitting together on a future panel by showing the predicted probability of citation for all values of each variable. The underlying probability of citing any given precedent is quite low, so it is important to understand the impact of collegiality relative to that scale. A precedent written by a colleague who is participating in the immediate case has a predicted probability of 0.033 compared to a current colleague who is not, where the predicted probability of citation is 0.029. So even though the difference between those is only 0.004, that is still a 14 percent increase relative to the baseline. Over the range of Pr(Future Panel), the probability of citation goes from 0.025 up to 0.072. In short, the increase of 0.047 represents a nearly threefold increase. To better understand the substantive import of such findings, we consider how a precedent fares in the aggregate. Each case in our dataset is available as a precedent that could be cited in many opinion-precedent

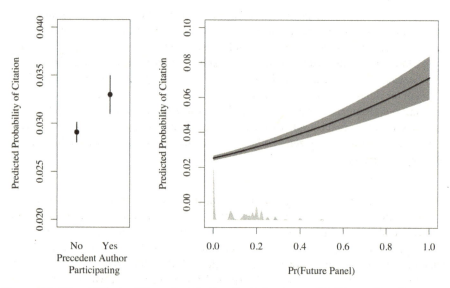

Figure 8.2 Direct Effects of Precedent Author Participating and Pr(Future Panel) on Citation, Courts of Appeals: This figure shows the predicted probability of a precedent being cited when the precedent is and is not participating in the immediate case (left-hand panel) and as Pr(Future Panel) varies (right-hand panel). The bars and shaded region depict the 95% confidence intervals. The density plot shows the distribution of Pr(Future Panel).

dyads. We count the number of dyads each precedent is in and then calculate the average of those numbers, which is 345. Using this measure of central tendency, we find that when the author is participating, an average precedent would get an estimated 11.4 citations compared to 10 citations when a current colleague is not participating. For Pr(Future Panel), the estimated number of total citations ranges from 8.6 all the way up to 24.8. These findings suggest that forward-looking behavior focused on maintaining relationships has a larger effect on citation decisions than the back-and-forth persuasion that can happen when two judges are on the same panel.

In the circuit court model, there is also some evidence of collegiality having a direct effect on citation that is in the opposite direction from what we expected. The authors of the two opinions having chambers in the same courthouse actually decreases the probability of citation. Along similar lines, when the two judges have served together, the length of that service is negatively correlated with citation. While not anticipated, these findings shed interesting light on collegiality and citation that is not necessarily inconsistent with our broader narrative. Judges in the same courthouse have more frequent and nuanced opportunities for building and maintaining good working relationships with their colleagues. It is possible that this renders the somewhat ham-handed technique of flattery through citation less necessary. The negative result for cotenure in the circuit courts may reflect the importance of future interactions as colleagues who have served together for a shorter time often anticipate working together longer in the future. While this may not be true for older judges, we have controlled for the age of the opinion author in our model. It is holding age constant that we find serving together a shorter time leads to more citations.

Next, we consider our conditional collegiality hypothesis. For citation decisions, we expect that our collegiality variables will have the most explanatory power when the opinion and precedent author are closer together in terms of ideology. Therefore, the conditional relationship we hypothesize emerges if a collegiality variable has a significant (and positive) effect for low levels of ideological distance but is not significant (or is smaller) at high levels of ideological distance. We find no support for this hypothesis in the circuit courts. Most of the collegiality variables have similar effects at low and high Ideological Distance. The two exceptions defy our expectations in two ways. The status of a colleague as current or former is only statistically significant for ideological foes rather than allies. Furthermore, under those conditions both current and former colleagues are less likely to be cited than judges with whom the opinion author never served. With respect to current colleagues, it is important to note that this finding pertains only to current colleagues who are not on the panel in the immediate case. As we discussed earlier, a precedent is more likely to be cited when the author is both a current colleague and participating in the case as hand. However, our results indicate that judges with different ideological perspectives do not necessarily gain respect for each other through shared service sufficient to increase citations to one another. Rather, serving with ideological foes in the present or past actually decreases willingness to cite their work.

Third, we examine whether the effect of Ideological Distance is dampened when two judges have closer collegial relationships. This hypothesis would be reflected in the effect of Ideological Distance (which we expect to be negative) being nonsignificant or closer to zero when two judges have high levels of a collegiality variable compared to low ones. Here we see consistent evidence that greater levels of Ideological Distance significantly decrease the probability of citation. But the model provides no indications that collegiality dampens that effect. The only condition where Ideological Distance is not statistically significant is when the opinion author never served with the judge who wrote the precedent. While it seems somewhat unlikely that circuit judges would not be aware of the ideological leaning of their predecessors, it is possible that this finding suggests diminished information or awareness where there is no personal connection. One final interesting point to note about the effect of Ideological Distance is that the size of its effects are all on a similar scale as the significant collegiality variables.

Finally, the effects of collegiality and ideology are even better understood in the context of other variables that affect citation. Figure 8.3 shows the changes in

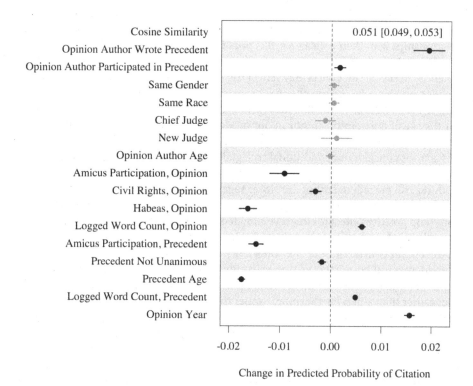

Change in Predicted Probability of Citation

Figure 8.3 Changes in Predicted Probability of Citation, Courts of Appeals, Control Variables: Estimates (and associated 95% confidence intervals) of the change in the predicted probability a majority opinion cites a precedent by moving each control variable from a low to high value while holding other variables at their median conditional on citation. Low and high values are 25th and 75th percentile conditional on citation for continuous variables and zero and one for binary variables. Estimates and confidence intervals in gray (instead of black) indicate that the confidence interval includes zero. Full regression estimates are available in Table 8.B.1 in the chapter appendix.

THE IMPACT OF RELATIONSHIPS ON THE USE OF PRECEDENT   217

predicted probability of citation generated by moving the control variables from a low (25th percentile or low value of a dichotomous variable) to a high (75th percentile or the high value of a dichotomous variable) value. The x-axis covers the same range as the previous figure so that the size of effects can easily be compared. Some of these variables have much larger effects than collegiality and ideology. This is not surprising in the context of citation decisions. The biggest determinant of citation by far is Cosine Similarity. This makes perfect sense since the relevance of a precedent is the sine qua non of citation. Opinion authors are also much more likely to cite precedents they wrote themselves. They also cite the cases they participated in more frequently, but that effect size is much smaller. One of the biggest negative effects is from the age of a precedent. This is nothing new. Precedents addressing habeas petitions are also substantially less likely to get cited, and those in civil cases are somewhat less likely to be cited than precedents in criminal cases. As we expect, longer precedents get cited more, and longer opinions refer to more precedents. It also appears that judges have become more prolific in their citations over time, although that may be an artifact of the data construction process.[13] The most surprising findings are that cases with amicus participation are both less likely to cite and be cited. While we assumed these cases were those in which the legal issues were more salient, it is possible that is not the case. Or perhaps in the circuit courts, amicus participation is a sort of last-ditch effort employed only under dire circumstances. All in all, we conclude that future research into amicus practice in circuit courts could prove very interesting.

Collegiality and Citation in the U.S. Supreme Court

Data

As in previous chapters, our Supreme Court analysis covers all orally argued cases from 1955 to 2009. The model specification is largely analogous to our circuit court study. Since the citation outcome is binary, we use a probit model. And, once again, we cluster on the opinion.

Our primary explanatory variables at the Supreme Court level reflect the more limited variation in collegial contacts. However, we can use a pair of indicator variables for former and current colleagues. Pairs of justices who never served together are the baseline. We can also control for cotenure by measuring the length of time two justices have served together (or did serve together in the past for former colleagues). We interact these collegiality variables with Ideological Distance, which is the absolute value of the difference between the JCS scores of the opinion author and precedent author.

We control for many of the same factors that we do in the circuit court model, but context requires some modification. Once again, we use cosine similarity to control for the legal relevance of a precedent. Since our Supreme Court dataset includes cases

---

[13] Since we pair each majority opinion with each previous one in the dataset, cases later in the data are paired with more cases, which means we are accounting for a larger percentage of the total available case law than we are in earlier cases in the data.

218 THE ELEVATOR EFFECT

from a wide variety of issue area, we also control for whether the opinion and precedent are within the same broad issue area. We account for whether the opinion author wrote the precedent or participated in that case. Next, we turn to past experiences, controlling for whether the opinion author previously clerked for the Supreme Court, worked in the courts of appeals, or worked in the D.C. Circuit specifically. As we discuss more fully in Chapter 5, these may be formative experiences for the way a justice interacts with colleagues. Current characteristics of the opinion author could affect citation too, so we account for whether they are the chief justice or new to the Court and their age. Finally, the model includes features of the opinion and precedent separately that could affect the probability of citation. We control for the salience and length of both the opinion and precedent as well as whether the precedent was not unanimous. Both salience variables use Clark, Lax, and Rice (2015)'s measure. The age and age-squared of the precedent and the year the opinion was issued round out the Supreme Court model. Summary statistics for all variables are available in Table 8.A.2 in the chapter appendix.

Results

We now look at how collegiality affects citation in the context of the Supreme Court. Our results for this analysis are available in Table 8.B.2. As we have observed throughout this book, there is less variation in interpersonal relationships at the Supreme Court level because all the justices work in the same courthouse and they generally all participate in each case. Nevertheless, they do vary in the amount of time they have served together. For purposes of citing precedent, they also vary in whether the opinion author is currently serving with the precedent author, served with them in the past, or whether their tenure on the Court did not overlap. Figure 8.4 provides the changes in predicted probabilities for our Supreme Court model. Overall, there is little evidence of collegiality influencing citation at this level. There is no evidence of collegiality having a direct effect on citation. In fact, many of the estimates are very close to zero (not merely imprecisely estimated).

However, there is one piece of evidence in favor of our conditional collegiality hypothesis. Recall that we expect collegiality indicators to have more of an effect between ideological allies. Our results show that Supreme Court justices are more likely to cite current colleagues compared to former or non-colleagues. But that effect is only statistically significant for low values of Ideological Distance. We further illustrate this relationship in Figure 8.5, which shows the marginal effect of a precedent being written by a current colleague over the range of Ideological Distance. This effect is only statistically significant when the Ideological Distance between the opinion and precedent authors is less than 0.5. However, as the density plot illustrates, the data are somewhat concentrated in this region. As a result, Current Colleague is statistically significant for 53 percent of the data. Next, we consider the size of the effect. The effect of a precedent being written by a current colleague is greatest when the two judges have precisely the same ideology score. Under these conditions, the marginal

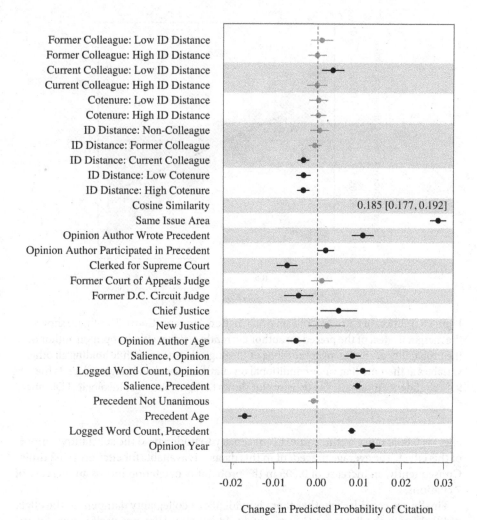

Figure 8.4 Changes in Predicted Probability of Citation, Supreme Court: Estimates (and associated 95% confidence intervals) of the change in the predicted probability a majority opinion cites a precedent by moving each variable from a low to high value while holding other variables at their median value conditional on citation. Changes produced by collegiality and ideology are presented at low and high values of the other to illustrate interactive effects. Low and high values are 25th and 75th percentile conditional on citation for continuous variables and zero and one for binary variables. Estimates and confidence intervals in gray (instead of black) indicate that the confidence interval includes zero. Full regression estimates are available in Table 8.B.2 in the chapter appendix.

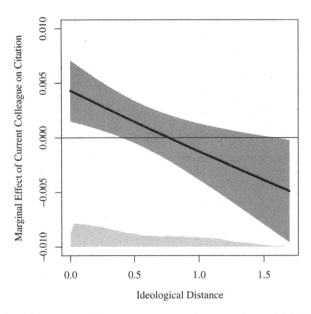

Figure 8.5 Effect of Current Colleague on Citation, Supreme Court: This figure shows the marginal effect of the precedent author currently serving with the opinion author on the probability of citation over the range of Ideological Distance (while holding all other variables at their median value conditional on citation). The shaded region depicts the 95% confidence intervals. The density plot shows the distribution of Ideological Distance.

effect is 0.005. Once again, context is necessary to understand the substantive import of this effect. The average precedent in this dataset is available for citation 1,408 times. Consequently, an increase of 0.005 in the probability of citation means an increase of 7 citations.

Finally, we consider whether there is evidence of collegiality dampening the effect of ideology in the Supreme Court context. Ideological Distance itself is not statistically significant in the regression table, but when all other variables are held at their median conditional on citation, the level of ideological disagreement between a pair of judges is a significant predictor of citing precedents written by current colleagues at both low and high values of shared time on the bench together. However, like in the circuit court model, there is no indication of ideological dampening. Once again, the type of colleague is the only collegiality variable that shows any variation in ideology. In the circuit courts, ideological distance is a significant predictor of citation to both former and current colleagues. For the Supreme Court, Ideological Distance is only significant for current colleagues. There is no evidence that citation to precedents written by either non-colleagues or former colleagues is shaped by ideological considerations. In the Supreme Court context, there is little chance this reflects a lack of knowledge about past justices. Rather, our results overall suggest that justices prefer to cite current colleagues who are ideological allies. Non-colleagues, former colleagues, and current colleagues on the other side of the ideological aisle are simply not likely to be cited. In short, any persuasion based on past interactions does not appear to sway justices in their selection of precedent.

The control variables show many of the same patterns that emerge in the circuit court model. More similar cases are cited more frequently. Here, our measure of whether two cases are in the same issue area is positive and significant in addition to the Cosine Similarity measure. We also see the same dynamics with opinion authors citing their own precedent much more frequently and, to a lesser degree, citing precedents from cases in which they participated. Longer opinions are cited more and contain more citations, older precedents are cited less, and there are more citations over time. Some differences emerge as well. Our indicator of salience is positive and significant as expected for both the opinion and the precedent. In the Supreme Court, older authors cite fewer precedents and chiefs cite more frequently. Neither of these measures was significant for circuit court judges. Lastly, some of the variables unique to this model reveal interesting patterns. Justices who clerked for a Supreme Court justice cite less frequently, as do justices who were elevated from the D.C. Circuit.

Conclusions

In this chapter, we theorized that collegiality would increase citation directly, that the effect would be most noticeable between ideological allies, and that the effect of ideology on citation would be dampened when two judges had or anticipated more frequent personal and professional contacts. One benefit of studying citation is that it is a type of judicial behavior that also allows us to distinguish between various mechanisms that might drive our hypothesized collegiality effect. We can compare the influence of judges who never served with an opinion author to those who were former colleagues, to those who are current colleagues. Forward-looking motivations designed to promote pleasant social discourse in the future will only manifest in behavior toward current colleagues, while any effects of collegiality that emerge with respect to former colleagues (compared to non-colleagues) must necessarily reflect the backward-looking mechanism of years of interactions informing and leading to a different behavior. We noted at the outset of this chapter that looking for evidence of collegiality across time is a tough test for our theory. Our results, summarized in Table 8.2, bear out this expectation.

Overall, this chapter makes three broad contributions. The first takeaway is that collegiality can affect citation decisions. Various features of how much an opinion and precedent author interact significantly affect the probability of citation. Perhaps more importantly, the second takeaway is *why* collegiality affects citation. Relationships appear to shape citation through the mechanisms of persuasion and maintenance of ongoing relationships, but not through influence based on past relationships. We find no evidence that respect and influence built through relationships change citations. When a precedent author is no longer on the court, whether they served with the opinion author does not make a statistically significant difference. Neither does more extensive time served together increase citation. However, there is evidence that judges cite with an eye toward persuasion (or are themselves persuaded by a colleague)

222 THE ELEVATOR EFFECT

Table 8.2 Summary of Results, Citing Precedent: A checkmark denotes a result that is statistically significant and in the direction we hypothesize. An "x" denotes a result that is significant, but in the opposite of the hypothesized direction.

	Direct Effect Collegiality	Conditional Effect Collegiality	Conditional Effect Ideology
Courts of Appeals			
Former Colleague		x	x
Current Colleague		x	x
Cotenure	x		
Same Courthouse	x		
Precedent Author Participated	✓		
Pr(Future Panel)	✓		
Supreme Court			
Former Colleague			
Current Colleague		✓	x
Cotenure			

because they are more likely to cite a precedent when its author is participating in the current case. Finally, judges cite in a forward-looking manner as evidenced by the finding that circuit judges are more likely to cite a colleague when they will be sitting with them on more panels in the future.

Finally, our third takeaway is that there are some key differences in how collegiality affects citation in different institutional contexts. Although colleague type and cotenure are the only consistent features across models, the differences are interesting. The way circuit judges cite their former colleagues is a bit unexpected. They are less likely to cite ideologically distant past colleagues (compared to non-colleagues). However, the Supreme Court model suggests that justices treat former and non-colleagues very similarly when it comes to citation. The difference between institutional context is most stark in terms of how authors cite their current colleagues. Circuit judges cite their current colleagues less frequently regardless of their ideological disagreements, while Supreme Court justices cite their current colleagues more frequently, but only if they are ideological allies. Finally, we consider Cotenure. In the circuit courts colleagues who serve together longer actually cite each other *less*, while in the Supreme Court Cotenure is not a significant predictor of citation.

The findings in this chapter help us to further understand collegiality by teasing apart potential mechanisms through analysis of a form of judicial interaction that stretches across time. They provide new and interesting information regarding the relationships among judges and how forward-looking concerns appear to take precedence over backward-looking behavior. This dynamic may be exclusive to the process of selecting citations, but it is suggestive for other areas of judicial behavior where it is more difficult to disentangle judges' motivations.

Appendix 8.A: Summary Statistics

Table 8.A.1 Summary Statistics for Courts of Appeals Search and Seizure Citation Dataset. Percentages may not add to 100% due to rounding.

Continuous Variables	Min.	25%	50%	75%	Max.
Cotenure	0	0	7	15	46
Ideological Distance	0.00	0.12	0.32	0.61	1.41
Pr(Future Panel)	0.00	0.00	0.08	0.20	1.00
Cosine Similarity	4.40	5.28	6.47	8.51	99.99
Opinion Author Age	37	56	63	70	96
Logged Word Count, Opinion	3.26	7.79	8.20	8.61	10.67
Precedent Age	0	5	12	21	57
Logged Word Count, Precedent	3.26	7.60	8.03	8.46	10.67
Opinion Year	1953	1989	1998	2005	2010

Dichotomous Variables	0	1			
Precedent Cited	99.2%	0.8%			
Same Courthouse	86%	14%			
Precedent Author Participating	95%	5%			
Opinion Author Wrote Precedent	97%	3%			
Opinion Author Participated in Precedent	95%	5%			
Same Gender	19%	81%			
Same Race	16%	84%			
Chief Judge	94%	6%			
New Judge	97%	3%			
Amicus Participation, Opinion	97%	3%			
Civil Rights, Opinion	71%	29%			
Habeas, Opinion	96%	4%			
Amicus Participation, Precedent	98%	2%			
Precedent Not Unanimous	85%	15%			

Categorical Variable	Percent				
Colleague Type					
Never a Colleague	16%				
Former Colleague	17%				
Current Colleague	67%				

224   THE ELEVATOR EFFECT

Table 8.A.2 Summary Statistics for Supreme Court Citation Dataset. Percentages may not add to 100% due to rounding.

Continuous Variables	Min.	25%	50%	75%	Max.
Cotenure	0	0	6	13	35
Ideological Distance	0.00	0.20	0.46	0.86	1.66
Cosine Similarity	6.0	7.05	8.47	10.92	88.43
Opinion Author Age	43	59	66	73	88
Salience, Opinion	−1.32	−0.59	−0.16	0.55	3.50
Logged Word Count, Opinion	4.71	8.16	8.48	8.80	10.74
Salience, Precedent	−1.32	−0.50	−0.29	0.39	3.50
Precedent Age	0	6	13	22	53
Logged Word Count, Precedent	4.71	7.94	8.34	8.71	10.74
Opinion Year	1955	1980	1988	1997	2009
Dichotomous Variables	**0**	**1**			
Precedent Cited	99.6%	0.4%			
Same Issue Area	81%	19%			
Opinion Author Wrote Precedent	94%	6%			
Opinion Author Participated in Precedent	56%	44%			
Clerked for Supreme Court	67%	33%			
Former COA Judge	41%	59%			
Former D.C. Circuit Judge	81%	19%			
Chief Justice	89%	11%			
New Justice	93%	7%			
Precedent Not Unanimous	33%	67%			
Categorical Variable	**Percent**				
Colleague Type					
Never a Colleague	22%				
Former Colleague	27%				
Current Colleague	51%				

Appendix 8.B: Regression Results

Table 8.B.1 Precedent Citation Model, Circuit Courts: Probit regression estimates of the effect of personal and professional contacts, Ideological Distance, their interaction, and a range of control variables on the probability an opinion will cite a precedent. The reported standard errors are robust standard errors that are clustered on the opinion and * denotes a p-value less than 0.05.

	Coef.	S.E.
Former Colleague	0.029	(0.019)
Ideological Distance	−0.030	(0.017)
Former Colleague × ID Distance	−0.104	(0.036)
Current Colleague	−0.020	(0.017)
Current Colleague× ID Distance	−0.062	(0.031)
Cotenure	−0.003	(0.001)
Cotenure × ID Distance	0.002	(0.001)
Same Courthouse	−0.081	(0.013)
Same Courthouse × ID Distance	0.003	(0.024)
Precedent Author Participating	0.059	(0.014)
Prec. Au. Participating × ID Distance	−0.037	(0.030)
Pr(Future Panel)	0.492	(0.048)
Pr(Future Panel) × ID Distance	−0.030	(0.105)
Cosine Similarity	0.075	(0.001)
Opinion Author Wrote Precedent	0.239	(0.016)
Opinion Author Participated in Precedent	0.025	(0.008)
Same Gender	0.007	(0.008)
Same Race	−0.015	(0.009)
Chief Judge	−0.019	(0.016)
New Judge	0.016	(0.023)
Opinion Author Age	−0.0003	(0.0005)
Amicus Participation, Opinion	−0.169	(0.031)
Civil Rights, Opinion	−0.051	(0.010)
Habeas, Opinion	−0.357	(0.027)
Logged Word Count, Opinion	0.118	(0.007)
Amicus Participation, Precedent	−0.306	(0.020)
Precedent Not Unanimous	−0.028	(0.006)
Precedent Age	−0.052	(0.001)
Precedent Age^2	0.0003	(0.00003)
Logged Word Count, Precedent	0.097	(0.004)
Opinion Year	0.016	(0.0004)
Intercept	−36.453	(0.796)
N		4,741,639
AIC		357882.9
BIC		358310.8

226 THE ELEVATOR EFFECT

Table 8.B.2 Precedent Citation Model, Supreme Court: Probit regression estimates of the effect of personal and professional contacts, Ideological Distance, their interaction, and a range of control variables on the probability an opinion will cite a precedent. The reported standard errors are robust standard errors that are clustered on the opinion and * denotes a p-value less than 0.05.

	Coef.	S.E.
Former Colleague	0.013	(0.016)
Ideological Distance	0.008	(0.016)
Former Colleague × ID Distance	−0.018	(0.022)
Current Colleague	0.047	(0.016)
Current Colleague × ID Distance	−0.061	(0.021)
Cotenure	0.0002	(0.001)
Cotenure × ID Distance	−0.0001	(0.001)
Cosine Similarity	0.069	(0.0005)
Same Issue Area	0.405	(0.008)
Opinion Author Wrote Precedent	0.099	(0.011)
Opinion Author Participated in Precedent	0.020	(0.010)
Clerked for Supreme Court	−0.076	(0.013)
Former COA Judge	0.011	(0.013)
Former D.C. Circuit Judge	−0.046	(0.018)
Chief Justice	0.049	(0.020)
New Justice	0.023	(0.021)
Opinion Author Age	−0.004	(0.001)
Salience, Opinion	0.067	(0.007)
Logged Word Count, Opinion	0.167	(0.012)
Salience, Precedent	0.082	(0.003)
Precedent Not Unanimous	−0.008	(0.006)
Precedent Age	−0.018	(0.001)
Precedent Age^2	0.0002	(0.0003)
Logged Word Count, Precedent	0.115	(0.005)
Opinion Year	0.007	(0.001)
Intercept	−19.423	(1.070)
N	7,989,134	
AIC	290876.3	
BIC	291237.5	

9

Taking Collegiality Seriously in Designing and Studying Courts

Introduction

Throughout this book, we have emphasized a fundamental fact about judging on the U.S. federal judiciary: a judge who wishes to maximize their influence in the long term should pay attention to their relationships with their colleagues in the short term. In this book, we used a combination of historical evidence, interview data, and quantitative analysis to examine the effects of judicial collegiality on judicial behavior. Knowing that collegiality is a broad concept, we focused our efforts on a simple conceptualization of the concept: the level of interpersonal contact between two judges. In examining judicial behavior, we cast our net widely to examine the decision to concur or dissent, vote to reverse a lower court judge, use harsh language, and cite the work of one's colleagues.

Our efforts were motivated by a simple fact: judges often say that collegiality is important for their work, but legal scholars and political scientists haven't devoted the attention to adjudicating the effects of collegiality that they have given to understanding the role of ideology, demographic characteristics, and legal considerations on judicial behavior. We hope our inquiry has demonstrated that collegiality plays an important role at nearly every stage of the judicial process in both the U.S. Courts of Appeals and the U.S. Supreme Court. In this chapter, we tie together our various analyses to draw some general conclusions about the role of collegiality in the U.S. federal courts, lay bare the limitations of our work, and discuss some pathways for future research that we hope will be fruitful as others advance our understanding of how interpersonal relationships among judges influence the judicial process.

Summary of Findings

We begin by outlining what we have found regarding the role of collegiality in judicial decision-making. Most of our analyses in the previous chapters have sought to answer one of three questions: First, what is the direct effect of collegiality (interpersonal contact) on judicial behavior? Second, how does the effect of collegiality vary according to the level of ideological disagreement between two judges? Third, do higher levels of collegiality dampen the effect of ideological disagreement on judicial behavior? In the following sections, we consider each of these questions in turn, drawing connections among our analyses to make some general conclusions. We have also sought to gauge the mechanisms that explain the effects of collegiality on judicial behavior and

The Elevator Effect. Morgan L.W. Hazelton, Rachael K. Hinkle, and Michael J. Nelson, Oxford University Press.
© Oxford University Press 2023. DOI: 10.1093/oso/9780197625408.003.0009

228   THE ELEVATOR EFFECT

to determine how these effects vary at different levels of the judicial hierarchy. Here, we discuss the lessons we have learned for each of these topics in turn.

Increased Collegiality May Foster Consensus

Throughout our empirical analyses, we hypothesized that increased personal and professional contacts would directly affect various kinds of judicial behavior. We theorized that collegiality would decrease public disagreement, reversal, and caustic rhetoric in dissents while increasing respectful language in dissents and citation. Throughout the book, we have uncovered evidence that increased levels of judicial collegiality can affect judges' voting patterns, citation decisions, and the language they use to express their disagreement with their colleagues.

Most of our evidence of collegiality directly affecting judges emerges when we look at the amount of time two judges have served together and how much they anticipate serving together in the future. Increased levels of cotenure are associated with a decrease in the likelihood of dissent for both circuit judges and Supreme Court justices. At the Supreme Court, for example, changing cotenure from its minimum to maximum values reduces the probability of dissent by about 5 percent; in the courts of appeals, that same change corresponds to a 3 percent decrease in the probability of a dissenting opinion. Compared to the baseline of dissents in both types of courts, these are notable decreases: they represent almost 25 percent of the dissent rate in the Supreme Court and nearly half the dissents that are typical in the courts of appeals.[1]

For circuit judges, we measured the importance of anticipated future interactions with how often a judge expects to be on a panel with any given colleague in the future. As we hypothesized, higher levels of anticipated future interaction decrease the probability of a dissenting opinion in the U.S. Courts of Appeals: a change from a pair of judges very unlikely to serve together on a given panel to a pair that is almost certain to serve together soon corresponds to a 6 percent decrease in the probability of a dissenting opinion. Further, when there is a dissent, the probability that the author will choose to use a rudely blunt sign-off of "I dissent" also decreases with the probability the pair of judges will serve together soon. And the effects of anticipated future interaction also color citation decisions: circuit judges are quicker to cite their current colleagues in circuits where they work together more frequently. Thus, when judges expect to see each other often, they are more likely to act in ways that maintain good relationships with their colleagues.

Still, interpersonal contact does not always have the direct effect on judicial behavior we expected. For example, we found scant evidence in any of our analyses that geographic proximity—whether two judges have chambers in the same courthouse— has a statistically significant direct effect. In fact, the only evidence of a direct effect is not in the direction we expected; circuit judges are actually less likely to cite precedents written by their colleagues in the same courthouse. We also found the circuit judges are more likely to cite precedents written by their colleagues who are on the

---

[1] In our Supreme Court data, 21% of votes are dissents, and in our circuit court data, 7% of votes are dissents.

TAKING COLLEGIALITY SERIOUSLY IN DESIGNING AND STUDYING   229

panel in the immediate case. Somewhat surprisingly, however, circuit judges become *less* likely to cite the precedents of colleagues the longer they serve on the same court.

The Effect of Collegiality Increases with Ideological Distance

Of course, direct effects are only part of the story. Even when collegiality does not affect judges across the board, it may matter selectively with respect to either ideological foes or allies. We now turn to providing a comprehensive look at where we find collegiality has a conditional impact on judicial decision-making. We hypothesized that the effects of collegiality would be greatest among ideological foes for voting behavior and in the language judges use to express their disagreement. By contrast, we expected collegiality to have the most noticeable impact among ideological allies when deciding which opinions to cite.

We found evidence that the effect of interpersonal contact increases with the level of ideological disagreement between two judges. First, we saw evidence in Chapter 3 that judges are less likely to dissent from ideological foes who work in the same building compared to those who are geographically distant. Second, when circuit judges do dissent from an ideological foe, they use an estimated 8.3 fewer negative emotional words in their opinion when they know they could run into the majority opinion author in the elevator or parking lot any day. Third, regarding cotenure, we find that Supreme Court justices who have served longer with each other and who are also ideologically distant are less likely to write concurring opinions. Finally, regarding our third indicator of collegiality, the probability of future panel service, we found that the likelihood of serving with a colleague in the future depressed the probability that a circuit judge will dissent for nearly all values of ideological distance, and that effect is largest when the two judges have strong ideological disagreements. These findings all align with our theory.

There are other findings with respect to the conditional effect of collegiality, as well. The status of a precedent author can conditionally impact the probability of citation. We hypothesized that current and former colleagues, especially those who are ideological allies of the opinion author, would be more likely to be cited. In the circuit courts, both former and current colleagues who are also ideologically distant are less likely to be cited than judges who were never colleagues of the majority opinion author. However, as we expected, Supreme Court justices are more likely to cite a current colleague compared to former or non-colleagues if the two judges are ideologically proximate.

We also found some effects regarding the conditional effect of collegiality that were contrary to our expectations. Two ideologically proximate judges who work in the same courthouse are more likely to concur compared to two who office separately. We hypothesized that such an effect would be negative and most notable between ideologically distant colleagues. There is evidence that, between ideological allies, increasing values of cotenure lead to a decrease in the probability that circuit judges and Supreme Court justices dissent in a polite manner and a decrease in the number of direct references to the majority in a Supreme Court dissent. Meanwhile, allies in the Supreme Court are more likely to dissent in a rude fashion. In all these contexts,

230 THE ELEVATOR EFFECT

we theorized that cotenure should matter most when two judges are ideologically distant, so these four findings where years served together is only significant for low levels of ideological distance are surprising. The direction of three of these results is unexpected as well. We hypothesized that increased familiarity gained through years of service together should make polite dissents more likely and rude dissents less likely. Instead, we observe the opposite. However, the finding that cotenure decreases direct references to the majority in the dissent, which are largely hostile and conflictual, is what we anticipated, even if we did expect it to emerge for foes rather than allies.

Collegiality Dampens the Effect of Ideological Disagreement

Our most robust conclusions emerge with respect to how the effect of ideological disagreement is conditioned by interpersonal contact. We expected that more extensive personal interactions would reduce the effect of ideological disagreement on each type of judicial behavior we examined. We found that close collegial relationships often render the effect of ideology nonexistent, or at least not statistically significant. Given the ubiquity of ideology as a powerful explanation for judicial behavior of many kinds, it is remarkable that we have uncovered such a wide variety of situations where it has no such explanatory power if judges have existing relationships. In fact, each of our three main indicators of collegiality show evidence of ideological dampening in the manner we hypothesize.

We begin by describing how working in the same courthouse can eliminate the effect of ideology on judicial decision-making. The probability that a circuit judge will concur, dissent, vote to reverse, and (if dissenting) write a polite dissent are all decisions that are only significantly affected by ideology when the relevant two judges do not have chambers in the same courthouse. When they do work in the same building, the effect of ideology is not just smaller, but essentially disappears. The only place where the converse pattern appears is in the case of negative language in dissenting opinions. However, for judges who work in close proximity, greater ideological distance actually decreases the amount of negative language used.

Next, the effect of ideology is conditional on how long two judges have served together. Interestingly, all four situations in which cotenure dampens ideology relate to the language of dissent. Ideological distance is only a significant predictor of the number of positive emotion words in a dissent for low values of cotenure. Similarly, ideology only significantly affects the probability of a polite dissent when two judges have served together a shorter amount of time. This finding appears in the context of both the circuit courts and the Supreme Court. In the Supreme Court, ideological distance is positively associated with the number of direct references to the majority in a dissent when cotenure is low. We expected the effect to be in this direction. Dissenters who are increasingly far from the majority opinion author should be more likely to resort to the more hostile and caustic rhetoric typically associated with directly calling out the majority. However, for very high levels of cotenure we see the direction flip: ideology has a negative effect on direct references to the majority.

Finally, the effect of ideological disagreements dissipates as judges become more likely to serve again with their panel members in the future. Here again, we see ideology have no effect—or less of an effect—for low values of this variable. When Pr(Future Panel) is low, judges' interpersonal relationships with their panel members are of less concern. As a result, there is less of a benefit for these judges to temper their behavior for the sake of a peaceful working environment. At higher values of Pr(Future Panel), by contrast, a judge knows they will sit with each colleague more often. In these circumstances, collegial concerns might begin to outweigh policy concerns. We see evidence of this in three ways. Ideology is only significant for low values of Pr(Future Panel) on the decision to concur, the number of positive words used in a dissent, and the usage of a polite form of dissent. For the decision of whether to dissent, circuit judges take ideology into account across the board, but its effect size is smaller when the probability of serving together in the future is higher.

Mechanisms

Our results also shed light on *why* collegiality matters. Throughout the book, we considered two types of explanations for why relationships matter. The first mechanism is persuasion. The longer two judges have served together, the better they might be able to persuade one another. There is evidence that persuasion affects the decision to dissent in both the circuit courts and the Supreme Court: increased cotenure reduces the probability of dissent in both contexts. Cotenure also decreases concurrences in the Supreme Court when a justice is ideologically distant from the majority opinion author. Finally, cotenure dampens the effect of ideology on several features of dissenting opinions which include the number of positive words in circuit dissents, the probability of a polite dissent in both types of courts, and the number of direct references to the majority in Supreme Court dissents. All these findings suggest that, as judges get to know each other sufficiently well, their increased persuasive ability is able to influence judicial behavior.

But persuasion is not the end of the story. A second mechanism through which collegiality can affect judicial decision-making is through forward-looking relationship management. In other words, judges may be more likely to follow the "golden rule," and treat others the way they would like to be treated, when they know they will have to interact with colleagues a substantial amount in the future. Public disagreement, reversals, and harshly framed dissents are all conflict-inducing behaviors that judges should minimize if they want to avoid doing damage to their professional relationships. Conversely, politely framed dissents and citing to colleagues are behaviors that might preserve or enhance future relationships. Our results suggest that judges act as if they care about their quality of life going forward and do not want to sour their relationships. When judges expect to spend more time together, they are less likely to dissent. And if they do dissent, they are less likely to do so rudely. They are also more likely to cite precedents written by their colleagues when they will have to see them more. Finally, larger values of Pr(Future Panel) lead to ideological dampening for the decisions to concur and dissent, the number of positive emotional words in a dissent, and the choice to use a polite form of dissent. All these findings are consistent with the explanation that judges are affected by collegiality because they care about good relations with their colleagues at a later date.

Ultimately, we find evidence that both personal and professional contact are important for decision-making, and collegiality influences judicial decision-making through both persuasion and suppression. These findings support theories of judicial behavior, like those put forward by Baum (1997) and Epstein, Landes, and Posner (2013), that suggest judges balance multiple goals. These findings help us understand why institutional context is important: different aspects of collegiality and related goals are important based on the type of court, interaction, and outcome.

Differences in Institutional Context

While we broadly theorize that collegiality affects judicial decision-making, there is reason to expect that its impact will vary depending upon institutional context. We studied the role of interpersonal interactions in two types of appellate courts. Circuit court judges are geographically dispersed, have higher caseloads, and have a strong norm of dissent avoidance. Supreme Court justices are quite different. They all work in the same courthouse, they decide all their cases together, they have a much lower caseload, and they more frequently air their disagreements publicly. These are only some of the differences that may lead to collegiality operating differently across levels of the judiciary. To some extent, the very differences make it difficult to compare and contrast the two contexts. However, our ability to examine the effect of cotenure across all of our models facilitates our ability to make cross-court comparisons.

In light of the differences between circuit courts and the Supreme Court, we begin by discussing the three places where we observed the same patterns in both contexts. First, in both types of court, judges who have served together longer are less likely to dissent from each other's opinions. Second, cotenure decreases the probability a dissenter will choose a polite form of dissent, but only among ideological allies. By contrast, we hypothesized that cotenure should increase the likelihood a dissenter will choose a polite form of dissent, especially when the majority opinion author is an ideological rival. While neither of these expectations were supported in our analysis, the fact that this pattern emerges in the circuit courts as well as the Supreme Court indicates we should take it seriously. Finally, the effect of ideology on the usage of polite forms of dissent is significant only for lower levels of cotenure, which indicates ideological dampening.

Unsurprisingly, the ways in which circuit courts and the Supreme Court are different are more numerous than the ways in which they are the same. There are six types of evidence that appear in one of the two contexts but are not statistically significant in the other. In the circuit courts, cotenure dampens the effect ideology has on the number of positive emotion words in a dissent and it decreases the probability of citation. In the Supreme Court models, cotenure has a range of impacts that are not evident in the circuit courts. Justices who have served longer in each other's company are less likely to concur, but only if they are ideologically distant. Longer cotenure also leads justices to use rude forms of dissent more frequently and fewer direct references to the majority when the dissenter is ideologically proximate to the majority opinion author. Finally, cotenure dampens the effect of ideology on the number of direct references to the majority.

Highlights of Our Findings

In the previous section, we have synthesized our results to draw some general conclusions, linking our findings across chapters. Here, we present two dozen of our most noteworthy findings in headline form for easy reference:

- The effect of ideology on a circuit judge's decision to write separately virtually disappears when two judges have office space in the same courthouse or when they estimate that they will serve with each other in 40 percent or more of future cases. However, when judges are physically dispersed and expect to work together less frequently, the effects of ideological distance are precisely what standard attitudinal theories of judicial decision-making predict.
- Circuit judges are less likely to dissent when they have served together longer and are more likely to serve in the future with the majority opinion author. This indicates that no single mechanism can explain the full effect of collegiality. Both persuasion and suppression appear to be at work.
- Supreme Court justices are less likely to dissent when they have served together longer with the majority opinion author. The size of this effect is similar in the circuit courts, an increase of 0.05 over the entire range of Cotenure, but the higher rate of dissent in the Supreme Court means this relationship has less relative impact than in the circuit courts.
- Supreme Court justices become less likely to concur from a colleague's opinions over the course of their shared service, but only when the two justices are ideologically distant.
- We uncover no evidence that the educational and professional credentials of a federal trial judge affect the probability that circuit judges will vote to reverse.
- There is no indication that whether a trial court judge reaches a result incongruent with their own ideology affects how circuit judges vote on appeal.
- The ideological distance between a circuit judge and the district judge who initially resolved the case is a significant factor in whether the circuit judge votes to reverse, but only if the circuit and district judges do not have chambers in the same courthouse. If they do, there is no indication that ideology plays a role in the decision to reverse.
- Both circuit and Supreme Court dissenters use the rude sign-off "I dissent" 21 percent of the time. However, circuit judges dissent with an explicitly polite sign-off in 53 percent of their dissents compared to 31 percent in the Supreme Court.
- Dissenters in the circuit courts are noticeably less willing to use a rude "I dissent" as they anticipate spending more time with the majority opinion author in the future.
- Circuit judges use less negative language when dissenting from an ideological rival who offices in the same building compared to one who is geographically at arm's length.

234   THE ELEVATOR EFFECT

- As two circuit judges who are ideological allies serve together longer, they become less likely to use explicitly polite forms of dissent. The same pattern emerges for Supreme Court justices. Over time, justices with similar ideological perspectives also become more likely to use rude forms of dissent. However, they use fewer direct references to the majority.
- In circuit courts, more extensive personal and professional contact between a dissenter and majority opinion author dampens the effect ideology has on how dissenters use positive emotional language and rudeness. Conversely, however, ideological distance leads to more negative emotional language in dissents, but only when the two judges work in the same courthouse.
- Circuit judges are more likely to cite a precedent written by a colleague who is serving in the case at hand or one whom they anticipate encountering more frequently in the future. They are less likely to cite a precedent written by a colleague with chambers in the same courthouse or a colleague with whom they have served for a longer period of time.
- In the circuit courts, opinion authors are less likely to cite a precedent written by an ideological foe if that judge is a current or former colleague compared to if they never served together at all.
- Supreme Court justices are more likely to cite their current colleagues compared to justices who are no longer on the court, but only if those current justices are also ideologically proximate to the opinion author.
- Justices who clerked in the Supreme Court at the beginning of their career dissent more frequently and cite less frequently than their colleagues without such experience.
- Justices who were elevated to the Court from one of the courts of appeals concur and dissent more frequently and their dissents are less polite, but they use fewer negative emotional words in their dissenting opinions.
- Former members of the D.C. Circuit who are promoted to the Supreme Court concur and dissent more frequently, are less likely to dissent in a rude fashion, use fewer direct references to the majority in their dissents, and use fewer citations in their majority opinions.
- Circuit judges are less likely to reverse trial court judges who are women but are more likely to vote to reverse judges of color.
- When two circuit judges are the same race, they are less likely to dissent and, if they dissent, less likely to do so in a rude fashion.
- Chief judges of the circuits typically behave like their colleagues with the one exception their dissenting opinions are less prone to directly refer to the majority.
- Supreme Court chief justices concur and dissent less than their peers. They also use less negative emotional language in their dissents and cite precedent more frequently.
- Judges are less likely to concur when they are new to a circuit and less likely to both concur and dissent when they are new to the Supreme Court. New justices also refer directly to the majority less in their dissents. However, in the rest of our analyses, they behave similarly to those with more experience.

Implications

Having described some of our most important findings, we now situate what we have learned in the broader literature on judicial politics. Here, our goal is to understand how our findings contribute to our shared understanding of judicial behavior, where our conclusions complement existing findings, and where they challenge current accounts. We also discuss several institutional reforms that have been proposed to alter the structure of the judiciary and discuss what our findings suggest about these proposals.

Implications for Theories of Judicial Behavior

Our results have important ramifications for existing accounts of judicial behavior. For decades, political scientists have sought to understand how judges decide cases. As discussed in Chapter 1, these efforts have led scholars to identify a set of factors, including legal considerations, policy preferences, strategic concerns, and background characteristics, that can predict how judges behave. Our primary goal in this book has been to contribute to this effort, identifying a factor we believe is an important determinant of judicial behavior—interpersonal relationships with colleagues—and demonstrating the effects of these relationships on a wide range of judicial behaviors. The most important argument of this book is that collegiality is a first-order consideration for judges, and scholars must account for judges' social concerns when theorizing and testing models of judicial behavior.

Aside from noting the importance of collegiality for judicial behavior, we have also emphasized the extent to which the bases of judicial behavior are *contextual*. Beginning in Chapter 1, we identified the major underpinnings of judicial behavior, paying special attention to discussing the conditions under which each of these factors is more or less important in the judicial calculus. Judicial behavior is complicated: courts, judges, and cases all differ. So too must theories and models of judging. Rather than spending time arguing whether "law matters" or "attitudes matter," political scientists (and legal scholars) would do well to focus their efforts on explaining *when* elements of the judicial calculus ebb and flow in their importance.

Our findings regarding ideological dampening provide a good example. Throughout this book, we have seen that the ideological distance between two judges varies widely—even among judges on the same court—in its ability to predict judicial behavior. We have argued that a key factor that conditions the influence of ideology is judges' levels of interpersonal contact with one another. Where judges have incentives to maintain good personal and professional working relationships, they are better able to overcome their policy disagreements and reach a publicly unified decision, and the effect of ideology is so small as to be imperceptible.

Our findings regarding ideological dampening provide an important limiting factor for the so-called attitudinal model of judicial behavior: even at the U.S. Supreme Court, the effect of ideology is not omnipresent. The extent to which judges' preferences are predictive of their behavior varies both across courts—something that political scientists have long known (e.g., Epstein, Landes, and Posner 2013; Zorn and

236 THE ELEVATOR EFFECT

Bowie 2010)—but also *depending on the configuration of colleagues with whom they are deciding the case*. In other words, attitudinal theories of judicial behavior should be adapted to the social dynamics of the panels in which judges decide cases; without accounting for judges' collegial concerns, attitudinal theories might overstate the influence of ideology on judicial behavior (or, at the very least, give a mistaken impression that the effects of ideology are omnipresent).

These implications extend beyond the judiciary. Scholars of legislative politics also turned an eye toward personal relationships as a way to turn down the heat in today's polarized legislatures (Masket 2008; Minozzi and Caldeira 2021). As we discussed in Chapter 5, communal living arrangements in the early republic are often cited to explain a greater level of consensus during early American history. Some have even suggested revisiting that arrangement:

> The comity in Washington is directly proportional to the amount of time elected officials spend with one another, and more specifically, with members of the opposite party. Nowadays, Democrats and Republicans are spending less and less time together, and it's one reason our politics have become so poisonous. If you want Washington to be less dysfunctional, then force members of Congress to get to know each other better (Cooper 2018).

While we do not think the members of the U.S. Senate will consent to living in a dorm anytime soon, our findings echo the conclusions of other studies that emphasize the importance of building strong interpersonal relationships among legislators as a way to improve the legislative environment in Washington, D.C., and in other legislative bodies across the country.

Further, a core finding throughout the book is the importance of interpersonal contact for consensus. Consensus has many salutary benefits for legal stability and development: nonunanimous opinions are received differently than unanimous decisions by other courts (Benjamin and Desmarais 2012). And there is also some evidence—itself not unanimous—that consensual opinions may be received more favorably by the public (Zink, Spriggs, and Scott 2009; Salamone 2014; c.f. Gibson, Caldeira, and Spence 2005). In this way, collegial relations among judges have both short-term effects in terms of the overall level of agreement among panel members, and also important long-term effects because unanimous rulings are more likely to be respected and implemented than fractured decisions more likely to be written under conditions of low collegiality. In this way, collegiality has important ramifications for judicial power and impact.

Implications for Institutional Reforms

Beyond the academic implications for theories of judicial behavior and legal development, our findings have broad implications for the structure of the judiciary and calls to reform the third branch of government. The most obvious set of implications come from the long-simmering debate over the ideal number and size of the circuits that populate the middle tier of the U.S. federal judiciary (see Edwards 2004; Kirkland

2014). Initially, a policy recommendation from our findings seems straightforward: a larger number of small circuits would be preferable. Smaller circuits would have more interpersonal contact among judges and, by extension, a more consensual and stable body of law. Similarly, many of the problems that judges have noted with our modern large circuits—difficulties keeping up with the circuit's changing caseload, large geographic differences across the larger circuits, and so forth—would be lessened by a system of more (and smaller) circuits.

But the solution is not that simple. Having smaller circuits requires *more* circuits, and there is a trade-off between small circuits with internally consistent decisions and a patchwork of conflicting national jurisprudence.[2] As Second Circuit Judge Jon O. Newman (1993, 188) has written, "As an appellate court of many judges inevitably breeds conflicts among its panels, a nation of many circuits inevitably breeds conflicts among its circuits. It is a threat that the Supreme Court cannot meet."

Weighing these competing considerations is not straightforward. On the one hand, a greater number of circuits would enable more consensual within-circuit decision-making, helping each circuit to develop clearer and more coherent bodies of precedent. But these smaller circuits may develop the law in conflicting directions, likely creating a greater level of cross-circuit conflicts against the current system. Thus, it is a problem that likely requires a "Goldilocks" solution whereby the size and number of circuits need to be "just right." Policymakers, scholars, and interested parties should consider how much dissent is healthy and weigh it against the cost of additional circuits. To do so, we need more studies both on the optimal size and number of circuits with regards to outcomes we care about, including the issuance of separate opinions and the creation of conflicts. Our findings indicate that the size of circuits matters regarding consensual decision-making, something that needs to be considered in these discussions.

Aside from creating a set of new, smaller circuits, another option is to institute some sort of divisional or regional calendaring system, which was briefly tried in the Ninth Circuit in the late 1970s. Such a system seems to initially provide the best of both worlds: the collegiality benefits of having judges sitting together on panels frequently and the jurisprudential benefits of having circuits covering larger geographic areas.

Unfortunately, however, the White Commission reports that the Ninth Circuit's experience was harmful to "circuit-wide collegiality and threatened the overall coherence of the circuit's substantive law" (Commission on Structural Alternatives for the Federal Courts of Appeals 1998, 50).[3] Perhaps most interestingly—and a consideration we have not given due attention to—is the Commission's note that the divisional system created "panel fever" caused by judges sitting with the same judges *too often*. This was a factor that came up in our interviews. J7 speculated based on their experiences that there is a happy medium with circuit size based in part on concerns that too small of a circuit could result in too much contact with a few judges.

---

[2] Cleveland (2013) provides a helpful, succinct summary of the arguments for and against larger and smaller circuit courts.

[3] The Commission on Structural Alternatives for the Federal Courts of Appeals, chaired by Justice Byron White, was created by Congress in 1997 to make recommendations about the size and configuration of the U.S. Courts of Appeals.

238 THE ELEVATOR EFFECT

Finally, our results have implications for the rules states and countries use to select and retain judges. One oft-discussed institutional reform, and the one reported most favorably out of the Biden Commission, is ending life tenure for Supreme Court justices (Savage 2021).[4] Here, our findings join a long line of political science evidence suggesting that term limits can have deleterious effects for political institutions (e.g., Kousser 2005; Carey, Niemi, and Powell 2000). Our results echo existing findings that such limits have adverse consequences for those who want political institutions to foster consensual policymaking.

Simply put, our results suggest that the institution that stays together decides together. The primary factor that changes between two judges over time is how well they know each other. This also indicates the importance of the meals and other social events colleagues share. While suggesting a return to the boardinghouse days of Chief Justice Marshall is hardly practical, especially in the federal circuits, there may be good reason for judges to gather for a meal, linger over dessert, or crack open another bottle of wine. Our findings indicate that this stability can generate increased consensus over time (see Meinke and Scott 2007). Imposing term limits on federal appellate court judges may lower levels of collegiality and increase dissensus on these courts, thereby threatening the stability of the law. As we noted in Chapter 2, collegiality and the related consensus may not always be normatively desirable. However, the possibility of increasing the existence of fractured opinions during a time of polarization and strife needs to be included in any such calculations.

Potential Reforms to Judicial Norms

Our results also have implications for some smaller—and more easily implementable—reforms. Perhaps the most notable involves the various ways in which judges (both on and off of the panel) discuss cases. Judicial norms regarding conversations about cases before oral arguments vary by circuits and judges and have changed over time. In circuits where the practice has moved toward discussing cases, some judges, especially older judges, may not participate in discussions before oral arguments. Most judges that we interviewed engaged in discussions before oral argument (J2, J4, J5, J6, and J7), but not all (J1 and J3).[5] Many judges (J2, J5, J6, and J7) explicitly stated that they thought such conversations were helpful.

Some examples from our interviewees are instructive. J2 reports that the norm "changed with time on the court" with the introduction of "new blood." "At first, I heard [other judges' views] first at oral arguments. There were unwritten rules, such

---

[4] President Joe Biden created a commission of judges, lawyers, and academics to study the U.S. federal judiciary. The commission held public hearings and issued a formal report in 2021. While the Commission did not endorse any structural changes to the Supreme Court, it provided an "analysis of the principal arguments in the contemporary public debate for and against Supreme Court reform, including an appraisal of the merits and legality of particular reform proposals" (Presidential Commission on the Supreme Court of the United States 2021, i).

[5] J3 said that in their circuit they "generally don't discuss cases before oral arguments with rare exceptions." As an example of such a rare exception, they cited "a jurisdiction issue [where they] need the attorneys to brief about it. We may discuss the case to head off a problem."

as [you would] affirm if didn't ask for oral argument. It didn't allow for changes of opinion or how to relay a quandary or if you were unsure about an issue." The "culture now" with "new blood" is much more willing to share beforehand. So, "colleagues know exactly where you are. It allows for discussion. It is the right way to go where we know where we stand before sitting." "The process [of speaking before oral arguments] gives [everyone] a heads up." The discussions before oral arguments are more specific but allow for a "full conversation" in the conferences after oral arguments.

J5 spearheaded a move to pre-argument communications in their circuit. They "want to know if they are on the wrong path and get set straight while my feet aren't in cement." It allows them to see if they can come to an "arrangement" but then clarified that "consensus would be a better word." In J5's estimation, "circuit culture changed for the better" after the move to such discussions. They noted a time when "one colleague brought up an important procedural issue that was unbriefed before [oral arguments] and it was educational."

Similarly, J6 identified the benefits of having such conversations as a "helpful sense of where colleagues are." They noted that judges often do this through clerks, so "why not [do this] through the judges who are better informed." When we asked about the costs of such an approach, J6 said they assume that "colleagues who won't [discuss cases before oral arguments] have concerns regarding avoiding influence and are coming in fresh." They always make clear that "until the ink is dry [their] vote is always subject to change."

Likewise, many judges have written of a common issue that leads to disunity among larger circuits: a decline in the norm of circulating draft opinions to the full circuit before they are issued (e.g., Wilkinson 1994; Rubin 1976). By receiving input from a broader set of circuit judges, opinion authors might find weaknesses in their opinions and get an early sense of whether their opinion will stand the test of time or be overturned *en banc*. J6 specifically brought up the importance of this practice when describing ways in which collegiality influences decision-making. They noted the norm and their circuit that "every draft opinion is circulated to the full circuit and not just the members of the panel. It is not infrequent that a judge from outside the panel comments." The judge specifically noted that their circuit was "in a sweet spot regarding size" to allow such a practice. They anticipated that it would not be practical in a very large circuit. The interviewee thought the practice helps "smooth over feathers." We asked if they thought this practice reduced the number of en bancs the circuit hears. The judge responded that "traditionally judges outside of the panel don't ask for an en banc poll" in their circuit while "in other circuits, it happens at the drop of the hat."

Judge Patricia M. Wald (1983, 785) of the D.C. Circuit suggested decades ago that circuits go a step further in their attempts to ensure coherent circuit law. She suggested that each circuit hold regular meetings among circuit judges, writing:

> It might make sense for the judges of the court to meet occasionally to discuss areas of law in the circuit that may need clarification, or have been left a bit murky. The purpose of sharing views on such topics would not be to establish a fixed agenda for action and definitely not to decide abstract issues. Rather, its purpose would be to make us more sensitive to our colleagues' interests and views, and perhaps to

240 THE ELEVATOR EFFECT

establish a general aura of agreement on our responsibility, as a court, to identify and to elucidate particular subjects. We might try such sessions once or twice a year, perhaps at the start of a new term. Our judicial conferences may have been originally designed for some such purpose, but now they are primarily social functions. Our monthly judges' meetings and Judicial Councils take up only administrative business.

Thus, additional input from circuit colleagues outside of the panel may be beneficial overall.

Based on our interviews and existing suggestions, we believe all circuits should seriously consider having panels circulate drafts, or otherwise discuss cases and the law, if they are not already doing so. This may allow for more clear statements of law from circuits and decreased use of en banc hearings that can strain relationships. Where circuits are too large to make such reviews possible or judges tend to read only the drafts of salient cases, the use of randomly sampled smaller divisions within the circuit may help.

The practice of having judges sit by designation has important implications regarding judicial collegiality and is another norm that both varies by circuit and deserves scrutiny. Some of our interviewees told us that their circuits, at times, ask district court colleagues to sit on their panels. J6 said that the circuit "used to be shorthanded in the past," which necessitated having district judges sit on panels. Now, "we bring in district judges so they can get a sense of how their papers will be graded." Similarly, J7 said they are "more isolated from district judges" than they used to be. "We used to ask the district judges to serve [by designation]." The circuit has a long backlog due to "slow confirmations" and extensive vacancies. Now, all vacancies have been filled and the circuit "[doesn't] need them." In fact, "senior judges complain they don't have enough cases."

But not all circuits have this practice. Harry T. Edwards (2004, 64) believed that having judges from outside of the D.C. Circuit sit on panels would harm the collegiality of that Court:

A rule that has been important to the rise in collegiality on the D.C. Circuit is an agreement among the judges that, absent a grave emergency, the court will not use visiting judges to decide cases on our docket. This rule is not meant to suggest any disrespect for our judicial colleagues from other courts. Rather, our judges believe that working without visiting judges allows us to interact with fewer distractions. [...] We are very open and forthright in our critiques of one another, confident in the understanding that all that we say is "in house" and "among family." Our thinking and writing thus benefit from a robust and healthy back-and-forth that makes for better individual opinions and a more coherent body of law generally. In short, to ensure expeditious issuance of our decisions, balanced work assignments among our judges, and coherence in the law of the circuit, we decided that only the judges of the court should do the work of our court.

Thus, there may also be trade-offs.

As indicated by our interviews and discussed in Chapter 6, designation is a means by which circuit judges learn about district judges, and it can help appellate judges

TAKING COLLEGIALITY SERIOUSLY IN DESIGNING AND STUDYING   241

build important assessments of the quality of their lower court colleagues.[6] Thus, designation may be a tool that helps both district and circuit judges learn about aspects of judicial decision-making. Based on the potential, it deserves further study and consideration. If empirical analyses indicate that such learning occurs, designation may be worth encouraging. Its deployment outside of times of need could be based on assessment of the understanding of judges regarding issues of facts, matters of law, and appellate review. Judge Edwards (2004, 64) disfavored having judges sit by designation due to the particular demands of the D.C. Circuit:

> The D.C. Circuit docket largely consists of very dense administrative law cases in appeals that often include huge records and numerous parties with their numerous briefs. It is not an inviting caseload for judges who are not used to it. We have also found that it is much easier to maintain the quality of our own work if we interact only with each other.

Thus, the types of cases in a circuit may need to be weighed against the potential learning from sitting by designation.

Opportunities for Future Research

This book advances our understanding of how interpersonal relationships among judges affect law and courts. But this book marks the beginning, not the end, of a conversation. We think there are many fruitful trails for future scholarship to blaze, and we outline some that we think could be particularly promising in the following sections.

Generalizability

One pressing opportunity for future research concerns the generalizability of our results with regards to the courts of appeals. Because we sought to eliminate potential confounding factors brought about by cross-issue variation (see Friedman and Martin 2011) and to allow for data collection over a longer period, we confined our analyses of circuit court judge behavior to a single issue area: search and seizure cases. While many well-known findings in the study of judicial politics rely on search and seizure cases (e.g., Segal and Spaeth 2002; Wahlbeck 1997; Bartels 2009), we acknowledge the limits to generalizability that arise from any single-issue study. We are very encouraged that our analyses regarding the Supreme Court, which include all issue areas, indicate that collegiality matters across a broad spectrum of legal cases.

Some of these limits may be theoretically interesting and demand follow-up research. For example, trade-offs between outcomes and rationales could well vary across issue areas; Choi and Gulati (2007) present evidence on this front with regard

---

[6] Additionally, for court of appeals judges, sitting as district judges helps them learn about the district judge perspective (J5).

242   THE ELEVATOR EFFECT

to the salience of a case. Likewise, other issue areas present issues in which judges vary more widely in the expertise they bring to the panel. By testing our theory on an issue in which all judges have some experience, we limited the confounding effects of expertise; across issues, however, expertise may mitigate or magnify the effects of collegiality on judicial behavior. Thus, we expect that the effects of collegiality on judicial behavior may vary by issue and encourage future scholars to investigate this possibility.

Collegiality and Judge Characteristics

Another important area for follow-up research concerns the demographic characteristics of judges. While our analyses reveal some important differences in judicial behavior according to the race and gender of judges, we did not give this topic nearly the attention it deserves. Studies suggest that demographic characteristics combine with institutional structures and interpersonal norms in ways that differentially affect the ability of women and nonwhite participants to have equal footing in deliberative environments (e.g., Karpowitz and Mendelberg 2014; Levine, Reypens, and Stark 2022); other research suggests that likability can affect group performance differently in all-male, all-female, and mixed-gender teams (Gerhards and Kosfeld 2020). Applied to our findings, this research would suggest that the effects of collegiality vary according to the sociodemographic characteristics of judges. In this way, demographic differences in the effects of collegiality may point to another consequence of judicial diversity.

Additionally, a burgeoning literature in the study of judicial behavior has analyzed the personality of judges and its effects on judicial behavior (see Hall 2018; Black et al. 2019). It seems likely to us that personality might interact with collegiality in many ways: for example, judges with higher levels of agreeableness might be more concerned with collegiality such that the effects of interpersonal contact increase with a judge's levels of that trait. On the other hand, judges who score highly on neuroticism may be less affected by collegial concerns. We look forward to future investigations of the effects of collegiality that account for judges' personality traits.

The effects of collegiality might also vary according to the prior professional characteristics of judges. While we did investigate the influence of Supreme Court justices' experiences on the courts of appeals and as Supreme Court clerks themselves in Chapters 5, 7, and 8, and the role of district court judge qualifications and circuit court judge experience on the district courts in Chapter 6, there are other types of experience that could be investigated. Justice Sandra Day O'Connor, for example, served as a leader in the Arizona state legislature before she was appointed to the U.S. Supreme Court. Early in her term, commentators made great note of this prior experience, suggesting that her legislative experience gave O'Connor "expertise and talent in building coalitions" that she could bring to the bargaining environment of the high court (Shea 1986, 12) or a "mellowing influence on the badly fragmented and highly independent Court" (Freilich, Cox, and Hall 1981, 627). Similarly, when Barack Obama nominated former Harvard Law School Dean Elena Kagan to the Supreme Court, much was made of her ability to forge consensus among the members of that highly fragmented elite law school faculty (Meckler 2010). Future work might investigate whether these and other types of experience affect the pull of collegiality on a judge's work.

Beyond the effects of one's past experiences, a judge's ambition might also shape the effects of collegiality. Recent studies have established that judges may alter their behavior in the hopes of "auditioning" for a place on a higher court (Epstein, Landes, and Posner 2013; Black and Owens 2016). For these judges, collegiality might be a double-edged sword. On the one hand, dissensus may help a judge stand out among her peers with a strongly worded dissenting opinion; on the other hand, weak consensual ties today might cause a judge problems in a later confirmation hearing. And, to the extent that presidents value "fighters" on the bench, abiding by norms of collegiality may have professional costs for auditioners. Thus, collegiality's effects might differ according to a judge's desire to serve on another court.

Throughout the book, we have taken it as a given that the benefits of collegiality are the same for all judges. They may not be. Our interviewees suggested that collegiality may be most important with respect to judges in the ideological center of a court. S4 speculated, based in part on public statements by Justice Kagan, that the loss of more moderate justices might decrease collegiality on the Court. "In the past, there were two swing justices in every case, moderates who could go to either side. [There were] professional reasons to be collegial—strategic reasons because you want those votes. That is not the case now." In other words, as collegial relationships in courts break down, judges may have less concern about accommodating their colleagues, thereby heightening the role of ideology on case outcomes and legal development. Future research should investigate the possibility that there is a partisan or ideological tinge to the effects of judicial collegiality.

Building and Maintaining Collegiality

We conceptualized collegiality as intrinsically linked with interpersonal contact, assuming that more contact is generally associated with heightened collegial concern. Future studies would do well to examine how other types of interpersonal contact might foster collegiality, whether collegiality might be fostered without interpersonal contact, and enrich our understanding of how collegial concerns ebb and flow between judges over time.

First, regarding other types of interpersonal contact, circuit conferences provide an important opportunity for judges to build relationships with their peers; the dynamics and effects of these consequences deserve future inquiry. J6 told us they found these conferences very valuable and would encourage opportunities for "formal socialization." They felt that the circuit conferences should include all different types of judges, circuit judges, magistrate judges, district judges, and bankruptcy judges; and, if they "had [their] druthers, these conferences would happen every year."

Additionally, we think committee service—both within and across circuits—is a prime candidate for future investigation. Every circuit has a committee structure to help carry out the circuit's business. Judges who work together on these committees may build professional relationships outside the confines of case deliberations that, in turn, shape the opinions they craft once they are assigned to the same panel. This is a

244   THE ELEVATOR EFFECT

type of interpersonal contact we did not measure in our analyses but may help to explain important social ties between judges.

Similarly, judges may get to know one another early in their career as they attend trainings for new judges, like "baby judges' school" (known formally as "Phase 1 Orientation Seminar") organized by the Federal Judicial Center (Gresko 2018). We have found some evidence throughout this book that new judges (defined as those in the first two years in their position) behave differently than their more experienced colleagues; they, for example, are less likely to concur in the U.S. Courts of Appeals. But it is also possible that judges make connections in these trainings that they draw upon as they begin their careers on the bench, in the way that many college students make friends for life on the Welcome Weekend that precedes their first week of college classes. We would not be surprised to learn, for example, that judges are more likely to cite the opinions of judges with whom they attended baby judges' school.

Our interviewees suggested that committee service at the *national* level might also help judges build relationships with one another. Many U.S. Court of Appeals judges sit on committees organized within the Judicial Conference of the United States, which acts as the national policymaking body for the federal courts (Administrative Office of the U.S. Courts 2002). There are committees on such important topics as Codes of Conduct, Criminal Law, and Judicial Resources. J6 told us that this type of committee work was a valuable avenue for the formation of relationships among judges and that they would increase those opportunities. There are "huge tradeoffs" regarding working in smaller groups and having broader contact. J3 also noted that committees on both the circuit and national level are great ways to get to know other judges: "You get to know other judges all around the nation. I have made life-long friends [this way]." The effects of cross-circuit interpersonal contacts on judicial behaviors like citation practices is an obvious path for future study.

Additionally, S4 believed that "justices' relationships before being on the Court" were important and worth investigating. Some of these relationships are "not starting from scratch." They noted that some justices, famously Ginsburg and Scalia and O'Connor and Rehnquist, came to the Court with strong preexisting relationships; many justices previously served together on the courts of appeals. They noted many justices come from the D.C. Circuit and suggested that background experience might affect Supreme Court justices' behavior: "There is a ton of interaction with the Supreme Court justices [by judges on the D.C. Circuit] due to the nature of the job." Additionally, they observed that Justice Kagan had relationships with conservative justices when she was the Dean of the Harvard Law School. Also, new justices may have fed clerks to the justices over the years and have built relationships with the justices through the clerk-selection process.

Second, our conceptualization of collegiality relies on interpersonal contact. As discussed in Chapter 2, we have a strong theoretical basis for treating collegiality and interpersonal contact as synonymous. But we acknowledge that interpersonal contact is not the only way to operationalize a judge's level of collegial concerns. It seems possible to us that collegial concerns might be activated even in the absence of interpersonal contact. For example, judges may have a desire to be seen in a good light by colleagues in other districts or circuits, even if they will never meet those judges in person. This desire to make a positive impression on another judge—even in the

TAKING COLLEGIALITY SERIOUSLY IN DESIGNING AND STUDYING 245

absence of interpersonal contact—might be a form of collegiality that shapes their behavior, perhaps by inspiring them to pull punches in a dissenting opinion or to suppress that dissent in the first place.

Finally, future scholarship should broaden our understanding of how collegial concerns ebb and flow between judges over time. At the beginning of the Biden administration, media reports spurred popular discussion about collegiality declining at the U.S. Supreme Court. In 2021, *CNN* reporter Joan Biskupic wrote that the justices "are increasingly impugning their colleagues' motives and sincerity" in a way that suggests that the Roberts Court "[a]ppears to be entering a new era of personal accusation and finger-pointing." *Slate* reporter Mark Joseph Stern, appearing on a podcast, said the current Court was "tense, touchy, and terrifying" even as the justices present the Court to the public as collegial: "[W]hen you read what they are saying and these opinions, they are mad at each other." Asked to rate the feuds on the current Court on a scale akin to Bravo's popular Real Housewives franchise, Stern said, "[I]t would be, like, an argument over dinner with a table flip at the end" (Sanders 2021). And then it got worse. Writing about the Court a year later, as the Court returned to in-person oral argument, *NPR* reporter Nina Totenberg (2022a) reported that the discord among the justices was obvious from their facial expressions: Elena Kagan's "anger is often palpable, the color literally draining from her face," while conservative justices are prone to roll their eyes during oral argument.

There was also a sense among some of our interviewees that collegiality in the judiciary is declining. C4 was concerned regarding "collegiality declining everywhere," which they attributed to Donald Trump and the pandemic. They told us: "Everyone is pissed all of the time. Even on the state court, it is now waning." They were unsure regarding the circuit.[7] They described the period they clerked in as "halcyon" and said people would "let things fly." Now, however, sharp dissents have become much more commonplace.

During the COVID pandemic, where in-person contact among judges was reduced, there were some stark examples regarding disputes between dissenters and majorities. For example, the Eleventh Circuit denied a petition for an en banc hearing and there was "a blistering dissent from Judge Robin Rosenbaum, who accused the majority of violating circuit precedent and even threatening the rule of law" (Moline 2020). As mentioned in Chapter 7, Judge Kevin Newsom bemoaned the uncollegial nature of the dissent and hoped for a more civil environment in the future (Moline 2020). Thus, external forces might influence issues of contact and collegiality.

Together, these anecdotes suggest to us that the level of collegiality on a court might grow or wane over time. As we discussed in Chapter 2, Judge Edwards on the D.C. Circuit was renowned for his ability to improve collegiality on that court. And John Roberts has frequently said that he views building and maintaining collegiality and consensus on the U.S. Supreme Court as an important job of the chief justice (e.g., Rosen 2007). Together, these experiences suggest that judicial leadership may play an important role in fostering collegiality, and changes in that leadership might account for variation in the level of collegiality on a court. Further, these experiences suggest

---

[7] The former clerk had state court and circuit experience. They were more sure that the state court was falling apart.

246 THE ELEVATOR EFFECT

that changes in judicial collegiality over time may not be adequately measured by the indicators we have employed, suggesting that collegiality on a court is a more global, court-level concept rather than the dyadic conception of collegiality we employ here. This is an important topic for future study.

Collegiality in Other Contexts

We have focused our study on the effects of collegiality on the bread-and-butter decisions made by appellate judges: the opinions they issue in cases decided by panels. But the effects of collegiality might be important in other places and on other types of judicial behaviors.

For example, en banc review provides one avenue for advancing our research on these issues. When the circuits sit en banc, they generally come together as a whole and deal with particularly contentious issues. In this way, these panels look more like the Supreme Court than the traditional three-judge panels that hear ordinary appeals, yet those decisions are still reviewable by the high court. Furthermore, where circuits come together for en banc proceedings, it provides a relatively rare opportunity to bring the full circuit (or a substantial subset) together outside of conferences. By studying en banc review, future researchers can get additional leverage on issues like the ramifications of group size on decision-making due to the variation in circuit size and institutional rules regarding assembling the panels. Harry T. Edwards (2004) suggests both that too much en banc review can harm the collegiality of a circuit and that too little may indicate that collegiality is not working properly.

Our interviewees suggested that en banc review is ripe with potential collegial effects. S2 noted that a "functional en banc system" helps collegiality. They described large circuits as having "dysfunctional" systems. C3 noted that conversations around en banc matters tended to "flair tensions." En banc was rare in the circuit and represented "the tip of the iceberg [that] hides bigger conflicts." The circuit had a "stable political breakdown that was razor-thin." So "no side had the ability to force [its will]." When considering such matters, the judges would fax "memoranda to each other." The judge would review the memos. There would be a "flurry of faxes over the next weeks." It was "at times contentious." C3 "could see collegiality mattering" in such cases. There were "explicitly appeals regarding collegiality and decorum." Judges would reference the circuit's norms regarding the rarity of en banc. There was the explicit use of "institutional norms to reduce breaches in collegiality."

The judges we interviewed emphasized how the en banc process brings collegial concerns to the forefront. J4 also described en banc review as implicating collegiality in the decision whether to grant review and "taking a toll on collegiality" because you are reviewing "a colleague's carefully written opinion. Did they get it right? Is it better to let sleeping dogs lie?" To this end, "it is like with precedent—when should you leave well enough alone or get it right? Collegiality is the thumb on the scale against fixing [it]."

Beyond the en banc process, collegiality may matter in other types of courts. The indicators of collegiality we use, based on frequent contact between a pair of judges, are easily adaptable to apex courts in the U.S. states and abroad. These courts have

TAKING COLLEGIALITY SERIOUSLY IN DESIGNING AND STUDYING   247

different institutional rules about panel assignment, deliberation practices, case selection, and judicial selection and retention that are ripe for future investigation. For example, the use of judicial elections in the United States gives judges an incentive to cultivate a personal vote, potentially pitting an individual judge's personal need for public support over the court's desire for consensus (Gibson and Nelson 2021). Or, consider the European Court of Justice whose judges hail from different countries and may be able to build personal relationships through shared language, religion, or international alliances that could color their behaviors in the courtroom. Understanding how other types of institutional arrangements affect collegiality in other judiciaries is a prime candidate for future study.

Additionally, collegiality might matter in chambers. C2 suggested, expressly based in part on their understanding that Supreme Court justices bounce ideas off of clerks instead of other justices, that "intra-office collegiality is the more important of the two types of collegiality [(intra and inter-office collegiality)]." C2 noted that intra-office collegiality mattered because for "harder" cases "the whole office was involved" and there was a lot of "batting around" of ideas. When asked about ways in which collegiality mattered to how cases were resolved, C3 noted that when the clerks and judge meet that they offered "different perspectives." They had "different ways of talking about [the issues] and thinking about them." They "respected each other. If someone needed to say something. We gave [them] the room to explain. We assumed it was important and not a rabbit hole." There would be "continuous arguments" with the judge regarding case outcomes. There would be "different configurations" regarding the sides in the arguments, sometimes the judge would be on one side with the clerks on the other, while other times the clerks would split. "No one saw it as a waste of time. No one was upset, it was totally ok. It is the only job I have had where a two-hour-long fight with my boss wasn't a problem." There was "no end time for those discussions."

C4 believed positive work relationships were important among clerks and interns. This was "especially [true] because [we were] overseeing interns and giving them feedback. It is important to develop trust and respect. [They are] still friends with one of the interns." C4 remembers a specific case where the work they did with an intern was important in drafting the opinion. They did go over "different revisions of opinions" with the judge. They would "go over the draft together." There was less "back and forth" and "wrestling with the issues" or "substantive wrestling" than C4 had experienced clerking on a state court.[8]

---

[8] Collegiality also appears to be a factor, at least in some courts, regarding which clerks work on specific cases. Similarly, C3 believed collegiality "mattered" when "work[ing] through cases." Within the chambers, there was a "draft selection system." Each clerk would write "quips" about incoming cases. These were one-paragraph summaries regarding the cases and "noteworthy features." Such features could include "high profile counsel" or if the case was "pro se." They would compile a list of the cases. Based on the quips, the clerks would select cases they wanted to work on. At lunch, "in snaking order," the clerks would pick cases. There were usually thirty-five to forty cases and each clerk would end up with roughly ten cases. The selection was based on "differing interests—business law vs. insurances vs. constitutional law. You could sense what people want." In any set of cases, there were usually approximately "four juicy cases." You might give one of these prized cases to someone else "based on their interests." In S5's chambers, the clerks divvied up the cases on their own based, in part, on interests.

So, too, might collegiality affect other types of judicial behaviors. Take, for example, case selection. The U.S. Supreme Court chooses most of its own docket according to the "rule of four" in which a minority of judges can force the full court to decide a case. As others have noted (e.g., Perry 1991; Black and Owens 2009a), the case-selection process is a rich strategic environment, and S4 told us that collegiality "definitely affected what cases were taken" at the U.S. Supreme Court, though, when pressed, they declined to elaborate. Join-3 votes, in which a judge agrees to vote to take a case if three of his colleagues agree, seem particularly ripe to be affected by collegial concerns (Black and Owens 2009b).

Similarly, collegiality might affect decision-making on the Court's so-called "shadow docket" (Baude 2015; Vladeck 2019). As many legal scholars have noted, the Supreme Court has begun deciding many important issues without oral argument or full briefing, instead issuing orders (sometimes without written rationale or an accounting of the justices' votes). S4 suggested that there has been a qualitative shift in the justices' behavior in this regard, saying in the past "dissents were mild and now are very critical of the process and opinions." This behavior, according to S4, is a symptom of declining collegiality at the Court.

Finally, collegiality might matter with regard to authorship and oral arguments. S4 noted that collegiality might influence opinion assignment and the influence of opinion writers. They said that "it has changed. There is a famous example with Brennan assigning opinions to the weakest link. If he assigned the opinion a light or skeptical justice, he would try to use collegiality to have the justice come around. Sometimes, it doesn't work, and sometimes perhaps there is [horse-trading.] [That is] strategy—no collegiality there." They also believed that "the opinion writer has some latitude regarding writing and the opinion." However, that latitude had become more limited: "In the past, Brennan would include little nuggets, that were seemingly innocuous, for future use. Justices are now wise." S3 stated that collegiality allowed questioning at oral argument to flow.

When it comes to "collegiality in terms of compromising of positions," S2 was "unsure if it was collegiality or game playing. Unsure of which bucket to put it in." They said they can "identify instances of justices taking positions that didn't align with their own to hold majorities or decide who would author." There are "those who engage" as "part of wooing justices" and are "willing to compromise to keep [another justice] with [them]."

At this point, it should be clear that we think there are lots of exciting paths for future research to take. It is clear from our findings that collegiality has an important role to play in understanding why judges behave as they do. We have just scratched the surface of this complicated, but vital, topic, and we look forward to seeing how this research agenda develops.

Final Thoughts

In the end, we believe relationships matter in human endeavors. We suspect this is not a shocking claim to readers, who likely encounter the truth of this sentiment daily.

However, the importance of relationships is often ignored when we design institutions and then study individuals within them. We find a mound of evidence, both qualitative and quantitative in nature, indicating this is a mistaken when it comes to federal appellate courts. Instead, we find that relationships matter to outcomes and appear to be effortful to maintain. While crafting policies and reforms should not end with considerations regarding relationships, it would be a good place to start.

Bibliography

Administrative Office of the U.S. Courts. 2002. "About the Judicial Conference." https://www.uscourts.gov/about-federal-courts/governance-judicial-conference/about-judicial-conference (accessed August 23, 2022).

Alder, Madison. 2022. "Judicial Opinion Barbs Reflect Political Divisions, Twitter Era." *Bloomberg Law*, February 1. https://news.bloomberglaw.com/us-law-week/judicial-opinion-barbs-reflect-political-divisions-twitter-era (accessed August 23, 2022).

Aldisert, Ruggero J. 1989. "Precedent: What It Is and What It Isn't: When Do We Kiss It and When Do We Kill It." *Pepperdine Law Review* 17 (3): 605–36.

American Association of University Professors. 2016. "On Collegiality as a Criterion for Faculty Evaluation." https://www.aaup.org/report/collegiality-criterion-faculty-evaluation (accessed August 23, 2022).

Andrews, Kyle R., Franklin J. Boster, and Christopher J. Carpenter. 2012. "Persuading in the Small Group Context." In *The Sage Handbook of Persuasion: Developments in Theory and Practice*, eds., James P. Dillard and Lijiang Shen. Thousand Oaks, CA: Sage Publications, Inc., 354–70.

Archer, Dawn. 2011. "Facework and Im/Politeness Across Legal Contexts: An Introduction." *Journal of Politeness Research* 7 (1): 1–19.

Asch, Solomon E. 1951. "Effects of Group Pressure Upon the Modification and Distortion of Judgments." In *Groups, Leadership and Men: Research in Human Relations*, ed., Harold Guetzkow. Pittsburgh, PA: Carnegie Press, 177–90.

Asch, Solomon E. 1955. "Opinions and Social Pressure." *Scientific American* 193 (5): 31–35.

Asch, Solomon E. 1956. "Studies of Independence and Conformity: I. A Minority of One Against a Unanimous Majority." *Psychological Monographs: General and Applied* 70 (9): 1–70.

Atkins, Burton M. 1973. "Judicial Behavior and Tendencies Towards Conformity in a Three Member Small Group: A Case Study of Dissent Behavior on the U.S. Court of Appeals." *Social Science Quarterly* 54 (1): 41–53.

Atkins, Burton M., and Justin J. Green. 1976. "Consensus on the United States Courts of Appeals: Illusion or Reality?" *American Journal of Political Science* 20 (4): 735–48.

Atkins, Burton M., and William Zavoina. 1974. "Judicial Leadership on the Court of Appeals: A Probability Analysis of Panel Assignment in Race Relations Cases on the Fifth Circuit." *American Journal of Political Science* 18 (4): 701–11.

Balkin, Jack M., and Sanford Levinson. 1995. "How to Win Cites and Influence People." *Chicago-Kent Law Review* 71 (3): 843–70.

Banks, Christopher P. 1999. *Judicial Politics in the D.C. Circuit Court*. Baltimore, MD: Johns Hopkins University Press.

Barnes, Robert. 2022a. "Clarence Thomas Says Supreme Court Leak Has Eroded Trust in Institution." *Washington Post*, May 14. https://www.washingtonpost.com/politics/2022/05/14/clarence-thomas-supreme-court-leak-roe-trust/ (accessed August 23, 2022).

Barnes, Robert. 2022b. "Sotomayor, Roberts Say They Did Not Ask Gorsuch to Wear a Mask on Supreme Court Bench." *Washington Post*, January 19. https://www.washingtonpost.com/politics/courts_law/neil-gorsuch-sonia-sotomayor-masks-supreme-court/2022/01/19/7977831a-7946-11ec-9102-d65488c31bb1_story.html (accessed August 23, 2022).

Barnes, Robert, and Lauren Lumpkin. 2022. "Alito Reluctant to Discuss State of Supreme Court After Roe Leak." *Washington Post*, May 12. https://www.washingtonpost.com/politics/2022/05/12/samuel-alito-roe-wade-leak/ (accessed August 23, 2022).

Bartels, Brandon L. 2009. "The Constraining Capacity of Legal Doctrine on the U.S. Supreme Court." *American Political Science Review* 103 (3): 474–95.

Bartels, Brandon L., and Christopher D. Johnston. 2013. "On the Ideological Foundations of Supreme Court Legitimacy in the American Public." *American Journal of Political Science* 57 (1): 184–99.

Bartels, Brandon L., and Christopher D. Johnston. 2020. *Curbing the Court: Why the Public Constrains Judicial Independence*. Cambridge University Press.

Bashman, Howard. 2022. "How Appealing." *Above the Law*, August 15. https://howappealing.abovethelaw.com/ (accessed August 23, 2022).

Baude, William. 2015. "Foreword: The Supreme Court's Shadow Docket." *New York University Journal of Law & Liberty* 9 (1): 1–63.

Baum, Lawrence. 1997. *The Puzzle of Judicial Behavior*. Ann Arbor, MI: University of Michigan Press.

Baum, Lawrence. 2006. *Judges and Their Audiences: A Perspective on Judicial Behavior*. Princeton University Press.

Baum, Lawrence. 2017. *Ideology in the Supreme Court*. Princeton University Press.

Beim, Deborah, Alexander V. Hirsch, and Jonathan P. Kastellec. 2014. "Whistleblowing and Compliance in the Judicial Hierarchy." *American Journal of Political Science* 58 (4): 904–18.

Beim, Deborah, Alexander V. Hirsch, and Jonathan P. Kastellec. 2016. "Signaling and Counter-Signaling in the Judicial Hierarchy: An Empirical Analysis of *En Banc* Review." *American Journal of Political Science* 60 (2): 490–508.

Benesh, Sara C., and Malia Reddick. 2002. "Overruled: An Event History Analysis of Lower Court Reaction to Supreme Court Alteration of Precedent." *Journal of Politics* 64 (2): 534–50.

Benesh, Sara C., Reginald S. Sheehan, and Harold J. Spaeth. 1998. "Equity in Supreme Court Opinion Assignment." *Jurimetrics* 39 (4): 377–90.

Benjamin, Stuart M., and Bruce A. Desmarais. 2012. "Standing the Test of Time: The Breadth of Majority Coalitions and the Fate of U.S. Supreme Court Precedents." *Journal of Legal Analysis* 4 (2): 445–69.

Berinsky, Adam J. 2015. "Rumors and Health Care Reform: Experiments in Political Misinformation." *British Journal of Political Science* 47 (2): 241–62.

Biskupic, Joan. 2018. "John Roberts Touts Collegiality, but Supreme Court's Record Suggests Otherwise." *CNN*, October 17. https://www.cnn.com/2018/10/17/politics/john-roberts-division (accessed August 23, 2022).

Biskupic, Joan. 2021. "Supreme Court Enters a New Era of Personal Accusation and Finger-Pointing." *CNN*, May 21. https://www.cnn.com/2021/05/21/politics/supreme-court-finger-pointing-kavanaugh-kagan-gorsuch/index.html (accessed August 23, 2022).

Black, Ryan C., Matthew E.K. Hall, Ryan J. Owens, and Eve M. Ringsmuth. 2016. "The Role of Emotional Language in Briefs Before the US Supreme Court." *Journal of Law and Courts* 4 (2): 377–407.

Black, Ryan C., and Ryan J. Owens. 2009a. "Agenda Setting in the Supreme Court: The Collision of Policy and Jurisprudence." *Journal of Politics* 71 (3): 1062–75.

Black, Ryan C., and Ryan J. Owens. 2009b. "Join-3 Votes and Supreme Court Agenda Setting." *SSRN*. https://papers.ssrn.com/sol3/papers.cfm?abstract_id=1568389 (accessed August 23, 2022).

Black, Ryan C., and Ryan J. Owens. 2012. "Consider the Source (and the Message): Supreme Court Justices and Strategic Audits of Lower Court Decisions." *Political Research Quarterly* 65 (2): 385–95.

BIBLIOGRAPHY 253

Black, Ryan C., and Ryan J. Owens. 2016. "Courting the President: How Circuit Court Judges Alter Their Behavior for Promotion to the Supreme Court." *American Journal of Political Science* 60 (1): 30–43.

Black, Ryan C., Ryan J. Owens, Justin Wedeking, and Patrick C. Wohlfarth. 2016. *U.S. Supreme Court Opinions and Their Audiences.* Cambridge University Press.

Black, Ryan C., Ryan J. Owens, Justin Wedeking, and Patrick C. Wohlfarth. 2019. *The Conscientious Justice: How Supreme Court Justices' Personalities Influence the Law, the High Court, and the Constitution.* Cambridge University Press.

Black, Ryan C., Ryan J. Owens, Justin Wedeking, and Patrick C. Wohlfarth. 2021. "On Estimating Personality Traits of US Supreme Court Justices." *Journal of Law and Courts* 9 (2): 371–96.

Black, Ryan C., and James F. Spriggs II. 2013. "The Citation and Depreciation of U.S. Supreme Court Precedent." *Journal of Empirical Legal Studies* 10 (2): 325–58.

Black, Ryan C., and Lee Epstein. 2005. "Recusals and the Problem of an Equally Divided Supreme Court." *Journal of Appellate Practice and Procedure* 7 (1): 75–99.

Blackstone, Bethany, and Paul M. Collins Jr. 2014. "Strategy and the Decision to Dissent on the U.S. Courts of Appeals." *Justice System Journal* 35 (3): 269–86.

Blankenship-Knox, Ann E., R. Eric Platt, and Hannah Read. 2017. "Rewarding Collegiality: The Use of Collegiality as a Factor in Faculty Evaluation and Employment Decisions." *Journal of Faculty Development* 31 (2): 37–42.

Boston, Joshua. 2020. "Strategic Opinion Language on the US Courts of Appeals." *Journal of Law and Courts* 8 (1): 1–26.

Boudin, Michael. 2011. "Friendly, J., Dissenting." *Duke Law Journal* 61 (2011): 881–901.

Bousfield, Derek. 2008. *Impoliteness in Interaction.* Amsterdam: John Benjamins Publishing Company.

Bowie, Jennifer Barnes, Donald R. Songer, and John Szmer. 2014. *View from the Bench and Chambers.* Charlottesville: University of Virginia Press.

Bowie, Jennifer Barnes, and Donald R. Songer. 2009. "Assessing the Applicability of Strategic Theory to Explain Decision Making on the Courts of Appeals." *Political Research Quarterly* 62 (2): 393–407.

Boyd, Christina L. 2015a. "Federal District Court Judge Ideology Data." *University of Georgia.* https://spia.uga.edu/faculty-member/christina-l-boyd/ (accessed August 23, 2022).

Boyd, Christina L. 2015b. "The Hierarchical Influence of Courts of Appeals on District Courts." *Journal of Legal Studies* 44 (1): 113–41.

Boyd, Christina L., Lee Epstein, and Andrew D. Martin. 2010. "Untangling the Causal Effects of Sex on Judging." *American Journal of Political Science* 54 (2): 389–411.

Brace, Paul, and Melinda G. Hall. 2001. "'Haves' Versus 'Have Nots' in State Supreme Courts: Allocating Docket Space and Wins in Power Asymmetric Cases." *Law & Society Review* 35 (2): 393–417.

Braman, Eileen, and Thomas E. Nelson. 2007. "Mechanism of Motivated Reasoning? Analogical Perception in Discrimination Disputes." *American Journal of Political Science* 51 (4): 940–56.

Bratton, Kathleen A., and Stella M. Rouse. 2011. "Networks in the Legislative Arena: How Group Dynamics Affect Cosponsorship." *Legislative Studies Quarterly* 36 (3): 423–60.

Bravin, Jess, and Laura Meckler. 2010. "Obama to Nominate Kagan to Seat on Supreme Court." *Wall Street Journal,* May 10. https://www.wsj.com/articles/SB10001424052748704307804575234301943175776 (accessed August 24, 2022).

Breeze, Ruth. 2012. "'With the Greatest Respect for My Colleagues': Politeness in Dissenting Opinions in International Arbitration Disputes." In *New Perspectives on (Im)politeness and Interpersonal Communication,* eds., Lucis Fernández Amaya, Maria de la O Hernández López, and Reyes Gómez Morón. Newcastle upon Tyne: Cambridge Scholars Publishing, 149–65.

254 BIBLIOGRAPHY

Brown, J. Robert, and Allison Herren Lee. 1999. "Neutral Assignment of Judges at the Court of Appeals." *Texas Law Review* 78 (5): 1037–116.

Brown, Penelope, and Stephen C. Levinson. 1987. *Politeness: Some Universals in Language Usage*. Cambridge University Press.

Brudney, James J., and Lawrence Baum. 2016. "Protean Statutory Interpretation in the Courts of Appeals." *William and Mary Law Review* 58 (3): 681–763.

Bryan, Amanda C., and Eve M. Ringsmuth. 2016. "Jeremiad or Weapon of Words: The Power of Emotive Language in Supreme Court Dissents." *Journal of Law and Courts* 4 (1): 159–85.

Cain, Àine. 2016. "We Asked and You Answered—Here Are 9 Horrifying Stories about Terrible Coworkers." *Business Insider*, August 28. https://www.businessinsider.com/horror-stories-about-terrible-coworkers-2016-8 (accessed August 23, 2022).

Caldeira, Gregory A. 1985. "The Transmission of Legal Precedent: A Study of State Supreme Courts." *American Political Science Review* 79 (1): 178–94.

Caldeira, Gregory A., and Samuel C. Patterson. 1987. "Political Friendship in the Legislature." *Journal of Politics* 49 (4): 953–75.

Caldeira, Gregory A., and Christopher J.W. Zorn. 1998. "Of Time and Consensual Norms in the Supreme Court." *American Journal of Political Science* 42 (3): 874–902.

Calvert, Randall L. 1985. "The Value of Biased Information: A Rational Choice Model of Political Advice." *Journal of Politics* 47 (2): 530–55.

Cameron, Charles M., Jeffrey A. Segal, and Donald R. Songer. 2000. "Strategic Auditing in a Political Hierarchy: An Informational Model of the Supreme Court's Certiorari Decisions." *American Political Science Review* 94 (1): 101–16.

Caminker, Evan H. 1994. "Why Must Inferior Courts Obey Superior Court Precedents?" *Stanford Law Review* 46 (4): 817–73.

Caminker, Evan H. 1999. "Sincere and Strategic Voting Norms on Multimember Courts." *Michigan Law Review* 97 (8): 2297–380.

Canes-Wrone, Brandice, and Tom S. Clark. 2009. "Judicial Independence and Nonpartisan Elections." *Wisconsin Law Review* 2009: 21–65.

Canes-Wrone, Brandice, Tom S. Clark, and Jason P. Kelly. 2014. "Judicial Selection and Death Penalty Decisions." *American Political Science Review* 108 (1): 23–39.

Canes-Wrone, Brandice, Tom S. Clark, and Jee-Kwang Park. 2012. "Judicial Independence and Retention Elections." *Journal of Law, Economics, & Organization* 28: 211–34.

Carey, John M., Richard G. Niemi, and Lynda W. Powell. 2000. *Term Limits in State Legislatures*. Ann Arbor, MI: University of Michigan Press.

Carp, Robert A. 1972. "The Scope and Function of Intra-Circuit Judicial Communication: A Case Study of the Eighth Circuit." *Law & Society Review* 6 (3): 405–26.

Carp, Robert A., and Russell Wheeler. 1972. "Sink or Swim: The Socialization of a Federal District Judge." *Journal of Public Law* 21 (2): 359–93.

Carrubba, Clifford J., and Tom S. Clark. 2012. "Rule Creation in a Political Hierarchy." *American Political Science Review* 106 (3): 622–43.

Casillas, Christopher J., Peter K. Enns, and Patrick C. Wohlfarth. 2011. "How Public Opinion Constrains the U.S. Supreme Court." *American Journal of Political Science* 55 (1): 74–88.

Chilton, Adam S., and Marin K. Levy. 2015. "Challenging the Randomness of Panel Assignment in the Federal Courts of Appeals." *Cornell Law Review* 101 (1): 1–56.

Choi, Stephen J., and G. Mitu Gulati. 2007. "Trading Votes for Reasoning: Covering in Judicial Opinions." *Southern California Law Review* 81 (4): 735–79.

Chown, Jillian D., and Christopher C. Liu. 2015. "Geography and Power in an Organizational Forum: Evidence from the U.S. Senate Chamber." *Strategic Management Journal* 36 (2): 117–96.

BIBLIOGRAPHY 255

Cialdini, Robert B., and Noah J. Goldstein. 2004. "Social Influence: Compliance and Conformity." *Annual Review of Psychology* 55 (1): 591–621.

Clark, Tom S. 2009. "A Principal-Agent Theory of En Banc Review." *Journal of Law, Economics, & Organization* 25 (1): 55–79.

Clark, Tom S. 2011. *The Limits of Judicial Independence*. Cambridge University Press.

Clark, Tom S., Jeffrey R. Lax, and Douglas Rice. 2015. "Measuring the Political Salience of Supreme Court Cases." *Journal of Law and Courts* 3 (1): 37–65.

Clegg, Joshua W. 2012. "The Importance of Feeling Awkward: A Dialogical Narrative Phenomenology of Socially Awkward Situations." *Qualitative Research in Psychology* 9 (3): 262–78.

Clermont, Kevin M., and Theodore Eisenberg. 2002. "Judge Harry Edwards: A Case in Point." *Washington University Law Quarterly* 80 (4): 1275–90.

Cleveland, David R. 2013. "Post-Crisis Reconsideration of Federal Court Reform." *Cleveland State Law Review* 61 (1): 47–100.

Cohen, Jonathan M. 2002. *Inside Appellate Courts*. Ann Arbor, MI: University of Michigan Press.

Collier, Helen V. 1992. "Collegiality Among Judges: No More High Noons." *The Judges Journal* 31(1): 4–7 & 37–38.

Collins Jr., Paul M., Kenneth L. Manning, and Robert A. Carp. 2010. "Gender, Critical Mass, and Judicial Decision Making." *Law & Policy* 32 (2): 260–81.

Collins Jr., Paul M. 2007. "Lobbyists Before the U.S. Supreme Court: Investigating the Influence of Amicus Curiae Briefs." *Political Research Quarterly* 60 (1): 55–70.

Commission on Structural Alternatives for the Federal Courts of Appeals. 1998. *Final Report*. https://www.law.berkeley.edu/wp-content/uploads/2019/03/Commission-on-Structural-Alternatives-for-the-Federal-Courts-of-Appeals-1998.pdf (accessed August 23, 2022).

Cooper, Rory. 2018. "Want to Drain the Swamp? Build Congress a Dorm." *Politico*, November 20. https://www.politico.com/magazine/story/2018/11/20/want-to-drain-the-swamp-build-congress-a-dorm-222641 (accessed August 23, 2022).

Corley, Pamela C. 2010. *Concurring Opinion Writing on the U.S. Supreme Court*. Albany, NY: State University of New York Press.

Corley, Pamela C., Amy Steigerwalt, and Artemus Ward. 2013. *The Puzzle of Unanimity: Explaining Consensus on the U.S. Supreme Court*. Redwood City, CA: Stanford University Press.

Corley, Pamela C., and Artemus Ward. 2020. "Intracourt Dialogue: The Impact of US Supreme Court Dissents." *Journal of Law and Courts* 8 (1): 27–50.

Cross, Frank B. 2007. *Decision Making in the U.S. Courts of Appeals*. Redwood City, CA: Stanford University Press.

Cross, Frank B., and James W. Pennebaker. 2014. "The Language of the Roberts Court." *Michigan State Law Review* 2014 (4): 853–94.

Cross, Frank B., James F. Spriggs II, Timothy R. Johnson, and Paul J. Wahlbeck. 2010. "Citations in the U.S. Supreme Court: An Empirical Study of Their Use and Significance." *University of Illinois Law Review* 2010 (2): 489–576.

Cross, Frank B., and Emerson H. Tiller. 1998. "Judicial Partisanship and Obedience to Legal Doctrine: Whistleblowing on the Federal Courts of Appeals." *Yale Law Journal* 107 (7): 2155–76.

Cross, Frank B., and Emerson H. Tiller. 2007. "Understanding Collegiality on the Court." *University of Pennsylvania Journal of Constitutional Law* 10 (2): 257–71.

C-SPAN. 2018. "Chief Justice Roberts Remarks at University of Minnesota Law School." *C-SPAN*, October 16. https://www.c-span.org/video/?451977-1/chief-justice-roberts-stresses-supreme-courts-independence-contentious-kavanaugh-hearings (accessed August 23, 2022).

BIBLIOGRAPHY

C-SPAN. 2019. "Supreme Court Justice Kagan at University of Colorado Law School." *C-Span Transcript*, October 22. https://www.c-span.org/video/?465467-1/supreme-court-justice-kagan-university-colorado-law-school (accessed August 23, 2022).

Curry, James M., and Jason M. Roberts. 2022. "Interpersonal Relationships and Legislative Collaboration in Congress." *Legislative Studies Quarterly*. https://onlinelibrary.wiley.com/doi/full/10.1111/lsq.12381 (accessed August 23, 2022).

Danescu-Niculescu-Mizil, Cristian, Moritz Sudhof, Dan Jurafsky, Jure Leskovec, and Christopher Potts. 2013. "A Computational Approach to Politeness with Application to Social Factors." *arXiv*: 1306.6078.

Danziger, Shai, Jonathan Levav, and Liora Avnaim-Pesso. 2011. "Extraneous Factors in Judicial Decisions." *Proceedings of the National Academy of Sciences* 108 (17): 6889–92.

Davis, John W. 1940. "The Argument of an Appeal." *ABA Journal* 26 (12): 895–99.

Dawson, Diane, Esteban Morales, Erin C. McKiernan, Lesley A. Schimanski, Meredith T. Niles, and Juan Pablo Alperin. 2022. "The Role of Collegiality in Academic Review, Promotion, and Tenure." *PLoS ONE* 17 (4): e0265506.

de Rohan Barondes, Royce. 2010. "ABA Judicial Ratings as the 'Gold Standard' or Fool's Gold: Federal District Judge Ratings and Reversals." *SSRN*. https://papers.ssrn.com/sol3/papers.cfm?abstract_id=1632752 (accessed August 23, 2022).

Denison, Alexander, Justin Wedeking, and Michael A. Zilis. 2020. "Negative Media Coverage of the Supreme Court: The Interactive Role of Opinion Language, Coalition Size, and Ideological Signals." *Social Science Quarterly* 101 (1): 121–43.

Denniston, Mark W. 2014. *Dialogue Among State Supreme Courts: Advancing State Constitutionalism*. El Paso, TX: LFB Scholarly Publishing LLC.

Driscoll, Amanda, and Michael J. Nelson. 2018. "There Is No Legitimacy Crisis: Support for Judicial Institutions in Modern Latin America." *Revista de La Sociedad Argentina de Análisis Político* 12 (2): 361–77.

Druckman, James N. 2001a. "On the Limits of Framing Effects: Who Can Frame?" *Journal of Politics* 63 (4): 1041–66.

Druckman, James N. 2001b. "Using Credible Advice to Overcome Framing Effects." *Journal of Law, Economics, & Organization* 17 (1): 62–82.

Dworkin, Ronald. 1986. *Law's Empire*. Cambridge, MA: Harvard University Press.

Dynel, Marta. 2015. "The Landscape of Impoliteness Research." *Journal of Politeness Research* 11 (2): 329–54.

Edwards, Harry T. 1998. "Collegiality and Decision Making on the D.C. Circuit." *Virginia Law Review* 84 (7): 1335–70.

Edwards, Harry T. 2003. "The Effects of Collegiality on Judicial Decision Making." *University of Pennsylvania Law Review* 151 (5): 1639–90.

Edwards, Harry T. 2004. "A Conversation with Judge Harry T. Edwards." *Washington University Journal of Law & Policy* 16 (1): 61–80.

Epstein, Lee, and Jack Knight. 1998. *The Choices Justices Make*. Washington, D.C.: CQ Press.

Epstein, Lee, William M. Landes, and Richard A. Posner. 2011. "Why (and When) Judges Dissent: A Theoretical and Empirical Analysis." *Journal of Legal Analysis* 3 (1): 101–37.

Epstein, Lee, William M. Landes, and Richard A. Posner. 2013. *The Behavior of Federal Judges*. Cambridge, MA: Harvard University Press.

Epstein, Lee, Andrew D. Martin, Kevin M. Quinn, and Jeffrey A. Segal. 2009. "Circuit Effects: How the Norm of Federal Judicial Experience Biases the Supreme Court." *University of Pennsylvania Law Review* 157 (3): 101–46.

Epstein, Lee, Andrew D. Martin, Jeffrey A. Segal, and Chad Westerland. 2007. "The Judicial Common Space." *Journal of Law, Economics, & Organization* 23 (2): 303–25.

BIBLIOGRAPHY 257

Epstein, Lee, Jeffrey A. Segal, and Harold J. Spaeth. 2001. "The Norm of Consensus on the U.S. Supreme Court." *American Journal of Political Science* 45 (2): 362–77.

Epstein, Lee, and Thomas G. Walker. 2018. *Constitutional Law for a Changing America: Rights, Liberties, and Justice.* Washington, D.C.: CQ Press.

Epstein, Lee, Thomas G. Walker, and Jason Roberts. 2021. "The U.S. Supreme Court Justices Database." *USC Gould School of Law.* https://epstein.usc.edu/justicesdata (accessed August 23, 2022).

Erskine, Ellena. 2021. "We Read All the Amicus Briefs in Dobbs so You Don't Have To." *SCOTUSblog,* November 30. https://www.scotusblog.com/2021/11/we-read-all-the-amicus-briefs-in-dobbs-so-you-dont-have-to/ (accessed August 23, 2022).

Farhang, Sean, and Gregory Wawro. 2004. "Institutional Dynamics on the U.S. Court of Appeals: Minority Representation Under Panel Decision Making." *Journal of Law, Economics, & Organization* 20 (2): 299–330.

Federal Judicial Center. 2022. "Biographical Directory of Article III Federal Judges, 1789–Present." *Judges.* https://www.fjc.gov/history/judges (accessed August 23, 2022).

Feldman, Noah. 2009. "When Arrogance Takes the Bench." *New York Times,* June 10. https://www.nytimes.com/2009/06/11/opinion/11feldman.html (accessed August 23, 2022).

Financial Services and General Government Appropriations for 2020: Hearings Before a Subcommittee of the Committee on Appropriations. 2020 116 Cong. (statement of Elena Kagan and Samuel Alito, Associate Justices, U.S. Supreme Court). https://www.govinfo.gov/content/pkg/CHRG-116hhrg38124/html/CHRG-116hhrg38124.htm (accessed August 24, 2022).

Finegan, Edward. 2020. "Legal Writing: Attitude and Emphasis: Corpus Linguistic Approaches to 'Legal Language': Adverbial Expression of Attitude and Emphasis in Supreme Court Opinions." In *The Routledge Handbook of Forensic Linguistics*, eds., Malcolm Coulthard and Alison Johnson. New York: Routledge, 65–77.

Fischman, Joshua B. 2011. "Estimating Preferences of Circuit Judges: A Model of Consensus Voting." *Journal of Law and Economics* 54 (4): 781–809.

Fischman, Joshua B. 2015. "Interpreting Circuit Court Voting Patterns: A Social Interactions Framework." *Journal of Law, Economics, & Organization* 31 (4): 808–42.

Ford, Matt. 2002. "The Rude Trump Judge Who's Writing the Most Bonkers Opinions in America." *The New Republic*, January 31. https://newrepublic.com/article/165169/lawrence-vandyke-judge-ninth-circuit-appeals-trump-bonkers-opinions (accessed August 23, 2022).

Fowler, James H., Timothy R. Johnson, James F. Spriggs II, Sangick Jeon, and Paul J. Wahlbeck. 2007. "Network Analysis and the Law: Measuring the Legal Importance of Supreme Court Precedents." *Political Analysis* 15 (3): 324–46.

Freilich, Robert H., Gregory D. Cox, and Elizabeth Hall. 1981. "1980–1981 Annual Review of Local Government Law: The Changing Federal Direction and Its Impact on Local Government." *The Urban Lawyer* 13 (4): 621–82.

Friedman, Barry. 2009. *The Will of the People: How Public Opinion Has Influenced the Supreme Court and Shaped the Meaning of the Constitution.* New York: Farrar, Straus; Giroux.

Friedman, Barry, and Andrew D. Martin. 2011. "Looking for Law in All the Wrong Places: Some Suggestions for Modeling Legal Decision-Making." In *What's Law Got to Do with It? What Judges Do, Why They Do It, and What's at Stake*, ed., Charles Gardner Geyh. Redwood City, CA: Stanford University Press, 143–72.

Friedman, Lawrence M., Robert A. Kagan, Bliss Cartwright, and Stanton Wheeler. 1981. "State Supreme Courts: A Century of Style and Citation." *Stanford Law Review* 33 (5): 773–818.

Galanter, Marc. 1974. "Why the Haves Come Out Ahead: Speculations on the Limits of Legal Change." *Law & Society Review* 9 (1): 95–160.

García, Francisco Fernández. 2014. "Impoliteness, Pseudo-Politeness, Strategic Politeness? On the Nature of Communicative Behaviour in Electoral Debates." *Círculo de Lingüística Aplicada a La Comunicación* 58: 60–89.

George, Tracey E. 2008. "From Judge to Justice: Social Background Theory and the Supreme Court." *North Carolina Law Review* 86 (5): 1333–67.

George, Tracey E., and Lee Epstein. 1992. "On the Nature of Supreme Court Decision Making." *American Political Science Review* 86 (2): 323–37.

Gerhards, Leonie, and Michael Kosfeld. 2020. "I (Don't) Like You! But Who Cares? Gender Differences in Same-Sex and Mixed-Sex Teams." *The Economic Journal* 130 (627): 716–39.

Gibson, James L. 1977. "Discriminant Functions, Role Orientations and Judicial Behavior: Theoretical and Methodological Linkages." *Journal of Politics* 39 (4): 984–1007.

Gibson, James L., Gregory A. Caldeira, and Vanessa A. Baird. 1998. "On the Legitimacy of National High Courts." *American Political Science Review* 92 (2): 343–58.

Gibson, James L., Gregory A. Caldeira, and Lester Kenyatta Spence. 2005. "Why Do People Accept Public Policies They Oppose? Testing Legitimacy Theory with a Survey-Based Experiment." *Political Research Quarterly* 58 (2): 187–201.

Gibson, James L., and Michael J. Nelson. 2014. "The Legitimacy of the U.S. Supreme Court: Conventional Wisdoms, and Recent Challenges Thereto." *Annual Review of Law and Social Science* 10 (1): 201–19.

Gibson, James L., and Michael J. Nelson. 2015. "Is the U.S. Supreme Court's Legitimacy Grounded in Performance Satisfaction and Ideology?" *American Journal of Political Science* 59 (1): 162–74.

Gibson, James L., and Michael J. Nelson. 2017. "Reconsidering Positivity Theory: What Roles Do Politicization, Ideological Disagreement, and Legal Realism Play in Shaping U.S. Supreme Court Legitimacy?" *Journal of Empirical Legal Studies* 14 (3): 592–617.

Gibson, James L., and Michael J. Nelson. 2018. *Black and Blue: How African Americans Judge the U.S. Legal System*. New York: Oxford University Press.

Gibson, James L., and Michael J. Nelson. 2021. *Judging Inequality: State Supreme Courts and the Inequality Crisis*. New York: Russell Sage Foundation.

Giles, Micheal W., Bethany Blackstone, and Richard L. Vining. 2008. "The Supreme Court in American Democracy: Unraveling the Linkages between Public Opinion and Judicial Decision Making." *Journal of Politics* 70 (2): 293–306.

Giles, Micheal W., Thomas G. Walker, and Christopher J.W. Zorn. 2006. "Setting a Judicial Agenda: The Decision to Grant En Banc Review in the U.S. Courts of Appeals." *Journal of Politics* 68 (4): 852–66.

Giles, Micheal W., Virginia A. Hettinger, and Todd C. Peppers. 2001. "Picking Federal Judges: A Note on Policy and Partisan Selection Agendas." *Political Research Quarterly* 54 (3): 623–41.

Giles, Micheal W., Virginia A. Hettinger, Christopher J.W. Zorn, and Todd C. Peppers. 2007. "The Etiology of the Occurrence of En Banc Review in the U.S. Court of Appeals." *American Journal of Political Science* 51 (3): 449–63.

Gillman, Howard. 1999. "The Court as an Idea, Not a Building (or a Game): Interpretive Institutionalism and the Analysis of Supreme Court Decision-Making." In *Supreme Court Decision-Making: New Institutionalist Approaches*, eds., Cornell W. Clayton and Howard Gillman. University of Chicago Press, 65–87.

Ginsburg, Ruth Bader. 1990. "Remarks on Writing Separately." *Washington Law Review* 65 (1): 133–50.

Ginsburg, Ruth Bader. 2010. "The Role of Dissenting Opinions." *Minnesota Law Review* 95 (1): 1–8.

Glynn, Adam, and Maya Sen. 2015. "Identifying Judicial Empathy: Does Having Daughters Cause Judges to Rule for Women's Issues." *American Journal of Political Science* 59 (1): 37–54.

BIBLIOGRAPHY 259

Goelzhauser, Greg. 2015. "Silent Acquiescence on the Supreme Court." *Justice System Journal* 36 (1): 3–19.

Goldman, Sheldon. 1968. "Conflict and Consensus in the United States Courts of Appeals." *Wisconsin Law Review* 1968: 461–82.

Goodman, Paul S., and Dennis P. Leyden. 1991. "Familiarity and Group Productivity." *Journal of Applied Psychology* 76 (4): 578–86.

Gorman, Anna. 2004. "Collegiality Is a Casualty in U.S. Legal Wars." *Los Angeles Times*, April 2. https://www.latimes.com/archives/la-xpm-2004-apr-02-me-onthelaw2-story.html (accessed August 23, 2022).

Gou, Angie, Ellena Erskine, and James Romoser. 2022. "STAT PACK for the Supreme Court's 2021–22 Term." *SCOTUSblog*, July 1. https://www.scotusblog.com/wp-content/uploads/2022/07/SCOTUSblog-Final-STAT-PACK-OT2021.pdf (accessed August 23, 2022).

Goźdź-Roszkowski, Stanisław. 2020. "Communicating Dissent in Judicial Opinions: A Comparative, Genre-Based Analysis." *International Journal for the Semiotics of Law—Revue Internationale de Sémiotique Juridique* 33 (2): 381–401.

Greenhouse, Linda. 2002. "The Nation; the Court: Same Time Next Year. And Next Year." *New York Times*, October 6. https://www.nytimes.com/2002/10/06/weekinreview/the-nation-the-court-same-time-next-year-and-next-year.html (accessed August 23, 2022).

Gresko, Jessica. 2018. "In This Classroom, Every Student's Name Is 'Judge.'" *Associated Press*, February 7. https://apnews.com/article/north-america-donald-trump-ap-top-news-courts-politics-fce2e7b2cf1f493db1183e6202549a68 (accessed August 23, 2022).

Grisales, Claudia. 2019. "'Game Recognizes Game': A Bipartisan Bond in the Age of Impeachment." *NPR*, September 27. https://www.npr.org/2019/09/27/764817694/game-recognizes-game-a-bipartisan-bond-in-the-age-of-impeachment (accessed August 23, 2022).

Gruenfeld, Deborah H., Elizabeth A. Mannix, Katherine Y. Williams, and Margaret A. Neale. 1996. "Group Composition and Decision Making: How Member Familiarity and Information Distribution Affect Process and Performance." *Organizational Behavior and Human Decision Processes* 67 (1): 1–15.

Haire, Susan B. 2001. "Rating the Ratings of the American Bar Association Standing Committee on the Federal Judiciary." *Justice System Journal* 22 (1): 1–17.

Haire, Susan B., Stefanie A. Lindquist, and Donald R. Songer. 2003. "Appellate Court Supervision in the Federal Judiciary." *Law & Society Review* 37 (1): 143–68.

Hall, Matthew E.K., Gary E. Hollibaugh, Jonathan D. Klingler, and Adam J. Ramey. 2021. "Considerations in Personality Measurement: Replicability, Transparency, and Predictive Validity." *Journal of Law and Courts* 9 (2): 397–405.

Hall, Matthew E.K. 2018. *What Justices Want: Goals and Personality on the U.S. Supreme Court*. Cambridge University Press.

Hall, Matthew E.K. and Jason H. Windett. 2016. "Discouraging Dissent: The Chief Judge's Influence in State Supreme Courts." *American Politics Research* 44 (4): 682–709.

Hall, Melinda Gann. 1987. "Constituent Influence in State Supreme Courts: Conceptual Notes and a Case Study." *Journal of Politics* 49 (4): 1117–24.

Hansford, Thomas G., and James F. Spriggs II. 2006. *The Politics of Precedent on the U.S. Supreme Court*. Princeton University Press.

Harris, Allison P. 2021. "Can Racial Diversity Among Judges Affect Sentencing Outcomes?" *Allison P. Harris*. https://www.allisonpharris.com/uploads/1/0/7/3/107342067/harris_diversitysentencing.pdf (accessed August 23, 2022).

Harris, Allison P., and Maya Sen. 2019. "Bias and Judging." *Annual Review of Political Science* 22: 241–59.

Harris, Peter. 1982. "Structural Change in the Communication of Precedent Among State Supreme Courts, 1870–1970." *Social Networks* 4 (3): 201–12.

260 BIBLIOGRAPHY

Harris, Peter. 1985. "Difficult Cases and the Display of Authority." *Journal of Law, Economics, & Organization* 1 (1): 209–21.

Harris, Sandra. 2001. "Being Politically Impolite: Extending Politeness Theory to Adversarial Political Discourse." *Discourse & Society* 12 (4): 451–72.

Harvey, Anna, and Barry Friedman. 2009. "Ducking Trouble: Congressionally Induced Selection Bias in the Supreme Court's Agenda." *Journal of Politics* 71 (2): 574–92.

Hazelton, Morgan L.W., and Rachael K. Hinkle. 2022. *Persuading the Supreme Court: The Significance of Briefs in Judicial Decision-Making*. Lawrence, KS: Kansas University Press.

Hettinger, Virginia A., Stefanie A. Lindquist, and Wendy L. Martinek. 2003. "Acclimation Effects and Separate Opinion Writing in the U.S. Courts of Appeals." *Social Science Quarterly* 84 (4): 792–810.

Hettinger, Virginia A., Stefanie A. Lindquist, and Wendy L. Martinek. 2004. "Comparing Attitudinal and Strategic Accounts of Dissenting Behavior on the U.S. Courts of Appeals." *American Journal of Political Science* 48 (1): 123–37.

Hettinger, Virginia A., Stefanie A. Lindquist, and Wendy L. Martinek. 2006. *Judging on a Collegial Court*. Charlottesville, VA: University of Virginia Press.

Hinkle, Rachael K. 2015. "Legal Constraint in the U.S. Courts of Appeals." *Journal of Politics* 77 (3): 721–35.

Hinkle, Rachael K. 2016. "Strategic Anticipation of En Banc Review in the U.S. Courts of Appeals." *Law & Society Review* 50 (2): 383–414.

Hinkle, Rachael K. 2021. "How Policy Influence Varies with Race and Gender in the US Courts of Appeals." *Research & Politics* 8 (3): 1–7.

Hinkle, Rachael K. 2022. "How to Extract Legal Citations Using Python (for the Complete Beginner)." *Law & Courts Newsletter* 32 (1): 12–4.

Hinkle, Rachael K. 2023. "Publication and Strategy in the U.S. Courts of Appeals." *Journal of Institutional and Theoretical Economics* 179 (1): 146—51.

Hinkle, Rachael K., Morgan L.W. Hazelton, and Michael J. Nelson. 2017. "Legal Scholarship Highlight: Getting to Know You—The Unifying Effects of Membership Stability." *SCOTUSblog*, May 26. https://www.scotusblog.com/2017/05/legal-scholarship-highlight-getting-know-unifying-effects-membership-stability/ (accessed August 23, 2022).

Hinkle, Rachael K., Andrew D. Martin, Jonathan D. Shaub, and Emerson H. Tiller. 2012. "A Positive Theory and Empirical Analysis of Strategic Word Choice in District Court Opinions." *Journal of Legal Analysis* 4 (2): 407–44.

Hinkle, Rachael K., and Michael J. Nelson. 2016. "The Transmission of Legal Precedent Among State Supreme Courts in the Twenty-First Century." *State Politics & Policy Quarterly* 16 (4): 391–410.

Hinkle, Rachael K., and Michael J. Nelson. 2018a. "How to Lose Cases and Influence People." *Statistics, Politics, and Policy* 8 (2): 195–222.

Hinkle, Rachael K., and Michael J. Nelson. 2018b. "The Intergroup Foundations of Policy Influence." *Political Research Quarterly* 71 (4): 729–42.

Hinkle, Rachael K., Michael J. Nelson, and Morgan L.W. Hazelton. 2020. "Deferring, Deliberating, or Dodging Review? Explaining Counterjudge Success in the U.S. Courts of Appeals." *Journal of Law and Courts* 8 (2): 277–300.

Horowitz, Michael, Brandon M. Stewart, Dustin Tingley, Michael Bishop, Laura Resnick Samotin, Margaret Roberts, Welton Chang, Barbara Mellers, and Philip Tetlock. 2019. "What Makes Foreign Policy Teams Tick: Explaining Variation in Group Performance at Geopolitical Forecasting."*Journal of Politics* 81 (4): 1388–404.

Hovland, Carl I., and Walter Weiss. 1951. "The Influence of Source Credibility on Communication Effectiveness." *Public Opinion Quarterly* 15 (4): 635–50.

BIBLIOGRAPHY 261

Howard, J. Woodford. 1981. *Courts of Appeals in the Federal Judicial System: A Study of the Second, Fifth, and District of Columbia Circuits.* Princeton University Press.

Hughes, Charles Evans. 1928. *The Supreme Court of the United States.* New York: Columbia University Press.

Hume, Robert J. 2019. "Disagreeable Rhetoric, Shaming, and the Strategy of Dissenting on the U.S. Supreme Court." *Justice System Journal* 40 (1): 3–20.

Hurley, Lawrence, and Andrew Chung. 2018. "Sparks or Harmony with Kavanaugh on the U.S. Supreme Court." *Reuters*, October 5. https://www.reuters.com/article/usa-court-kavana ugh-impact-analysis-idINKCN1MF2OH (accessed August 23, 2022).

Indeed. 2022. "10 Tips for How to Get Along with Coworkers." *Career Guide.* https://www.ind eed.com/career-advice/career-development/how-to-get-along-with-coworkers (accessed August 23, 2022).

Janis, Irving L. 1972. *Victims of Groupthink: A Psychological Study of Foreign-Policy Decisions and Fiascoes.* Boston, MA: Houghton Mifflin.

Janis, Irving L. 1982. *Groupthink: Psychological Studies of Policy Decisions and Fiascoes.* Boston, MA: Houghton Mifflin.

Jarvenpaa, Sirkka L., Thomas R. Shaw, and D. Sandy Staples. 2004. "Toward Contextualized Theories of Trust: The Role of Trust in Global Virtual Teams." *Information Systems Research* 15 (3): 250–67.

Johnson, Ben, and Logan Strother. 2021. "The Supreme Court's (Surprising?) Indifference to Public Opinion." *Political Research Quarterly* 74 (1): 18–34.

Johnson, Charles A. 1987. "Law, Politics, and Judicial Decision Making: Lower Federal Court Uses of Supreme Court Decisions." *Law & Society Review* 21 (2): 325–40.

Johnston, Richard E., and Robert L. Peabody. 1976. "Supreme Court Voting Behavior: A Comparison of the Warren and Burger Courts." In *Cases in American Politics*, ed., Robert L. Peabody. New York: Praeger, 71–110.

Kahn, Jeffrey H., Renee M. Tobin, Audra E. Massey, and Jennifer A. Anderson. 2007. "Measuring Emotional Expression with the Linguistic Inquiry and Word Count." *American Journal of Psychology* 120 (2): 263–86.

Kanter, Rosabeth Moss. 1977. "Men and Women of the Corporation Revisited." *Management Review* 26 (2): 257–63.

Karpowitz, Christopher F., and Tali Mendelberg. 2014. *The Silent Sex: Gender, Deliberation, and Institutions.* Princeton University Press.

Kassow, Benjamin, Donald R. Songer, and Michael P. Fix. 2012. "The Influence of Precedent on State Supreme Courts." *Political Research Quarterly* 65 (2): 372–84.

Kastellec, Jonathan P. 2007. "Panel Composition and Judicial Compliance on the U.S. Courts of Appeals." *Journal of Law, Economics, & Organization* 23 (2): 421–41.

Kastellec, Jonathan P. 2011. "Hierarchical and Collegial Politics on the U.S. Courts of Appeals." *Journal of Politics* 73 (2): 345–61.

Kastellec, Jonathan P. 2013. "Racial Diversity and Judicial Influence on Appellate Courts." *American Journal of Political Science* 57 (1): 167–83.

Kay, Stanley. 2018. "The Highest Court in the Land." *Sports Illustrated*, July 25. https://www. si.com/nba/2018/07/25/supreme-court-building-basketball-court (accessed August 23, 2022).

Keltner, Dacher, Lisa Capps, Ann M. Kring, Randall C. Young, and Erin A. Heerey. 2001. "Just Teasing: A Conceptual Analysis and Empirical Review." *Psychological Bulletin* 127 (2): 229–48.

Kim, Pauline T. 2009. "Deliberation and Strategy on the United States Courts of Appeals: An Empirical Exploration of Panel Effects." *University of Pennsylvania Law Review* 157 (5): 1319–81.

BIBLIOGRAPHY

Kim, Pauline T. 2011. "Beyond Principal-Agent Theories: Law and the Judicial Hierarchy." *Northwestern University Law Review* 105 (2): 535–75.

Kirkland, Justin H. 2014. "Chamber Size Effects on the Collaborative Structure of Legislatures." *Legislative Studies Quarterly* 39 (2): 169–98.

Klein, David E. 2002. *Making Law in the United States Courts of Appeals*. Cambridge University Press.

Klein, David E., and Robert J. Hume. 2003. "Fear of Reversal as an Explanation of Lower Court Compliance." *Law & Society Review* 37 (3): 579–606.

Klein, David E., and Darby Morrisroe. 1999. "The Prestige and Influence of Individual Judges on the U.S. Courts of Appeals." *Journal of Legal Studies* 28 (2): 371–91.

Kluger, Richard. 2011. *Simple Justice: The History of Brown v. Board of Education and Black America's Struggle for Equality*. New York: Vintage Books.

Kosma, Montgomery N. 1998. "Measuring the Influence of Supreme Court Justices." *Journal of Legal Studies* 27 (2): 333–72.

Kousser, Thad. 2005. *Term Limits and the Dismantling of State Legislative Professionalism*. Cambridge University Press.

Kozinski, Alex. 1993. "What I Ate for Breakfast and Other Mysteries of Judicial Decision Making." *Loyola of Los Angeles Law Review* 26 (4): 993–99.

Krewson, Christopher N. 2019. "Strategic Sensationalism: Why Justices Use Emotional Appeals in Supreme Court Opinions." *Justice System Journal* 40 (4): 319–36.

Kritzer, Herbert M., and Mark J. Richards. 2003. "Jurisprudential Regimes and Supreme Court Decisionmaking: The *Lemon* Regime and Establishment Clause Cases." *Law & Society Review* 37 (4): 827–40.

Kritzer, Herbert M., and Mark J. Richards. 2005. "The Influence of Law in the Supreme Court's Search-and-Seizure Jurisprudence." *American Politics Research* 33 (1): 33–55.

Kurzon, Dennis. 2001. "The Politeness of Judges: American and English Judicial Behaviour." *Journal of Pragmatics* 33 (1): 61–85.

Lakoff, Robin T. 1989. "The Limits of Politeness: Therapeutic and Courtroom Discourse in Linguistic Politeness." *Multilingua* 8 (2–3): 101–29.

Landes, William M., Lawrence Lessig, and Michael E. Solimine. 1998. "Judicial Influence: A Citation Analysis of Federal Courts of Appeals Judges." *Journal of Legal Studies* 27 (2): 271–332.

Lane, Charles. 2001. "Disorder in the Court." *Washington Post*, November 12. https://www.washingtonpost.com/archive/politics/2001/11/12/disorder-in-the-court/195e3461-6d19-43ca-b83e-32517ce934ad/ (accessed August 23, 2022).

Lawless, Jennifer L., Sean M. Theriault, and Samantha Guthrie. 2018. "Nice Girls? Sex, Collegiality, and Bipartisan Cooperation in the U.S. Congress." *Journal of Politics* 80 (4): 1268–82.

Lax, Jeffrey R., and Charles M. Cameron. 2007. "Bargaining and Opinion Assignment on the US Supreme Court." *Journal of Law, Economics, & Organization* 23 (2): 276–302.

Levine, Sheen S., Charlotte Reypens, and David Stark. 2022. "Who Cooperates with Whom in Diverse-Gender Teams: Paying to Cross the Gender Gap." *Academy of Management Proceedings* 2022 (1). https://doi.org/10.5465/AMBPP.2022.11099abstract (accessed August 23, 2022).

Levy, Leo. 1960. "Studies in Conformity Behavior: A Methodological Note." *Journal of Psychology* 50 (1): 39–41.

Levy, Marin K. 2017. "Panel Assignment in the Federal Courts of Appeals." *Cornell Law Review* 103 (1): 65–116.

Levy, Marin K. 2020. *Twitter*. December 2020. https://twitter.com/marinklevy/status/1334668658187046912 (accessed August 23, 2022).

Li, Siyu. 2020. "A Separation-of-Powers Model of U.S. Chief Justice Opinion Assignment." *Justice System Journal* 41 (1): 3–21.

Lindquist, Stefanie A. 2006. "Bureaucratization and Balkanization: The Origins and the Effects of Decision-Making Norms in the Federal Appellate Courts." *University of Richmond Law Review* 41 (3): 659–706.

Lindquist, Stefanie A., and Rorie Spill Solberg. 2007. "Judicial Review by the Burger and Rehnquist Courts: Explaining Justices' Responses to Constitutional Challenges." *Political Research Quarterly* 60 (1): 71–90.

Liptak, Adam. 2003. "Order Lacking on a Court: U.S. Appellate Judges in Cincinnati Spar in Public." *New York Times*, August 12. http://www.nytimes.com/2003/08/12/us/order-lacking-on-a-court-us-appellate-judges-in-cincinnati-spar-in-public.html (accessed August 23, 2022).

Liptak, Adam. 2022. "Justice Jackson, a Former Law Clerk, Returns to a Transformed Supreme Court." *New York Times*, July 18. https://www.nytimes.com/2022/07/18/us/politics/ketanji-brown-jackson-scotus.html?smid=tw-share (accessed August 23, 2022).

Lithwick, Dahlia. 2022. "I Am Embarrassed for the Supreme Court." *Slate*, March 29. https://slate.com/news-and-politics/2022/01/scotus-masking-roberts-denial-takeaway.html (accessed August 23, 2022).

Lithwick, Dahlia. 2018. "The Elmo Antidote." *Slate*, March 6. https://slate.com/news-and-politics/2018/03/sonia-sotomayors-message-of-empathy-listening-and-compromise-is-what-we-need.html (accessed August 23, 2022).

Locher, Miriam A., and Richard J. Watts. 2005. "Politeness Theory and Relational Work." *Journal of Politeness Research* 1 (1): 9–33.

Lupia, Arthur, and Mathew D. McCubbins. 1998. *The Democratic Dilemma*. Cambridge University Press.

Maltzman, Forrest, James F. Spriggs II, and Paul J. Wahlbeck. 2000. *Crafting Law on the Supreme Court: The Collegial Game*. Cambridge University Press.

Maltzman, Forrest, and Paul J. Wahlbeck. 1996. "Strategic Policy Considerations and Voting Fluidity on the Burger Court." *American Political Science Review* 90 (3): 581–92.

Maltzman, Forrest, and Paul J. Wahlbeck. 2004. "A Conditional Model of Opinion Assignment on the Supreme Court." *Political Research Quarterly* 57 (4): 551–63.

Manning, Christopher D., Prabhakar Raghavan, and Hinrich Schütze. 2008. *Introduction to Information Retrieval*. Cambridge University Press.

Manz, William H. 2001. "The Citation Practices of the New York Court of Appeals: A Millennium Update." *Buffalo Law Review* 49 (3): 1273–313.

Martin, Andrew D., and Kevin M. Quinn. 2002. "Dynamic Ideal Point Estimation via Markov Chain Monte Carlo for the U.S. Supreme Court, 1953–1999." *Political Analysis* 10 (2): 134–53.

Martin, Andrew D., Kevin M. Quinn, Theodore W. Ruger, and Pauline T. Kim. 2004. "Competing Approaches to Predicting Supreme Court Decision Making." *Perspectives on Politics* 2 (4): 761–67.

Martinek, Wendy L. 2010. "Judges as Members of Small Groups." In *The Psychology of Judicial Decision Making*, eds., David E. Klein and Gregory Mitchell. New York: Oxford University Press, 73–94.

Masket, Seth. 2008. "Where You Sit Is Where You Stand: The Impact of Seating Proximity on Legislative Cue-Taking." *Quarterly Journal of Political Science* 3 (3): 301–11.

Masood, Ali S., Benjamin J. Kassow, and Donald R. Songer. 2017. "Supreme Court Precedent in a Judicial Hierarchy." *American Politics Research* 45 (3): 403–34.

Matthews, Donald R. 1960. *United States Senators and Their World*. Chapel Hill, NC: University of North Carolina Press.

Matthews, Donald R., and James A. Stimson. 1975. *Yeas and Nays: Normal Decision-Making in the U.S. House of Representatives*. New York: Wiley.

Mauro, Tony. 2018. "Justice Kavanaugh May Find Rough Start with New Colleagues." *National Law Journal*, October 7. https://www.law.com/nationallawjournal/2018/10/07/justice-kavanaugh-may-find-rough-start-with-new-colleagues/ (accessed August 24, 2022).

Maveety, Nancy, Charles C. Turner, and Lori Beth Way. 2010. "The Rise of the Choral Court: Use of Concurrence in the Burger and Rehnquist Courts." *Political Research Quarterly* 63 (3): 627–39.

Mayer, Roger C., James H. Davis, and F. David Schoorman. 1995. "An Integrative Model of Organizational Trust." *Academy of Management Review* 20 (3): 709–34.

McBride, Kelly. 2022. "NPR Reporting on Supreme Court Mask Controversy Merits Clarification." *NPR*, January 20. https://www.npr.org/sections/publiceditor/2022/01/20/1074540207/npr-reporting-on-supreme-court-mask-controversy-merits-clarification (accessed August 24, 2022).

McDonald, R. Robin. 2020. "'Good Grief': 11th Circuit Judges Get into Scathing Exchange over Transgender Inmate." *The Daily Report*, December 3. https://www.law.com/dailyreportonline/2020/12/03/good-grief-11th-circuit-judges-get-into-scathing-exchange-in-fractious-order/ (accessed August 24, 2022).

McDonald, Ruth, Kath Checkland, Stephen Harrison, and Anna Coleman. 2009. "Rethinking Collegiality: Restratification in English General Medical Practice 2004–2008." *Social Science & Medicine* 68 (7): 1199–205.

McGrath, Joseph E. 1997. "Small Group Research, That Once and Future Field: An Interpretation of the Past with an Eye to the Future." *Group Dynamics: Theory, Research, and Practice* 1 (1): 7–27.

McGuire, Kevin T., and James A. Stimson. 2004. "The Least Dangerous Branch Revisited: New Evidence on Supreme Court Responsiveness to Public Preferences." *Journal of Politics* 66 (4): 1018–35.

McPherson, Miller, Lynn Smith–Lovin, and James M. Cook. 2001. "Birds of a Feather: Homophily in Social Networks." *Annual Review of Sociology* 27 (1): 415–444.

Meinke, Scott R., and Kevin M. Scott. 2007. "Collegial Influence and Judicial Voting Change: The Effect of Membership Change on U.S. Supreme Court Justices." *Law & Society Review* 41 (4): 909–38.

Merryman, John H. 1977. "Toward a Theory of Citations: An Empirical Study of the Citation Practice of the California Supreme Court in 1950, 1960, and 1970." *Southern California Law Review* 50 (3): 381–428.

Miller, Gary J. 2005. "The Political Evolution of Principal-Agent Models." *Annual Review of Political Science* 8: 203–25.

Minozzi, William, and Gregory A. Caldeira. 2021. "Congress and Community: Coresidence and Social Influence in the U.S. House of Representatives, 1801–1861." *American Political Science Review* 115 (4): 1292–1307.

Moline, Michael. 2020. "Transgender FL Inmate's Appeal Leaves 11th Circuit Judges at Each Others' Throats." *The Florida Phoenix*, December 4. https://floridaphoenix.com/2020/12/04/transgender-fl-inmates-appeal-leaves-11th-circuit-judges-at-each-others-throats/ (accessed August 24, 2022).

Mondak, Jeffrey J. 1990. "Perceived Legitimacy of Supreme Court Decisions: Three Functions of Source Credibility." *Political Behavior* 12 (4): 363–84.

Monnappa, Avantika. 2022. "How Facebook Uses Big Data: The Good, the Bad, and the Ugly." *Simplilearn*, July 27. https://www.simplilearn.com/how-facebook-is-using-big-data-article (accessed August 24, 2022).

Morgan, Donald G. 1953. "The Origin of Supreme Court Dissent." *William and Mary Quarterly* 10 (3): 353–77.

Morison, John, and Adam Harkens. 2019. "Re-Engineering Justice? Robot Judges, Computerised Courts and (Semi) Automated Legal Decision-Making." *Legal Studies* 39 (4): 618–35.

Murphy, Michael R. 2000. "Collegiality and Technology."*Journal of Appellate Practice and Process* 2 (2): 455–61.

Murphy, Walter F. 1964. *Elements of Judicial Strategy*. Chicago: University of Chicago Press.

Nagel, Stuart S. 1962. "Sociometric Relations Among American Courts." *Southwestern Social Science Quarterly* 43 (2): 136–42.

Nagel, Stuart S. 1974. "Multiple Correlation of Judicial Backgrounds and Decisions." *Florida State University Law Review* 2 (2): 258–80.

Nash, Jonathan Remy. 2022 "Measuring Judicial Collegiality Through Dissent." *Buffalo Law Review* 70 (4): 1561–635.

Nelson, Michael J., and Lee Epstein. 2022. "Human Capital in Court: The Role of Attorney Experience in US Supreme Court Litigation." *Journal of Law and Courts* 10 (1): 61–85.

Nelson, Michael J., and James L. Gibson. 2019. "How Does Hyper-Politicized Rhetoric Affect the US Supreme Court's Legitimacy?" *Journal of Politics* 81 (4): 1512–16.

Nelson, Michael J., and James L. Gibson. 2020. "Measuring Subjective Ideological Disagreement with the US Supreme Court." *Journal of Law and Courts* 8 (1): 75–94.

Nelson, Michael J., Morgan L.W. Hazelton, and Rachael K. Hinkle. 2022. "How Interpersonal Contact Affects Appellate Review." *Journal of Politics* 84 (1): 573–77.

Nelson, Michael J., and Rachael K. Hinkle. 2018. "Crafting the Law: How Opinion Content Influences Legal Development." *Justice System Journal* 39 (2): 97–122.

Nelson, Michael J., and Patrick Tucker. 2021. "The Stability and Durability of the U.S. Supreme Court's Legitimacy." *Journal of Politics* 83 (2): 767–71.

Nelson, Michael J., and Alicia Uribe-McGuire. 2017. "Opportunity and Overrides: The Effect of Institutional Public Support on Congressional Overrides of Supreme Court Decisions." *Political Research Quarterly* 70 (3): 632–43.

Newman, Jon O. 1993. "1,000 Judges—The Limit for an Effective Federal Judiciary." *Judicature* 76 (4): 187–88.

Niblett, Anthony. 2010. "Do Judges Cherry Pick Precedents to Justify Extra-Legal Decisions? A Statistical Examination." *Maryland Law Review* 70 (1): 234–71.

Niblett, Anthony, and Albert H. Yoon. 2015. "Judicial Disharmony: A Study of Dissent." *International Review of Law and Economics* 42: 60–71.

Nielson, Aaron. 2017. "D.C. Circuit Review—Reviewed: 'Breyer, Alito, and Their Pals'." *Notice and Comment,* March 25. http://yalejreg.com/nc/d-c-circuit-review-reviewed-breyer-alito-and-their-pals/ (accessed August 24, 2022).

Note. 2011. "From Consensus to Collegiality: The Origins of the Respectful Dissent." *Harvard Law Review* 124 (5): 1305–26.

NPR. 2022. "Transcript: Gorsuch Didn't Mask Despite Sotomayor's COVID Worries, Leading Her to Telework." *NPR,* March 21. https://www.npr.org/transcripts/1073428376 (accessed August 24, 2022).

Orso, Anna. 2018. "Kagan, Sotomayor Bemoan Court Polarization." *Philadelphia Inquirer,* October 6. A1.

Ortiz-Ospina, Esteban. 2020. "Who Do We Spend Time with Across Our Lifetime?" *Our World in Data,* December 11. https://Ourworldindata.org/Time-with-Others-Lifetime (accessed August 24, 2022).

Owens, Ryan J. 2010. "The Separation of Powers and Supreme Court Agenda Setting." *American Journal of Political Science* 54 (2): 412–27.

Owens, Ryan J., and Patrick C. Wohlfarth. 2019. "The Influence of Home-State Reputation and Public Opinion on Federal Circuit Court Judges." *Journal of Law and Courts* 7 (2): 187–214.

Pang, Xun, Barry Friedman, Andrew D. Martin, and Kevin M. Quinn. 2012. "Endogenous Jurisprudential Regimes." *Political Analysis* 20 (4): 417–36.

Parigi, Paolo, and Patrick Bergemann. 2016. "Strange Bedfellows: Informal Relationships and Political Preference Formation Within Boardinghouses, 1825–1841." *American Journal of Sociology* 122 (2): 501–31.

Patrice, Joe. 2022. "Partner Seems Pretty Ticked Off in This Voice Mail." *Above the Law*, July 20. https://abovethelaw.com/2022/07/partner-seems-pretty-ticked-off-in-this-voicemail/ (accessed August 24, 2022).

Patry, William. 2005. "How to Learn from Dick Posner." *Patry Copyright Blog*, May 5. http://williampatry.blogspot.com/2005/05/how-to-learn-from-dick-posner.html (accessed February 22, 2023).

Pennebaker, James W., Roger J. Booth, and Martha E. Francis. 2007. "Linguistic Inquiry and Word Count: LIWC [Computer Software]." https://www.liwc.app/ (accessed August 24, 2022).

Peresie, Jennifer L. 2005. "Female Judges Matter: Gender and Collegial Decisionmaking in the Federal Appellate Courts." *Yale Law Journal* 114 (7): 1759–90.

Perry Jr., H.W. 1991. *Deciding to Decide: Agenda Setting in the United States Supreme Court.* Boston, MA: Harvard University Press.

Poole, Keith T. 1998. "Recovering a Basic Space from a Set of Issue Scales." *American Journal of Political Science* 42 (3): 954–93.

Pornpitakpan, Chanthika. 2004. "The Persuasiveness of Source Credibility: A Critical Review of Five Decades' Evidence." *Journal of Applied Social Psychology* 34 (2): 243–81.

Posner, Richard A. 1990. "A Tribute to Justice William J. Brennan, Jr." *Harvard Law Review* 104 (1): 13–5.

Posner, Richard A. 2008. *How Judges Think*. Boston, MA: Harvard University Press.

Presidential Commission on the Supreme Court of the United States. 2021. *Final Report*. https://www.whitehouse.gov/wp-content/uploads/2021/12/SCOTUS-Report-Final-12.8.21-1.pdf (accessed August 24, 2022).

Prison Fellowship. 2019. "Reps. Doug Collins and Hakeem Jeffries Presented with Colson Advocate Award." December 10. https://www.prisonfellowship.org/2019/12/reps-doug-collins-and-hakeem-jeffries-presented-with-colson-advocate-award/ (accessed August 24, 2022).

Pryor, Tom. 2017. "Using Citations to Measure Influence on the Supreme Court." *American Politics Research* 45 (3): 366–402.

Randazzo, Kirk A. 2008. "Strategic Anticipation and the Hierarchy of Justice in U.S. District Courts." *American Politics Research* 36 (5): 669–93.

Ray, Laura Krugman. 1989. "The Justices Write Separately: Uses of the Concurrence by the Rehnquist Court." *UC Davis Law Review* 23 (4): 777–832.

Rehnquist, William H. 1974. "Is an Expanded Right of Privacy Consistent with Fair and Effective Law Enforcement: Or Privacy, You've Come a Long Way, Baby." *University of Kansas Law Review* 23 (1): 1–22.

Rehnquist, William H. 2000. "Remarks by William H. Rehnquist at the College of William and Mary." *Supreme Court of the United States*, October 6. https://www.supremecourt.gov/pub licinfo/speeches/viewspeech/sp_10-06-00 (accessed August 24, 2022).

Revesz, Richard. 1999. "Ideology, Collegiality, and the D.C. Circuit: A Reply to Chief Judge Harry T. Edwards." *Virginia Law Review* 85 (5): 805–51.

Rice, Andrew. 2021. "Merrick Garland vs. Trump's Mob." *New York Magazine*, July 2. https://nymag.com/intelligencer/article/merrick-garland-justice-department-insurrection.html (accessed August 24, 2022).

Richards, Mark J., and Herbert M. Kritzer. 2002. "Jurisprudential Regimes in Supreme Court Decision Making." *American Political Science Review* 96 (2): 305–20.

Roberts, John G. 2006. "What Makes the D.C. Circuit Different? A Historical View." *Virginia Law Review* 92 (3): 375–89.

Robinson, Kimberly Strawbride. 2018. "No Halloween Trick, Attorney Argues for Himself at Supreme Court." *Bloomberg Law*, February 27. https://news.bloomberglaw.com/us-law-week/no-halloween-trick-attorney-argues-for-himself-at-supreme-court (accessed August 24, 2022).

Rogowski, Jon C., and Betsy Sinclair. 2012. "Estimating the Causal Effects of Social Interaction with Endogenous Networks." *Political Analysis* 20 (3): 316–28.

Rosen, Jeffrey. 2007. "Roberts's Rules." *The Atlantic*, February 15. https://www.theatlantic.com/magazine/archive/2007/01/robertss-rules/305559/ (accessed August 24, 2022).

Routt, Garland C. 1938. "Interpersonal Relationships and the Legislative Process." *Annals of the American Academy of Political and Social Science* 195 (1): 129–36.

Rubin, Alvin B. 1976. "Views from the Lower Court." *UCLA Law Review* 23 (3): 448–64.

Rubin, Richard. 2016. "Physician Burnout and the Loss of Collegial Relationships: A Reversible Trend?" *Huron*, February 8. https://www.huronlearninglab.com/resources/articles-and-industry-updates/insights/february-2016/physician-burnout-and-the-loss-of-collegial-relati (accessed August 24, 2022).

Saad, Lydia. 2014. "The '40-Hour' Workweek Is Actually Longer—By Seven Hours." *Gallup*, August 29. https://news.gallup.com/poll/175286/hour-workweek-actually-longer-seven-hours.aspx (accessed August 24, 2022).

Sala, Brian R., and James F. Spriggs II. 2004. "Designing Tests of the Supreme Court and the Separation of Powers." *Political Research Quarterly* 57 (2): 197–208.

Salamone, Michael F. 2014. "Judicial Consensus and Public Opinion: Conditional Response to Supreme Court Majority Size." *Political Research Quarterly* 67 (2): 320–34.

Salamone, Michael F. 2018. *Perceptions of a Polarized Court: How Division among Justices Shapes the Supreme Court's Public Image*. Philadelphia, PA: Temple University Press.

Sanders, Sam. 2021. "The Real Justices of SCOTUS." NPR, *It's Been a Minute*, May 25. https://www.npr.org/transcripts/999078292 (accessed August 24, 2022).

Savage, Charlie. 2021. "Biden's Supreme Court Commission Shows Interest in Term Limits for Justices." *New York Times*, November 18. https://www.nytimes.com/2021/11/18/us/politics/supreme-court-term-limits-biden.html (accessed August 24, 2022).

Scalia, Antonin. 1994. "The Dissenting Opinion." *Journal of Supreme Court History* 19 (1): 33–44.

Schroeder, James C., and Robert M. Dow Jr. 1999. "Arguing for Changes in the Law." *Litigation* 25 (2): 37–41 & 67–68.

Schulz-Hardt, Stefan, Andreas Mojzisch, and Frank Vogelgesang. 2008. "Dissent as a Facilitator: Individual- and Group-Level Effects on Creativity and Performance." In *The Psychology of Conflict and Conflict Management in Organizations*, eds., Carsten K.W. DeDreu and Michele J. Gelfand. Mahwah, NJ: Taylor & Francis Group/Lawrence Erlbaum Associates, 149–77.

Schwartz, Bernard. 1983. *Super Chief: Earl Warren and His Supreme Court: A Judicial Biography*. New York University Press.

Segal, Jeffrey A. 1984. "Predicting Supreme Court Cases Probabilistically: The Search and Seizure Cases, 1962–1981." *American Political Science Review* 78 (4): 891–900.

Segal, Jeffrey A. 1997. "Separation-of-Powers Games in the Positive Theory of Congress and Courts." *American Political Science Review* 91 (1): 28–44.

Segal, Jeffrey A., and Albert D. Cover. 1989. "Ideological Values and the Votes of U.S. Supreme Court Justices." *American Political Science Review* 83 (2): 557–65.

Segal, Jeffrey A., and Harold J. Spaeth. 2002. *The Supreme Court and the Attitudinal Model Revisited*. Cambridge University Press.

268   BIBLIOGRAPHY

Sen, Maya. 2014. "How Judicial Qualification Ratings May Disadvantage Minority and Female Candidates." *Journal of Law and Courts* 2 (1): 33–65.

Sen, Maya. 2015. "Is Justice Really Blind? Race and Appellate Review in U.S. Courts." *Journal of Legal Studies* 44 (1): 187–229.

Shea, Barbara C.S. 1986. "Sandra Day O'Connor—Woman, Lawyer, Justice: Her First Four Terms on the Supreme Court." *University of Missouri, Kansas City Law Review* 55 (1): 1–32.

Sherry, Suzanna. 2006. "Logic Without Experience: The Problem of Federal Appellate Courts." *Notre Dame Law Review* 82 (1): 97–154.

Slothuus, Rune, and Claes H. de Vreese. 2010. "Political Parties, Motivated Reasoning, and Issue Framing Effects." *Journal of Politics* 72 (3): 630–45.

Smith, Joseph L. 2006. "Patterns and Consequences of Judicial Reversals: Theoretical Considerations and Data from a District Court." *Justice System Journal* 27 (1): 28–46.

Smith, Joseph L., and Emerson H. Tiller. 2002. "The Strategy of Judging: Evidence from Administrative Law." *Journal of Legal Studies* 31 (1): 61–82.

Smyth, Russell, and Vinod Mishra. 2011. "The Transmission of Legal Precedent Across the Australian State Supreme Courts over the Twentieth Century." *Law & Society Review* 45 (1): 139–70.

Smyth, Russell, and Ingrid Nielsen. 2019. "The Citation Practices of the High Court of Australia, 1905-2015." *Federal Law Review* 47 (4): 655–95.

Solberg, Rorie Spill, Jolly A. Emrey, and Susan B. Haire. 2006. "Inter-Court Dynamics and the Development of Legal Policy: Citation Patterns in the Decisions of the U.S. Courts of Appeals." *Policy Studies Journal* 34 (2): 277–93.

Songer, Donald R. 1982. "Consensual and Nonconsensual Decisions in Unanimous Opinions of the United States Courts of Appeals." *American Journal of Political Science* 26 (2): 225–39.

Songer, Donald R., and Susan B. Haire. 1992. "Integrating Alternative Approaches to the Study of Judicial Voting: Obscenity Cases in the U.S. Courts of Appeals." *American Journal of Political Science* 36 (4): 963–82.

Songer, Donald R., Jeffrey A. Segal, and Charles M. Cameron. 1994. "The Hierarchy of Justice: Testing a Principal-Agent Model of Supreme Court--Circuit Court Interactions." *American Journal of Political Science* 38 (3): 673–96.

Songer, Donald R., and Reginald S. Sheehan. 1992. "Who Wins on Appeal? Upperdogs and Underdogs in the United States Courts of Appeals." *American Journal of Political Science* 36 (1): 235–58.

Songer, Donald R., Reginald S. Sheehan, and Susan B. Haire. 1999. "Do the Haves Come Out Ahead over Time—Applying Galanter's Framework to Decisions of the U.S. Courts of Appeals, 1925-1988." *Law & Society Review* 33 (4): 811–32.

Spaeth, Harold J., Lee Epstein, Andrew D. Martin, Jeffrey A. Segal, Theodore J. Ruger, and Sara C. Benesh. 2021. "2020 Supreme Court Database, Version 2021 Release 01." *Washington University Law.* http://supremecourtdatabase.org (accessed August 24, 2022).

Spitzer, Matthew, and Eric Talley. 2000. "Judicial Auditing." *Journal of Legal Studies* 29 (2): 649–83.

Spitzer, Matthew, and Eric Talley. 2013. "Left, Right, and Center: Strategic Information Acquisition and Diversity in Judicial Panels." *Journal of Law, Economics, & Organization* 29 (3): 638–80.

Spriggs II, James F., and Thomas G. Hansford. 2001. "Explaining the Overruling of U.S. Supreme Court Precedent." *Journal of Politics* 63 (4): 1091–111.

Srinivasan, Sri, Pamela Harris, and Daphna Renan. 2021. "A Model of Collegiality: Judge Harry T. Edwards." *Judicature* 105 (1): 76–79.

Stanchi, Kathryn M. 2006. "The Science of Persuasion: An Initial Exploration." *Michigan State Law Review* 2006 (2): 411–56.

BIBLIOGRAPHY 269

Stapleton, Walter K. 1995. "The Federal Judicial System in the Twenty-First Century." *Delaware Lawyer* 13 (3): 34–39.

Stephens, Richard B. 1952. "The Function of Concurring and Dissenting Opinions in Courts of Last Resort." *University of Florida Law Review* 5 (4): 394–410.

Stohr, Greg, and Jennifer Epstein. 2018. "Kagan Says Loss of Centrist Could Harm Perception of High Court." *Bloomberg Law*, October 5. https://www.bloomberg.com/news/articles/2018-10-05/supreme-court-needs-to-stay-out-of-politics-two-justices-say (accessed August 24, 2022).

Sunstein, Cass R., David Schkade, Lisa M. Ellman, and Andres Sawicki. 2006. *Are Judges Political?: An Empirical Analysis of the Federal Judiciary*. Washington, D.C.: Brookings Institution Press.

Sutton, Jeffrey S. 2010. "A Review of Richard A. Posner, *How Judges Think* (2008)." *Michigan Law Review* 108 (6): 859–76.

Swalve, Tilko. 2022. "Does Group Familiarity Improve Deliberations in Judicial Teams? Evidence from the German Federal Court of Justice." *Journal of Empirical Legal Studies* 19(1): 223–49.

Szmer, John, Robert K. Christensen, and Samuel Grubbs. 2020. "What Influences the Influence of U.S. Courts of Appeals Decisions?" *European Journal of Law and Economics* 49 (1): 55–81.

Taber, Charles S., and Milton Lodge. 2006. "Motivated Skepticism in the Evaluation of Political Beliefs." *American Journal of Political Science* 50 (3): 755–69.

Tate, C. Neal. 1981. "Personal Attribute Models of the Voting Behavior of U.S. Supreme Court Justices: Liberalism in Civil Liberties and Economics Decisions, 1946–1978." *American Political Science Review* 75 (2): 355–67.

ten Brummelhuis, Lieke L., Jarrod M. Haar, and Tanja van der Lippe. 2010. "Collegiality Under Pressure: The Effects of Family Demands and Flexible Work Arrangements in the Netherlands." *International Journal of Human Resource Management* 21 (15): 2831–47.

The Recorder. 2021. "In Fiery Dissent, Lawrence VanDyke Chastises 9th Circuit for 'Distorted' Precedent." *Law.com*, November 21. https://www.law.com/therecorder/2022/06/14/in-fiery-dissent-lawrence-vandyke-chastises-9th-circuit-for-distorted-precedent/ (accessed August 24, 2022).

Tillman, Elizabeth A., and Rachael K. Hinkle. 2018. "Of Whites and Men: How Gender and Race Impact Authorship of Published and Unpublished Opinions in the US Courts of Appeals." *Research & Politics* 5 (1): 1–7.

Tjoflat, Gerald Bard. 1993. "More Judges, Less Justice: The Case Against Expansion of the Federal Judiciary." *ABA Journal* 79 (7): 70–73.

Totenberg, Nina. 2022a. "Gorsuch Didn't Mask Despite Sotomayor's COVID Worries, Leading Her to Telework." *NPR*, January 18. https://www.npr.org/2022/01/18/1073428376/supreme-court-justices-arent-scorpions-but-not-happy-campers-either (accessed August 24, 2022).

Totenberg, Nina. 2022b. "Supreme Court Hears Arguments on Campaign Finance Law, Issues Statement on NPR Report." *NPR*, March 29. https://www.npr.org/2022/01/19/1074169348/supreme-court-hears-arguments-on-campaign-finance-law-issues-statements-on-npr-r (accessed August 24, 2022).

Tracy, Karen. 2011. "A Facework System of Minimal Politeness: Oral Argument in Appellate Court." *Journal of Politeness Research* 7 (1): 123–45.

Truman, David B. 1956. "The State Delegations and the Structure of Party Voting in the United States House of Representatives." *American Political Science Review* 50 (4): 1023–45.

Turner, Charles C., Lori Beth Way, and Nancy Maveety. 2010. "Beginning to Write Separately: The Origins and Development of Concurring Judicial Opinions." *Journal of Supreme Court History* 35 (2): 93–109.

BIBLIOGRAPHY

Tushnet, Mark. 2008. *I Dissent: Great Opposing Opinions in Landmark Supreme Court Cases.* Boston, MA: Beacon Press.

Tushnet, Mark, and Katya Lezin. 1991. "What Really Happened in *Brown v. Board of Education.*" *Columbia Law Review* 91 (8): 1867–930.

Ulmer, S. Sidney. 1971. "Earl Warren and the Brown Decision." *Journal of Politics* 33 (3): 689–702.

United States Courts. 2022. "Federal Court Management Statistics." https://www.uscourts.gov/statistics/table/na/federal-court-management-statistics/2022/03/31 (accessed August 24, 2022).

Urofsky, Melvin I. 1988. "Conflict Among the Brethren: Felix Frankfurter, William O. Douglas and the Clash of Personalities and Philosophies on the United States Supreme Court." *Duke Law Journal* 1988 (1): 71–113.

Urofsky, Melvin I. 2017. *Dissent and the Supreme Court: Its Role in the Court's History and the Nation's Constitutional Dialogue.* New York: Pantheon Books.

Valley, Kathleen L., Margaret A. Neale, and Elizabeth A. Mannix. 1995. "Friends, Lovers, Colleagues, Strangers: The Effects of Relationships on the Process and Outcome of Dyadic Negotiations." In *Research on Negotiation in Organizations* Greenwich, eds., Robert J. Bies, Roy Lewicki, and Blair Sheppard. CT: JAI Press, 65–94.

Varsava, Nina. 2021. "Professional Irresponsibility and Judicial Opinions." *Houston Law Review* 59 (1): 103–74.

Vass, Holly. 2017. "Lexical Verb Hedging in Legal Discourse: The Case of Law Journal Articles and Supreme Court Majority and Dissenting Opinions." *English for Specific Purposes* 48: 17–31.

Verbrugge, Louis M. 1997. "The Structure of Adult Friendships." *Social Forces* 56 (2): 576–97.

Vladeck, Stephen I. 2019. "The Solicitor General and the Shadow Docket." *Harvard Law Review* 133 (11): 123–63.

Wahlbeck, Paul J. 1997. "The Life of the Law: Judicial Politics and Legal Change." *Journal of Politics* 59 (3): 778–802.

Wahlbeck, Paul J. 2006. "Strategy and Constraints on Supreme Court Opinion Assignment." *University of Pennsylvania Law Review* 154 (6): 1729–55.

Wahlbeck, Paul J., James F. Spriggs II, and Forrest Maltzman. 1999. "The Politics of Dissents and Concurrences on the U.S. Supreme Court." *American Politics Research* 27 (4): 488–514.

Wald, Patricia M. 1983. "The Problem with the Courts: Black-Robed Bureaucracy, or Collegiality Under Challenge." *Maryland Law Review* 42 (4): 766–86.

Wald, Patricia M. 1984. "Thoughts on Decisionmaking." *West Virginia Law Review* 87 (1): 1–12.

Wald, Patricia M. 1987. "Some Thoughts on Judging as Gleaned from One Hundred Years of the *Harvard Law Review* and Other Great Books." *Harvard Law Review* 100 (4): 887–908.

Wald, Patricia M. 1999. "A Response to Tiller and Cross." *Columbia Law Review* 99 (1): 235–61.

Walker, Thomas G., Lee Epstein, and William J. Dixon. 1988. "On the Mysterious Demise of Consensual Norms in the United States Supreme Court." *Journal of Politics* 50 (2): 361–89.

Walsh, David J. 1997. "On the Meaning and Pattern of Legal Citations: Evidence from State Wrongful Discharge Precedent Cases." *Law & Society Review* 31 (2): 337–61.

Ward, Artemus, and David L. Weiden. 2006. *Sorcerers' Apprentices: 100 Years of Law Clerks at the United States Supreme Court.* New York University Press.

Wasby, Stephen L. 1980. "Internal Communication in the Eighth Circuit Court of Appeals." *Washington University Law Quarterly* 58 (3): 583–605.

Wasby, Stephen L. 1987. "Communication in the Ninth Circuit: A Concern for Collegiality." *Puget Sound Law Review* 11 (1): 72–138.

Wedeking, Justin, and Michael A. Zilis. 2018. "Disagreeable Rhetoric and the Prospect of Public Opposition: Opinion Moderation on the U.S. Supreme Court." *Political Research Quarterly* 71 (2): 380–94.

Westerland, Chad, Jeffrey A. Segal, Lee Epstein, Charles M. Cameron, and Scott Comparato. 2010. "Strategic Defiance and Compliance in the U.S. Courts of Appeals." *American Journal of Political Science* 54 (4): 891–905.

White, G. Edward. 1984. "The Working Life of the Marshall Court, 1815–1835." *Virginia Law Review* 70 (1): 1–52.

Wilkinson, J. Harvie. 1994. "The Drawbacks of Growth in the Federal Judiciary." *Emory Law Journal* 43 (4): 1147–88.

Wolf, Richard. 2020. "Opera, Travel, Food, Law: The Unlikely Friendship of Ruth Bader Ginsburg and Antonin Scalia." *USA Today*, September 20. https://www.usatoday.com/story/news/politics/2020/09/20/supreme-friends-ruth-bader-ginsburg-and-antonin-scalia/584 4533002/ (accessed August 24, 2022).

Wood, Diane P. 2012. "When to Hold, When to Fold, and When to Reshuffle: The Art of Decisionmaking on a Multi-Member Court." *California Law Review* 100 (6): 1445–78.

Yalof, David A., Joey Mello, and Patrick Schmidt. 2011. "Collegiality on the U.S. Supreme Court: An Early Assessment of the Roberts Court." *Judicature* 94 (6): 1–11.

Young, James Sterling. 1966. *The Washington Community, 1800–1828*. New York: Harcourt Brace Jovanovich.

Zilis, Michael, and Justin Wedeking. 2020. "The Sources and Consequences of Political Rhetoric: Issue Importance, Collegial Bargaining, and Disagreeable Rhetoric in Supreme Court Opinions." *Journal of Law and Courts* 8 (2): 203–27.

Zink, James R., James F. Spriggs II, and John T. Scott. 2009. "Courting the Public: The Influence of Decision Attributes on Individuals' Views of Court Opinions." *Journal of Politics* 71 (3): 909–25.

Zorn, Christopher J.W., and Jennifer Barnes Bowie. 2010. "Ideological Influences on Decision Making in the Federal Judicial Hierarchy." *Journal of Politics* 72 (4): 1212–21.

Index

For the benefit of digital users, indexed terms that span two pages (e.g., 52–53) may, on occasion, appear on only one of those pages.

Tables and figures are indicated by *t* and *f* following the page number

ABA ratings, 142
agreement, emphasizing in language of
    dissents, 165
Alito, Samuel Anthony, Jr., 4, 112–13
ambition, collegiality and, 243
amicus curiae briefs, 41, 65–66, 216–17
appellate courts. *See* collegiality; Courts of
    Appeals; intercourt relations; publicizing
    disagreements; Supreme Court
Archer, Dawn, 168
Asch, Solomon E., 31–32
Atkins, Burton M., 84
attitudinal theories of judicial behavior, 7–8,
    70, 235–36. *See also* ideology
authorship, collegiality and, 248

baby judges' school, 244
background characteristics
    collegiality and, 242–43
    influence on judicial behavior, 10–11
    and willingness to dissent or concur, 52–
      53, 65
Balkin, Jack M., 202, 203–4
Bashman, Howard, 161–62
Batchelder, Alice, 1–2
Baum, Lawrence, 76, 232
Biden Commission, 238n.4
binding precedents, 202–3
Biskupic, Joan, 245
Black, Hugo Lafayette, 123
Black, Ryan C., 7
Blackmun, Harry, 166
Boarding house years, 27–28, 110, 111*f*, 236
Boggs, Danny J., 1–3
Bowie, Jennifer Barnes, 82
Boyd, Christina L., 10, 138n.3
Breeze, Ruth, 164
Brennan, William J., Jr., 52n.3, 166, 167, 248
Brown, Penelope, 163–64, 168
Brown v. Board of Education, 112

Bye, Kermit E., 165
Byrd, John W., Jr., 1–2

Cain, Àine, 18
Caldeira, Gregory A., 27–28, 203
Calvert, Randall L., 143
Caminker, Evan H., 138n.3
Carp, Robert, 56, 146
case context
    and language of dissents, 174–75
    reasons to cite precedents, 203
    and willingness to dissent or concur, 65–66
caseload, and willingness to dissent or
    concur, 65–66
case selection, 248
caustic language in dissents, 169. *See also*
    rude language in dissents
chambers, collegiality in, 247
Choi, Stephen J., 241–42
Christensen, Robert K., 203–4, 207–8
circuit conferences, 243
circuit courts. *See* citations; collegiality;
    Courts of Appeals; intercourt relations;
    language of dissent; publicizing
    disagreements
circulating draft opinions, 239–40
citations
    in Courts of Appeals, 211–17, 213*f*, 214*f*, 216*f*
    effect of collegiality as increasing with
      ideological distance, 229
    general discussion, 221–22, 222*t*
    impact of collegial relationships on, 204–
      9, 208*t*
    importance of studying, 201–2
    overview, 14, 199–201
    reasons to cite precedents, 202–4
    regression results, 225
    research design, 209–11
    summary statistics, 223
    in Supreme Court, 217–21, 219*f*, 220*f*

274 INDEX

Clark, Tom S., 174–75
Clay, Eric, 2–3
Clegg, Joshua W., 31–32
clerks
  collegiality among in Supreme
    Court, 129–31
  as conduits in Supreme Court, 131
  experiential factors shaping justice
    behavior, 123–24, 127
  interview questions used with, 45–47
  interviews with regarding collegiality, 22–
    27, 22t, 113–22
  intra-office collegiality, 247
  perspectives on collegiality, 47
  public statements on collegiality by, 21
Clermont, Kevin M., 15n.3
Cohen, Jonathan M., 56–57
collaborative nature of judicial behavior, 11
collegiality. *See also* citations; intercourt
    relations; language of dissent;
    publicizing disagreements
  book roadmap, 12–14
  building and maintaining, 243–46
  clerks' perspectives on, 47
  collaborative nature of judicial
    behavior, 11
  defining, 17–18
  existing evidence on effects of, 27–34
  future research opportunities, 241–48
  general discussion, 42–43, 248–49
  implications of findings, 235–41
  importance of, 18–27, 22t
  influences on judicial behavior, 5–11
  interview methods used to study, 43–44
  interview questions used to study, 44–47
  overview, 1–5, 15–17, 227
  pros and cons of, 33–34
  summary of findings, 227–34
  theory of, 34–42
Collier, Helen V., 19
Collins, Doug, 11
Collins, Paul M., Jr., 56
colorful language in dissents, 168. *See also*
    rude language in dissents
committee service, 243–44
communal living arrangements, 27–28, 236
communicative element of citation, 202
concurring opinions, 71t, 104t, *See also*
    publicizing disagreements
  and collegiality in Supreme Court, 122

conditional effect of collegiality, 66–68,
    67f, 88–91, 89f, 90f, 91f
conditional effect of ideology, 68, 69f, 91–
    94, 92f, 93f
control variables, 99
costs of, 51–53
cumulative effect of collegiality, 94–99, 95f,
    97f, 98t
differences between concurring and
    dissenting, 55
direct effects of collegiality, 66, 87, 88f
overview, 50–51, 160
regression results from Supreme Court
    model, 125–28, 126f, 133t, 135t
relationship between reversal and, 143–44
conferences, 35–36, 243
conformity effects, 33
Congress, as constraint on judicial
    behavior, 8–9
congressional delegation (CODEL)
    travel, 27–28
consensus. *See* unanimous decisions
contact among colleagues. *See* collegiality;
    future contact; interpersonal contact;
    past contact; publicizing disagreements
contextual bases of judicial behavior, 235
conversations about cases before oral
    arguments, 238–39
Corley, Pamela C., 55, 161
cosine similarity scores, 210–11, 212
cotenure
  collegiality as dampening effect of
    ideology, 230
  and collegiality in Supreme Court, 108,
    120, 122–23, 123f, 125–27, 128
  conditional effect of collegiality, 89–90, 90f
  conditional effect of ideology, 91–93, 92f
  differences in institutional context, 232–33
  direct effects of collegiality, 87, 88f
  effect of collegiality as increasing with
    ideological distance, 229–30
  empirical strategy, 85–86, 86f
  impact on citations, 215
  importance of collegiality in context of, 20
  increased collegiality as fostering
    consensus, 228
  and language of dissents, 173–74, 177–83,
    178f, 182f, 184–87, 185f, 186f, 189
  and persuasion, 80–81, 231
  and probability of dissent, 13

INDEX 275

regression results from Supreme Court model, 126*f*, 133*t*, 135*t*

counterideological lower court decisions, 148–49, 150, 151*f*

courthouse, judges working in same. *See* Same Courthouse measure of collegiality

courts

collegiality in different types of, 246–47

importance of collegiality in, 19–27, 22*t*

legitimacy of, 9n.19, 20–21, 32, 51

similarity between, as reason for citations, 203

Courts of Appeals (U.S.). *See also* citations; intercourt relations; language of dissent; publicizing disagreements

attitudinal considerations and judicial behavior, 8

circuit size and future professional contact, 82–84, 83*f*, 84n.9

citations, impact of relationships on, 200–1, 209, 210, 211–17, 213*f*, 214*f*, 216*f*, 222, 223*t*, 225*t*

differences in institutional context, 232–33

experiential factors shaping justice behavior, 124, 127

group dynamics in, 11

highlights of findings, 233–34

implications for reform of, 237–38, 239–41

importance of collegiality in, 15–16

increased collegiality as fostering consensus, 228–29

influence of law on judicial behavior, 6

institutional differences in collegiality, 40–42, 108–9, 113–14

internal constraints on judicial behavior, 10

interviews regarding collegiality in, 22–27

language of dissent, 160, 172–73, 174–81, 176*f*, 177*f*, 178*f*, 180*f*, 181*f*, 182*f*, 183*f*, 188*t*, 190*t*, 192*t*, 193*t*, 194*t*

sitting by designation, 145–46n.8, 240–41

COVID pandemic, 245

credentials, relationship between reversal and, 142, 144, 148, 150, 151*f*, 154

Cross, Frank B., 10, 17, 40, 167, 203

cross-court relationships. *See* intercourt relations

culture, of judicial circuits, 22–23

current colleagues, citation of, 207–9, 208*t*, 211–12, 215, 218–21, 220*f*

Curry, James M., 27–28

daily lives, collegiality in, 18–19

Davis, James H., 29, 30, 39

Davis, John W., 139–40

D.C. Circuit, 15–16, 60, 124, 127, 137

deference, in language of dissents, 164–65

demographic characteristics, 10, 242–43. *See also* personal characteristics

de Rohan Barondes, Royce, 142

designation, sitting by, 145–46n.8, 240–41

direct address to majority in dissents, 171–72, 181, 183*f*, 187, 187*f*, 194*t*, 197*t*

directness, in language of dissents, 166–67

disagreements. *See* concurring opinions; dissenting opinions; publicizing disagreements; suppression of disagreement

discussions before oral arguments, 238–39

dissenting opinions, 71*t*, 104*t*, *See also* language of dissent; publicizing disagreements

benefits of, 159

and collegiality in Supreme Court, 122, 125

conditional effect of collegiality, 66–68, 67*f*, 88–91, 89*f*, 90*f*, 91*f*

conditional effect of ideology, 68, 69*f*, 91–94, 92*f*, 93*f*

context and complexity of dissent, 160–63

control variables, 99

costs of, 51–53

cumulative effect of collegiality, 94–99, 95*f*, 97*f*, 98*t*

differences between concurring and dissenting, 55

direct effects of collegiality, 66, 87, 88*f*

and internal constraints on judicial behavior, 10

overview, 12–13, 50–51

regression results from Supreme Court model, 125–28, 126*f*, 133*t*, 135*t*

District Courts (U.S.). *See* Courts of Appeals; intercourt relations

Douglas, William O., 110–11, 123, 165

draft opinions, circulating, 239–40

Dumbauld, Edward, 199

Edwards, Harry T., 5, 15–16, 17, 19, 21, 34, 40, 78, 240–41, 245–46

276 INDEX

efficiency of judges, effect of collegiality on, 26
Eisenberg, Theodore, 15n.3
emotional language in dissenting opinions, 170, 172, 172*f*, 175–77, 176*f*, 182–83, 184*f*, 192*t*, 195*t*
en banc review, collegiality in, 246
Epstein, Lee, 5, 6, 8, 15n.3, 19, 50, 56, 147, 232
everyday lives, collegiality in, 18–19
experiential factors
　collegiality and, 35–37, 242–43
　judicial behavior and, 10–11
　language of dissents and, 174
　shaping justice behavior, 123–24, 127
external audiences, language of dissent and, 163
external constraints on judicial behavior, 8–10, 109

face-threatening acts (FTAs), 164
familiarity. *See also* interpersonal contact
　as key component of collegial environment, 56
　and relationship of collegiality to outcomes, 29–30
fear of reversal, 138n.3, *See also* intercourt relations
federal judges. *See* collegiality; Courts of Appeals; judicial behavior; Supreme Court
Feldman, Noah, 110–11
Finegan, Edward, 165–66
flattery, as motive for citations, 205–7
former colleagues, citation of, 205–7, 208*t*, 215, 220–21, *See also* past contact
Frankfurter, Felix, 110–11
Friedman, Barry, 61
Friedman, Lawrence M., 201–2
Friendly, Henry, 159
future contact
　collegiality as dampening effect of ideological disagreement, 231
　conditional effect of collegiality, 90–91, 91*f*
　conditional effect of ideology, 93, 93*f*
　direct effects of collegiality, 87, 88*f*
　empirical strategy, 85–86, 86*f*
　impact on citations, 211–15, 214*f*
　increased collegiality as fostering consensus, 228
　and language of dissents, 168–69, 173–74, 177–81, 178*f*, 181*f*, 182*f*

as motive for citations, 207–8
suppression and, 80, 81–85, 83*f*, 101, 101*t*
why collegiality matters, 231–32

Garland, Merrick, 162
generalizability of results, 241–42
geography and collegiality. *See also* proximity and collegiality; Same Courthouse measure of collegiality
　measuring hierarchical collegiality, 145–47, 147*t*
　overview, 55–58
George, Tracey E., 6
Gibbons, Julia Smith, 165
Ginsburg, Ruth Bader, 11, 125, 244
Glynn, Adam, 10
"going along". *See* suppression of disagreement
Gorman, Anna, 19
Gorsuch, Neil, 20–21
Greenhouse, Linda, 107
group dynamics
　effect on judicial behavior, 11
　and willingness to dissent or concur, 52–53
groupthink, 33
Grubbs, Samuel, 203–4, 207–8
Gruenfeld, Deborah H., 29–30
Grutter v. Bolinger, 2–3
Gulati, G. Mitu, 241–42
Guthrie, Samantha, 28

Haar, Jarrod M., 17–18, 19
Haire, Susan B., 142
Harlan, John Marshall, 159
Harlan II, John Marshall, 123
Harris, Peter, 202
Hazelton, Morgan L.W., 10–11
hedging language in dissents, 164
heuristics, use by appellate judges, 138, 139–41
hierarchical collegiality. *See* intercourt relations
Hinkle, Rachael K., 6, 10–11, 162–63, 211
Hovland, Carl I., 141
Hughes, Charles Evans, 162–63
Hume, Robert J., 169

identity
　and collegiality, 242–43
　heuristics used by appellate judges, 139–41
　influence on judicial behavior, 10–11

and language of dissents, 174
and willingness to dissent or concur, 52–53, 65
ideology, 71t
and breakdown of collegial relationships, 243
collegiality as dampening effect of disagreement, 70, 230–31, 235–36
collegiality as dampening effect of ideological disagreement, 5, 12, 16–17
and collegiality in Supreme Court, 125, 127
conditional effect of collegiality, 66–68, 67f, 88–91, 89f, 90f, 91f
conditional effect on publicizing disagreement, 68, 69f, 91–94, 92f, 93f
cumulative effect of collegiality, 94–99, 95f, 97f, 98t
effect of collegiality as increasing with difference in, 229–30
effect on publicizing disagreements, 53–54, 100–1
impact on citations, 206, 208–9, 211–14, 215–17, 218–21, 220f
implications for theories of judicial behavior, 235–36
influence on judicial behavior, 7–8
interpersonal contact and publicizing disagreement, 49–50
and language of dissents, 169, 174, 175–81, 182f, 184–87, 186f, 188–89
and level of interpersonal contact, 102
and probability of separate opinion, 100–1
regression results from Supreme Court model, 126f, 133t, 135t
relationship between reversal and, 138–39, 142, 143, 144–45, 148–49, 150–56, 151f, 152f, 153f
research design, 63, 64, 64f, 67f, 69f
in theory of collegiality and judicial behavior, 38–42
and willingness to dissent or concur, 52
impolite language in dissents, 165–67
influence, citations as reflecting, 202, 205–6, 207, 221–22
In re Byrd (6th Cir. 2001), 1–2
Inskeep, Steve, 20–21
institutional context and collegiality
citations, 222
differences in balancing ideology and collegiality, 40–42

features of courts making relationships important, 20–21
interview evidence regarding collegiality, 113–14
overview, 232–33, 246–47
Supreme Court, 108–10
institutional reforms, 236–38
intensifying words, in language of dissents, 166–67
intercourt relations
assessments, collegiality, and ideology, 144–45
building assessments, 141–44
conditional effect of ideology by assessments, 150–54, 153f
control variables, 154, 155f
data and research design, 148–50
direct effects of reputation, 150, 151f, 152f
general discussion, 154–56
measuring hierarchical collegiality, 145–47, 147t
overview, 13, 137–39
regression results, 157
results, 150–54, 151f, 152f, 153f, 155f
reversal and reputation, 139–41
summary statistics, 156
internal constraints on judicial behavior, 8–10
interns, work relationships with, 247
interpersonal contact. *See also* collegiality; future contact; past contact; publicizing disagreements
and collegiality in Supreme Court, 118–20
conditional effect of ideology on reversal, 152–54
existing evidence on effects of, 27–30
impact on citations, 204–9, 211–12
and language of dissents, 168–69, 173–74, 177–79
measuring hierarchical collegiality, 145–47, 147t
relationship between reversal and, 143–44, 149, 149t, 155–56
relationship of collegiality to, 34–38, 49
and relationships among clerks and justices, 116–17
intra-office collegiality, 247

Jacobs, Dennis, 165
Jeffries, Hakeem, 11
Johnson, Charles A., 6, 8

278 INDEX

Jones, Nathaniel R., 1–2, 166
judges
  interviews with regarding collegiality, 22–27, 22t
  public statements on collegiality by, 21
judicial behavior. *See also* citations; collegiality; intercourt relations; language of dissent; publicizing disagreements
  book roadmap, 12–14
  collaborative nature of, 11
  implications of research for theories of, 235–36
  influences on, 5–11
  leading theories of, 4–5
Judicial Common Space (JCS) scores, 63, 148, 174
Judicial Conference of the United States, 244
judicial hierarchy, and willingness to dissent or concur, 65–66
judicial leadership, role in fostering collegiality, 245–46
judicial norms, potential reforms to, 238–41
judicial panels. *See* panels
judicial personality, 55–56
judiciary, implications for reform of, 236–38
justices. *See also* Supreme Court
  clerk observations about, 117–18
  contact and relationships among clerks and, 116–17
  interview evidence regarding operation and importance of collegiality, 117–18

Kagan, Elena, 4, 107, 242–43, 244, 245
Kastellec, Jonathan P., 10
Kluger, Richard, 112
Knight, Jack, 8
knowledge of other individual's perspective, 29–30
Kosma, Montgomery N., 202
Krewson, Christopher N., 169
Kritzer, Herbert M., 6
Kurzon, Dennis, 167, 170–71

Landes, William M., 5, 8, 15n.3, 19, 50, 56, 232
language of dissent
  collegiality and, 167–69
  context and complexity of dissent, 160–63
  data and methods, 172–75
  differences in institutional context, 232

general discussion, 188–89, 188t
impact of language on relationships, 163–67
measuring politeness and rudeness, 169–72, 172f
overview, 13–14, 159–60
regression results, 192
summary statistics, 190
Supreme Court results, 181–87, 184f, 185f, 186f, 187f
U.S. Courts of Appeals results, 175–81, 176f, 177f, 178f, 180f, 181f, 182f, 183f
law, influence on judicial behavior, 6–7
Lawless, Jennifer L., 28
Lax, Jeffrey R., 174–75
leadership, role in fostering collegiality, 245–46
legal correctness, assessment of by appellate judges, 142–43
legal development
  consequences of separate opinions for, 51
  role of precedent in, 201–2
legislative behavior, effect of collegiality on, 27–28
legitimacy of courts
  public perception of, 9n.19
  and role of collegiality, 20–21, 32
  and unanimous decisions, 51
Levinson, Sanford, 202, 203–4
Levinson, Stephen C., 163–64, 168
Levy, L., 42
Levy, Marin K., 84–85
Lezin, Katya, 112
Lindquist, Stefanie A., 56
lobbying, through citations, 207
Locher, Miriam A., 165–66
Lupia, Arthur, 141–42

majority opinions. *See also* publicizing disagreements
  ability of collegiality to improve, 26
  and costs of publicizing disagreement, 52
  direct address in dissent, 171–72, 181, 183f, 187, 187f, 194t, 197t
  overview, 50–51
  relationship between separate opinions and, 161
  in research on citations, 209–10
Maltzman, Forrest, 7, 10, 76–77, 102
Manning, Kenneth L., 56

INDEX 279

Marshall, John, 110
Martin, Andrew D., 10, 61
Martinek, Wendy L., 40–41
Masket, Seth, 27–28
Matthews, Donald R., 27
Mauro, Tony, 107
Mayer, Roger C., 29, 30, 39
McCubbins, Mathew D., 141–42
Mello, Joey, 164
Minozzi, William, 27–28
Moore, Karen Nelson, 2–3
Murphy, Michael R., 49

Nash, Jonathan Remy, 40
negative tone, in language of dissents, 163, 170, 175–79, 176f, 177f, 182–83, 184f
Nelson, Michael J., 10–11, 162–63
Newman, Jon O., 82–83, 237
Newsom, Kevin, 162, 245
Niblett, Anthony, 203–4
nonrandom assignment to panels, 84–85

O'Connor, Sandra Day, 242–43, 244
office arrangements, in Supreme Court, 119
opinion writing. See also citations; concurring opinions; dissenting opinions; publicizing disagreements
    consequences of collegiality in Supreme Court, 121–22, 128–29
    effect of collegiality on, 23–24, 26–27, 248
    experiential factors shaping justice behavior, 123–24
    external constraints affecting, 9–10
    implications for reform of, 239
    institutional differences in, 114
    overview, 50–51
    regression results from Supreme Court model, 125–28, 126f, 133t, 135t
O'Sullivan, Clifford, 165
Owens, Ryan J., 7

panels. See also probability of future panel service
    and collegiality in Courts of Appeals, 49
    group dynamics in Courts of Appeals, 11
    importance of collegiality in, 20
    interview evidence on assignment to, 72–74
    opinion writing by, 50–51
    relationship between reversal and composition of, 149–50

sitting by designation, 145–46n.8, 240–41
suppression and and future professional contact, 82–85, 83f
past contact. See also cotenure
    empirical strategy, 85–86, 86f
    impact on citations, 205–7, 211–12
    and language of dissents, 168
    and persuasion, 80–81
Pennebaker, James W., 167
personal attacks, in language of dissents, 167–68. See also rude language in dissents
personal characteristics
    and collegiality, 242–43
    influence on judicial behavior, 10–11
    and language of dissents, 174
    and willingness to dissent or concur, 52–53, 65
personal costs, role in suppression, 31–32
personal encounters, relationship of collegiality to, 36, 37–38
personal experiences, relationship between reversal and, 143–44
personality, collegiality and, 242
personal relationships. See also citations; collegiality; intercourt relations; language of dissent; publicizing disagreements
    conditional effect of collegiality, 88–91, 89f, 90f, 91f
    conditional effect of ideology, 91–94, 92f, 93f
    cumulative effect of collegiality, 94–99, 95f, 97f
    and decision to publicize disagreement, 75, 99–100, 101–2
    direct effects of collegiality, 87, 88f
    measuring, 79
    versus professional relationships, 76–77
persuasion
    citations, role in, 202, 205–7, 208, 208t, 221–22
    and collegiality in Supreme Court, 128
    and decision to publicize disagreement, 75–76, 77–78, 101–2
    existing evidence on effects of collegiality, 29–30
    overview, 12, 231
    past contact and, 80–81
    and Same Courthouse measure of collegiality, 79

280 INDEX

physical proximity and collegiality. *See also* Same Courthouse measure of collegiality
  measuring hierarchical collegiality, 145–47, 147t
  overview, 55–58
  in Supreme Court, 119
policymaking, studies of collegiality in, 27–28
politeness in language of dissents
  collegiality and, 167, 168–69
  differences in institutional context, 232
  general discussion, 188–89
  impact of language on relationships, 163–65
  measuring, 169–72, 173
  U.S. Courts of Appeals results, 175–81, 180f
  U.S. Supreme Court results, 184–86, 185f, 186f
positive emotional language, in dissents, 170, 175–79, 176f, 178f, 182–83, 184f
Posner, Richard A., 5, 8, 15n.3, 19, 50, 52, 56, 111, 232
precedents
  in Courts of Appeals, 211–17, 213f, 214f, 216f
  effect of collegiality as increasing with ideological distance, 229
  general discussion, 221–22, 222t
  impact of collegial relationships on, 204–9, 208t
  importance of studying citations, 201–2
  overview, 14, 199–201
  reasons to cite, 202–4
  regression results, 225
  research design, 209–11
  summary statistics, 223
  in Supreme Court, 217–21, 219f, 220f
principal-agent theory, 138, 139–41
probability of future panel service
  collegiality as dampening effect of ideological disagreement, 231
  conditional effect of collegiality, 90–91, 91f
  conditional effect of ideology, 93f, 93
  direct effects of collegiality, 87, 88f
  empirical strategy, 85–86, 86f
  impact on citations, 212–15, 214f
  increased collegiality as fostering consensus, 228
  and language of dissents, 173–74, 177–81, 178f, 181f, 182f
  and suppression, 101, 101t
  why collegiality matters, 231–32

professional costs, role in suppression, 32
professional experiences
  collegiality and, 35–37, 242–43
  judicial behavior and, 10–11
  language of dissents and, 174
  shaping justice behavior, 123–24, 127
professionalization, and importance of collegiality, 114–15
professional relationships. *See also* citations; collegiality; intercourt relations; language of dissent; publicizing disagreements
  conditional effect of collegiality, 88–91, 89f, 90f, 91f
  conditional effect of ideology, 91–94, 92f, 93f
  cumulative effect of collegiality, 94–99, 95f, 97f, 98t
  and decision to publicize disagreement, 75, 99–100, 101–2
  direct effects of collegiality, 87, 88f
  measuring, 80–85, 83f
  versus personal relationships, 76–77
  persuasion and, 80–81
  suppression and, 80, 81–85, 83f
proximity and collegiality. *See also* Same Courthouse measure of collegiality
  measuring hierarchical collegiality, 145–47, 147t
  overview, 55–58
  in Supreme Court, 119
Pryor, Tom, 203–4, 205–6
publicizing disagreements. *See also* concurring opinions; dissenting opinions; language of dissent; opinion writing
  collegiality and costs of, 50–53
  collegiality and ideological disagreement, 53–54
  conditional effect of collegiality, 66–68, 67f, 88–91, 89f, 90f, 91f
  conditional effect of ideology, 68, 69f, 91–94, 92f, 93f
  control variables, 99, 100f
  cumulative effect of collegiality, 94–99, 95f, 97f, 98t
  data and research design, 60–68, 61f, 63f, 64f, 67f
  descriptive results, 63–64
  detailed data collection description, 72
  differences between concurring and dissenting, 55

direct effects of collegiality, 66, 87, 88f
empirical strategy, 85–86, 86f
general discussion, 69–70, 99–102
institutional differences, 114
interview evidence on panel
    assignment, 72–74
measuring mechanisms, 79–85, 83f, 85t
multivariate analysis, 64–68, 67f, 71
overview, 12–13, 49–50, 160
personal versus professional
    relationships, 76–77
persuasion and suppression, 77–79
proximity and collegiality, 55–58
reasons for effects of collegiality, 75–76
regression results, 104
Same Courthouse measure of
    collegiality, 58–59
summary statistics, 103
public opinion as constraint on judicial
    behavior, 9
public statements on collegiality, 21

qualifications, relationship between reversal
    and, 142, 144, 148, 150, 151f, 154
quality of decisions, assessment of by
    appellate judges, 141–43

reforms
    institutional, 236–38
    to judicial norms, potential, 238–41
regret, in language of dissents, 170–71
Rehnquist, William H., 60, 110, 125, 244
Reinhardt, Stephen, 167
relationships, impact of language on, 163–
    67. See also collegiality; interpersonal
    contact
reputation, reversal and
    direct effects on reversals, 150, 151f, 152f
    measuring hierarchical collegiality, 146–47
    overview, 139–41
respect, in language of dissents, 164–
    65, 170–71
reversal decisions
    assessments, collegiality, and
        ideology, 144–45
    building assessments, 141–44
    conditional effect of ideology by
        assessments, 150–54, 153f
    control variables, 154, 155f
    data and research design, 148–50
    direct effects of reputation, 150, 151f, 152f

fear of reversal, 138n.3
general discussion, 154–56
measuring hierarchical collegiality, 145–47
overview, 137–39
regression results, 157
reputation and, 139–41
results, 150–54, 151f, 152f, 153f, 155f
summary statistics, 156
Revesz, Richard, 15n.3
review, as constraint on judicial behavior, 9–
    10. See also intercourt relations
Rice, Andrew, 162
Rice, Douglas, 174–75
Richards, Mark J., 6
Roberts, Jason M., 27–28
Roberts, John Glover, Jr., 3, 20–21, 110, 124,
    137, 162, 164, 245–46
Rogowski, Jon C., 28
Rosenbaum, Robin, 245
Rubin, Alvin B., 34–35, 83
Rubin, Richard, 18–19
rude language in dissents
    collegiality and, 168–69
    general discussion, 188–89
    impact of language on
        relationships, 165–67
    measuring, 169–72, 173
    overview, 161–62
    U.S. Courts of Appeals results, 175–81,
        180f, 181f
    U.S. Supreme Court results, 184–87, 185f

salience, and language of dissents, 174–75
Same City variable, 59
Same Courthouse measure of collegiality, 58f
    collegiality as dampening effect of
        ideological disagreement, 230
    conditional effect of collegiality on
        publicizing disagreement, 66–67, 67f,
        89, 89f
    conditional effect of ideology on
        publicizing disagreement, 68, 69f, 91, 92f
    conditional effect of ideology on
        reversal, 152–54
    direct effects of collegiality on publicizing
        disagreement, 87
    direct effects of reputation on reversals,
        150, 151f
    impact on citations, 215
    and language of dissents, 173–74, 175–81,
        177f, 178f, 182f

282 INDEX

Same Courthouse measure of collegiality (*cont.*)
  measuring hierarchical collegiality, 145–46
  overview, 58–59
  personal relationships, measuring, 79
  regression results, 71*t*
  relationship between reversal and, 149, 149*t*
  variation in over time and space, 62–63, 63*f*
Scalia, Antonin Gregory, 11, 52n.3, 125, 244
Schmidt, Patrick, 164
Schoorman, F. David, 29, 30, 39
Schwartz, Bernard, 112
search and seizure cases, 60–62, 61*f*
Segal, Jeffrey A., 6, 7, 8
Sen, Maya, 10, 142, 151–52, 154
separate opinions. *See* concurring opinions; dissenting opinions; language of dissent; opinion writing
shadow docket, Supreme Court, 248
shared interests, and intercourt relations, 138–39, 141–42
Sherry, Suzanna, 140
sign-offs, in dissents, 170–71, 172, 179–81, 180*f*, 182*f*, 184–86, 185*f*, 186*f*, 193*t*, 196*t*
similarity between cases and courts, role in citations, 203
Sinclair, Betsy, 28
sitting by designation, 145–46n.8, 240–41
Sixth Circuit, 1–3
skills, and intercourt relations, 138–39
Smith, Joseph L., 9–10, 138n.3
social distance, and language of dissents, 168
social events, relationship of collegiality to, 36
socialization, and importance of collegiality, 114–15
Songer, Donald R., 78–79, 82
Sotomayor, Sonia, 20–21
source credibility, 138–39, 141–42
Spaeth, Harold J., 7, 8
spicy language in dissents, 168. *See also* rude language in dissents
Spriggs, James F., II, 7, 10, 76–77, 102
Stapleton, Walter K., 5, 80
stare decisis, 201–3
Stern, Mark Joseph, 245
Stevens, John Paul, 165

strategy
  influence on judicial behavior, 7n.18, 8–10
  and willingness to dissent or concur, 52
summary declaration of dissent, 170–71, 172, 179–81, 180*f*, 182*f*, 184–86, 185*f*, 186*f*, 196*t*
suppression of disagreement
  and collegiality in Supreme Court, 128
  and decision to publicize disagreement, 75–76, 78–79, 101–2
  existing evidence on effects of collegiality, 30–32
  and future professional contact, 80, 81–85, 83*f*
  overview, 12
  and Same Courthouse measure of collegiality, 79
  unwarranted, concerns about, 33–34
  why collegiality matters, 231–32
Supreme Court (U.S.). *See also* citations
  attitudinal considerations and judicial behavior, 7, 8
  case selection, 248
  citations, impact of relationships on, 200–1, 209, 217–21, 219*f*, 220*f*, 222, 224*t*, 226*t*
  collegiality and institutional context, 108–10
  data and research design, 122–25, 123*f*
  decline in collegiality in, 245
  descriptive statistics, 125
  external and internal constraints on judicial behavior, 8–9, 10
  general discussion, 128–29
  highlights of findings, 233–34
  historical accounts regarding collegiality, 110–13, 111*f*
  implications for reform of, 238
  importance of collegiality in, 3–4, 20–21
  increased collegiality as fostering consensus, 228
  influence of law on judicial behavior, 6
  institutional differences in collegiality, 40–42, 113–14, 232–33

interview evidence regarding collegiality in, 113–22

interview results, 129–31

language of dissent, 160, 172–73, 174–75, 181–87, 184f, 185f, 186f, 187f, 188t, 191t, 195t, 196t, 197t

multivariate research, 125–28, 126f

overview, 13, 107–8

regression results, 133

results of collegiality research, 125–28, 126f

shadow docket, 248

summary statistics, 132

Sutton, Jeffrey, 52

Swalve, Tilko, 30

Szmer, John, 82, 203–4, 207–8

ten Brummelhuis, Lieke L., 17–18, 19

term limits, 238

Theriault, Sean M., 28

Thomas, Clarence, 112

three-judge panels. *See* panels

Tiller, Emerson H., 9–10, 17, 40

Tjoflat, Gerald Bard, 82, 164

tone of dissents, 170, 172, 172f

Totenberg, Nina, 20–21, 110–11, 245

trainings for new judges, 244

trial courts. *See* intercourt relations

Truman, David B., 28

trust, and relationship of collegiality to outcomes, 29–30

Tushnet, Mark, 112

Ulmer, S. Sidney, 112

unanimous decisions. *See also* persuasion; suppression of disagreement

attitudinal considerations, 8

costs of publicizing disagreement, 51

effect of collegiality on, 26, 228–29, 236

reasons for suppression, 32

in Supreme Court, 112

U.S. Courts of Appeals. *See* citations; collegiality; Courts of Appeals; intercourt relations; language of dissent; publicizing disagreements

U.S. Supreme Court. *See* Supreme Court

van der Lippe, Tanja, 17–18, 19

VanDyke, Lawrence, 161–62

Wahlbeck, Paul J., 7, 10, 76–77, 102

Wald, Patricia M., 21, 29, 30–31, 239–40

Walsh, David J., 199

Ward, Artemus, 161

Warren, Earl, 112

Wasby, Stephen L., 56, 58–59

Watts, Richard J., 165–66

Weis, Joseph F., Jr., 199

Weiss, Walter, 141

Wheeler, Russell, 146

whistle-blowing function of dissenting opinions, 52, 53–54, 65–66

White, Byron, 166

White, G. Edward, 110

White Commission on Structural Alternatives for the Federal Courts of Appeals, 84, 237

Wilkey, Malcolm R., 165

Wilkinson, J. Harvie, 35, 83

Wood, Diane, 21, 31

wooing, through citations, 207

work relationships. *See* collegiality

Yalof, David A., 164

Yoon, Albert H., 203–4

Zavoina, William, 84